THE MODEL OMBUDSMAN

*To Larry Guillot,
Another Model Ombudsman*

From Larry Hill
Jan. 12, 1977

It must not be forgotten that it is especially dangerous to enslave men in the minor details of life. For my own part, I should be inclined to think freedom less necessary in great things than in little ones, if it were possible to be secure of the one without possessing the other.

Subjection in minor affairs breaks out every day, and is felt by the whole community indiscriminately. It does not drive men to resistance, but it crosses them at every turn, till they are led to surrender the exercise of their own will. Thus their spirit is gradually broken and their character enervated.

—Alexis de Tocqueville, *Democracy in America*

THE MODEL OMBUDSMAN

Institutionalizing New Zealand's Democratic Experiment

LARRY B. HILL

PRINCETON UNIVERSITY PRESS
PRINCETON, NEW JERSEY

1976

Copyright © 1976 by Princeton University Press
Published by Princeton University Press, Princeton, New Jersey
In the United Kingdom: Princeton University Press, Guildford, Surrey

All Rights Reserved

Library of Congress Cataloging in Publication Data will
be found on the last printed page of this book

Publication of this book has been aided by the Andrew W.
Mellon Foundation

This book has been composed in Caledonia

Printed in the United States of America
by Princeton University Press, Princeton, New Jersey

*To Susan and
Brian Wellington, a Genuine Kiwi,
who shared the field experience with me*

Contents

| | Tables | xi |
| | Preface | xiii |

Part 1
PROLOGUE

One	Democracy, Bureaucracy, and the Ombudsman	3
	Images of Bureaucracy	4
	The Ombudsman	8
Two	A Political-Anthropological Approach to the Ombudsman	16
	Theoretical Perspectives: The Transfer of Institutions and Institutionalization	18
	Fieldwork: Watching the Ombudsman	27
	Research Design: The Ombudsman's Authority System	35
Three	Creating the Social Field: The Ombudsman in New Zealand	47
	Receptivity to the Ombudsman	48
	Traditional Appeals Agencies	53
	The Politics of Transfer	67
	Conclusions	73

Part 2
THE OMBUDSMAN CRUCIBLE

Four	Inputs: The Complaints	79
	Complaint Levels	80
	Targets of Complaint	81

CONTENTS

	Complaints and Departmental Classifications	87
	Subjects of Complaints	93
	Conclusions	99
Five	Access to the Ombudsman: His Clients	101
	Clients' Identities	105
	Demographic Origins	106
	Sexual Composition	109
	Age Distribution	110
	Educational Background	112
	Marital Status	114
	Racial-Ethnic Background	116
	Class-Occupational Background	119
	Civil Service Employment	124
	Conclusions	125
Six	Exchange Processes: The Ombudsman and His Clients	130
	Extensiveness of Interaction	130
	Perceptions of the Ombudsman	132
	Client Attitudes	135
	Client Strategies	138
	Nature of Relationship	145
	Conclusions	149
Seven	Exchange Processes: The Bureaucracy and the Ombudsman	153
	Investigations and Targets	155
	Extensiveness of Interaction	172
	Pervasiveness of Complaint's Threat	174
	Nature of the Ombudsman's Demands	177
	Departmental Reaction	179
	Conclusions	182
Eight	Outcomes: The Ombudsman's Impact	185
	The Meaning of the Ombudsman's Decisions	186
	Helping and Its Correlates	194
	The Ombudsman and Administrative Reform	204
	Conclusions	239

CONTENTS

Part 3
THE OMBUDSMAN AND HIS PUBLICS

Nine The Ombudsman's "Victims": The
Bureaucrats   245

The Perceptual Context	247
Psychosocial Distance from the Ombudsman	250
The Ombudsman's Impact upon the Civil Service	253
Evaluation of the Ombudsman's Jurisdiction	259
General Affect for the Ombudsman	260
Conclusions	265

Ten Honorable Members and the
Ombudsman   267

Putting the Ombudsman in Context	268
Psychosocial Distance from the Ombudsman	275
Interaction with the Ombudsman	277
The Ombudsman's Impact upon Political Life	281
The Ombudsman's Effectiveness, Status, and Jurisdiction	285
Affection for the Ombudsman	290
Conclusions	295

Eleven The Queen's Ministers and the
Ombudsman   298

Ministers as Grievance Men	298
The Ombudsman and Ministerial Responsibility	301
Assessing the Ombudsman	306
Conclusions	310

Part 4
EPILOGUE

Twelve Evaluations: Program, Institutionalization,
and Transfer   317

Program Evaluation	318

CONTENTS

Alternative Measures of Institutionalization	323
Of Time and the Threshold of Institutionalization	338
Transfer, Transformation, and the Future	343

Appendices

   A. In Retrospect: A Commentary by Sir Guy Powles   347
   B. The Ombudsmen Act 1975   353

Select Bibliography   387

Index   405

Tables

3-1.	Public Attitudes toward the Power of the Public Service	51
4-1.	Complaints to the Ombudsman by Governmental Organization	82
4-2.	Complaints to the Ombudsman against Unscheduled Organizations	86
4-3.	Scheduled Complaints to the Ombudsman by Type of Organization	92
4-4.	Offensive Complaints to the Ombudsman	94
4-5.	Defensive Complaints to the Ombudsman	97
5-1.	Demographic Origins of the Ombudsman's Clients	107
5-2.	Age Distribution of the Ombudsman's Clients	111
5-3.	Marital Status of the Ombudsman's Clients	115
5-4.	Class-Occupational Backgrounds of the Ombudsman's Clients	120
6-1.	Types of Appeals Invoked by the Ombudsman's Clients	141
7-1.	Departmental Targets of Complaint and Investigation	157
8-1.	Classification of the Ombudsman's Decisions	187
8-2.	Departmental Targets of Administrative Reform	216
8-3.	Synoptic Chart of the Ombudsman's Substantive Policy Impacts upon Selected Major Impact Targets	218
8-4.	The Content of Procedural Reforms	234
9-1.	Department Heads' Attitudes on Ombudsman's Jurisdiction	261
9-2.	Department Heads' Mean Responses to Ombudsman Attitude Statements	262

TABLES

10-1.	Subjects of the Three Most Usual Grievances Brought to M.P.s	272
10-2.	Members' Attitudes on the Ombudsman's Jurisdiction	289
10-3.	M.P.s' Mean Responses to Ombudsman Attitude Statements	291
11-1.	Ministers' Mean Responses to Ombudsman Attitude Statements	309

Preface

Some nine years ago, when the fieldwork upon which this book about the New Zealand Ombudsman is based was initiated, I would have challenged the possible applicability to me of Evans-Pritchard's comment that an intensive study of this sort normally takes about a decade to reach finally published form.[1] "Perhaps a sluggard could require that much time," I would have contended if I had known of the generalization, "but it will not take me that long." The course of events was, however, only somewhat more rapid than Evans-Pritchard prophesied.

Following the eighteen months of field experience in New Zealand it was necessary to code and keypunch interviews and other data, to perform a computer analysis of them, to blend those "hard" data with "softer" but no less empirical materials gained through participant observation, to place all of this within a broad historical-social context, to measure the resulting mélange of social facts—to use Durkheim's term—against important theoretical conceptions, and finally to put the result in the form of a Ph.D. dissertation—that cultural artifact which the modern day apprentice scholar must produce as a *rite de passage* before full-fledged academic status is granted. All of these operations did require a considerable amount of time; the thesis that fathered this book was submitted in 1970.

A virtue of the thesis format is that, while setting out fully the salient features of the system under analysis, I was allowed to include much rich, descriptive material without regard to arbitrary space limitations. Such preliminary ethnological documents tend toward prolixity,

---

[1] E. E. Evans-Pritchard, *Social Anthropology and Other Essays* (New York: Free Press, 1962), p. 76.

PREFACE

however; the one I produced ran to 900 pages. Despite the further delay in publication occasioned by the necessity to condense and revise completely the original tome, that requirement has been propitious in two main ways.

First: it has forced me to sharpen the theoretical argument and prune away large pieces of descriptive underbrush which were impedimenta to the central focus. During the revisions, I have presented preliminary versions of some of the materials at annual meetings of the American Society for Public Administration and of the American, the Midwest, the Southern, and the Southwestern Political Science Associations. Furthermore, The *American Political Science Review*, the *Journal of Comparative Administration*, *Political Studies*, the *Urban Affairs Quarterly*, the *New Zealand Journal of Public Administration*, and *Political Science* have been hospitable to my articles on the Ombudsman (papers appearing in the first two journals listed are incorporated into the following presentation). These oral and written forums have been valuable opportunities for honing my interpretations of the Ombudsman against the questions, and sometimes the criticisms, of other scholars.[2]

Second: the delay in publication has allowed me to evaluate the Ombudsman's institutionalization over a much longer time perspective, while the passage of time has not invalidated the original analysis. Thanks to the office's detailed annual *Reports* and to other material supplied by the Ombudsman, by bureaucrats, by politicians, and by academicians, I have been able to update continually much of the data that I collected in the field; this is particularly true of the analysis of the Ombudsman's policy impact upon public administration, which is presented in Chapter 8.

[2] Readers who are titillated by confrontations between academicians may wish to examine Frederick C. Thayer's letter to the editor about one of my articles and my response. Both appear in the *American Political Science Review* 69 (June 1975), 580–83.

PREFACE

This book evaluates the first twelve and one-half years of the New Zealand Ombudsman's existence. The cut-off point for most portions of the research, 31 March 1975, happens to coincide very nearly with the passage of the Ombudsmen Act 1975, on 26 June. The revised statute, which appears as Appendix B below, consolidates and amends the original 1962 act in several respects, e.g., the requirement that clients pay a two-dollar fee when complaining is dropped. But the most important change is the creation of multiple Ombudsmen to handle the increase in workload caused by the extension of the office's jurisdiction into local government matters. The actual significance for the office of these changes remains to be seen, but probable implications are explored below—especially in Chapter 12. Whatever the future may hold for the Ombudsmen, the expansions of the institution's structure and jurisdiction are votes of confidence in the performance of New Zealand's first Ombudsman. Furthermore, although the concept of the office is not altered, these changes mark a critical juncture in the Ombudsman's organizational development; mid-1975 thus constitutes an appropriate point for ending this analysis. Despite the fact that New Zealand now has a troika of Ombudsmen, only one existed during this study, and the term is used below in the singular.

Not only has this book been a long time in the making, but also it is my pleasure to acknowledge that a number of organizations and individuals have had a hand in its production. The fieldwork was initially sponsored by a United States Government grant under the Fulbright-Hays Act (administered by the U.S. Educational Foundation in New Zealand), and additional support in the field was provided by Tulane University, by the Internal Research Committee of the Victoria University of Wellington, and by Victoria's School of Political

PREFACE

Science and Public Administration. Since leaving New Zealand, the National Endowment for the Humanities and several entities at the University of Oklahoma—including the College of Arts and Sciences, the Faculty Research Fund, the Masters of Public Administration Research and Development Fund, and the Department of Political Science—have contributed to my support.

Furthermore, my personal indebtednesses are many. The greatest is to the first Anglo-Saxon Ombudsman, Sir Guy Powles, who has become Chief Ombudsman under the new Act. He and his staff suffered under my seemingly interminable microanalysis of their behavior with continual good humor. I thank my friends (and unpaid research associates) Stuart Aikman, First Assistant; J. D. Armstrong, Administrative Officer; the late Leslie Smith, Legal Officer; and Thea Slevin and Wendy Alerdice, Secretaries. In my judgment, New Zealand is fortunate to have appointed as her first Ombudsman a man of the moral, intellectual, and professional caliber of Sir Guy. And I second the sentiments he has expressed in his annual *Reports* about the dedication and competence of his staff.

Within government, major appreciation is expressed to the Members of Parliament—all eighty submitted to my interview. The late Hon. Ralph Hanan (then Minister for Justice) and the Hon. Alan McCready of the National Party and the Hon. Whetu Tirakatene-Sullivan (subsequently Minister for Tourism) and the Hon. Phil Amos (subsequently Minister of Education) of the Labor Party were most helpful in giving advice and arranging interviews. Also, the permanent heads of the principal government agencies and their staffs generously gave of their time and allowed me to peruse their records. Several made special efforts on my behalf: since I bothered the Social Welfare Department most extensively, special thanks are recorded to it and

PREFACE

especially to George Brocklehurst, C. A. Oram, and John Grant.

Outside government circles I am grateful to A. C. Brassington and A. F. Manning of the Constitutional Society and to Dan Long of the Public Service Association for their information. Thanks are also due to the editor of the *Evening Post* for allowing me access to its clippings library.

My former colleagues in the School of Political Science and Public Administration at the Victoria University were instrumental in giving me whatever education in the New Zealand political system I have acquired. I particularly thank Alan Robinson, John Roberts, Ralph Brookes, Les Cleveland, and Don McAllister—all of whom contributed more than they realize.

Additionally, a large debt is owed to Laurie Brown, until recently Professor of Psychology at Victoria, who not only assisted in the development of several of the coding categories for the analysis of the Ombudsman's files, but also valiantly coded many of the cases himself after I had to leave New Zealand. Pat Morrison contributed importantly to the coding of the Ombudsman's bureaucratic impact, and three other research assistants—Stephenie Colston, Betsy Gunn and Michael Fitzgerald—also provided general assistance. The lion's share of the typing of this manuscript's many versions has been borne—with unfailing good grace—by Geri Rowden and Betty Anderson.

In addition to those already named, individuals who have over the years provided helpful comments upon portions of the manuscript include William Gwyn (my thesis director), Stanley Anderson, Ralph Braibanti, Morris Davis, Bernard Frank, Karl Friedmann, Walter Gellhorn, Susan Hill, Robert Lineberry, Geoffrey Marshall, Richard Merritt, John Moore, Charldean

PREFACE

Newell, Alan Robinson, Donald Rowat, Sanford Thatcher, and Alan Wyner. Among my Oklahoma colleagues, the useful advice of David Bailey, Oliver Benson, Samuel Kirkpatrick, Hugh MacNiven, David Morgan, and William Watson must be mentioned.

To bear fruit, scholarship demands—in my experience at least—an affective environment that is supportive. This requirement has been ably met by my family, Susan, Brian, and Eric; by my political science colleagues; and by Shirley Pelley and other friends on the staff of the University of Oklahoma Libraries.

This recitation of assistance is not intended to parcel out the blame. I cheerfully accept responsibility for all of the following.

LARRY B. HILL
Norman, Oklahoma

Part 1
PROLOGUE

CHAPTER ONE

Democracy, Bureaucracy, and the Ombudsman

THIS book is about democracy, about bureaucracy, and about the ombudsman—that originally Scandinavian "grievance man" advertised as a solution to the modern problem of how to maintain democracy in bureaucratic society. In general terms, the focus is upon a central problem in classical political theory: the proper relationships between the governors and the governed. More specifically, this book is an inquiry into the institutions and processes through which citizens, either voluntarily or involuntarily, become involved with the state. Governing and being governed is viewed as a political production-consumption process.[1] From the citizens' perspective the material sufficiency or the justice of the governmental outputs that they consume may be analyzed; from the governmental perspective the same things may be investigated but with regard to their impact upon such matters as the level of support for the regime. Whichever viewpoint is assumed, an analysis of the relations between the governors and the governed is no less important for understanding modern political life than it was for Plato and Aristotle.

History records the development of several multipurpose institutions that control arbitrary governmental actions. These include popular and representative assemblies, public opinion enlightened by a free press, a loyal opposition, independent political parties, competing groups organized to express political interests, writ-

[1] For a thoughtful analysis of political consumption and involvement see Herbert Jacob, *Debtors in Court: the Consumption of Government Services* (Chicago: Rand McNally, 1969); see especially Chapter 1.

ten constitutions, and the rule of law, including courts. The existence of a successfully functioning pattern of such governmental control mechanisms traditionally has been used to distinguish democratic from authoritarian regimes, but the burgeoning of the administrative state—which is the most significant political development of modern times—challenges the usefulness of these distinctions.

Whatever the formal political arrangements may be, in all complex societies man is governed by corps of professional administrators; and that ancient tension between Leviathan's demands for authority and administrative efficiency on one hand and the democrats' goals of executive accountability and responsiveness on the other has been intensified by the bureaucracy's growth. A normative gulf separates those who fear the emerging brave new world of technological bureaucracy from those who insist upon forging beyond such socially distracting concepts as individual freedom and dignity; but on both sides of the gulf the objective analysis is similar: pervasive social control through organization is the future's salient political phenomenon. A wide range of critics contend that the traditional, unspecialized agencies of governmental control are inadequate in the face of bureaucracy. Many reformers feel that specialist bureaucratic control institutions, such as the ombudsman, are needed.

Images of Bureaucracy

It is ironic that bureaucracy has come to be regarded with suspicion; according to the conventional view, professional administration was an indicator of political maturity. Max Weber pointed to the following bureaucratic characteristics: strict spheres of jurisdiction and specialization of work, the use of generalized rules and procedures, the establishment of an official hierarchy and of graded levels of authority, and the use of the criterion of competence (and further training) as a guide for recruitment and promotion.[2] Weber viewed such "rational-legal" systems as salutary, and generations of public administration specialists have dedicated themselves to fostering his ideals. Governance based upon these precepts does seem preferable to dilettantism, caprice, incompetence, and favoritism. Precisely what, then, explains the concern about bureaucracy?

First, just bureaucracy's meteoric increase both in absolute size and in functional scope sometimes appears alarming. With but few exceptions, mainly military ones, prior to the 1930s government administration was primarily small-scale. Since then, important new political entities consisting of thousands of employees have been created. Many people find it difficult to understand the complexities of large-scale organization. To them, government bureaucracy seems incomprehensible and threatening, as do several other aspects of modern life related to bigness, including private bureaucracy and urbanism.[3] Furthermore, whether one attributes it to a diabolical plot or to compliance with society's demands for additional services, as most academic writers do, it is clear that modern governments increasingly intrude upon areas of their citizens' lives that previously were considered private. Certainly, such aversive forms of control as taxation breed little affection for the bureaucratic instrumentalities; but even rewarding contacts, such as social security benefits, remind citizens of their increasing dependence upon government largess. The public cannot escape the awareness that their primary linkages

[2] H. H. Gerth and C. Wright Mills, *From Max Weber: Essays in Sociology* (New York: Oxford University Press, 1946), pp. 196–99.

[3] One unsympathetic organization theorist claims that such individuals are frustrated by their inability to personalize bureaucracy and that they suffer from "a kind of social disease which we propose to call 'bureausis.'" Victor A. Thompson, *Modern Organization* (New York: Alfred A. Knopf, 1961), pp. 170–73.

PROLOGUE

to the state are as subjects and as consumers of services; this heightened awareness has created a climate favorable to bureaucratic critics.

Second, government administration often is depicted as unresponsive or incompetent. In 1930 Harold Laski defined bureaucracy in the *Encyclopedia of the Social Sciences* as "the term usually applied to a system of government the control of which is so completely in the hands of officials that their power jeopardizes the liberties of ordinary citizens." Bureaucratic characteristics allegedly were "a passion for routine in administration, the sacrifice of flexibility to rule, delay in the making of decisions, and a refusal to embark upon experiments."[4] As the scope of contacts between administrators and citizens has multiplied, the pejorative usage of the term *bureaucracy* has increased. Writing one-third of a century after Laski, William A. Robson listed the following additional "bureaucratic maladies": "An excessive sense of self-importance on the part of officials or an undue idea of the importance of their offices; an indifference toward the feelings or the convenience of individual citizens; . . . a preoccupation with particular units of administration and an inability to consider the government as a whole; a failure to recognize the relations between the governors and the governed as an essential part of the democratic process."[5] Considerably more extravagant citations of bureaucratic insensitivity, inefficiency, and "red tape" have become commonplace in popular literature. However grim this image of bureaucracy is, most of those "evils" theoretically seem to be capable of correction.

But it is sometimes alleged that there is a third bureaucratic aspect that is endemic: dehumanization. Weber himself listed as a social consequence of bureau-

[4] Harold Laski, "Bureaucracy," *Encyclopaedia of the Social Sciences*, Vol. 3 (New York: Macmillan, 1930), p. 70.

[5] William A. Robson, *The Governors and the Governed* (Baton Rouge: Louisiana State University Press, 1964), p. 18.

DEMOCRACY, BUREAUCRACY, AND OMBUDSMAN

cratic control "the dominance of a spirt of formalistic impersonality, *sine ira et studio,* without hatred or passion, and hence without affection or enthusiasm. The dominant norms are concepts of straightforward duty without regard to personal considerations. Everyone is subject to formal equality of treatment; that is, everyone in the same empirical situation."[6] Weber celebrated this attitude as the "spirit in which the ideal official conducts his office," but others have come to regard as offensive this impersonal, automatic, professionalized, increasingly pervasive bureaucratic machine. That is, they feel that contacts with the government have become *dehumanized;* symbolic of it is the increasing incidence of government-citizen interaction through numeric codes and computers.[7]

Fourth, many critics are concerned about bureaucracy because they fear that it enjoys certain strategic advantages over the traditional institutions charged with controlling it. The sheer volume of decisions that a large, geographically dispersed government department must make and make quickly concerning a variety of complex and often technical matters makes it unlikely that a small group of generalists, say on a legislative committee, could act as an effective monitor of the overall operations. Even on specific matters, such as investigating citizens' grievances, the bureaucracy could marshal superior reservoirs of information, expertise, and technological and other resources. The traditional control agencies achieve occasional triumphs, but many feel that they are inherently disadvantaged. This conclusion appears so compelling to several scholars that they devote their primary hopes for a responsible public administration to attempts

---

[6] Max Weber, *The Theory of Social and Economic Organization,* trans. by A. M. Henderson and Talcott Parsons, ed. by Talcott Parsons (New York: Oxford University Press, 1947), p. 340.

[7] As an example of these kinds of criticisms, see George E. Berkley, *The Administrative Revolution* (Englewood Cliffs, N.J.: Prentice-Hall, 1971), p. 13.

PROLOGUE

to socialize the bureaucracy into accepting the precepts of democratic morality.[8]

Hence there are four views, which may be held concurrently, about why bureaucracy poses a threat: bureaucracy's gargantuan growth dwarfs the individual; bureaucracies are politically unresponsive or inefficient; bureaucratic relationships are inherently dehumanizing; and bureaucracy enjoys strategic power advantages over the traditional governmental control devices. These are the maladies for which the ombudsman has been prescribed as the cure.

THE OMBUDSMAN

Reinhard Bendix, writing on the subject of the political control of public officials in the *International Encyclopedia of the Social Sciences*, declared in 1968: "The need for an opportunity to redress individual grievances is widely recognized, but the institution of the ombudsman is not easily transferred from one constitutional framework to another."[9] Precisely that—the transfer and the subsequent institutionalization of the ombudsman into the New Zealand political system—is this book's subject.

Ombudsmen first were transferred within Scandinavia. After its invention in Sweden in 1809, the institution appeared in Finland in 1919, in Denmark in 1954, and in

---

[8] Robert S. Lorch contends: "Without doubt the overshadowing question of modern democracy is: How can the public control administrators? . . . Legislators are too much in the dark to ask intelligent questions about what administrators are doing, and even if they were not in the dark they would not have *time* to ask intelligent questions. . . . If there is to be democratic procedure within the enormous piece of the law-making function which is controlled by administrators it must be for the most part invented, fostered, practiced, championed by the administrators themselves." *Democratic Process and Administrative Law* (Detroit: Wayne State University Press, 1969), pp. 99–100.

[9] Reinhard Bendix, "Bureaucracy," *International Encyclopedia of the Social Sciences*, Vol. 2 (New York: Macmillan and Free Press, 1968), p. 217.

DEMOCRACY, BUREAUCRACY, AND OMBUDSMAN

Norway in 1963. In 1962 the New Zealand official became the first non-Scandinavian ombudsman (the Norwegian and New Zealand transfers really were contemporaneous). His success provided the initial evidence that the institution was not dependent upon a uniquely Scandinavian constellation of cultural and political factors. Since then, the institution has become *au courant*, and the New Zealand official has become the primary model, in both structural and behavioral terms, for the world's newer ombudsmen.

In a structural sense, the New Zealand statute not only strongly influenced the forms of the other early Anglo-Saxon ombudsmen—e.g., Great Britain, Hawaii, Alberta —which themselves later became models for even newer officials,[10] but also the New Zealand statute was a principal foundation for several "model statutes," which subsequently became highly influential in their own right— e.g., Ralph Nader's Connecticut ombudsman bill introduced in 1963, the Harvard Student Legislative Research Bureau's state ombudsman statute (also instigated by Nader),[11] Walter Gellhorn's annotated model ombudsman statute,[12] and the Model Ombudsman Statute for State Governments (which was drafted by Yale Legislative Services in collaboration with the American Bar Association).

[10] A comparison of the statutes makes the New Zealand influence obvious; particularly, the Alberta legislation is very nearly a direct copy of the model. In addition to the apparent similarities, the New Zealand example is known by students of the institutions to have been important during the drafting stages; for an account of the New Zealand influence upon the British official's creation, see Frank A. Stacey, *The British Ombudsman* (Oxford: Clarendon Press, 1971).

[11] "A State Statute to Create the Office of Ombudsman," *Harvard Journal on Legislation*, 2 (June 1965), 213–38; reprinted as an appendix to the 7 March 1966 *Hearing on Ombudsman* of the United States Senate Judiciary Subcommittee on Administrative Practice and Procedure, at pp. 336–61.

[12] Walter Gellhorn, "Appendix: Annotated Model Ombudsman Statute," in Stanley V. Anderson, ed., *Ombudsmen for American Government?* (Englewood Cliffs, N.J.: Prentice-Hall, 1968), pp. 159–73.

PROLOGUE

In a behavioral sense, the New Zealand Ombudsman's written reports, which have been widely diffused, and his speeches (including the giving of legislative testimony in various countries) and published articles[13] have generally publicized the office; and, more importantly, they have provided role models for ombudsmen entering their novitiate. Testifying to the New Zealand Ombudsman's properties as a role model, Herman S. Doi, Hawaii's Ombudsman and the most experienced American ombudsman, has commented as follows:

> The Obudsman concept and its implications are not self-evident. Yet, New Zealand in 1962 boldly implemented the concept with the appointment of Sir Guy Powles as Ombudsman. New Zealand's experiment proved to the English-speaking world that the Ombudsman concept would beneficially complement and improve a basically sound and responsive Government. To those bold experimenters, to those who supported the institution through its formative years, and to Sir Guy Powles, we who followed their lead owe a vote of thanks.[14]

Because he is the model ombudsman and because of his relative longevity, which provides necessary historical perspective, it is appropriate to select this first Anglo-Saxon ombudsman for detailed study.

On the national level, the ombudsman has been transferred not only throughout Scandinavia and to New Zea-

---

[13] For example, one of his early speeches was twice reprinted in scholarly journals: Sir Guy Powles, "The Citizen's Rights Against the Modern State and Its Responsibilities to Him," an address delivered to the Royal Institute of Public Administration, Canberra, Australia, on 14 November 1963. It was published in the *International and Comparative Law Quarterly* 13 (July 1964), 761–97; and in *Public Administration* 23 (1964), 42–68.

[14] *Official Record of Proceedings of the Conference of Australasian and Pacific Ombudsmen*, Wellington, New Zealand, 19–22 November 1974 (Wellington: Office of Ombudsman, 1975), p. 10.

land, but also to Great Britain, Guyana, Tanzania, Northern Ireland, Israel, Mauritius, France, and Fiji. New constitutions in Bangladesh, Greece, Pakistan, and the Philippines provide for the office. Also, West Germany has a military ombudsman, and Canada has a "Commissioner of Official Languages." On the subnational level, four American states (Hawaii, Nebraska, Iowa, and Alaska), eight Canadian provinces (Alberta, New Brunswick, Newfoundland, Ontario, Quebec, Manitoba, Nova Scotia, and Saskatchewan), and all of the Australian states except for Tasmania have ombudsmen. Such cities as Zurich, Switzerland; Jerusalem and Tel Aviv, Israel; Atlanta, Georgia; Dayton, Ohio; Seattle, Washington; San Jose, California; and Kansas City, Missouri have municipal ombudsmen. At least one hundred ombudsmen exist on the campuses of American colleges and universities.

Merely keeping track of the plethora of ombudsman proposals has become a major undertaking. The Ombudsman Committees of the American Bar Association and the International Bar Association, which have taken on that chore, reported in 1975 upon ombudsman news of various types in 128 non-American jurisdictions, mainly national ones. In addition to several proposals at the American federal level, by 1975 ombudsman bills had been introduced into the legislatures of all but eight of the American states.[15] In short, there is a worldwide ombudsman movement which has reached such proportions that some have labeled it "ombudsmania."[16]

---

[15] See Bernard Frank, American Bar Association and International Bar Association Ombudsman Committees, "Ombudsman Survey July 1, 1974—June 30, 1975" (Allentown, Pennsylvania, 1975). See also the committees' reports for previous years.

[16] Donald C. Rowat, "Recent Developments in Ombudsmanship," *Canadian Journal of Public Administration* 10 (1967), 35. The volume Rowat edited, *The Ombudsman: Citizen's Defender* (Toronto and London: University of Toronto Press and Allen and Unwin, 1965), has been an important document in the ombudsman movement. Two other such documents are the papers presented in 1967 at Columbia University's

PROLOGUE

A key to understanding the ombudsman's popularity is the concept's relative simplicity; "grievance man," "mediator," and "citizens' defender" are commonly used and not inaccurate synonyms. The 1974 edition of the *Encyclopaedia Britannica,* which offers a more structural definition, states that an ombudsman is a "legislative commissioner for investigating citizens' complaints of bureaucratic abuse."[17] In developing a more comprehensive definition, I have isolated several defining characteristics: the classical ombudsman is 1) legally established, 2) functionally autonomous, 3) external to the administration, 4) operationally independent of both the legislature and the executive, 5) specialist, 6) expert, 7) nonpartisan, 8) normatively universalistic, 9) client-centered but not antiadministration, and 10) both popularly accessible and visible. The institution's mission is to generate complaints against government administration, to use its extensive powers of investigation in performing a postdecision administrative audit, to form judgments that criticize or vindicate administrators, and to report publicly its findings and recommendations but not to change administrative decisions.[18] Indeed, one of the institution's most interesting puzzles is its apparent effectiveness despite minimal coercive capabilities.

American Assembly on the Ombudsman, which are collected in Anderson, ed., *Ombudsmen for American Government?;* and the papers in Roy V. Peel, ed., "The Ombudsman or Citizens' Defender: A Modern Institution," *Annals of the American Academy of Political and Social Science* 377 (May 1968).

[17] Stanley V. Anderson, "Ombudsman," *Encyclopaedia Britannica, Micropaedia,* 1974, Vol. 7, p. 530.

[18] See also Donald C. Rowat's somewhat more legalistic listing of the ombudsman's "essential features." Preface to Second Edition, in Rowat, ed., *The Ombudsman: Citizen's Defender,* rev. ed. (Toronto: University of Toronto Press, 1968), p. xxiv; and Stanley V. Anderson's more functionally based "essential characteristics" in *Ombudsman Papers: American Experience and Proposals* (Berkeley: University of California, Institute of Governmental Studies, 1969), pp. 3–4.

DEMOCRACY, BUREAUCRACY, AND OMBUDSMAN

According to the ombudsman's advocates, these characteristics qualify him to treat the maladies of the modern administrative state; his expertise, powers of investigation, etc. allegedly can penetrate the bureaucracy's defenses. From a functional viewpoint, the ombudsman is said to possess both popular and administrative virtues. Not only does he right specific wrongs, bring humanity into administrative relationships, and lessen alienation by acting as a community psychiatrist; but also he improves administration both in particular instances and generally, acts as a watchdog preventing bureaucratic abuses, and bolsters administrative morale by demonstrating that civil servants often are unfairly accused.

The ombudsman sometimes has been dismissed as merely the latest in a series of administrative palliatives—including the city manager and the planning-programming-budgeting system—embraced by frustrated political engineers and utopian administrators. But the institution tends not to make enemies, and very little ombudsman writing of a critical nature exists. In sifting the literature, William B. Gwyn noted six supposedly undesirable consequences of the ombudsman: knowledge of his presence increases civil servants' timidity in making decisions; he inclines administrators to "cover" themselves by creating unnecessarily extensive records and "red tape"; he tends to overextend himself by substituting his judgments on complex policies for those of technical experts; his role of citizens' advocate promotes an adversary relationship with administrators who will create defenses against him; because the ombudsman is not an administrator, his proposals may be viewed as those of an idealistic and impractical outsider; and his existence may create complacency, distracting policy makers from other needed reforms.[19]

[19] William B. Gwyn, "Transferring the Ombudsman," in Anderson, ed., *Ombudsmen for American Government?*, pp. 43–45. These dys-

PROLOGUE

Furthermore, sometimes it is alleged that the ombudsman wastes the time of busy administrators with complaints from frivolous or grasping clients, or that his lobbying for a particular complaint may coerce the department into distorting their priorities so that individuals who complain gain an unfair advantage over those in similar circumstances who do not. From another perspective, it has been claimed that because the ombudsman can only recommend changes and not reverse decisions, he is not powerful enough to warrant serious consideration. Perhaps the harshest criticism is that of radical theorists who claim that the ombudsman is a liberal or conservative institution designed to legitimate and make more palatable the existing order; thus the ombudsman is counterrevolutionary.

The mushrooming of interest in and experimentation with the ombudsman as a monitor of the relationships between the governors and the governed establishes the office as an appropriate subject of policy analysis. The extensive interest in the subject, however, has been thus far mainly of the normative-speculative type,[20] and the level of scholarship generally has been descriptive. Although the main points of contention can be framed in researchable terms—i.e., what kinds of people complain, what is the ombudsman's impact upon the bureaucracy

---

functional consequences were culled from Walter Gellhorn's two books, *When Americans Complain: Governmental Grievance Procedures* (Cambridge, Mass.: Harvard University Press, 1966); and *Ombudsmen and Others: Citizens' Protectors in Nine Countries* (Cambridge, Mass.: Harvard University Press, 1966).

[20] A perusal of even the titles of the rapidly expanding ombudsman literature clearly reveals its normative thrust. Counting only the items from scholarly or semischolarly sources, Stanley Anderson's 1969 bibliography contains nearly 250 listings, and it now is quite incomplete. See *Ombudsman Papers*, pp. 381–407. The most influential early popularizing article was Henry J. Abraham, "A Peoples' Watchdog Against Abuse of Power," *Public Administration Review* 20 (Summer 1960), 152–57.

14

and his clients, or what do politicians think about him—little such research has been undertaken. Empirical research often has been discouraged by the new ombudsmen's legal secrecy requirements and by their sometimes overly cautious estimations of the sensitivity of materials in their files.[21] The competing claims of the ombudsman's advocates and detractors raise important public policy considerations about what kind of institution an ombudsman really is. This book's goal is to find out.

[21] The inaccessibility of files for extended research does not, of course, mean that no valuable work can be done. The ombudsmen themselves provide useful data in their annual reports, and they often have cooperated with scholars by granting interviews and sometimes providing additional statistical data. The classic comparative study remains Walter Gellhorn, *Ombudsmen and Others*. Britain's Parliamentary Commissioner, who took office after Gellhorn's book was completed, is analyzed in William B. Gwyn, "The British PCA: 'Ombudsman or Ombudsmouse?'," *Journal of Politics* 35 (February 1973), 45–69; and in Roy Gregory and Peter Hutchesson, *The Parliamentary Ombudsman: A Study in the Control of Administrative Action* (London: Allen and Unwin, 1975). Stacey's book cited above, *The British Ombudsman*, mainly treats the creation and early days of the office.

The University of California's Ombudsman Activities Project, sponsored by the Office of Economic Opportunity (Stanley V. Anderson, Principal Investigator), which has provided technical assistance to the new American ombudsmen, is not hampered by such research limitations. See Alan J. Wyner's slender monograph *The Nebraska Ombudsman: Innovation in State Government* (Berkeley: University of California, Institute of Governmental Studies, 1974); and John E. Moore's report on the Hawaiian Ombudsman, forthcoming.

CHAPTER TWO

A Political-Anthropological Approach to the Ombudsman

It would be easy to quote works of high repute . . . in which wholesale generalisations are laid down before us, and we are not informed at all by what actual experiences the writers have reached their conclusion. No special chapter or paragraph is devoted to describing to us the conditions under which observations were made and information collected. I consider that only such ethnographic sources are of unquestionable scientific value, in which we can clearly draw the line between . . . the results of direct observation and . . . the inferences of the author.

—BRONISLAW MALINOWSKI, *Argonauts of the Western Pacific*

THE preceding introduction of the ombudsman's significance was couched in political terms, and the following analysis is explicitly political in substance. In spirit, however, I have approached my subject from an anthropological perspective. Anthropologists typically have conducted in "primitive" societies investigations which are intensively focused, which feature extended research, and which systematically analyze particular aspects of behavior within the broadest social context. For reasons to be detailed below, I undertook such an investigation of the New Zealand Ombudsman.

An epochal event in the history of anthropology was the publication in 1922 of Bronislaw Malinowski's *Argonauts of the Western Pacific*. In that book, based upon nearly three years of study among the Trobriand Islanders, Malinowski certainly redefined the mission of the anthropologist; many claim that his research was so superior to all that preceded it that he actually invented modern fieldwork techniques. Hortense Powdermaker, one of Malinowski's students, has noted that this study

A POLITICAL-ANTHROPOLOGICAL APPROACH

"set new standards for field workers which continue to operate." As a result of his influence, "field work came to mean immersion in a tribal society—learning, as far as possible, to speak, think, see, feel, and act as a member of its culture and, at the same time, as a trained anthropologist from a different culture."[1]

In the Introduction to *Argonauts*—entitled "The Subject, Method and Scope of this Inquiry"—Malinowski exhorted anthropologists to make full and candid disclosures of their methods; and, in the course of a lengthy and highly personalized memoir of his own techniques, he revealed the "secret of effective field-work." Three methodological principles could be isolated, he said:

> First of all, naturally, the student must possess real scientific aims, and know the values and criteria of modern ethnography. Secondly, he ought to put himself in good conditions of work; that is, in the main, to live without other white men, right among the natives. Finally, he has to apply a number of special methods of collecting, manipulating and fixing his evidence.[2]

If one acknowledges that the venue of ethnographic study can be moved from the "primitive isolate" to a modern, developed society, then the applicability of Malinowski's principles to our ombudsman study can be easily grasped. In accordance with his admonitions, this methodological chapter describes 1) the project's grounding in social science theory, 2) the conditions of fieldwork, and 3) the construction of a research design.[3]

---

[1] Hortense Powdermaker, "Field Work," *International Encyclopedia of the Social Sciences*, Vol. 5 (New York: Macmillan and Free Press, 1968), p. 418.

[2] Bronislaw Malinowski, *Argonauts of the Western Pacific: An Account of Native Enterprise and Adventure in the Archipelagoes of Melanesian New Guinea* (New York: E. P. Dutton, 1922), p. 6; a Dutton Everyman Paperback edition was published in 1961.

[3] The epigraphs that introduce the chapter's divisions are from the Introduction to *Argonauts*.

PROLOGUE

Theoretical Perspectives: The Transfer of Institutions and Institutionalization

Good training in theory, and acquaintance with its latest results, is not identical with being burdened with "preconceived ideas." . . . Preconceived ideas are pernicious in any scientific work, but foreshadowed problems are the main endowment of a scientific thinker, and these problems are first revealed to the observer by his theoretical studies.

Change of various types has become such a preeminent feature of modern life that it is hardly a contradiction to call it a constant. Especially during the past three decades, the type of change that has held political scientists fascinated is the politics of development. The introduction into traditionally structured political systems of modern technology such as the mass media and mechanized agriculture, of new values such as equality and democracy, and of innovative organizational patterns including political parties and factories, brought highly visible political changes that had far-reaching consequences for the systems affected. Perceptible discontinuities between the (usually modern) donor and the (usually premodern) recipient societies highlight these sorts of change processes, but such political changes are only particular instances of more general types of change.

The general category of political change under scrutiny here is exogenously inspired change, which may be divided into three subtypes:[4] *coercive* change may be in-

---

[4] This typology of social change is related to but distinct from both Milton J. Esman, "Some Issues in Institution Building Theory," in D. Woods Thomas, Harry R. Potter, William L. Miller, and Adrian F. Aveni, *Institution Building: A Model for Applied Social Change* (Cambridge, Mass.: Schenkman, 1972), pp. 65–67; and Everett M. Rogers, *Modernization Among Peasants: The Impact of Communication* (New York: Holt, Rinehart and Winston, 1969), pp. 5–7.

A POLITICAL-ANTHROPOLOGICAL APPROACH

duced through tactics such as foreign military aggression or subversion; *guidance* change, in Milton Esman's terms, or *directed contact* change, in Everett Rogers', is caused by the attempts of outside change agents or social engineers, in cooperation with local leaders, to promote change according to the formers' prescriptions; when change that is exogenous and *voluntary* occurs, local elites become convinced that a foreign solution to a social problem is demonstrably superior to the endogenous product and decide to adopt it. The Scandinavian ombudsman was voluntaristically transferred to New Zealand, and the following theoretical discussion concentrates upon that type of change, but the similarities with other types are apparent.

Having established an interest in voluntarily accepted political change of exogenous origin, it remains to identify the substance of change and to specify the change processes. As societies cope with perennial political problems, more or less enduring and rationalized structural solutions evolve or are created to respond to them. Here we are concerned with those solutions that are given organizational form and that commonly are called political institutions.[5] Societies' institutions can be compared, and if we conceive of them as economic commodities, it is apparent that there is a thriving international exchange market in political institutions. Historically those, such as Roman law or the Australian ballot,

[5] Most of the following theoretical discussion focuses upon organizations; yet much of it is also pertinent to analyses of less "organized" institutions. For an enlightening interpretation of institutions (broadly conceived) and structures and of their relationships to such concepts as function and process and also for an extensive review of the thoughts of such writers as Almond, Eisenstadt, Esman, Friedrich, Huntington, de Jouvenel, La Palombara, Lasswell and Kaplan, Miller, Mitchell, Myrdal, Parsons, Pennock, Riggs, and Selznick, see Ralph Braibanti, "External Inducement of Political-Administrative Development: An Institutional Strategy," in Braibanti, ed., *Political and Administrative Development* (Durham, N.C.: Duke University Press, 1969), pp. 52–58.

that appear to possess certain relative advantages over indigenous techniques have been widely diffused. In this sense, such techniques as the parliamentary and the presidential governmental systems can be described as competitive. The intersocietal diffusion of political technique long has been commonplace, but various factors—particularly technological advances in communications—have caused the present to be an age of the explosion of that process. Civil service commissions, kibbutzim, panchayats, courts of arbitration, communist parties—all have been widely diffused and are perceived of internationally as being available for transfer.[6]

[6] The origins of social institutions is a subject that has fascinated anthropologists since the discipline's beginnings. During the nineteenth and early twentieth centuries controversy raged between the evolutionists, who believed that societies independently evolved their own cultures, and the diffusionists, who argued that institutions were diffused from a few cultural centers. E. E. Evans-Pritchard, himself a nonbeliever, has summarized the contentions of the diffusionists as follows (*Social Anthropology and Other Essays* [New York: Free Press, 1962], pp. 46–47; originally published in 1951): "Where we know the history of an invention, whether in technology, art, thought, or custom, we almost invariably find that it has not been made independently by a number of peoples in different places and at different times but by one people in one place and at a particular moment of their history, and that it has spread, wholly or in part, from this people to other peoples. When we look into the matter further we find that there have been a limited number of centres of important cultural development and diffusion, and also that in the process of borrowing and incorporation into other cultures the diffused traits may undergo all sorts of modifications and changes."

In its extreme form, diffusionism became a *reductio ad absurdum*; grandiose flights of fancy occurred as the origin of every institution was traced to its alleged source—usually ancient Egypt. Lucy Mair's conclusions about the intellectual battle are apt (*An Introduction to Social Anthropology*, 2nd ed. [Oxford: Clarendon Press, 1972], p. 20): "The whole discussion now seems rather unreal, ignoring as it does the obvious fact that the imitation of tools and techniques is something very different from the 'taking over' of institutions or myths. In fact most of the writers whose work has lived have recognized that the history of society must have been a mixture of independent development and the effects of external influences."

A POLITICAL-ANTHROPOLOGICAL APPROACH

At the highest theoretical level this book focuses upon the international transfer of political institutions; that increasingly prevalent phenomenon is best understood as a complex social communications process. Adopting a generalized overview of the communications net, the following elements can be identified.[7] First, a functioning political institution, the *source*, actively or passively emits messages about itself. Secondly, the *transmitter* or foreign inducer decodes those messages and encodes a signal. Thirdly, having been processed through a variety of political *channels*, the signal encounters the network's fourth major element; the *receiver* (host country) selectively interprets or decodes the signal and encodes or prepares to act on it. Finally, the receiver's message constitutes the *response*, which, if the communications process was successful, becomes a new political institution and a potential source for future transmissions.[8] Of course, in either the transmitter or receiver the signal may undergo substantial alteration due to encoding or decoding errors or to intentional modulations. Also, distortion may occur through the introduction of noise at any

[7] For an amplification of the model outlined here, see Larry B. Hill, "The Inter-Systematic Transfer of Political Institutions: A Communications Strategy for the Analysis of Political Change" (Paper delivered at the 66*th* Annual Meeting of the American Political Science Association, Los Angeles, 8–12 September 1970).

[8] This model's primary departure from Lasswell's useful early formulation, "Who / says what / in which channel / to whom / with what effect?" (Harold D. Lasswell, "The Structure and Function of Communication in Society," in Lyman Bryson, ed., *The Communication of Ideas* [New York: Harper, 1948], p. 37) is that it bifurcates his "who" and conceptually distinguishes source from transmitter. Furthermore, the proposed model may be differentiated from the usual unilinear model of information theory in which, as Warren Weaver (Claude E. Shannon and Warren Weaver, *The Mathematical Theory of Communication* [Urbana: University of Illinois Press, 1939], p. 98) has stated: "the *information source* selects a desired *message* out of a set of possible messages." The present formulation considers the source to be the *origin* of the communication but not necessarily its *initiator*. That role usually is fulfilled by a discrete agent of transmission.

point, especially in the channel. As in the parlor game "Telephone," the new institution may bear only a faint resemblance to the original source's message.

This broad conceptualization of the process of transfer permeates the following treatment, but I shall not attempt a systematic consideration of the entire communication process. Instead, I begin toward the end of it—when an exogenous institution is being "received" in the host political system. We shall inquire how the receiver decoded the signal and what response was encoded; these are very complex phenomena. The embryonic structure that is created must be integrated into the receiver's cultural-structural matrix. That integration process is called institutionalization. Whatever else it may be, institutionalization is a dynamic, or in anthropological terms a diachronic, phenomenon; it is an institution in the process of *becoming*.

This study focuses upon one principal aspect of the process of institutionalization, upon the political structure's relationship with its environment. The other main thrust of the institutionalization literature is upon internal structural integration. Nelson Polsby exemplifies this thrust in his study of the institutionalization of the House of Representatives in which he states: "Over the life span of this institution, it has become perceptibly more bounded, more complex, and more universalistic and automatic in its internal decision making."[9] Additionally, of Samuel Huntington's four criteria of institutionalization, two are internal: complexity and coherence.[10] Such

---

[9] Nelson W. Polsby, "The Institutionalization of the U.S. House of Representatives," *American Political Science Review* 62 (March 1968), 145.

[10] Samuel P. Huntington, "Political Development and Political Decay," *World Politics* 17 (April 1965), 394. The portions of this influential article that pertain to institutionalization are reprinted, with some revisions, in Huntington's book *Political Order in Changing Societies* (New Haven: Yale University Press, 1969), pp. 12–24.

measures of organizations' internal structures and capabilities clearly are material, particularly since large, intrinsically important structures including legislatures, political parties, bureaucracies, and armies are the usual units of analysis. Nevertheless, if one's focus is upon the political implications for a society of attempting to create a new institution, then a study of the nascent institution's linkages with its milieu may appear to be a higher research priority than analyses of the above-enumerated internal matters. It might even be argued that the salient aspects of the organization's internal capabilities are likely to be reflected in its external performance.

I conceive of the organization (the incipient institution) as a behaving entity or actor in an environment populated with other potentially competitive actors. Clearly, an institution must successfully defend itself against depredations from the environment, and some theorists view the organization's environmental relationships in defensive terms. Huntington's two final criteria of institutionalization are primarily defensive: adaptability (a function of chronological age, generational leadership succession, and ability to take on new functions while discarding obsolete ones), and autonomy ("the development of political organizations and procedures that are not simply expressions of the interests of particular social groups").[11] If, in addition to internal complexity and coherence, organizations attain high degrees of adaptability and autonomy in the face of environmental challenges, then Huntington contends they are institutionalized.

In my view, however, the development of defensive capabilities is a necessary yet not a sufficient index of institutionalization. Not only must an organization *defend*

[11] "Political Development and Political Decay," p. 401. It should be noted that Polsby's first criterion, well-boundedness, is not strictly internal; it is related to Huntington's environmental concept of autonomy.

itself against its environment, but also it must acquire an *offensive* capability. "From the very beginning," S. N. Eisenstadt has observed, "any bureaucratic organization is put in what may be called a power situation in relation to its environment and has to generate processes of power on its own behalf."[12] Only those organizations that succeed in generating sufficient power to affect their environment in significant respects—whether or not the effects are the ones desired by the creators—have the potential for institutionalization as the concept will be used here. I say "potential" because I limit the concept of institutionality to those organizations whose ability to affect the environment is based upon a particular type of power: authority, or rightful power. *Institutionalization is a process that occurs over time in which the organization creates authority relationships vis-à-vis the environmental actors.* That is, the organization attains a level of internal structural integration sufficient for the performance of its other functions; it manages to cope with any incursions from environmental actors; and through the exercise of whatever resources of power and influence are available, it succeeds in establishing itself as an authority figure.[13]

An institution's coercive power quotient may be high or low, but its ability to affect environmental actors is not primarily based upon coercion but rather upon the respect that those actors display toward the institution. Authority is above all else a subjective phenomenon, and

[12] *Essays on Comparative Institutions* (New York: John Wiley, 1965), p. 187. This focus upon the organization's offensive capability parallels Ralph Braibanti's ("External Inducement of Political-Administrative Development," p. 55) discussion of "permeative dynamism" and the "propelled rediffusion of norms from one institution to others."

[13] The conception of authority that is used here is indebted to Max Weber. See *The Theory of Social and Economic Organization*, trans. by A. M. Henderson and Talcott Parsons, ed. by Talcott Parsons (New York: Oxford University Press, 1947), Chapter 3.

A POLITICAL-ANTHROPOLOGICAL APPROACH

the best gauge of an organization's institutionalization is the willingness of environmental actors to defer to it. This is not to imply that the successful organization, the institution, exercises anything like sovereignty over its environment. Minimally, it does mean that the legitimacy of its existence is acknowledged. Furthermore, the institution has created the expectation among the environment's members that its actions and demands will fall within the boundaries of a shared normative framework, so that predispositions toward at least negotiated compliance are established.[14]

[14] In its subjective aspect, this definition of institutionalization is related to Philip Selznick's often-cited conception: "Organizations become institutions as they are *infused with value*, that is, prized not as tools alone but as sources of direct personal gratification and vehicles of group integrity." (*Leadership in Administration: A Sociological Interpretation* [New York: Harper and Row, 1957], p. 40; Selznick's italics.) Selznick's primary orientation is toward the internal consequences of valuing and prizing, as is true of most writers who have been influenced by him. For example, Huntington (citing Selznick at p. 396 of "Political Development and Political Decay") declares: "Institutionalization makes the organization more than simply an instrument to achieve certain purposes. Instead its leaders and members come to value it for its own sake, and it develops a life of its own quite apart from the specific functions it may perform at any given time."
  A distinctive contribution of the institution-building (IB) strand of literature, which has a pronounced social engineering bias, is that it extends Selznick's "infused with value" criterion into the organization's environment. In his essay "The Elements of Institution Building" (in Joseph W. Eaton, ed., *Institution Building and Development: From Concepts to Application* [Beverly Hills: Sage Publications, 1972], p. 28), Milton Esman—who has been IB's principal theoretician—has said that the two fundamental principles of institutionality, the end state of IB, are: "(1) new norms and action patterns must be established both within the organization and in its relevant environment, and (2) both the organization and the innovations for which it stands must become institutionalized, prized in the environment. This means that both the organization and the innovations it fosters are 'infuse[d] with value beyond the technical requirements of the task at hand,' to use Selznick's celebrated phrase." The Inter-University Research Program in Institu-

PROLOGUE

Finally, some implications of that part of our definition which portrays institutionalization as "a process that occurs over time" should be made explicit. I recommend, with Eisenstadt, that rather than conceiving of the phenomenon as an end point we should "talk about the *process of institutionalization* and look on it as a process of continuous crystallization of different types of norms and frameworks."[15] As Huntington has reminded us ("Political Development and Political Decay"), political structures atrophy and decay perhaps more commonly than they develop. Because political organizations are vulnerable to so many environmental and internal vicissitudes, we cannot with confidence examine Organization Y at Time Z and certify it as finally institutionalized in the sense that it is vulcanized against further change. Although reaching even the lowest measurable level of institutionalization is a notable achievement (this point is treated more extensively in Chapter 12), the continuous, developmental character of the process cannot be neglected. It requires that we also allow for institutional decay, or deinstitutionalization.

---

tion Building, whose members are Indiana, Michigan State, Pittsburgh, and Syracuse Universities, has been financed by the Ford Foundation and has had close ties with the Agency for International Development. Most of the program's papers have been distributed in mimeographed form; many of them have been collected in the recently published books edited by Thomas, et al., and by Eaton, which were cited above.

The present book's perspective on institutionalization was developed independently of the IB approach, but the two are compatible in many respects. Authority, however, seems preferable to value as a basis for institutionalization because of the former term's historical political connotations: specifically, it evokes images of deference and compliance. Furthermore, authority is normatively neutral in the sense that an organization may be treated as an authority figure (respected and obeyed) yet not be liked (valued and prized) by many of its environmental actors; e.g., internal security organizations often fit this category.

[15] *Essays on Comparative Institutions*, p. 32. Also see Selznick's similar statement in *Leadership in Administration*, p. 16.

A POLITICAL-ANTHROPOLOGICAL APPROACH

Fieldwork: Watching the Ombudsman

As the natives saw me constantly every day, they ceased to be interested or alarmed, or made self-conscious by my presence, and I ceased to be a disturbing element in the tribal life which I was to study. . . . They finished by regarding me as part and parcel of their life, a necessary evil or nuisance, mitigated by donations of tobacco. Living in the village with no other business but to follow native life, one sees the customs, ceremonies and transactions over and over again. . . . The Ethnographer is enabled to add something essential to the bare outline of tribal constitution, and to supplement it by all the details of behaviour, setting and small incident.

It is good for the Ethnographer sometimes to put aside camera, note book and pencil, and to join in himself in what is going on. He can take part in the natives' games, he can follow them on their visits and walks, sit down and listen and share in their conversations.

Based upon the portrait of the ombudsman presented in Chapter 1, we would not expect the office's policy impacts to be so profound as to be easily discernible; concomitantly, the process of institutionalization—as it has just been sketched—is a subtle, developmental phenomenon whose extent could be accurately measured only by the application, over an extended period, of the most sensitive analytical techniques. Thus, my choice of an anthropological approach was epistemologically based: I concluded that the fieldwork perspective offered a superior means of knowing about the ombudsman, of attaining the deepest possible understanding of the consequences for the New Zealand political system of creating the office.[16]

---

[16] The selection of this methodological approach follows the advice W. Richard Scott ("Field Methods in the Study of Organizations," in

PROLOGUE

The decision to undertake an institutional study based upon fieldwork that would meet standards accepted by modern anthropologists carried with it a deep personal commitment, for it is generally presumed that about one year is the minimum period of field research likely to be profitable and that two years or more—including time spent in language study—is preferable.[17] Anthropologists are convinced that intensive observation of such duration is necessary to unravel from its context the meaning of the behavior under analysis. The seriousness with which anthropologists assume the duty of immersing themselves in their research is revealed in Evans-Pritchard's remark that if there is not sorrow on the part of both the fieldworker and his subjects when he says goodbye, the anthropologist has failed: "he can only establish this intimacy if he makes himself in some degree a member of their society and lives, thinks, and feels in their culture."[18]

Because the Maoris, the original Polynesian inhabi-

James G. March, ed., *Handbook of Organizations* [Chicago: Rand McNally, 1965], pp. 269–70) gave to those deciding whether "sustained" or "transitory" methods were more appropriate to their circumstances: "The researcher interested in characterizing the total situation and examining the nature of that 'totalness' will typically plan to engage in sustained interaction with subject group members, since this approach provides better opportunities for observing many aspects of the situation and for tracing through the connections among phenomena." Furthermore, Scott (p. 270) recommended: "If the system under examination is relatively small and change is considered an important element of the study design, sustained participation by the researcher will be the more satisfactory approach."

[17] Evans-Pritchard, *Social Anthropology*, p. 78. Because of the nature of the phenomenon I have chosen to study, my methodological discussion may sometimes be less descriptive of the American discipline of *cultural* anthropology than of the predominantly British study of *social* anthropology—which Raymond Firth once said might as well be labeled "micro-sociology." *Elements of Social Organization* (New York: Philosophical Library, 1951), p. 17.

[18] Evans-Pritchard, *Social Anthropology*, p. 79.

A POLITICAL-ANTHROPOLOGICAL APPROACH

tants, have intrigued generations of scholars, New Zealanders are used to anthropologists.[19] I hope my New Zealand friends will understand that in saying I studied government anthropologically and in using fieldwork terminology commonly applied to primitive societies, I do not in any way imply that the Kiwis are an underdeveloped people. The fact that New Zealand is a developed society facilitated my research in many ways, and not having to learn a new language saved time. During nineteen months of fieldwork, I wrestled with the twin problems of the Ombudsman's performance and institutionalization.

The establishment of a high level of rapport with the "natives" is crucial to the success of any extended anthropological effort; without the active support of a large number of New Zealanders in public life, this study could not have been done. Most important, of course, was the cooperation of the Ombudsman himself, Sir Guy Powles, who independently decided to allow it, and of his staff. Sir Guy graciously allowed me to use his office on The Terrace as my headquarters between the airy heights of the Victoria University and the nether regions of the government offices on Lambton Quay. He allocated me a room in his office complex where much of this research was done.

A peculiarly American question very often asked in discussions about the institution is, "But who will watch the ombudsman?" From the beginning of 1967 through August 1968, I watched the New Zealand Ombudsman. My approach featured sustained participation of an intensive character. I estimate that I averaged spending about thirty hours per week, including hours after closing

---

[19] As an academic subject, anthropology has flourished in New Zealand universities. A notable New Zealand–born (and New Zealand–educated at the undergraduate and master's levels) anthropologist is Raymond Firth, who became one of Malinowski's early doctoral students and later assumed his mentor's chair at London University.

PROLOGUE

time, in the office. During that time I observed the entire process of interaction, participated in staff meetings, and discussed general office policies as well as the handling of specific cases—all the while consuming innumerable cups of tea. Sir Guy allowed me complete access to his files and library and assisted in what most reasonable men surely would have regarded as an excruciatingly extended investigation of themselves. Under the terms of our agreement Sir Guy reserved the right to approve my usage of materials from his files. In the event, however, not one word was censored.

In short, my arrangement with the Ombudsman and his staff was ideal, I had all necessary access, and both professional and social rapport were excellent. The merits of having the observer become involved on a sustaining basis as a contributing participant in the activities under scrutiny are matters of debate among fieldworkers. However close my relationships were, I was not a staff member. The significance of some data probably escaped me because I did not become as intimately involved with the cases as I would have been if I had been either an employee or an intern in a public administration training program. Nevertheless, I became sufficiently expert at the office's *modus operandi* that upon reading a letter of complaint I normally could predict how it would be dealt with. Viewing my independence positively, it freed me from the tedium of routine cases and allowed me to schedule my movements independently. Even more important—I retained my objectivity and, I hope, triumphed over the fieldworker's natural inclination to bias the results by overidentifying with his subject. Although there was never any hostility, neither I nor the Ombudsman's office ever forgot that I was conducting a dispassionate political audit of the institution. Furthermore, this independence was crucial in establishing my credibility with the bureaucracy.

Because of the nature of the Ombudsman institution,

A POLITICAL-ANTHROPOLOGICAL APPROACH

much of the politically significant activity, such as interaction with government departments or Members of Parliament, could be monitored from his office. This simplified the research design, but I was not satisfied merely to observe the Ombudsman. I also did fieldwork in the government agencies that had the most contact with the Ombudsman, again with the objective of measuring his impact. Additionally, I interviewed the civil servants who were the directors of those agencies and also all eighty Members of Parliament, including the Ministers of the Crown. A fuller description of each of these project phases appears below.

Despite my success at gaining close access and maintaining rapport, I was continually made aware that the fieldworker's role always is a "marginal" one.[20] New Zealand politics is intimate politics; at the higher governmental levels, interpersonal communication ("old boy") networks are exquisitely intricate. The close-knit character of the political elite simplified my access to them, but it also was threatening in a subtle sense. Unfavorable as well as favorable messages about the investigator or the project could be transmitted quickly, and I was dependent upon maintaining close rapport over a long period of time. Furthermore, unlike traditional anthropologists dealing with "unsophisticated" peoples, I was demanding substantial amounts of time and forbearance from many modern, well-educated professionals who counted their time as a valuable commodity. The knowledge was constant that an unintentional offense, an event beyond my control, or even a sudden realization that I had been hanging around for a ridiculously long time could evaporate my entrée. The most prominent feature of my research design was a complex coding system

---

[20] See the personalized accounts of fieldwork experience contained in Morris Freilich, ed., *Marginal Natives: Anthropologists at Work* (New York: Harper and Row, 1970).

PROLOGUE

for the Ombudsman's cases that was not finally developed and put into operation until near the end of my stay. In other respects, too, the project's pieces were so interrelated that, like a house of cards, the failure of any one could cause the entire structure to collapse. Thus I felt highly vulnerable to a sudden loss of rapport.[21]

Nothing of the kind occurred. To the contrary, the support that I continued to receive up to the end of my research from the Ombudsman,[22] bureaucrats, and politicians was exemplary. The fact that no individual in pub-

[21] After I had been at work for several months the Ombudsman decided that, according to law, my oral pledge not to disclose the contents of his files might be insufficient, and I was sworn to confidentiality under the Official Secrets Act. Since the decision was precipitated by the request of another student to do a brief study of "my"—note the proprietary adjective—Ombudsman, I felt doubly threatened. One of my reactions to such feelings of malaise was to undertake, during the course of the interviews with Members of Parliament about the Ombudsman, an extremely time-consuming role analysis of the parliamentarians' jobs, as a hedge against the possible collapse of the original project. Of course this was not really secure either, because the party leaders could at any time revoke permission to interview.

The essays in *Marginal Natives* indicate that such anxiety feelings are common, perhaps inevitable, results of the length and intensity of the field experience. I cannot recommend fieldwork to those who are already emotionally insecure; Malinowski's report (*Argonauts*, p. 4) of the generalized depression he sometimes suffered parallels my own experience: "I well remember the long visits I paid to the villages during the first weeks; the feeling of hopelessness and dispair after many obstinate but futile attempts had entirely failed to bring me into real touch with the natives, or supply me with any material. I had periods of despondency, when I buried myself in the reading of novels, as a man might take to drink in a fit of tropical depression and boredom."

[22] Since I have mentioned my occasional flashes of paranoia, I should stress that in general my relationship with Sir Guy was a comfortable, even a joking, relationship. I recall that once, while reviewing the draft of my code for his cases, Sir Guy pointed to the category "Nature of Complaint" and noted that there was no entry to fit the two women who occasionally came into the office only to use the ladies' room. He supposed theirs should be coded as "Complaint Against Nature."

lic life, from the Prime Minister on down, refused my request for an interview is an index of the cooperation I received. Furthermore, I found that officials normally would allow me access to interesting materials that were confidential but not highly politically sensitive, if they were convinced that I could be relied upon to use them circumspectly. In fact, I was faced with a surfeit of data and constantly had to face difficult decisions about what was vital and what was peripheral.

I stressed to all groups my role as a neutral investigator and took care not to advertise the extensiveness of my contacts with the Ombudsman, knowledge of which might have made my independence suspect. That I began my research from a position of neutrality was generally accepted, and I jealously guarded the reputation. At the same time, however, I recalled Rosalie Wax's insight that fieldwork involves the building of reciprocal relationships and tried to provide incentives for people to present their positions in detail. I maintained "the attitude of one who was willing to be convinced that the person with whom I was talking was on the side of right and justice"[23] and in other ways implied that I might be converted to their point of view.

As a practical matter, reconciling my high degree of involvement with the goal of scientific detachment sometimes proved difficult. While discussing cases with an agency or with the Ombudsman it sometimes developed that one or the other party misunderstood the other's position. Since both parties might know that I was doubly informed, it was inappropriate merely to make a mental note of their misunderstanding; sometimes I acted as a communications channel. This only expedited understanding, and did not constitute intervention in the sense

[23] Rosalie H. Wax, "Reciprocity as a Field Technique," *Human Organization* 11 (Fall 1952), 37. This perspective is given extended treatment in Rosalie H. Wax, *Doing Fieldwork: Warnings and Advice* (Chicago: University of Chicago Press, 1971).

of advocacy of a point of view. Nevertheless, my knowledgeability helped me establish an image as a potentially useful source rather than as just an exotic parasite. I also was favorably situated to relay gossip among various groups—e.g., bureaucrats, the Ombudsman and his staff, parliamentarians, and members of the university faculty. Most everyone relishes such juicy conversational tidbits as colorful, informal reactions and preannouncements of impending decisions, but I was constantly reminded that today's listener is tomorrow's informant and nobody respects or cooperates with those who cannot be trusted to hold their tongue.

Apart from occasionally providing some interesting or useful information, there was little of a substantive nature that I could offer my informants in reciprocation for their help (I could not offer tobacco as Malinowski did, or money as some anthropologists do in tribal areas). But the intangible rewards of cooperation were sufficient. Many informants found it amusing or distracting to have some connection with a scientific project, others felt rewarded just by the experience of assisting a stranger who asked for help, and yet others seemed to hold the mistaken belief that talking to me might somehow help them. In addition to several of the motives just mentioned, the Ombudsman's deep involvement with my project was probably stimulated by a Messianic belief in publicizing the office's mission (based upon confidence that my report would, inevitably, be favorable) and by the commendably open attitude that such an office (created to monitor the activities of other government agencies) ought itself to be open to public scrutiny.

Certain aspects of my objective status were useful in gaining access and promoting rapport. The role of Fulbright scholar enhanced my legitimacy as did my connection with the School of Political Science and Public Administration of the Victoria University of Wellington, where I was appointed Junior Lecturer and taught the course in American politics for one term. Also, I became a

A POLITICAL-ANTHROPOLOGICAL APPROACH

minor celebrity through agreeing on various occasions (e.g., following the assassinations of Martin Luther King, Jr. and Robert F. Kennedy) to pose as resident expert on American politics for the New Zealand Broadcasting Corporation. Many bureaucratic and political respondents commented on the television and radio exposure, and identification with the N.Z.B.C. added to my credibility. The university tie was important practically too, because my colleagues used their close governmental relationships on my behalf to arrange interviews.

Furthermore, as an American I was an outsider, an innocent observer who reasonably could ask for full explanations, and yet one who was transient and therefore not a potential threat. It was also to my advantage that New Zealand bureaucrats have scarcely been studied. Some were visibly flattered at my interest in their work; others labored under the impression, which I certainly did not correct, that I was an official visitor to whom every courtesy was due. The politicians were more used to being studied, but they too cooperated fully. Several Members of Parliament asked when it would be their turn to be interviewed, and it appeared that some considered it prestigious to be seen being interviewed.

RESEARCH DESIGN: THE OMBUDSMAN'S AUTHORITY SYSTEM

The whole area of tribal culture in all its aspects has to be gone over in research. The consistency, the law and order which obtain within each aspect make also for joining them into one coherent whole. An Ethnographer who sets out to study only religion, or only technology, or only social organisation cuts out an artificial field for inquiry. Each phenomenon ought to be studied through the broadest range possible of its concrete manifestations; each studied by an exhaustive survey of detailed examples. If possible, the results ought to be tabulated into some sort of synoptic chart, both to be used as an

PROLOGUE

instrument of study, and to be presented as an ethnological document. With the help of such documents and such study of actualities the clear outline of the framework of the natives' culture in the widest sense of the word, and the constitution of their society, can be presented. This method could be called the method of statistic documentation by concrete evidence.

The unit of analysis adopted by early anthropologists usually was an entire small-scale society, typically a village or tribe. As larger entities were encountered, the scope of the phenomena under investigation had to be narrowed, and the concept of a field of social relations was developed.[24] That concept, too, has been narrowed analytically; Swartz, Turner, and Tuden have suggested that attention be focused upon the political field, which they conceive of as a "spatial-temporal continuum."

> A political field does not operate like clockwork, with all the pieces meshed together with finely tooled precision. It is, rather, a field of tension, full of intelligent and determined antagonists, sole and corporate, who are motivated by ambition, altruism, self-interest, and by desire for the public good, and who in successive situations are bound to one another through self-interest, or idealism—and separated or opposed through the same motives. At every point in this process we have to consider each unit in terms of its independent objectives, and we also have to consider the entire situation in which their interdependent actions occur.[25]

This book does not attempt comprehensive coverage of the New Zealand political field, although the Om-

[24] See Meyer Fortes, *The Dynamics of Clanship Among the Tallensi* (London: Oxford University Press, 1945), Chapter 13.

[25] Marc J. Swartz, Victor W. Turner, and Arthur Tuden, Introduction to Swartz, Turner, and Tuden, eds., *Political Anthropology* Chicago: Aldine, 1966), p. 8.

budsman's strategic location astride society's most sensitive pressure points insures that our narrative contains substantial amounts of general political analysis. Our focus is upon a particular aspect of the political field: those activities that have any significant bearing upon the office of Ombudsman.

The Ombudsman can be thought of as a cybernetic device for mediating the relationships between the governors and the governed. Such a systems conception accurately describes his position in the larger political context and also can be useful for examining the office's performance and institutionalization. Unlike most intensive, extended studies of organizations (which mainly focus upon what life is like for those who work or live inside the organization), I conceive of the office as an organization in action[26] and focus upon the Ombudsman's "foreign" relations. When the Ombudsman was created, it became the new organization's mission to interact with and develop regularized authority relationships with certain other political actors. This pattern of relationships we may label the Ombudsman's authority system—a subsystem, or subfield, of the larger political field.[27]

[26] See James D. Thompson, *Organizations in Action* (New York: McGraw-Hill, 1967).

[27] For an extended discussion, see Larry B. Hill, "The New Zealand Ombudsman's Authority System," *Political Science* 20 (September 1968), 40–51. Some organization theorists (e.g., Thompson, *Organizations in Action*, pp. 27–29) might call this authority system the Ombudsman's task environment.

Earlier I criticized the institution-building tradition's theoretical grounding upon a rather weak sociological concept, but the research designs of the IB engineers sometimes seem, in actuality, to study authority instead of value. For example, two proposed tests of institutionality are *influence* (the extent to which the organization affects decisions in its functional area and its ability to enlarge its sphere of action) and *impact* or spread effect (the degree to which its values and actions become normative within the environment). See Milton J. Esman and Hans C. Blaise, "Institution Building Research: The Guiding Concepts," Mimeographed (Pittsburgh: University of Pittsburgh, Graduate School of Public and International Affairs, 1966), pp. 6–7.

PROLOGUE

In carving out this analytical slice of social relationships we are, of course, creating "an artificial field of inquiry"—precisely the operation that Malinowski warned against in the above epigraph. Nevertheless, we shall be concerned with the relatedness of the various pieces of our analysis to the larger social whole. And, more to the point, we shall examine nearly the full range of relationships within our action system, giving particular attention to those factors that contribute toward what Malinowski called "joining them into one coherent whole." Even though the systemic relationships are, in the main, segmental—e.g., the Ombudsman and the bureaucrats usually interact only in their professional roles—from the viewpoint of the authority system, the perspective is holistic. Within-action-system-holism is a rather infelicitous term, but it is reasonably accurate as a description of my perspective.[28]

The book's plan can be set out briefly as follows. Chapter 3 completes the Prologue by placing the Ombudsman in context within the New Zealand political environment and telling the story of the birth of an institution. Part 2 assumes that if we scrutinize the interactions, transactions, or exchanges[29] between a putative institution and the other actors in its environment, we can draw some objective and reasonably reliable inferences about the strength of authority relationships: consequently, Chap-

[28] Anthropologists recently have become interested in complex societies, but little research yet has been done; nor is there any consensus upon the discipline's role in this new field. A reviewer inquires: "Must the anthropologist who studies a complex society become no more (and no less) than a coordinator of other specialists? Must 'holism,' perhaps an ephemeral idea at best, be utterly neglected in favor of segmental analyses of institutions, networks, or social categories?" Gilbert Kushner, "The Anthropology of Complex Societies," in Bernard J. Siegel, ed., *Biennial Review of Anthropology, 1969* (Stanford: Stanford University Press, 1970), p. 81.

[29] For an interpretation of institutionalization as an exchange process see Eisenstadt, *Essays on Comparative Institutions*, Chapter 1, Part 1. Esman discusses linkages and transactions in "The Elements of Institution Building," pp. 28–34.

ter 4 analyzes the Ombudsman's complaints, Chapter 5 examines his clients from a sociological perspective, Chapters 6 and 7 trace the exchange relationships between the Ombudsman and the clients and those between the bureaucracy and the Ombudsman, and Chapter 8 probes into the Ombudsman's policy impact upon both the clients and the bureaucracy. Part 3 represents an attempt to assess the normative dimensions of the office's authority through an investigation of the organizationally related attitudes, values, beliefs, and expectations of key individuals in the environment: the reactions to the Ombudsman of his principal targets, the bureaucrats, are considered in Chapter 9; and the Ombudsman opinions of Members of Parliament and Ministers of the Crown are presented in Chapters 10 and 11. Finally: the Epilogue evaluates the Ombudsman's performance as a social program, inquires into the degree of institutionalization, and explores the extent to which transformation or real institutional transfer have occurred.

Having announced that an investigation was undertaken of the behavioral and attitudinal linkages that have developed over time between the Ombudsman and the other actors in the authority system is not the same thing as saying *how* the investigation was conducted. Several alternative methods could have been chosen for the collection and presentation of such data. Malinowski (epigraph) made the intriguing suggestion that "synoptic charts," consisting of compilations of detailed examples of concrete behavior, be created as a means of revealing cultural patterns. Neither in *Argonauts* nor in his later work, however, did he actually construct charts that went beyond chronologies, genealogies, and the simplest analytical presentations.[30]

---

[30] E.g., Bronislaw Malinowski, *The Dynamics of Culture Change: An Inquiry into Race Relations in Africa*, ed. by Phyllis M. Kaberry (New Haven: Yale University Press, 1945), "Synoptic Chart for Problems of Native Diet in Their Economic Setting," pp. 104–5.

PROLOGUE

In fact, like the next generation of anthropologists, Malinowski's scientific approach was characterized by what Max Gluckman has called the "method of apt illustration." That is, following extensive observation and data collection, a general framework for the analysis of the society or culture was constructed:

> We then used the apt and appropriate case to illustrate specific customs, principles of organization, social relationships, etc. Each case was selected for its appropriateness at a particular point in the argument; and cases coming close together in the argument might be derived from the actions or words of quite different groups or individuals. There was no regularly established connection between the series of incidents in cases cited at different points in the analysis.[31]

In addition to the lack of connectedness of such cases, it should be apparent that in this methodology much hinges upon the fieldworker's capabilities as an accurate observer, upon his ability to focus upon significant problems, and upon the typicality of the cases selected.

Recognizing the theoretical limitations of the method of apt illustration, the "Manchester school" of social anthropology—under Max Gluckman's leadership—has developed the "extended-case method," which features detailed analyses of the connectedness of social relationships over time. Gluckman has contended that "the most fruitful use of cases consists in taking a series of specific incidents affecting the same persons or groups, through a long period of time, and showing how these incidents, these cases, are related to the development and change of social relations among these persons and groups, act-

---

[31] Max Gluckman, "Ethnographic Data in British Social Anthropology," *Sociological Review* 9 (March 1961), 7–8; a revised version of much of this article appears in Max Gluckman, Introduction to A. L. Epstein, ed., *The Craft of Social Anthropology* (London: Tavistock Publications, 1967), pp. xi–xx.

ing within the framework of their social system and culture."[32]

The following analysis of the relationships in the Ombudsman's authority system employs a version of the extended-case method. Of course, the chore of the organizational analyst is somewhat easier than that of the general observer of society, for organizations are defined by their formalized activities; and these activities become focal points of analysis. Among organizations, the Ombudsman has tasks that are in a structural sense highly patterned and repetitive, although in substance every complaint is unique. The work is analogous to a court's activities: complaints are lodged, some sort of deliberative or investigative process—involving various political actors—occurs, and a ruling is made which disposes of the case. Over time, a clear pattern of relationships develops, including the growth of a body of "case law." At an early stage in the fieldwork I confirmed that the files on each case were a veritable gold mine of information about the Ombudsman's functioning and that questions about the content of the complaints, the sociological identities of the clients, the client-Ombudsman-bureaucratic exchange relationships, and the office's impact upon both clients and the bureaucracy all could be monitored through a close analysis of the files. That such an approach made it possible to chart how the office's pertinent relationships had developed over time was also propitious.[33]

---

[32] Gluckman, "Ethnographic Data," p. 10. An excellent example (really an "apt illustration") of the use of the extended-case approach is J. Van Velsen, *The Politics of Kinship: A Study in Social Manipulation Among the Lakeside Tonga of Nyasaland* (Manchester: Manchester University Press for the Rhodes-Livingston Institute, 1964).

[33] Many early social anthropologists, such as Malinowski and Radcliffe-Brown, held an exaggerated conception of the functional unity of the systems they studied. The creation of the Ombudsman was intrusive as far as the government actors in his authority system were concerned (although perhaps from a more elevated and long-term perspec-

PROLOGUE

Following some weeks of more-or-less random observation, during which I "immersed myself in the data," picked the brains of a number of informants who were reputed to be astute, and ruminated about how to study the office, I began to formulate a plan of attack—a detailed code for the case analysis that would bare the Ombudsman's life history. As a conscientious student, I searched for models, but could not find a previous study that utilized a similarly intensive and comprehensive approach to institutional biography. Although some works on content analysis and data processing were suggestive, I was, in the end, left to my own devices.

As I observed the office and discussed it with bureaucrats and others, I began to note what looked like regularized patterns of behavior and formulated a great lot of questions about various possible relationships. These were often framed in hypothetical terms, but I acknowledge that my approach was largely exploratory. The principal explanation for this was that no base of previous, behavioral research on ombudsmen existed from which hypotheses could be generated. Strangely, even the available descriptive writings were, in the main, so normative or legalistic in nature that they contained few speculations about possible organizational relationships. However pleased I may feel in retrospect at having been a pioneer, during the fieldwork period such feelings were tempered by the insecurities of traveling through uncharted territory.

Unfortunately, some of the questions that occurred to me could not be answered by the data; my approach had

---

tive, the development may be viewed as "functional"—in the sense that it promotes stability for the political system). In my view the potential for conflict is, in a general sense, inherent in such systems, and the question of how much tension or cooperation is characteristic of a particular system is a matter for empirical investigation. As Gluckman notes ("Ethnographic Data," p. 15), the extended-case method is especially useful for revealing such relationships.

A POLITICAL-ANTHROPOLOGICAL APPROACH

to be both inductive and deductive. Over the course of more than a year, I developed a code that was, in effect, a questionnaire for "interviewing" the files. Inevitably, the code went through innumerable drafts, each of which was given several trial runs. During the development process, the questions of whether a given phenomenon occurred often enough to be worth the burden of coding it and whether the coding categories that had evolved were exhaustive of the empirical or logical possibilities were omnipresent. The former question was complicated by the understanding that much about the office might be revealed through documenting how seldom a particular circumstance occurred; for example, it was not until the final stages that I realized it was important to record that the Ombudsman's clients very seldom asked for favoritism—unlike many complainants to legislators.

While the code was being fashioned, I was researching the institution's origins, conducting case studies of some government agencies' experiences with the Ombudsman (reported in Chapter 7), and beginning to investigate its relations with Parliament. These activities continually led me to add to, or otherwise refine, the coding instrument and also contributed to the development of the questionnaires for interviewing the bureaucrats and parliamentarians. Those interviews were begun before the coding of the cases started, so they too provided useful leads for the coding instrument.

The Ombudsman Act 1962 required that complaints be made in writing. Instead of filling out a bureaucratic form, however, citizens merely write a letter stating their grievance in their own words. Although the idiosyncratic character of the letters greatly complicated the coding process, they provided important data about many of the clients' social and some psychological attributes. As we shall see below, even though no complaint form was provided (or perhaps *because* none was available), clients tended to have the outline of a form in mind while writing. Thus, they usually provided in their letters a considerable amount of information about themselves, and it is possible to draw important inferences from these personalized documents. During the latter stages of developing the coding instrument, I learned that Dr. Laurie Brown, Professor of Psychology at the Victoria University of Wellington, also was interested in analyzing the letters of complaint. Several of the loosely social-psychological variables that are analyzed in Chapters 5 and 6 were developed in collaboration with Professor Brown; some should be credited to him exclusively. As finally revised, the coding instrument was extensive; I attempted to collect ninety-six separate pieces of information about each case.

Apart from developing a coding instrument, the other main problems of the case analysis were the structuring of the sample and the determination of its size. Since there was no firm knowledge of the actual distribution of the cases' important characteristics, there was no mandate for structuring the sample in a particular fashion. Because of the project's focus upon institutionalization, a longitudinally based procedure—which would be sensitive to change over time—was adopted.[34]

There was no indication, statistical or otherwise, as to an optimum sample size. On intuitive grounds, it was decided that about one-tenth of the total complaints lodged would constitute a sample sufficiently large to be representative.[35] In the end, 450 cases—11 percent of the

[34] The chronological procedure also was convenient, since the cases were numbered and filed sequentially. Not only would a random sample have masked changes over time, it also would have forced an early cut-off of the pool of cases that had a chance to be included; during the study, the universe grew by 1,500 cases.

[35] For a statistical test of the sample in which its results are compared with the Ombudsman's report of the figures for the total actual cases on an important variable, see note 1, Chapter 8.

total cases processed at the conclusion of our analysis—were coded and are used in the following exploration.[36]

To conclude, my approach to the Ombudsman represents a melding of the traditional anthropological perspective with the perspectives held by modern, quantitatively-oriented sociologists and political scientists. Because of the time and attention devoted to the design of the questionnaires and the coding instrument, it might seem that I intended to exemplify the following maxim: "The fieldworker who knows precisely how to put his questions has also come to know a large proportion of the correct answers."[37] Such was not, however, my

[36] The original intention was to sample 20 percent of the cases. Thus, coding began on the 3,000-odd cases that existed at that time; cases 0005, 0010, 0015, etc., were taken in order. As the coding approached 200 complaints (case 1,000), it became apparent that the time required to code the cases would, at that rate, exceed the time available. Simply to proceed until time ran out was undesirable because of a wish to examine the process of institutionalization over the longest time span possible. Therefore, the decision was taken to jump two bodies of cases. (The alternative would have been to change the basis of sampling, but this would have caused some cases that were already coded to be discarded.) According to the revised procedure, every fifth case from 0005 to 1,000 (September 1962 to February 1964) was coded; cases 1,005 to 2,000 were skipped; 2,005 to 3,000 (July 1965 to February 1967) were coded; 3,005 to 4,000 were skipped, and 4,005 to 4,280 (September 1968 to March 1969) were coded.

The original purpose of the sampling procedure, to note trends over time, can be served in two ways. First: we can compare the three main time groups. Second: we can look for patterns within the nine batches of fifty coded cases. In either event, the gaps that exist because the intervening cases were not analyzed will accentuate any changes that may occur. To save space, the book's tables do not depict the time perspective; any important changes over time are presented textually.

To keep readers from foundering amid a surfeit of numbers, the percentage figures presented below usually have been rounded to the nearest whole percent. Exceptions occur when they are compared with other exact figures, such as census reports. This rounding explains why some totals may equal slightly more or less than 100 percent.

[37] Rosalie Wax (*Doing Fieldwork*, p. 26) believes that this piece of professional folklore originated with Sidney and Beatrice Webb.

PROLOGUE

intention. Although I had gained—through general observation and intuitive insight—some important understandings about the Ombudsman, I did not trust to these impressions but used them as the framework for the systematic collection of data that were "hard" and intersubjectively transmissible. The quantitative approach was convenient because it focused and simplified the analysis; the quantity of data available was so great that patterns often were difficult to discern impressionistically. But the computer analysis of the complaints not only reduced the data to manageable proportions, it also yielded many findings that were a surprise to me and to the Ombudsman and his staff.

Having taken our bearings and set the course for our study in the Antipodes, let us begin the ethnological report.

CHAPTER THREE

Creating the Social Field: The Ombudsman in New Zealand

NEW Zealand is a modern "developed" society,[1] and politics takes place within a context in which government is very actively and deeply involved in society.[2] The ubiquitous welfare state might come into direct contact with individuals on such matters as installing a telephone, granting a pension, obtaining a loan on a house, or writing a last will and testament. These and many other disparate services require a large governmental establishment, and New Zealand has the world's highest percentage of its working-age population employed by its various government and public enterprises.[3] Considerable financial resources are also required, and New Zealand's extractive as well as distributive capabilities are well developed. It is the third- or fourth-ranking nation and is close to the leaders in the measure (by different methods) of both governmental revenue and expenditure as a percentage of the Gross National Product.[4]

[1] New Zealand was placed first among fifty countries on a "social evolution" scale derived from Parsonian theory. See Gary L. Buck and Alvin L. Jacobson, "Social Evolution and Structural-Functional Analysis: An Empirical Test," *American Sociological Review* 33 (June 1968), 348.

[2] For a more detailed exploration see Larry B. Hill, "Political Culture-and-Personality: Theoretical Perspectives on Democratic Stability from the New Zealand Pattern," in Samuel A. Kirkpatrick and Lawrence K. Petitt, eds., *The Social Psychology of Political Life* (Belmont, Calif.: Duxbury Press, 1972), pp. 140–56.

[3] Bruce M. Russett, et. al., *World Handbook of Political and Social Indicators* (New Haven: Yale University Press, 1964), Table 19, p. 70.

[4] Ibid., Table 14, p. 62; Table 15, p. 63; Table 16, p. 64; and Table 17, p. 65. For a discussion of the welfare state, see C. Westrate, *Portrait of A Modern Mixed Economy: New Zealand* (Wellington: Sweet and Maxwell, 1959).

PROLOGUE

One might guess that the bureaucracy's pervasiveness was responsible for New Zealand's adoption of the ombudsman. Certainly, the extensive citizen-government contacts were a relevant consideration, but the explanation of why New Zealand chose an ombudsman is much more complicated than this. In pursuing the explanation, this chapter will examine several aspects of the political environment that also are important in understanding the ombudsman's institutionalization. The chapter's three sections inquire into New Zealand's cultural receptivity to the ombudsman, into the structure of the traditional governmental appeals agencies, and into the political processes of transferring the ombudsman.

Receptivity to the Ombudsman

Since it became an essentially independent nation in the mid-nineteenth century, New Zealand has developed or has been among the first to adopt a number of political institutions. Prominent among them have been 1) the neglected and dependent children legislation, 1867; 2) the Government Life Insurance Department, 1869; 3) the Public Trust Office, 1872; 4) women's suffrage, 1893; 5) the Court of Arbitration, 1894; 6) Old Age Pensions Act, 1898; 7) Family Allowances Act, 1926; 8) government health care program implemented, 1938–41; and 9) unicameral legislature, 1950.[5]

New Zealand has thereby gained an international reputation for innovativeness, a reputation as a laboratory of democracy fairly seething with political experiments. Despite such political experiments, however, social critics have long contended that New Zealand is not a truly innovative society. Instead, they identify certain conservative social characteristics including Victorian standards

---

[5] See the Chronological Table in J. L. Robson, ed., *New Zealand: The Development of Its Laws and Constitution*, 2nd ed. (London: Stevens, 1967), pp. xv–xx.

of morality and of treatment of women and children, an insular cultural smugness, a lack of economic initiative, and oppressive community pressures toward conformism.[6] Without entering into arguments about the accuracy of this sociological analysis, it is appropriate to point out that there is no evidence indicating that a country's social and political propensities toward innovation necessarily correspond.

Criticizing New Zealand's innovativeness from another perspective, in 1904 André Siegfried commented:

> A people can advertise itself, just as a merchant or a manufacturer can. The New Zealanders are quite aware of it. . . .
>
> They are proud of their innovations and their trials of what had been tried nowhere else; they enjoy being able to smile at the timidity of old countries, and to believe that they are giving them lessons. Votes for women? Why not? It is new; it is something to try. . . . And it is the same with all kinds of measures. For this strange rage for novelty lies at the inception of most of their laws.[7]

The purpose here is not to judge the "genuineness" of New Zealand's commitment to political change. Taking into account her small size (the population was about 2.3 million in 1960, and the land area is about equal to that of the state of Colorado) and remoteness from large centers of population (even Australia is 1,200 miles away), the degree of overcompensation is perhaps not unnatural. In any event, the presence of the cultural norm of political innovation is highly significant. Over forty years after

[6] See, for example, David P. Ausubel, *The Fern and the Tiki: An American View of New Zealand National Character, Social Attitudes and Race Relations* (New York: Holt, Rinehart and Winston, 1960), p. 6.

[7] André Siegfried, *Democracy in New Zealand* (London: G. Bell, 1913), pp. 61–62, quoted in J. B. Condliffe, *New Zealand in the Making*, 2nd ed. (London: Allen and Unwin, 1959), p. 184.

PROLOGUE

Siegfried commented about New Zealand's "strange rage for novelty," Lipson was to observe that that trait still existed and that it could be strategically used by the agent of change: "In his advocacy he can suggest that if his plan is adopted, New Zealand will be starting a new experiment and thus will again lead the world."[8] Expectations of innovation are created and further experimentation may become a self-fulfilling prophecy. Hence, innovations such as the ombudsman could be expected to be considered sympathetically if their applicability to a particular situation that was perceived as a political problem were demonstrated.

Since the ombudsman had evolved as an institution for the control of bureaucracy, it is imperative to probe New Zealand's image of bureaucracy. Although there are few data bearing directly upon this subject, it is apparent that one strand of the political culture disagrees with the academicians'[9] sympathetic view of the public service. In fact, Professor Campbell has described it as a New Zealand tradition "that the civil service should be widely regarded with fear, contempt, and dislike as a host of unproductive, socialistic, power-hungry bureaucrats."[10] Colored by his British perspective, this assessment seems to be somewhat overdrawn.

---

[8] Leslie Lipson, *The Politics of Equality* (Chicago: University of Chicago Press, 1948), p. 498. He also claimed to perceive a corollary of this argument that tended to inhibit change: "If you propose some change, you may hear the retort that you should let well alone and should not interfere with that which is already better than what other countries possess."

[9] See R. J. Polaschek, *Government Administration in New Zealand* (Wellington and London: New Zealand Institute of Public Administration and Oxford University Press, 1958), pp. 277–88: "Occasionally, a petty official is arrogant and lazy, but for all that, much of government is warm and human."

[10] Peter Campbell, "The New Zealand Public Service Commission," *Public Administration* 34 (Summer 1956), 165.

CREATING THE SOCIAL FIELD

TABLE 3-1
Public Attitudes toward the Power of the Public Service (percents)

Attitude	Labor Voters n = 337	National Voters n = 438	Total (includes all others) n = 861
Too Powerful	31	31	31
Not Too Powerful	43	44	42
No Opinion	25	25	26
Total	99[a]	100	99[a]

[a] Totals are less than 100 percent because of rounding.

Table 3-1 presents survey data that probe popular attitudes toward the civil service.[11] Almost a third of the voters interviewed agreed with the statement, "Public servants have got too much power and are exploiting the situation in their own interests." Most strikingly, the degree of dissatisfaction that this finding represents was shared in identical proportions by both parties' voters! Over two-fifths of both parties' voters supported the public service. The high rate of "no opinion" indicates that cleavages were not sharply defined on this issue. It is remarkable that partisan identification made almost no difference in the answers. Whereas one might have expected Labor voters—whose party contributed so much to the welfare state—to be more protective of the public service, National voters actually were slightly more favorable. Precisely what behavioral consequences these data might presage was difficult to determine; and these

[11] This question was included in a postelection survey conducted by the School of Political Science and Public Administration of the Victoria University of Wellington in 1963. The findings reported here are from random samples of two urban electorates in Wellington, Karori (an upper-middle-class electorate) and Miramar (a mixed middle-class and working-class electorate). It is thought that the two are reasonably representative of New Zealand urban opinion. I am indebted to the School for access to the unpublished results.

data were not available to political leaders at the time the ombudsman was being considered. Nevertheless, New Zealand politicians did not need a poll to tell them that a large sector of the electorate was (on other than partisan grounds) apprehensive about the growth of and the power of the bureaucracy.

During the late 1950s, in addition to the feelings of the representative samples of voters discussed above, a number of prominent public figures became increasingly uneasy about the degree to which the welfare state was ordering the lives of individuals. It was feared that successive Labor and National Governments had excessively used (or had been used by) the governmental apparatus to promote social equality and state regulation of the economy to the detriment of individual freedom. Symptomatic of this feeling was the decision of the 1957 Convention of the New Zealand Institute of Public Administration to discuss as its theme bureaucracy in New Zealand.[12] The Convention specifically focused upon the exercise and control of administrative discretion.

The Institute, whose members include an important stratum of the political, administrative, and academic elite, considered the adequacy of existing administrative controls. Several improvements, such as an administrative court system, a written constitution, a bill of rights, a restoration of the second chamber, and an increase in the investigative powers of Members of Parliament, received at least passing attention at the conference; but none were fully developed or officially advocated. In fact, these and other similar feelings would have been best described as vague malaise, rather than as acute dissatisfaction with the status quo. They had not been brought into focus by any particular bureaucratic fiasco in any way similar to

[12] The papers presented there are collected in R. S. Milne, ed., *Bureaucracy in New Zealand* (Wellington: New Zealand Institute of Public Administration, 1957). See especially the discussion recorded after the presentation of each paper.

Britain's Crichel Down affair.[13] Nevertheless, this malaise seemed to offer a fertile environment for the introduction of some new device for the control of bureaucracy.

Traditional Appeals Agencies

The pervasiveness of bureaucracy necessarily created friction between the governors and the governed, and procedures had evolved to ameliorate it. Citizens with grievances traditionally had access to six principal appeals institutions: Members of Parliament, Ministers, internal departmental appeals channels, Parliamentary Petitions Committees, the ordinary courts, and administrative tribunals.

Members of Parliament. Although the eighty members, including four special Maori members, of New Zealand's unicameral (since 1950) Parliament had little independent impact upon public policy,[14] they were very close to their constituents. Perhaps this was at least partly due to New Zealand's single-member constituency, first-past-the-post electoral system as contrasted with the Scandinavian proportional representation systems. Most Members returned to their electorate almost every weekend where—among a myriad of other activities—they listened to citizens' grievances against the government. In cases in which the Member decided to intervene personally, he might have initially contacted the

[13] One of the papers presented at the Institute's conference (by a man who was later to become an Attorney-General under the National Government) extensively summarized the Crichel Down affair and pointed to its lessons for New Zealand. See D. J. Riddiford, "A Citizen's Point of View," Ibid., pp. 71–74.

[14] In fact, the preponderance of the only major book on Parliament is devoted to the question of "whether the New Zealand Member of Parliament possessed any power or even influence in the public life of his country." See Robert N. Kelson, *The Private Member of Parliament and the Formation of Public Policy: A New Zealand Case Study* (Toronto: University of Toronto Press, 1964), p. vii.

PROLOGUE

local branch office of the department involved, with whose officer he would have established a personal relationship.

If he chose to approach the department in Wellington he might have contacted the permanent head or a subordinate whom he knew. Departments usually were generous about directly giving out information to M.P.s—even to the Opposition—at least when it involved only an individual case rather than broader policy matters. Usually the M.P. could expect success only if he could present new information, convince them that they had made a mistake in applying regular procedures, or—in the case of a discretionary decision—persuade them that certain facts were misinterpreted or that others should have been more heavily weighted.

Because Ministers' offices were located in Parliament, M.P.s often took complaints directly to them. Usually such contacts were made in writing, but the case was often discussed personally with the Minister or his secretary. Although an M.P. might have been allowed to see the department's file on the complainant, this would have been rare. He usually asked for a written reply that could be passed on to the complainant as proof that he had at least tried. If the Minister refused to reverse the ruling, the Member usually simply commiserated with his constituent. Introducing a notice of motion or a private Member's Bill theoretically was possible, but impracticable.

A more likely action would have been to ask a parliamentary question. Questions to Ministers were used for many purposes; the most usual ones were political. For the years 1957 to 1960 a mean of about 61 percent of the total were explicitly or implicitly party political,[15] and

[15] Computed from Tables 3 and 4 of the Appendix of Robin Frontin-Rollet, "Questions in the House of Representatives," an unpublished Honors research paper, Victoria University of Wellington, 1967. The following discussion of questions refers to the years before 1962, the

CREATING THE SOCIAL FIELD

85 percent were asked by the Opposition. An analysis revealed that questions on government administration represented only a small proportion of the total, less than 5 percent over a sixteen-year period ending in 1961, and that the percentage was diminishing.[16] The actual annual number that probed various areas of administration ranged from only twelve to thirty-two; this indicated that the subject was hardly an obsession with Members. In addition, there were some procedural difficulties. The purpose of the oral question session held each Wednesday was to discuss the written replies to previously submitted questions. But Ministers were not compelled to reply directly to criticisms, and in the five minutes allowed they could discuss questions in any order or even all at once. Supplementary questions were not possible. Also, pursuing an attack during the adjournment debate was not an option as in Britain.[17]

Ministers. In addition to continuing their own constituency work, Ministers served as a court of appeal in dealing with complaints. Many clients did not, however, deign to complain to lesser officials but began at the top. Personalized attention by the Minister was one of the characteristics of New Zealand's intimate political life that many citizens came to regard as a perquisite. As an indication of the volume of citizen complaints that were filtered through the Minister, an annual mean of 2,880 pieces of ministerial correspondence was processed by one department, the State Advances Corporation, between 1957 and 1961. Just the fact that the Minister read

---

year in which important procedural changes were made to bring New Zealand closer to British practice.

[16] I am grateful to Mr. Peter V. O'Brien for the data which were taken from materials for his LL.B. thesis, "Parliamentary Control of Administrative Action in New Zealand: Questions to Ministers 1946–67," Victoria University School of Law, in preparation 1968.

[17] See Kelson, *The Private Member*, p. 70.

PROLOGUE

the letters (and perhaps the accompanying reports as well) before signing them acted as a check on the administration.

Ministers did have substantive powers to remedy grievances and could thoroughly investigate complaints. All departmental files could be called for and the department could be forced to defend its actions. Thus the Minister could completely reassess the decision, although considerations of time made a complete ministerial review of each case impossible. The fact that universalistic procedural norms were so thoroughly ingrained in the New Zealand administrative elite also limited the Minister's powers of intervention. The rare ministerial pressure to give special treatment to a complainant would have run into departmental counterpressures. This internal restraint on the illegitimate settling of complaints and the fact that Ministers were so busy that on most cases they only had time to skim the departmental report on the matter (which was ordinarily a defense of its action) constituted limitations on the usefulness of the Minister as an appeals agent. He did sometimes reverse departmental recommendations, however, and the mere fact that he personally signed most reports on complaints may have made citizens feel efficacious.

Complaints from the entire nation were received by the Prime Minister, and he stood at the pinnacle of the administrative system. The New Zealand Prime Minister traditionally has prided himself upon helping resolve complaints and providing the personal touch. The letters of citizens who complained to the Prime Minister were normally forwarded to the appropriate Minister for action. The Prime Minister might possibly have been appealed to by a Member of Parliament, or even by an ordinary citizen, about a Minister's decision. In such cases a meeting between all the parties involved, including departmental representatives, might have been held in the Prime Minister's office. It should be noted that, in spite of

CREATING THE SOCIAL FIELD

the Prime Minister's authority and prestige, his effectiveness as an appeals agent was subject to the same limitations as other Ministers.

Some comments in a speech prepared for Prime Minister Keith Holyoake provide insight into the increasing pressures on the time of Ministers, including the Prime Minister:

> There are a lot of problems which Departments are able and competent to handle but there seems to be a feeling that these should be side-stepped and that a personal interview be had with the Minister concerned. This practice has grown to the point where Ministers often find themselves with all too little time to ponder on problems of policy.[18]

These relatively mild remarks accurately reflected the opinions of many people in public life, but it is interesting that they were not delivered. Perhaps Mr. Holyoake felt that his advisers had erred; in any event, he did not come out against the norm of intimacy in politics.

Departments. Another of the agencies that protected the individual against arbitrary governmental actions was the appeals procedures of the department complained against. The permanent head of the department was constitutionally and politically responsible to his Minister for his department's actions. He, or his immediate staff, normally read all written complaints[19] and directed the in-

---

[18] An advance release of the Prime Minister's address to the Constitutional Society's Convention, Wool House, Wellington, Tuesday, 26 May 1963, 2:30 P.M., on the duties and responsibilities of Cabinet Ministers. The quoted sentences were skipped; and a reporter, who provided the advance text for me and wished to remain anonymous, crossed them out in accordance with the ground rules, which were to check against delivery.

[19] The request on the letterhead of the Head Office of the Inland Revenue Department is typical: "Please Address All Correspondence to The Commissioner of Inland Revenue."

PROLOGUE

vestigation. Depending upon the circumstances, the investigation might have been as thorough as that received by a ministerial inquiry. Officials were aware that dissatisfied citizens were likely to carry their appeal to a Member of Parliament, to their Minister, or to some other appeals agent.[20]

The existence of the various controls, both internal and external, on the bureaucracy were important factors in securing a fair and impartial administrative process,[21] but these negative limitations were not the sole explanation. Lipson called attention to "that 'inner check' which springs from the civil servant's professional devotion to the ideal of the public interest."[22] The internalization of these norms was an important factor in preventing mistakes and abuses and in ensuring that those that were discovered were corrected.

Parliamentary petitions. The traditional right of the subject to petition Parliament for a redress of grievances was imported from Britain. The bulk of the individual grievance complaints and the "political" ones were sent to the two alphabetically divided Petitions Committees. An analysis of the 108 petitions presented between 1957 and 1961 reveals that they declined from a high of 34 in 1957 to a low of only 15 in 1960.[23] Unlike the historical

[20] Other agencies that controlled departments included Cabinet Committees, Caucus Committees, Parliament's Public Accounts (later Expenditures) Committee, the Controller and Auditor-General, and the Treasury.

[21] See Peter Campbell, "Politicians, Public Servants, and the People in New Zealand, II," *Political Studies* 4 (1956), 26–29; see also Polaschek, *Government Administration in New Zealand,* pp. 283–84.

[22] Lipson, *The Politics of Equality,* p. 479.

[23] The petitions statistics have been compiled from the *Reports of the Public Petitions A to L and M to Z Committees, 1957–61* (Wellington, R. E. Owen, Government Printer). Following the Committees' method, eighty-five separate but identical petitions presented in 1961 have been dealt with here and subsequently as a single petition.

CREATING THE SOCIAL FIELD

experience in Great Britain where petitioning had largely become a mass political exercise,[24] 65 percent of the New Zealand petitions bore but a single signature.[25] In 70 percent of them the complainant(s) had some personal interest in the outcome of the petition. Some change in policy would have to be made to satisfy over half, and a smaller percentage, 44, pleaded for compensation from the government. Pressure groups were seldom (7 percent) directly involved, at least not to the extent of attaching their name to a petition; petitioning in New Zealand has been primarily the preserve of the individual, and of *ad hoc* groups.[26]

Committee hearings, which normally were held *in camera*, occurred on about eight or ten Wednesday mornings during Parliament's session.[27] On the appointed date the relevant department would be ready with its report,

[24] See Colin Leys, "Petitioning in the Nineteenth and Twentieth Centuries," *Political Studies* 3 (1955), 45–64.

[25] The median of the others was 166 signatures. During this period only ten petitions having over 1,000 signatories were presented. The four largest were 1) 80,004, "For the immediate cessation of the use of 1080 and associated poisons for the attempted extermination of deer in New Zealand and a public inquiry into the issue," 1960; 2) 61,366, "That the House of Representatives will take no step towards joining the International Monetary Fund without the authority of a referendum of electors," 1961; 3) 13,489, "Praying for a written constitution for New Zealand and a Second Chamber of Parliament," 1961; and 4) 11,640, "Praying for legislation to abate the broken bottle menace . . . ," 1957.

[26] An illustrative petition would be that of G. Hallett in 1958, "Praying for compensation for alleged unlawful arrest and detention and for loss." Many of them might have been appealable to an ombudsman if one had existed.

[27] Interviews conducted in 1967 with Members, former Members, and the Committee staff provide the basis for the discussion of the Committee's procedure. Also the author is grateful to the Committee for allowing a stranger to sit in on two of their sessions. For a more detailed account see Larry B. Hill, "Parliamentary Petitions, the Ombudsman, and Political Change in New Zealand," *Political Studies* 22 (September 1974), 337–46.

which would be read immediately after the petition was read by the Committee's Clerk. Following the reading of the petitioner's formal submissions, an indirect exchange of views took place between the parties. This discussion was filtered through the chairman, and the Committee questioned both adversaries. A Minister was normally present for guidance and consultation. Following this, the petitioner was asked to leave the room so that the Committee could confer privately with the departmental representatives. Although the Committee had the power to subpoena any public or even private records, in only about 10 percent of the cases was any research done for information not provided by either party.

It is generally acknowledged that only those petitions recommended to the government for "most favorable" consideration had any appreciable likelihood of being acted upon.[28] Though 57 percent of the petitions were rejected or given "no recommendation," a substantial 15 percent were given the Committees' highest endorsement.[29] There was no established procedure by which the government's final disposition of the Committees' recommendations was reported. Sir Guy Powles has reported[30] data for the five-year period 1958–62, which are the most reliable that have been gathered. Seventeen petitions received a "most favorable" recommendation; of those, six were substantially granted by the government.

[28] In rare instances those reported for "favorable" consideration were acted upon; Kelson (*The Private Member*, p. 156) has recounted one or two examples of petitions placed in other categories which were granted by the government.

[29] About an equal number were withdrawn, often after the complainant had been more fully appraised of the reasons for a departmental action.

[30] "The Citizen's Rights Against the Modern State and Its Responsibilities to Him," an address delivered to the Royal Institute of Public Administration, Canberra, Australia, 14 November 1963, p. 5. Reprinted in the *International and Comparative Law Quarterly* 13 (1964), 761–66.

Four of those were cases in which compensatory grants were made. An additional four of the seventeen were partially implemented, but the remaining seven were rejected by the Government.

Thus, very few people actually had their grievances resolved through the petitions process each year, and the deprecatory opinions many Members of Parliament expressed toward the Committees[31] suggested that a vested interest structure would not necessarily oppose an ombudsman. (There were no data that would indicate whether or not the M.P.s themselves might view an ombudsman as a threat to their role as grievance handlers.) Furthermore, citizens' long experience with the petitions process meant that there was a reservoir of popular familiarity with such a complaints process.

Courts. The administratively aggrieved New Zealander also had the option of seeking redress in the courts. The facts that the orderly procedures of the rule of law were so firmly imbedded and that citizens were so habituated to peaceable behavior patterns are relevant to an understanding of the role of the courts.[32] The judiciary was independent, even fiercely so, both of the executive and of other political pressure;[33] but it was not an aggressive actor in the political process.[34] The common-law proclivity to follow precedent, which was inherited from

---

[31] See Kelson, *The Private Member*, p. 156.

[32] An artifact of both circumstances is that during the five-year period from 1957 to 1961 a mean of only 1.6 convictions and sentences for the crime of murder were handed down each year. Compiled from *New Zealand Statistics of Justice—1965*, Department of Statistics publication (Wellington: Government Printer, 1967), Table 13, p. 16.

[33] See K. J. Scott, *The New Zealand Constitution* (Oxford: Clarendon Press, 1962), Chapter VI, for a cogent summary of the courts' function in the political system.

[34] Of course the New Zealand courts were passive in that a litigant must initiate a case; the point here is that they have narrowly defined their field of action in a manner unlike that of the American courts.

Britain, is highly visible. This, along with their allied preference for adhering to the very letter of the law, has meant that the New Zealand courts have been quite a conservative body.[35]

As in Britain, complaints against administration were tried in the ordinary courts. The court's primary charge in such cases was to ascertain whether the administrative action under review was within the powers granted by the relevant Act. The complainant's best hope was that the court would find that the administrator acted *ultra vires* (beyond power). Success was most unlikely unless it could be demonstrated that an official exceeded his statutory powers, or that he exercised them "in bad faith or for an improper purpose, or on irrelevant or extraneous considerations, or without taking into account relevant considerations."[36]

As the following authority indicates, the legal grounds themselves were very narrowly circumscribed:

> Even if the authority has made an error of law or of fact, or has acted in the absence of evidence, the courts will not intervene unless the error of law or fact has the effect of giving the authority a jurisdiction that it would not have had if the error had not been made.[37]

New Zealand Acts tend to confer very wide discretionary powers upon public officials,[38] and the phrase making a

---

[35] See Polaschek, *Government Administration*, pp. 276–77.

[36] Gordon Orr, *Report on Administrative Justice in New Zealand* (Wellington: Government Printer, 1964), p. 107. In a most unusual case a decision could be quashed on the grounds that it was "grossly unreasonable." Further, if an error of law that was "apparent on the face of the record" were uncovered, the court might have intervened. The problem with this is that administrators usually did not detail the legal grounds upon which they made decisions, so this possibility was seldom applicable.

[37] C. C. Aikman, "Administrative Law—I," in Robson, ed., *New Zealand: The Development of Its Laws and Constitution*, 2nd ed., p. 188.

[38] See Polaschek, *Government Administration*, pp. 279–80. Orr, *Report*, pp. 108–9, has reported that discretionary powers were classified as either "objective" or "subjective." The administrator was charged in

statute "judge proof" was sometimes used to refer to the practice of rendering an action immune from judicial review by making the basis of decisions discretionary.

An attendant difficulty of using the courts to have administrative grievances rectified was that of Crown privilege of documents. Very often in such proceedings it might have been impossible for the litigant or for the court to comprehend such vital matters as the source and content of the information upon which an action was based. The department involved would have expected little difficulty in convincing their Minister that the departmental files should not be made public.[39] Even routine documents, such as Social Security files whose disclosure would not have been likely to prejudice defense or national security—matters on which Crown privilege had traditionally been claimed—could have been and sometimes were held confidential.

Many cases arose through applications for the traditional prerogative writs: mandamus, certiorari, and prohibition.[40] But they could be used only in very narrow circumstances; the requirement of proving that a duty to act judicially existed was a primary limitation that eliminated cases of administrative discretion. Orr's comment on the writs' inadequacy is representative: "They have become so encrusted with historical limitations as to ren-

---

the former category with the necessity to "have reasonable grounds to believe" that a state of affairs existed, and those grounds might be challenged in court. In the case of the now more numerous subjective powers it was only required that a set of specified circumstances existed "in his opinion," or "if it appears" to have existed. It would indeed have been an inept administrator who could not have convinced a court that he had based his decision on the evidence as he interpreted it at the time.

[39] See Orr, *Report*, p. 110.

[40] Habeas corpus is, of course, also available to the citizen who has been incarcerated. The newer writ of declaration was a further possibility. For discussions of the writs see Aikman, "Administrative Law—I," pp. 188–92; Orr, *Report*, pp. 110–12; Polaschek, *Government Administration*, pp. 275–76; and Powles, "The Citizen's Rights," p. 708.

der them only partly effective in dealing with modern problems."[41]

Sir Guy Powles conducted a survey of the significant reported New Zealand administrative law cases for the decade 1952–1962. Of the total of fifty-six cases, about 43 percent were successful, so the effectiveness of the writs should not be disparaged.[42] Nevertheless, it must be recognized that the number of complainants applying for each writ was quite small for a ten-year period. Certainly New Zealand lawyers were aware of the limitations on the courts' role as adjudicators of administrative grievances, and they undoubtedly advised most prospective litigants to try the political avenues of redress. In combination, these factors lowered the usefulness of the courts as an administrative appeals agency. It is true, however, that access to the courts was comparatively cheap and simple in New Zealand and that judges were guided by libertarian principles. It would seem that the concept of the ombudsman would have appeared to be congruent with and complementary to the judicial system.

Administrative tribunals. Concomitantly with the expansion of the modern multiservice state in New Zealand as elsewhere, a mélange of administrative tribunals grew up. Their major advantages over regular courts are that they are cheap, quick, and may have specialist expertise. It was conceded that their procedures varied widely, and some administrative lawyers had criticized their independence and objectivity.[43] Nonetheless, there was no

[41] Orr, *Report,* p. 107.
[42] Powles, "The Citizen's Rights," p. 7. Of the twenty-four successful cases, certiorari was granted six times, mandamus three times, declaration twice, prohibition and injunction once, and eleven cases were classified as other and miscellaneous.
[43] J. L. Robson and K. J. Scott, "Public Administration and Administrative Law," in Robson, ed., *New Zealand: The Development of Its Laws and Constitution,* p. 126; see also Polaschek, *Government Administration,* p. 279.

notable domestic pressure to consider reform. The publication of Britain's Franks Report[44] stimulated the New Zealand Justice Department to undertake a survey of tribunals in 1959. It was finally published in 1965—almost without analysis—in a departmental report, "The Citizen and Power." The following is based upon an analysis of those data.[45]

The 64 tribunals that were discovered can be allocated among the following eight functional categories: licensing ($N = 14$), judging conditions of employment and salaries of civil servants ($N = 9$), judging misconduct of civil servants ($N = 4$), policy formation and/or general inquiry ($N = 10$), granting benefits or compensation ($N = 6$), assessing duty, tax costs ($N = 3$), evaluating trade practices ($N = 3$), miscellaneous administrative decision making ($N = 15$). Twenty-eight percent of them were designed to handle appeals from administrators' actions and hence were similar to the kinds of review authorities that have been discussed above; 20 percent were appellate bodies that reviewed the actions of other administrative tribunals; and over half, 52 percent, exercised original decision-making jurisdiction.

One circumstance that might tend to call into question the tribunals' independence was that 52 percent of them met in a room belonging to the department. The aggrieved citizen could have drawn more comfort from the fact that in 94 percent of the cases the department had to present *all* of its evidence and reasoning in an open hearing and could not present a secret report after the complainant had withdrawn. In replying to the very broad question of whether or not the tribunal received policy instructions from the Minister, only two (the Local Authorities Loans Board and the Price Tribunal) admitted

[44] *Report of the Committee on Administrative Tribunals and Enquiries in the United Kingdom*, Cmnd. 218, 1958, H.M.S.O.
[45] For convenience, the five tribunals that were created after the Ombudsman was appointed have been included.

that they did. It would, however, be very surprising if several others were inattentive to government policy.[46]

Although only 5 percent of the tribunals were limited to the strict rules of evidence that would be applied in a court of law, in other respects the complainant's rights were likely to be protected. He usually could be represented by a lawyer (86 percent), subpoena witnesses on his behalf (82 percent), and always have them cross-examined. But public hearings were held in only 45 percent of the cases, and written reasons for a decision were not given in 21 percent.

Only two-thirds of the tribunals were allowed to take a case to the courts on a question of law *even on their own initiative*. Specific provision for an appeal to the courts on *any* basis was made for only about one-fifth of them. About a third of their Acts even exempted the tribunals from applications for the prerogative writs except on a contention that related to the tribunal's jurisdiction! Four Acts (those of the Shops and Offices Exemptions Tribunal, the Public Service Appeal Board, the Special Board of Appeal, and the Government Railways Appeal Board) entirely excluded the tribunals from the courts' jurisdiction by providing that no writs be issued. Of those ten tribunals that felt able to answer the Justice Department's final question (which asked if there were a right of appeal what proportion was successful) only one estimated one-half, and the others ranged between one-third and one-tenth.

This brief analysis has indicated that administrative tribunals' independence from the executive, their protection of individual legal rights, their operating procedures, and their provisions for appeal to the courts varied greatly. Their existence did not make the ombudsman

[46] See Robson and Scott, "Public Administration," pp. 114–17, for a discussion of the "Lewis case," a well-known example of government interference with the policies of a Land Sales Committee in 1946.

concept superfluous, nor was it unacceptable. Instead, the ombudsman could have been interpreted as filling some of the gaps in the procedure of appeals to tribunals.

Other channels. In addition to the six primary appeals agencies, other channels, such as appeals to a lawyer, to a newspaper, or specifically to the Leader of the Opposition, also should be mentioned. With all of these various options the citizen's prospects of having the basis for his grievance carefully reviewed were high. It is even possible that he could on one complaint have access to *all* of the possible appeals agents.

On the other hand, although the list of appeals agencies covered the gamut of the administrative process, it also was true that there were deficiencies and that the various agencies did not function as a true system. Particularly when a department gained the support of its Minister in defending a disputed discretionary decision (the most usual type of decision), the political appeals agencies (the first four examined above) were likely to be inefficacious, the ordinary courts would be most unlikely to intervene for the reasons discussed in that section, and administrative tribunals (in the rare instances in which an appeal on this sort of decision would lie to one) were beset with further problems as appeals agents. Possible proponents of the ombudsman or of some other solution could thus capitalize upon the identifiable (but difficult to measure precisely) amount of popular dissatisfaction with the rule of the "bureaucrats" and could claim that their innovation was ideal for filling this lacuna.

The Politics of Transfer

The foremost international actor in the transfer of the ombudsman to New Zealand was Denmark's Ombudsman, Stephan Hurwitz.[47] Between 1956 and 1961 Hurwitz disseminated at least nine articles about his office through internationally circulated English-language publications, and several New Zealand individuals who later became advocates learned of the ombudsman through them. The first, which attracted the attention of several members of the legal profession, especially academics and those in some government departments, appeared in the British journal *Public Law*, and was entitled "Control of the Administration in Denmark: The Danish Parliamentary Commissioner for Civil and Military Government Administration."[48] This article would have been seen somewhat earlier by those lawyers who were members of the New Zealand section of the International Commission of Jurists, for it had originally appeared in the international body's *Journal*.[49]

The New Zealand Labor Party's Attorney-General, the Hon. H. G. R. Mason, and the Deputy Secretary for Justice, Dr. J. L. Robson, were directly exposed to the idea of the ombudsman through a supranational agency, the United Nations Seminar on Judicial and Other Remedies Against the Illegal Exercise or Abuse of Administrative Authority, which was held at Kandy, Ceylon, during 4–15 May 1959. Working papers for the seminar's consideration had been prepared by Professor C. J. Hamson, a leading British academic lawyer, and by Stephan Hurwitz. Hamson's paper focused on the ombudsman among

---

[47] For a comparative analysis of the transfers of the principal national ombudsmen, see Larry B. Hill, "The International Transfer of the Ombudsman: A Communications Analysis," in Richard L. Merritt, ed., *Communication in International Politics* (Urbana: University of Illinois Press, 1972), pp. 295–317.

[48] *Public Law* 3 (Autumn 1958), 236–53. J. D. B. Mitchell's editorial comment, p. 209, also served to popularize the idea of the ombudsman.

[49] Stephan Hurwitz, "Control of the Administration in Denmark," *Journal of the International Commission of Jurists* 1 (Spring-Summer 1958), 224–43.

other administrative remedies, while Hurwitz generally described his work.[50]

Upon returning to New Zealand, Robson gave his copy of the Hurwitz paper to the editor of *Political Science*, the journal of the School of Political Science and Public Administration at the Victoria University in Wellington, and it was reprinted in the September 1960 issue. The article, which was entitled "The Scandinavian Ombudsman," focused upon the Danish experience and attained wide currency in New Zealand intellectual circles, while popularizing the name *ombudsman*.

The report of a British Broadcasting Corporation interview with Hurwitz, which was printed in the British *Listener* of 16 July 1959, also attracted some New Zealand attention. Thus far, however, awareness of the ombudsman had penetrated only a small segment of the political elite. After 27 July 1959, the size of the ombudsman-aware public was greatly increased by *Time* magazine's ombudsman story, which was a condensation of the *Listener* article and was the first ombudsman piece to be circulated in New Zealand on a mass scale. Focusing upon the increasing frustrations of citizens exposed to bureaucratic tyranny, the article lamented the inadequacies of the existing parliamentary remedies and reported that many British citizens were looking "longingly" at Scandinavia's answer to this problem, the ombudsman. Following a pronunciation guide, *Time* reproduced some highlights of the interview with Hurwitz, including a brief description of his job and an explanation of some of the differences between the Swedish, Finnish, and Danish ombudsmen.

Subsequent to these early acquaintance stimuli, in

[50] The papers and the discussion are printed in United Nations, "1959 Seminar on Judicial and Other Remedies Against the Illegal Exercise or Abuse of Administrative Authority," (ST/TAO/HR/4), Peradeniya (Kandy), Ceylon, 4–15 May 1959. Both papers were discussed by the conference in their authors' absence.

PROLOGUE

1959 the newly formed Constitutional Society began to lobby among the leaders of both political parties for an ombudsman. The Labor Government rejected the proposal saying only that an ombudsman was not needed because of the comprehensive nature of existing methods of citizen protection. The National Party, however, some of whose leaders such as the Hon. J. R. Marshall had developed an independent interest in the ombudsman, decided that the institution might make a good proposal for the upcoming election. Such a proposal appealed to National for a number of reasons—not the least of which was the fact that it might mollify the Constitutional Society and others on its right flank for their failure to obtain more far-reaching programs, such as a written constitution and the restoration of the second chamber; and an ombudsman plank was included in National's election platform.

The 1960 election campaign was generally a dull one in which neither the participants nor the electorate worked up much enthusiasm.[51] The ombudsman plank seems to have been a peculiarly nonpolitical one and was apparently hardly mentioned in the campaign. There is no record of Labor speaking against the proposal.[52]

Following National's victory, the Justice Department—by then headed by Dr. Robson, who had come

[51] See R. M. Chapman, W. K. Jackson, and A. V. Mitchell, *New Zealand Politics in Action: The 1960 General Election* (London: Oxford University Press, 1962). According to their assessment (pp. 100, 104, and 107), "Very few of the policy proposals in these manifestos excited much discussion or attention. . . . The electorate in 1960 showed little interest in the comparatively short list of policy proposals laid before it. . . . One of the quietest election campaigns for many years closed on 25 November with the final speeches and messages of the party leaders."

[52] In their quite complete analysis of the campaign issues in the press, on radio, and in candidates' speeches Chapman, Jackson, and Mitchell only mention the ombudsman proposal three times in passing. See pp. 91, 94, and 131.

to favor strongly the ombudsman concept—was charged to draft a Bill. The major basis of the draft was the Danish Act. It was scrutinized on a clause-by-clause basis, and deviations from the pattern occurred only when the department perceived the necessity of allowing for differences between New Zealand and Denmark on particular details. After exhaustive debate, Cabinet decided to alter the draft in two important ways—to exempt Ministers from the ombudsman's jurisdiction and to retain the Crown's prerogative to claim privilege in the release of documents. The Hon. J. R. Hanan, Attorney-General and the Minister in charge of the Bill, introduced it to Parliament on 29 August 1961.

After a first reading debate, the Bill was allowed to lapse without proceeding any further at that session of Parliament. The two reasons for this were that other more important measures consumed the parliamentary calendar and that the government had been a bit chastened by some critical responses to the weaknesses of their Bill. These criticisms were led by some of New Zealand's most important newspapers—particularly the Wellington *Evening Post*, the *Auckland Star*, and the Christchurch *Press*.

The only direct opposition to the ombudsman concept came from the Public Service Association. At the early stages of the campaign, its *Journal* published some rather intemperate editorials criticizing this "no-goodsman," but these tended to exaggerate the Association's true policy. Pragmatically recognizing that an ombudsman would be established, the Association directed its energies toward ensuring that he would not become an inquisitor or anti–civil servant creature.[53]

After further intense governmental debate, the Bill was

[53] See Larry B. Hill, "The Role of Pressure Groups in the Policy Process: the New Zealand Public Service Association and the Adoption of the Ombudsman," *New Zealand Journal of Public Administration* 34 (March 1972), 46–58.

reintroduced in the new session on 14 June 1962, with Crown privilege against the ombudsman effectively removed but with the exemption of Ministers retained. In his introductory speech Hanan noted with pride that Britain's prestigious Whyatt Report[54] had reproduced his Bill in full, but he was pleased that New Zealand would not adopt Whyatt's ombudsman. Sensing that the most prevalent popular and Opposition mood was that his Bill had not been strong enough, he cited two deficiencies of Whyatt's puny ombudsman:

> For instance, that committee recommended that nobody should be able to make a complaint to the appeal authority except through a member of Parliament. Well, we will have none of that. We want to provide wider access to the Parliamentary Commissioner for Investigations. Also, curiously enough, the British recommendations provided that a Minister should have power of veto, power to stop the appeal authority inquiring into a matter. Members will therefore see that there are substantial differences between our Bill and the English proposals.[55]

A major theme of the government's parliamentary strategy was to align themselves directly with the Scandinavian model. Hanan later said: "Of all the different [Scandinavian ombudsmen] systems, we have found that the Danish one most nearly suits our own needs and conditions, and this Bill follows very broadly the approach of the Danish Law." Thus, no doubts were allowed to remain in anyone's mind that an attempt at institutional transfer was in process. Indeed, Hanan was anxious to prove that his official, whatever he might be called, would be a real Danish ombudsman, rather than "an

[54] Sir John Whyatt, *The Citizen and the Administration: The Redress of Grievances—A Report by Justice* (London: Stevens, 1961).
[55] New Zealand, Parliament, *Parliamentary Debates* 330 (14 June 1962), 118–20.

anemic and ineffective version of the model." Despite some obviously necessary modifications to fit local conditions, "the provisions of the Bill are similar in scope, and in some respects this Bill goes further than its Danish prototype."[56] Continuing to stress this linkage, another government speaker, Mr. Riddiford, noted that Sweden's ombudsman had stood the test of time, but Denmark's version had been brought up to date and was ideal for New Zealand's conditions: "We may rely fairly safely on the example found satisfactory in Sweden and Denmark over a considerable period of time, and amongst a people similar to ourselves in democratic ideas, language and race."[57]

The Opposition did not strongly object to the Bill except that it came to contend that the government was not following the Danish model closely enough. This contention was their primary theme in the major parliamentary debate on the revised Bill. The most important partisan clash developed over the name *ombudsman*. It is an important index to the level of intensity of the debate that after that issue was won, on a rare free vote, Labor did not force a recorded vote on the final Bill.

Conclusions

The preceding examination of the cultural and structural aspects of New Zealand's ombudsman-relevant political environment and the synopsis of the politics of transfer did not reveal any compelling arguments for introducing an ombudsman. There were indications that some people felt the pervasive government administration was becoming insensitive and "bureaucratic," but it was conceded to be highly efficient and honest. Attention had not focused upon any celebrated administrative fiasco, and the

[56] Ibid. (25 July 1962), pp. 1118–20.
[57] Ibid., p. 1121.

existence of a reasonable pattern of appeals agencies was well known.

Surely the vague popular and elite uneasiness about bureaucracy and the cultural characteristic of political innovativeness are elements in explaining why the ombudsman was adopted. The institution's advocates capitalized upon both during the adoption campaign, and the main part of the explanation is a political one. After being convinced of the ombudsman's virtues by exogenous sources, which they regarded as prestigious, key members of the political elite pushed for an ombudsman. The timing of the interest in the subject was propitious, for it surfaced as planning decisions were under way for a political campaign. Since no real opposition emerged, creating an ombudsman was merely one of the matters the new National Government did, and was expected by all to do, in fulfilling its electoral mandate.

Two aspects of the New Zealand political-administrative environment, which are relevant to the ombudsman's later institutionalization, merit emphasis. First: New Zealand politics is stable. There are no important ethnic divisions (as in Switzerland), social divisions (as in Great Britain), economic divisions (as in the United States), regional divisions (as in Italy), religious divisions (as in Germany), ideological divisions (as in France), or linguistic divisions (as in Canada). A usual pattern of research on these countries is to focus upon such divisions; since they are relatively unimportant in New Zealand we are, in effect, using them as control variables. Whereas Samuel Huntington focused upon institutionalization from the perspective of creating political order in changing societies,[58] our perspective involves the study of political change in an orderly society. If the only important change is the introduction of an exogenous institution, its effects can be assessed with some confidence.

[58] Samuel P. Huntington, *Political Order in Changing Societies* (New Haven: Yale University Press, 1969).

Second: the ombudsman's congruence with the established political value patterns and its apparent lack of threat to other actors in the political system facilitated its adoption and appears positive for institutionalization. The ombudsman was created as a supplement, not a replacement, for the existing grievance agents.

Finally, theorists who stress the importance of the reaction of the "vested interest structures" to attempts at institutional change, sometimes give the impression that successful transfer is almost impossible.[59] They ignore, however, the political importance of leadership;[60] once a political institution has been formally adopted, certain strains toward institutionalization usually are set in motion. During the adoption campaign, opposition to the institution may have been normative, but once it is approved the burden falls upon the actors in its task environment to grant it legitimacy, at least in operational terms, or to show cause why they should not. The dedication of political innovators sometimes makes institutions work when according to all indicators they should not. Nevertheless, these "strains toward institutionalization" are not guarantees. In addition to the possibility of institutionalization, after formal adoption institutions may simply wither or have their functions transformed.

Parliament unanimously appointed Sir Guy Richardson Powles, K.B.E., C.M.G., as New Zealand's Ombudsman on 1 October 1962. The appointment was generally regarded as a distinguished one. Sir Guy had been a lawyer, a successful officer during World War II,

[59] See, for example, Talcott Parsons, *The Social System* (Glencoe, Ill.: Free Press, 1951), p. 496. Certainly it is true that what we may call the political residues of the adoption campaign should be investigated. In this case we have seen that there were no important residues that would seem to be inimical to the ombudsman's success.

[60] See Glenn D. Paige, "The Rediscovery of Politics," in John D. Montgomery and William J. Siffin, eds., *Approaches to Development: Politics, Administration, and Change* (New York: McGraw-Hill, 1966), pp. 49–51.

PROLOGUE

and a highly esteemed administrator-diplomat. He had served for eleven years as the High Commissioner of Western Samoa when it was a United Nations trust territory under New Zealand's tutelage, and he was, in fact, its governor. Sir Guy's diplomatic career was capped by his selection as New Zealand's first ambassador to India. Although a distinct aura of success clung to his name, he returned to New Zealand as a rather unknown quantity to many bureaucrats and politicians. The succeeding chapters explore his fate as Ombudsman.

Part 2

THE OMBUDSMAN CRUCIBLE

CHAPTER FOUR

Inputs: The Complaints

"What is an ombudsman?" is a question that already has been asked, and a skeletal definition was given in the first chapter. Nevertheless, through inquiring more specifically what kind of institution the New Zealand Ombudsman has become, the next several chapters will attempt to answer the general question more comprehensively. This chapter investigates the Ombudsman's intake, his complaints. Although the Ombudsman has the power to be self-activating, nearly all of his investigations are initiated by citizens' complaints. Hence it is scarcely an exaggeration to say that the Ombudsman's role is largely determined by his complaints.

Most of the rhetoric about the need for an ombudsman is rather vague about the kinds of matters citizens would be likely to bring to him. But that rhetoric's dominant theme is that he is a "Citizens' Protector" against the depredations of government. Frequently cited examples of types of cases in which he would intervene on the hapless citizen's behalf include unjust prosecution or incarceration, excessive taxation, "bureaucratic" legal demands, and general harassment. In B. F. Skinner's terms, the Ombudsman is conceptually a part of the "literature of freedom," because he is seen as providing escape from aversive governmental controls.[1] Our findings will indicate that the Ombudsman's activities as a guardian against bureaucratic restraints on traditional liberties, constitute only a small—although not an unimportant—part of his work. Therefore, the conventional conception of the Ombudsman's role must be recast. This chap-

[1] B. F. Skinner, *Beyond Freedom and Dignity* (New York: Alfred A. Knopf, 1971); see Chapter 2.

ter provides a brief overview of the findings; subsequent chapters will relate the complaints to the clients, to the Ombudsman-bureaucratic relationship, and to their outcomes.

COMPLAINT LEVELS

Preliminary to the complaints' content, let us examine their level. "What if they had an ombudsman and nobody complained?" Fortunately for the Ombudsman, that interesting possibility did not occur. Before he had been in office a month, well over 100 complaints had arrived; and 334 were received during the first six months. For the first full governmental reporting year, which was 1964 (New Zealand government agencies report to Parliament on the basis of a year ending 31 March), 692 new complaints were registered. For the next six years the totals fluctuated somewhat around that figure but remained close to it: 1965—743 complaints; 1966—685 complaints; 1967—713 complaints; 1968—637 complaints; 1969—620 complaints; 1970—759 complaints. Apparently, 1971 represented a watershed in the Ombudsman's attractiveness to citizens; for the first time, over 1,000 complaints were lodged. During the last five years, clients presented the following numbers of grievances: 1971—1,107 complaints; 1972—1,135 complaints; 1973—1,246 complaints; 1974—855 complaints; and 1975—1,163 complaints.[2]

No completely satisfactory explanation for the dramatic increase during the last five years is apparent, but the following factors seem to share responsibility. First: through conducting and reporting on two special investigations during 1970 and 1971 (the police handling of the

[2] Compiled from the yearly *Report of the Ombudsman* (Wellington: Government Printer, 1964–1975), Appendix B. The annual statistics have been adjusted to exclude from each year's totals those complaints that remained under investigation at the end of the previous year.

INPUTS: COMPLAINTS

demonstrations against United States Vice President Spiro Agnew and an investigation of the Paremoremo maximum security prison), the Ombudsman received an unusual amount of favorable media exposure. Second: the Ombudsman was appointed Race Relations Conciliator as an additional duty in 1970; this also increased the visibility of the Ombudsman Office (Race Relations complaints are not, however, included in the above totals). Third: this period coincided with what appears to have been a worldwide growth of "consumerism," and some citizens may have come to view the Ombudsman as an accessible manifestation of this political movement. Finally: we may speculate that a threshold phenomenon was at work. Perhaps after seven and one-half years, awareness of the Ombudsman as a possible grievance agent had so permeated society that more people who would have complained earlier if they had had a reason to, had time for an actual complaint to arise.

Unfortunately, we have no definite criteria for judging whether this level of complaints is high or low. It is clear that enough citizens did invoke the Ombudsman's services to keep his small staff busy, but the finding that New Zealand citizens have lodged some 10,000 grievances with their Ombudsman during twelve and one-half years may seem less than spectacular. This level of utilization is, however, consistent with the experiences of the original Scandinavian models.[3]

TARGETS OF COMPLAINT

Having established that substantial numbers of complaints were lodged, let us begin to identify them. A perusal of Table 4-1 reveals that more than two-thirds of the grievances have been against eighteen government

[3] See "Appendix: Statistics on Existing Ombudsman Systems" in Donald C. Rowat, ed., *The Ombudsman: Citizen's Defender*, 2nd ed. (Toronto: University of Toronto Press, 1968), pp. 329-37.

TABLE 4-1
Complaints to the Ombudsman by Governmental Organization
1 October 1962 to 31 March 1975

Organizations	Mean Annual Complaints	Annual Range of Complaints	Total Complaints Received n	%	Total Sample Complaints n	%
Total Major Complaint Organizations	613	464–1,033	7,361	68	287	64
Social Welfare[a]	115	87– 172	1,374	13	71	16
Justice	66	21– 214	786	7	21	5
Education	59	39– 142	704	7	29	7
Inland Revenue	45	26– 102	535	5	32	7
State Services Commission	35	31– 50	425	4	17	4
Police	34	19– 49	408	4	9	2
Post Office	34	14– 55	403	4	13	3
Labor	31	18– 53	367	3	23	5
Health	29	14– 53	347	3	13	3
Housing Corporation[b]	28	15– 44	334	3	9	2
Customs	27	14– 49	318	3	14	3
Works and Development[c]	26	20– 55	306	3	16	4
Railways	17	8– 28	205	2	5	1
Government Superannuation Fund Board	16	7– 44	197	2	8	2
Transport	15	3– 27	184	2	4	1
Lands and Survey	14	9– 27	163	2	7	2
State Insurance Office	13	5– 30	154	1	1	—
Defense	13	2– 28	151	1	6	1
Total Other Scheduled Organizations	107	72– 179	1,281	12	65	14
Total Unscheduled Organizations and Obscure	178	107– 256	2,134	20	98	22
Grand Total	898	620–1,409	10,776	100	450	100

Compiled from the annual *Report of the Ombudsman* (Wellington: Government Printer, 1964–1975), Appendix B.

[a] The agency was called the Social Security Department until 1973.
[b] The agency was called the State Advances Corporation until 1975.
[c] The agency was called the Ministry of Works until 1974.

departments, each of which had more than 150 complaints lodged against it.[4] The "major complaint organizations" are the primary institutions of New Zealand's highly developed welfare state. Chapter 7 evaluates what kinds of complaint targets are presented by several of those departments whose complaints have been most often investigated by the Ombudsman.

Nearly twice as many complaints have been made about decisions of the Social Welfare Department as against Justice, its closest competitor. It should be noted, however, that until 1972 Social Welfare had no separate appeals agency; whereas the Tax Court displaced much of the Ombudsman's jurisdiction over Inland Revenue, a similarly constituted department. A longitudinal analysis—not shown in the table—indicated that some changes have occurred in the departments' relative rankings; inferences about them can be drawn from the relationships between the departments' mean and range of complaints. But Social Welfare's hegemony has been steady; its share of the total complaints lodged did not dip below 12 percent until 1975, when only 9 percent of the Ombudsman's grievances were against Social Welfare. Whether this result was fortuitous or presaged a trend—possibly due to the creation of an internal appeal authority—is as yet impossible to determine.

A tracing of the Justice Department's complaints over time does reveal a trend: complaints have increased markedly. Justice complaints constituted less than 6 percent of the annual total until 1972, when they increased to 9 percent. The increase was to be permanent; it re-

[4] The sample more properly should be compared with the total actual complaints reported in 1969, because this was the sample's last year. Although some departmental changes in complaint levels have occurred, overall totals changed relatively little in the interim. Thus the table records that through 1975, 68 percent of the complaints were against the major complaint organizations; the corresponding percentage for 1969 was 66.

flected the Ombudsman's new attention to prison problems. During the subsequent years, Justice complaints represented 15, 13, and 9 percent, respectively, of the Ombudsman's caseload. Conversely, complaints against the Education Department show no trend, although the fluctuations are considerable. Inland Revenue's complaints are declining, however. The top of the range, a figure that was a larger proportion of the total caseload (9 percent) than has since occurred, was reached in the first year. Probably, potential complainants have become increasingly aware of the Tax Court's limitations on the Ombudsman's jurisdiction. Of the remaining major complaint organizations, either no long-range tendency is discernible or the numbers become too small for detailed trend analysis. Two exceptions should be mentioned; Health and Customs complaints have declined considerably, for unknown reasons.

Since the Ombudsman's creation, fewer than 150 complaints have been made against each of thirty-seven other organizations within his jurisdiction.[5] Why so few complaints should have been made against several of them—such as the Government Life Insurance Office, the Public Trust Office, or the Tourist and Publicity Department—is puzzling.

[5] Those organizations and their total complaints follow: Agriculture and Fisheries 115; Public Trust Office 114; Internal Affairs 111; Education Boards 108; Hospital Boards 92; Maori and Island Affairs 88; Trade and Industry 58; Marine 48; Earthquake and War Damage Commission 48; Electricity 44; Valuation 43; Government Life Insurance Office 43; National Provident Fund Board 39; Mines 39; Rehabilitation Board 37; Forest Service 33; Treasury 33; National Roads Board 28; Foreign Affairs 25; Land Settlement Board 22; Maori Trust Office 21; Scientific and Industrial Research 14; Decimal Currency Board 10; Soil Conservation and Rivers Control Council 9; Audit 9; Tourist and Publicity 9; Accident Compensation Commission 8; Legislative 6; Statistics 6; National Parks Authority 4; Government Printing Office 4; Rural Banking and Finance Corporation 4; Prime Minister's Department 3; Government Stores Board 2; Maori Affairs Board 2; Crown Law Office 1; Water Allocation Council 1.

INPUTS: COMPLAINTS

One-fifth of the complaints received by the Ombudsman—a proportion of the caseload that has remained relatively stable over the years—have been directed against organizations or people that the Ombudsman found to be outside of his jurisdiction. The targets of those complaints are indicated in Table 4-2. Because those departments that are included within the jurisdiction are named in a schedule appended to the Ombudsman Act, the others usually are called "unscheduled" agencies.

More than one-fifth of the unscheduled complaints were not against government at all, but against private businesses, individuals, or associations. Seldom would it have appeared to most observers that the target was governmental, and it must be concluded that these complainants were quite ignorant of the Ombudsman's jurisdiction. This conclusion is not necessarily true, however, for those who have complained against the unscheduled national governmental organizations. Knowing exactly the state organizations whose activities he could not investigate might require a sophisticated knowledge of the Ombudsman's jurisdiction; this would be true of even a large number of the court complaints, because of the difficulty of separating the Justice Department's housekeeping functions from those of the courts as an independent entity.

Furthermore, New Zealanders tend not to differentiate sharply between national and local government, which often are in fact intermingled; so it is no surprise that one-quarter of the unscheduled complaints were against local government. Almost since the Ombudsman's establishment, it had been proposed that his jurisdiction be expanded to include local education and hospital boards; thus it is not unexpected that a number of complaints about their activities should be received before they were brought within the jurisdiction in 1969. Similarly, in later years the controversy concerning the inclusion

TABLE 4-2
Complaints to the Ombudsman against Unscheduled Organizations
1 October 1962 to 31 March 1975

Complaint Target	Total Complaints Received n	%
Total Nongovernmental	461	22
Private Business Firms	178	8
Legal Firms	115	5
Private Individuals	105	5
Insurance Companies	35	2
Trade Unions	11	1
Banks	9	—
Other	8	—
Total National Government	612	29
Court Decisions	415	19
War Pensions Board	95	4
Reserve Bank	27	1
Broadcasting Corporation	25	1
Universities	12	1
Other	38	2
Total Local Government	537	25
Municipalities and City Councils	269	13
County Councils	162	8
Education Boards[a]	33	2
Electric Power Boards	25	1
Hospital Boards[a]	22	1
Other	26	1
Miscellaneous and Obscure	535	25
Grand Total	2,145	101[b]

Compiled from the annual *Report of the Ombudsman* (Wellington: Government Printer, 1964–1975), Appendix C. Eleven more unscheduled complaints are reported here than are indicated in Appendix B of the 1975 *Report*. This is because some minor adding errors occurred during the preparation of earlier *Reports*.

[a] These complaints were lodged prior to 18 December 1969, when the Ombudsman's jurisdiction was extended to include local education and hospital boards.

[b] Total exceeds 100 percent because of rounding.

within the Ombudsman's ambit of various local government agencies created understandable confusion as to whether such bodies as locally elected councils could be complained against. If the volume of local government complaints lodged before such matters were a part of the Ombudsman's jurisdiction is any indicator of the level of popular dissatisfaction, one may reasonably expect that the revised statute (this portion went into effect on 1 April 1976), which put virtually all of local government within the Ombudsman's jurisdiction, will cause the office to become heavily involved with complaints against local government. According to the table, the largest remaining untapped reservoir of unscheduled governmental complaints is those against court decisions. There is, however, no powerful sentiment for following the Swedish precedent and allowing the Ombudsman to investigate judges.

Complaints and Departmental Classifications

In identifying the targets of complaint we observed that most complaints were against the major welfare state agencies, but that fact alone provides little information about the content of the complaints. Both Social Welfare and Inland Revenue are involved in the politics of redistribution, but since they deal with different phases of it, we would expect them to attract quite different kinds of complaints. What is needed is a set of criteria for classifying government agencies. Scholars long have been interested in such matters; but primarily because of the intractability of the problem, no truly satisfactory criteria exist.

The existing typology that is most useful for our purposes has been developed by Peter M. Blau and W. Richard Scott, whose classification is based upon the identity of the organization's prime beneficiary. Two of their four types of organizations interest us here: "service" and "commonweal" organizations.[6] Service organizations have as their primary goal promoting the welfare of their "public-in-contact"; these clients, who may be patients, beneficiaries, students, etc., usually are in direct contact with the organization. In contrast, "the distinctive characteristic of commonweal organizations is that the public-at-large is their prime beneficiary, often, although not necessarily, to the exclusion of the very people who are the object of the organization's behavior."[7] In serving the public interest, these commonweal organizations usually perform communitywide protective functions or act as an administrative arm.

This classification does appear to be relevant. Complaints that Social Welfare delayed payment of a benefit, that Education had improperly refused to grant a School Certificate, or that Health refused to pay for dental treatment *do* seem to have more in common with each other than with complaints that Works and Development was mislocating a bridge, that Railways was not keeping to its timetable, or that Post Office should hire more letter carriers. Accordingly, when departments are divided into the two categories, service and commonweal, we find that nineteen of the government organizations are primarily service departments and thirty-six are primarily commonweal. But, whereas the service departments constitute about one-third of the total organizations, they have accounted for 43 percent of the complaints to the Ombudsman against scheduled departments.[8]

Although the Blau-Scott classification has considerable merit, their distinctions are not entirely satisfactory for our purposes. Nearly all governmental agencies—in-

[6] *Formal Organizations: A Comparative Approach* (San Francisco: Chandler, 1962), pp. 40–45. "Mutual-benefit associations" and "business concerns" are their two other types.

[7] Ibid., p. 54.

[8] Table 4-3 is designed for rather different purposes, but the agencies now called "service" departments are listed in its first column. The "commonweal" departments are contained in the second two columns.

cluding service agencies—also are commonweal organizations. It is because government became convinced that it was in the *public interest* as well as in individuals' interests to provide for income maintenance, education, health care, and so on, that these organizations were created in the first place. This does not mean that service departments cannot be distinguished on the basis of their primary orientation toward clients (I believe they can be), but making such distinctions often may be tenuous.

For example, I categorize Agriculture and Fisheries as a commonweal agency, because it functions primarily to promote farming, which will lead to increased exports and help the national balance of payments. Because of its role as a welfare agency for farmers, however, it also could be categorized as a service department. On balance, the former function is in New Zealand considerably more important than the latter. The multifunctional character of government departments is, of course, an inherent limitation of this sort of classification system. This discussion of a commonweal agency having contact with clients leads to another difficulty with the classification system: it ignores some important differences *among* commonweal organizations. The functions performed by Customs and Police are very different from those of Treasury and Statistics, yet all four are "commonweal" organizations.

Let us make more explicit our goals in classifying agencies. We want to try to understand why some kinds of departments are more often complained against than others. The major explanatory variable would seem to be the nature of the organization's relationship with the public-in-contact. We shall see that inquiring about clientele contacts is related to but distinct from the Blau-Scott *cui bono* criterion. Three types of organizations—all of which are commonweal—are suggested: "client-serving," "client-attending," and "non-client-oriented" organizations.

The first type, client-serving agencies, are the previously discussed service departments that have as their mission the furthering of the public interest through aiding individuals, who are perceived as objects of concern in themselves.

Secondly, client-attending organizations have as their primary mission the achievement of some public goal, but what is distinctive about them is that in performing this mission they necessarily come into direct contact with large numbers of individual citizens. Clients tend not to be valued personally but to be attended to as customers (Post Office, Railways, Tourist and Publicity) or as appellants (Inland Revenue, Justice, Police). Often they have become clients involuntarily, and they may regard themselves as victims rather than beneficiaries. In other cases the contact usually may be nonaversive (Labor, Lands and Survey, Agriculture and Fisheries), but helping individuals is an incidental by-product of pursuing a broader public purpose. The third type, non-client-oriented agencies, seldom come into direct contact with the general public. Their primary mission usually is to produce goods or services. Often these products, such as a new highway or sewerage plan, are not ordinarily consumed by individual citizens but by the public as a whole or some aggregate segment of it. Also the products may be intermediary ones, such as statistics or legislation, destined to be consumed by other government agencies.[9]

---

[9] This typology cuts across Katz and Kahn's distinction between "people-molding" or processing, and "object-molding" organizations. Education and Superannuation, for example, both are client-serving, but the latter agency is not involved in energy transformations that mold people. Of the client-attending agencies, Justice molds people through its prisons, but Customs does not. Defense, among the non-client-oriented departments, molds people, but they are not clients. Works and Development clearly is involved in object molding, but that would be a gross oversimplification of Treasury's role. See Daniel Katz and Robert L. Kahn, *The Social Psychology of Organizations* (New York: John Wiley and Sons, 1966), pp. 115–17. Their distinction is related to an

INPUTS: COMPLAINTS

We would hypothesize that client-attending departments would provide the most complaints because of the often aversive nature of their contact with citizens, that client-serving agencies would be second, and that non-client-oriented agencies rarely would offend the public. This hypothesis is only partially supported by the data in Table 4-3; the organizations are ranked within categories according to the number of complaints received.

As predicted, few complaints were lodged against non-client-oriented departments—even though that classification contained more departments, twenty-four, than either of the others. The distribution of the remainder among the nineteen client-serving and the twelve client-attending departments, however, did not fulfill our expectations. The two classifications attracted nearly equal shares of the complaints, but slightly more were against the client-serving than against the client-attending organizations. The horizontal bars in each column separate the major complaint organizations from the other scheduled departments, and it is apparent that half of the former are client-attending departments. During twelve and one-half years, the fluctuations in the percentages of the complaints against each of the three types of organizations were minor, and no trend was discernible.

These findings that the Ombudsman's complaints are not mainly against departments that often are involved in restraining the citizen's liberties—although a large portion are against such departments—call into question the traditional concept of the Ombudsman's role mentioned in the beginning of the chapter. But perhaps that role concept can be rescued, at least partially, if most of the complaints against the client-attending organizations are

---

earlier differentiation by Talcott Parsons between "production" organizations (whose materials are physical objects) and "service" organizations (whose materials are people). See *Structure and Process in Modern Societies* (New York: Free Press, 1960), pp. 20–21.

THE OMBUDSMAN CRUCIBLE

TABLE 4-3
Scheduled Complaints to the Ombudsman by Type of Organization
1 October 1962 to 31 March 1975

Client-Serving Organizations	Client-Attending Organizations	Non-Client-Oriented Organizations
Social Welfare	Justice	Works and Development
Education	Inland Revenue	Transport
Health	State Services Commission	Defense
Housing Corporation	Police	
Government Superannuation Fund Board	Post Office	Internal Affairs
State Insurance Office	Labor	Trade and Industry
	Customs	Marine
Public Trust Office	Railways	Electricity
Education Boards	Lands and Survey	Mines
Hospital Boards		Valuation
Maori and Island Affairs	Agriculture and Fisheries	Forest Service
Earthquake and War Damage Commission	Decimal Currency Board	Treasury
Government Life Insurance Office	Tourist and Publicity	National Roads Board
National Provident Fund Board		Foreign Affairs
Rehabilitation Board		Scientific and Industrial Research
Land Settlement Board		Soil Conservation and Rivers Control Council
Maori Trust Office		Audit
Accident Compensation Commission		Legislative
Rural Banking and Finance Corporation		Statistics
Maori Affairs Board		National Parks Authority
		Government Printing Office
		Prime Minister's Department
		Government Stores Board
		Crown Law Office
		Water Allocation Council

| Total N = 3,736 % = 43 | Total N = 3,744 % = 43 | Total N = 1,162 % = 13 |
| Sample N = 148 % = 42 | Sample N = 145 % = 41 | Sample N = 59 % = 17 |

Compiled from *Report of the Ombudsman* (Wellington: Government Printer, 1975), Appendix B. The total scheduled complaints equaled 8,642; the total for the sample was 352.

INPUTS: COMPLAINTS

civil libertarian types and if the client-serving complaints principally involve such matters as "bureaucratic" arrogance, unfairness, or incompetence. This classification of government departments is, however, insufficiently sensitive to answer such questions. A means of classifying the subjects of the individual complaints is needed.

SUBJECTS OF COMPLAINTS

Complaining is a kind of demand behavior. Although political scientists are beginning to develop typologies for classifying policies, similar attention has not yet been given to creating categories for demands. The attempt to devise subject coding categories that were the most common denominators of the complaints was this project's most difficult and most time-consuming assignment. Without knowing much about the details of the cases in advance—although work was begun with the information contained in Appendix C of the Ombudsman's annual *Reports*—a large number of cases were read, and the present subject categories evolved. The dilemma of steering a course between being either too specific or too general, while providing for all important contingencies, was omnipresent. After very extensive preliminary coding, it emerged that the complaints fell into two major groupings: "offensive" claims and "defensive" ones. It should be stressed that, as the categories constantly were rearranged, this seemed to be a natural division; it was not reached by *a priori* assumptions. In fact, this insight long was denied me, because my perceptual set inclined me toward the view that the Ombudsman normally would act as a "Citizens' Protector."

The questions asked of each complaint were, does the complainant wish either to *extract* something *from* the department or to criticize an action or the quality of an action it has taken; or does he wish to *defend* or protect himself *against* an action or contemplated action? An example of a difference between the two is that a claim for an increase in the amount of a benefit is coded as offensive, while an appeal from a decision to reduce or cancel a benefit is defensive. In the latter case, the complainant had developed a vested interest in the benefit; other perceived threats or restraints upon civil or economic freedoms are regarded as defensive. Sometimes complaints seemed to be mixed offensive and defensive, but each complaint finally was assigned to one or the other heading.

The most general finding to emerge from the analysis is that the Ombudsman's complaints are predominantly offensive. Whereas it traditionally has been assumed that an Ombudsman would be most often asked to protect the citizen from governmental encroachment upon his freedoms, in fact, only 28 percent of the sample's complaints were of that type. Instead, 72 percent were offensive. The relative distribution of offensive and defensive complaints has not changed over time.

According to Table 4-4, two-thirds of the offensive complaints were primarily about a disagreement with a

TABLE 4-4
Offensive Complaints to the Ombudsman

Subject of Complaint	n	%
Total Complainants' Disagreements with Department's Decision	213	66
Question of Eligibility for Benefit—Satisfaction of Criteria such as Age, Residence, Experience, Membership, etc.	47	15
Question of Eligibility for Benefit—Satisfaction of Means Test	21	7
Claim for Rebate of Payments Made to Department	14	4
Refusal of Promotion or Increase in Wages	12	4
Refusal to Pay Compensation—Other Than Personal	12	4

INPUTS: COMPLAINTS

TABLE 4-4—continued

Subject of Complaint	n	%
Denial of Competence or Suitability for Bursary, Exam, Adoption, Citizenship	10	3
Refusal to Sell or Lease or Unjust Price of Goods or Services under Department's Control	9	3
Claim for Collection of Arrears, Nonpayment, Underpayment, Retrospective Payment	8	2
Claim for Increase in Amount of Benefit	8	2
Claim for Reimbursement for Expenses—Legal, Moving, etc.	6	2
Refusal to Provide Services	6	2
Claim that Method of Computing Benefit is Unfair	5	2
Refusal of Appeal or of Reopening of or Right to Appeal	4	1
Refusal to Employ	4	1
Refusal to Award Contract, Lease, License, etc.	3	1
Refusal to Pay Compensation for Personal Injury	2	1
Restriction of Access to or Use of Property under Department's Control	2	1
Miscellaneous: Refusal or Failure to Perform an Act or to Recommend or Assist—or Persistence in Objectionable Acts or Methods	40	12
Total Complainants' Criticisms of Quality of Department's Action	47	15
Alleged Mistreatment as Employee, Inmate, Customer, Client—Includes Partiality, Interference, Unfairness	16	5
Failure to Properly Fulfill Prescribed Duties under Act or Agreement	11	3
Low Standard of Service—Neglect, Poor Maintenance, Slow Mail, etc.	4	1
Failure to Supervise Personnel Properly	2	1
Failure to Regulate Outside Groups under Departmental Control	2	1
Miscellaneous: General Criticisms of Quality of Administration, Incompetence, Misinformation, etc.	12	4
Unscheduled Offensive Complaints	63	20
Grand Total	323	100

decision taken during the implementation of policy. More of the offensive complaints related to various aspects of the complainant's eligibility for a benefit than to any other subject. In total, those first two items in the table account for 22 percent of the offensive complaints; several other categories concern additional aspects of different governmental benefits. In a highly developed welfare state which distributes many kinds of income payments and services, it should be expected that disputes over the process of allocation would be commonplace. The table's subcategory "claim for rebate" requires a brief explanation: refunds requested for alleged overpayments for goods or services were coded as offensive, since clients wanted money from the department, rather than the reverse. Also, the circumstances were such that it did not seem to be a matter of clients paying under protest and then complaining to the Ombudsman about the department's overcharging. The remaining subcategories, which should be self-explanatory, cover the wide gamut of decisions made in administering any complex government.

The second large category of offensive complaints is distinguished from those discussed above by the fact that their thrust appeared to be more against *how* the action was taken than against the act itself. Included here are such matters as unfairness, delay, and "bureaucratic" incompetence. The British often subsume many of these defects under the label of "maladministration," and it has been assumed that they would be principal sources of complaint to an Ombudsman. Sometimes it was not immediately apparent which departmental actions the complainant found most objectionable—e.g., was his complaint really that the agency denied his claim for a benefit or that it unduly delayed any decision? Although it was not unusual for clients to charge that there was some element of maladministration in their case, careful scrutiny revealed that few—only one-seventh of the total

INPUTS: COMPLAINTS

offensive complainants—made such allegations the principal basis of their complaint.

The data in Table 4-5 indicate the distribution of the 28 percent of the Ombudsman's total complaints that were

TABLE 4-5
Defensive Complaints to the Ombudsman

Subject of Complaint	n	%
Principle of or Extent of Liability to Pay Taxes, Duty, Damages, etc.	47	37
Refusal to Permit Complainant to Act, Sell, Import, Enter New Zealand	12	9
Unjust Attempt to Enforce Bond	5	4
Decision to Deport or Issue of Deciding upon Deportation	4	3
Department's Decision to Exercise Power of Eminent Domain	4	3
Price of Property Acquired	3	2
Department's Attempt to Reduce Benefit	3	2
Decision to Prosecute Complainant	3	2
Decision to Terminate Employment	3	2
Decision to Commit or to Retain Complainant in Mental Hospital	2	2
Department's Demand for Refund of Overpayment	2	2
Decision to Call Up Complainant for Military Service	2	2
Decision to Retain Complainant in Prison	1	1
Attempt to Enforce Terms of Contract, Lease, or License	1	1
Miscellaneous: Unjust Claims Including Various Methods, Requirements of Rules and Regulations	8	6
Unscheduled Defensive Complaints	27	21
Total	127	100

defensive in nature. Over one-third of them were about the question of paying money to the department (or the amount involved). What often was mentioned was the department's demand for tax, customs, or damages payments. Taxation law is so complex and many citizens' understanding of it is so limited that the lowness of the figure seems surprising. Likewise, the second largest category, which consisted of those who contended that they were prohibited from taking some action by a departmental decision, seems sparsely populated when one considers the scope of government's proscriptions. Complaints about the enforcement of bond agreements, the third highest type of defensive complaint, are most likely to come from students who have agreed to accept Education Department money to be trained as teachers on condition that they teach afterward. It is striking that no other category of defensive complaints constituted more than 3 percent of the total. For included in the list are such matters as deportation, the taking of private land, prosecution, dismissal, and confinement in prison[10] or a mental hospital. One might assume that such complaints would provide a large percentage of the Ombudsman's clientele. This underscores the findings reported earlier that most complainants are motivated by an aggressive desire to get something *from* a department, rather than by a protective reaction.

When the complaints' subjects are cross-tabulated with the classification of departments, some significant differences emerge. As indicated above, 28 percent of the total complaints were defensive, and it is not unexpected that only 16 percent of those against client-serving departments were defensive. Furthermore, whereas we may have suspected that most of the grievances against the client-attending agencies would be complaints against "repression," in fact only 41 percent of them were defensive.

Although the matter has not yet been specifically addressed, it should be apparent by now that money has been an important element in the Ombudsman's com-

[10] For his 1972 annual *Report* (p. 17) the Ombudsman prepared a summary of complaints from prisoners. The totals for the years 1964–1972 follow: 2, 0, 2, 7, 4, 14, 15, 20, 91. The increase during 1972 was dramatic, and I would expect more such complaints to appear in a currently drawn sample.

INPUTS: COMPLAINTS

plaints. A quite constant total over time of 56 percent of them made some financial claim upon the government. As we might expect, many more of the complaints against client-serving departments (72 percent) made financial claims. Even 42 percent of the complaints against non-client-oriented agencies were financial. Based upon the findings thus far, one would expect the financial claims to be predominantly offensive in nature, and they were in total. But the pattern is unlike what we would expect; in fact, slightly fewer of the financial complaints (70 percent) were offensive than of the whole sample (72 percent).

CONCLUSIONS

Now that we know what kinds of cases come to the Ombudsman, we can begin to answer more fully the question posed at the beginning of this chapter: "What is an ombudsman?" Simply from an analysis of his inputs, we know that the New Zealand Ombudsman is not principally a defender of the helpless citizen entangled in the bureaucracy's relentless clutches and trying to escape. How does this finding affect the institution's social value; does it mean that the Ombudsman is unworthy of the popular and academic attention he has received? Such a conclusion is unwarranted. Although the Ombudsman is not *principally* a "Citizens' Defender," nearly one-third of the total complaints (41 percent of those against client-attending agencies) *did* seek to defend themselves against the bureaucracy—enough so that this function must be considered a significant component of the institution's role.

What of the finding that most complaints are offensive demands for money from client-serving agencies? This determination may be upsetting to those who have viewed the Ombudsman as a modern incarnation of such ancient libertarian principles as habeas corpus, but it does not necessarily lessen the legitimacy of the work the office does do. Because he attempts to attain for citizens all of the benefits to which they are entitled, the Ombudsman is in the tradition of democratic governmental control agencies. The circumstances of modern life more often bring citizens into contact with government as consumers than as subjects. The comment often is made that the growth of the welfare state has created new relationships between the governors and the governed, and the Ombudsman's distribution of complaints reflects those shifting relationships.

These findings provide a preliminary basis for determining what kind of institution the New Zealand Ombudsman has become, but our understanding is incomplete until the clients also are identified. Then clients and complaints can be juxtaposed. These are the objectives of the following chapter.

CHAPTER FIVE

Access to the Ombudsman: His Clients

Now that we know how many and what kinds of cases the Ombudsman has had to work with, this chapter considers the further major question: who uses the Ombudsman? These matters are interrelated, for the complaints cannot be interpreted properly when divorced from those who lodge them—the Ombudsman's clients. To make more explicit the previous chapter's theoretical thrust, these clients are involved in a pattern of consumption of political services that can be identified as demand behavior.[1] Because they essentially define the Ombudsman's institutional parameters, identifying the clients is of cardinal importance.

Whom we would expect to complain, depends upon our understanding of what it means to complain to the Ombudsman. All we know for certain about the clients from the mere fact of their complaint is that they were unable to cope personally with bureaucracy and sought the assistance of an outside agent. Two principal alternative interpretations of this behavior come to mind: 1) complaining to the Ombudsman is the action of a responsible citizen, so that—except for any structural barriers to access—clients are likely to represent a reasonable cross section of the citizenry; or 2) complaining is a deviant act that is likely to attract an unrepresentative group of clients.

No extended investigations with a similar intent have been undertaken as far as I am aware, but plausible ar-

[1] For a theoretical discussion of consumption as demand behavior see Herbert Jacob, *Debtors in Court: The Consumption of Government Services* (Chicago: Rand McNally, 1969), pp. 5–9.

guments can be constructed to support both presumptions. On the one hand, in their study of bureaucratic-clientele relations in Israel, Brenda Danet and Harriet Hartman note that bureaucracies always are somewhat inefficient, and that a certain level of complaints is to be expected. They conclude that "the competent client is one who takes action or complains when he feels he has been treated unjustly."[2]

On the other hand, one can hypothesize as follows. The primary and accepted participatory role for the citizen in bureaucratic states is that of the recipient and consumer of governmental services. To engage in further participation, such as lodging a complaint, after a bureaucratic agency has rendered a decision, is an action that on its face must be interpreted as at least somewhat deviant. Since it is the Ombudsman's *raison d'être* to institutionalize such deviant behavior by encouraging complaints against the government, it seems reasonable that his clients would not constitute a representative social sample. Indeed, certain of the impressionistic evidence we have about clients supports this expectation. Walter Gellhorn has reported that "some of the [Swedish] Ombudsman's clients are steady customers—'querulents'—whose repeated communications may reflect emotional disturbance or mental disease. . . . Many are 'crank' letters, sometimes altogether incoherent or filled with fanciful tales of high-level conspiracies and persecutions."[3] This chapter's goal is to determine which of these interpretations best fits the New Zealand clients.

Sociologists of the law tend to approach from a structural perspective such matters as speculating about the sectors of society from which the Ombudsman's clients

---

[2] Brenda Danet and Harriet Hartman, "Coping with Bureaucracy: The Israeli Case," *Social Forces* 51 (September 1972), 9.

[3] Walter Gellhorn, *Ombudsmen and Others: Citizens' Protectors in Nine Countries* (Cambridge, Mass.: Harvard University Press, 1966), p. 210; see also p. 217.

would be recruited. They usually describe these concerns as questions of access to legal services or the mobilization or invocation of legal remedies.[4] Sometimes provisions exist for automatically invoking legal appeals, but this is seldom the case. Unless the Ombudsman should, for example, spot a newspaper story and initiate an investigation, gaining access to his services always requires purposive behavior on the part of the client or his agent.

The actual barriers to complaining are few, but significant. Initially, the restrictions upon his jurisdiction must be recalled. As discussed in the previous chapter, the activities of the courts, the military's personnel matters, and a few other state organizations are outside his purview (most local government was excluded until 1976). But the main corpus of the state bureaucracy is included, and within these boundaries his scope encompasses "any decision or recommendation made . . . relating to a matter of administration." After a complaint is lodged, the Ombudsman himself or some other actor decides whether or not complaints are within the jurisdiction, but the difficulty for many laymen of knowing in advance if a matter lies within the Ombudsman's competence must be counted as a barrier to complaining.

Another restriction immediately relevant to a prospective client's consideration of whether or not to complain is the Act's requirement that "every complaint to an Ombudsman shall be made in writing." Furthermore, until 1975 a fee of two dollars was payable unless the Ombudsman waived it. The former was intended to insure that clients were responsible for their complaints; the latter was directed against frivolous complaints. An unin-

[4] See Leon H. Mayhew, *Law and Equal Opportunity: A Study of the Massachusetts Commission Against Discrimination* (Cambridge, Mass.: Harvard University Press, 1968); and Kenneth Dolbeare, *Trial Courts in Urban Politics: State Court Policy Impact and Functions in a Local Political System* (New York: John Wiley, 1967).

tended consequence of the writing requirement is that it discriminates against those who are unable to express themselves adequately on paper and who are unfamiliar with the requisite strategies; the fee deterred those who considered two dollars a sufficiently important amount of money that its possible loss became a significant factor in their complaint decision. On their faces, these requirements would appear to discourage lower-class complaints.

Otherwise, there are few structural limitations upon access to the Ombudsman.[5] Those confined to correctional or mental institutions even are guaranteed by law the right to send him letters which their custodians may not open. Also, attempts have been made to reduce the overt risks involved in complaining. Investigations are conducted in private and the Ombudsman is constrained by the Official Secrets Act to keep information given to him confidential. Clients should know, however, that it almost never is possible to keep their identity secret in investigating any matter that affects them personally. This nonstructural bar to complaining, the risk of possible retribution, surely deters some potential clients.

Beginning in ignorance, this study was truly exploratory, and this chapter's goal is to create a composite portrait of the clients. Such a mosaiclike arrangement of numerous bits of data found in the complainants' files will illuminate the public policy question of what kind of institution the Ombudsman has become and enable us to

[5] The Ombudsman may in his discretion refuse to investigate a complaint if "there is an adequate remedy or right of appeal, other than the right to petition Parliament, to which it would have been reasonable for the complainant to resort; or [if] . . . having regard to all the circumstances of the case, any further investigation is unnecessary." Furthermore, complaints which are more than twelve months old, "trivial," "frivolous," "vexatious," "not made in good faith," or in which the complainant "has not a sufficient personal interest in the subject-matter," may be rejected. The last provision does not necessarily require that clients have legal "standing."

determine in which senses the complainants are deviant or representative New Zealanders.

Clients' Identities

Having established in the previous chapter that substantial numbers of complaints were lodged, let us begin to identify the appellants. An analysis of the sample revealed that the overwhelming total of 78 percent were individuals acting on their own behalf. Thus, the expectations of the Ombudsman's proponents that he would provide the missing link in the grievance procedures for the individual citizen are largely fulfilled.

The second largest category, 14 percent, was of those who were acting as agents for other individuals. Complaining for a close relative, such as a wife, son, or mother, accounted for half of that general category. As could be expected, it was sometimes apparent that the complaint was made without the knowledge of the intended beneficiary—especially in the case of elderly mothers. Perhaps surprisingly, lawyers seldom have taken advantage of the Ombudsman as a cheap legal research service; in only 5 percent of the cases did they complain on behalf of a client. Similarly, it is especially interesting that only three Members of Parliament complained to the Ombudsman as surrogates for constituents. Furthermore, neighborhood busybodies have not bothered the Ombudsman; only 1 percent of the complaints were from those whose relationship could be best described as neighbor or friend. Despite what one might predict from the potential political activism of the following organizations, the sample contained only one complaint each on behalf of individuals from businesses, unions, voluntary organizations, and political organizations or pressure groups.

Only 5 percent of the clients were organizations complaining *qua* organizations. Businesses have been the most anxious to ask for the Ombudsman's assistance, but their complaints constituted only 3 percent of the total. This seems surprisingly low in view of the manifold possibilities of disagreement with the government on such matters as taxation, import restrictions, custom duties, wage payments, etc. Various voluntary and political organizations and pressure groups lodged only 2 percent of the total complaints. Taking into account not only the large number of voluntary civic action groups in New Zealand, but also the importance of various political and pressure groups—and especially that of trade unions—the extent of their interaction with the Ombudsman is very low. The conclusion is inescapable that they have chosen to continue to use the particular channels of complaint that each has found effective over the years without trying the Ombudsman.

Demographic Origins

Since New Zealand's South Island has been growing in population at a much slower rate than has the North Island, it could be hypothesized that more complaints might come from the South—the rationale being that this island's residents might feel frustrated that the North Island was leaving them behind economically and that it was getting too large a share of government money. Thus, complaining to the Ombudsman on specific matters could be used as a vehicle for venting generalized frustrations. This has not occurred, however; 69.3 percent of the complaints came from the North and 28.2 percent from the South Island. The census reports their respective shares of the population as 70.7 percent and 29.3 percent.[6] On this geographical basis, those who complain to the Ombudsman certainly are representative of New Zealand.

[6] The national distribution is cited in *New Zealand Census of Population and Dwellings, 1966—Increase and Location of Population* (Wellington: Department of Statistics, 1967), p. 3 (hereinafter cited as *Increase and Location of Population*).

ACCESS: CLIENTS

Adopting as a definition of urbanization the commonly used criterion of percentage of population living in cities over 20,000, New Zealand is the world's sixth most urban country; the United Kingdom is fourth and the United States ranks ninth.[7] At the 1966 census, 62.6 percent of the population was urban,[8] but we learn from Table 5-1

TABLE 5-1
Demographic Origins of the Ombudsman's Clients Compared with the National Population

Demographic Origin	Ombudsman's Clients %	n	National Population[a] %
Four Main Centers	50.9	(229)	40.1
Other Urban Areas	19.8	(89)	22.5
Rural	19.1	(86)	22.7
Towns	7.8	(35)	14.8
Outside New Zealand	2.4	(11)	—
Total	100	(450)	100

[a] The national total equals 2.7 million.

that a total of 70.7 percent of the Ombudsman's clients were urban. Thus, the Ombudsman has become predominantly an urban complaints mechanism.[9] Furthermore, the table indicates that nearly 11 percent more of the sample's complaints came from the four main centers—Auckland, Wellington, Christchurch, and Dunedin—than would be the case if complaints were accurately distrib-

[7] Bruce Russett, et. al., *World Handbook of Political and Social Indicators* (New Haven: Yale University Press, 1964), p. 50.
[8] Computed from the data in *Increase and Location of Population*, pp. 3 and 16.
[9] For a fuller discussion, see Larry B. Hill, "Complaining to the Ombudsman as an Urban Phenomenon: An Analysis of the New Zealand Ombudsman's Clients," *Urban Affairs Quarterly* 8 (September 1972), 123–27.

uted according to population. The smaller urban areas, whose populations range from 27,615 for Nelson to 114,628 for Hutt, were the source of only slightly fewer complaints than would be allocated according to their actual population. Further analyses of all of New Zealand's eighteen urban areas also revealed an impressive correspondence between the cities' rankings on population and numbers of Ombudsman complaints.[10]

Wellington had the largest positive difference between the number of complaints it "deserved" according to its population quota and the number received. Taking into account the facts that it is the site of the Ombudsman's office and that as the capital it attracts politically conscious transients from all over the country, the difference, which was 6 percent, does not seem great. Just the circumstances that the Ombudsman is so readily accessible either by telephone or in person would lead one to hypothesize an even greater difference for Wellington.

Rural areas were the source of nearly as many complaints as they "deserved" to have. The towns, however, which range from 1,000 to Masterton's 17,596 (there is a gap of over 10,000 between the population of the largest town and the smallest urban area), were the most underrepresented. According to their share of the country's population, almost twice as many townspeople should have complained. The most reasonable explanation for the disparity is that people in the urban areas come into potentially acerbic contact with the government more often because of the mass character of life there. Also, possibly urbanites' ties to intermediate groups, which might act as alternative appeals channels, are relatively weak.[11] In such an isolated situation, writing to the Ombudsman may seem appealing. The fact that these ties are

[10] Using Spearman's rho, the coefficient of rank correlation was .77.
[11] See the discussion in William Kornhauser, "The Politics of Mass Society," in Harry Eckstein and David E. Apter, eds., *Comparative Politics—A Reader* (New York: Free Press, 1965), pp. 227–33.

likely to be particularly strong in small towns may help to explain the small number of protests from them.

Does being urban or nonurban affect the types of complaints? Although we might suspect that urban clients would complain disproportionately against client-serving agencies, such as Social Welfare, Health, or Education, this was not the case. They were significantly more likely than their nonurban fellows, however, to complain against client-attending departments (the comparative percents were 37 and 23); it is understandable that urban people would be more likely than nonurban people to have contacts with agencies such as Police and Labor. The reverse of that pattern was found with regard to the non-client-oriented organizations; only 10 percent of the urban complaints were against them, but 21 percent of the nonurban ones were. It is not surprising that nonurban people would have frequent encounters with agencies such as Works and Development, Forest Service, and Soil Conservation and Rivers Control Council. Furthermore, we might expect that urban clients would make offensive claims and demand money from government significantly more often than nonurban clients. Neither expectation was found to be true.

SEXUAL COMPOSITION

Although the census finds almost exactly as many women as men in New Zealand (99.2 females per 100 males),[12] politics, at least until very recently, has been the traditional preserve of the male. Few women were politically active before the 1970s, when a movement toward greater female participation started gaining momentum. It has been found that New Zealand women have less political information than men and are less exposed to politics through the mass media; also, except with their family,

[12] *Increase and Location of Population,* p. 7.

they discuss political events less.[13] Furthermore, because of their lesser involvement in the work force, women would presumably incur fewer grievances of the kind that might be taken to the Ombudsman than men. Taking these factors into account, it might be expected that men would complain to the Ombudsman in disproportionate numbers. This presumption is fully justified: 71 percent of the Ombudsman's individual complainants have been men as compared with 26 percent women (an additional 3 percent complained jointly as husband and wife). But significantly more women were among the urban than nonurban complainants; 30 percent as compared with 20 percent.

Possibly as a reflection of their possession of less political information, women were significantly more likely (30 percent) to complain against unscheduled organizations than men (20 percent). Also, more women (41 percent) than men (31 percent) pressed their grievance against a client-serving agency; many welfare state benefits, such as Widows' Pensions and the Family Benefit, are aimed principally at women. But men were more likely than women to choose as their target of complaint both client-attending and non-client-oriented departments.

These findings generally are in accord with traditional sex role stereotyping, as is the additional finding that women were more likely, 68 percent, than men, 55 percent, to make a financial claim. The sexes were very nearly equal, however, with regard to their proportions of offensive and defensive complaints.

Age Distribution

In comparison with the national population, the data in Table 5-2 indicate that the Ombudsman's clients over-

[13] A. D. Robinson and A. H. Ashenden, "Mass Communications and the 1963 Election: A Preliminary Report," *Political Science* 16 (September 1964), p. 19.

ACCESS: CLIENTS

TABLE 5-2
Age Distribution of the Ombudsman's Clients Compared with the National Population over Age 15

Age Category	Ombudsman's Clients %	n	National Population over Age 15[a] %
Retirement Age (Pension, Superannuitant, etc.)	22.2	(92)	12.4
Middle Age (Working, Family, etc.)	73.9	(306)	71.7
Young (Student, etc.)	3.9	(16)	15.9
Total	100	(414)	100

[a] The national total equals 1.7 million.

represent the older elements of society and underrepresent the younger group.[14] This seems reasonable since individuals under twenty-one are more likely to be still in school and since they have fewer contacts with government than do other citizens. There has been an important change over time, however. At the very beginning, almost one-third of the clients were of retirement age, but by the final of the sample's nine periods, almost all of the overrepresentation had disappeared. It seems that at the Ombudsman's inception a number of elderly people who had been awaiting the opportunity took their problems, usually pertaining to long-standing pension matters, to him. Since that time, their proportions have declined

[14] The national data are computed from *New Zealand Census of Population and Dwellings—1966: Summary Results* (Wellington: Department of Statistics, 1968), p. 3 (hereinafter cited as *Summary Results*). The census categories that correspond to those used in the table are ages 65+, 21–65, and 15–21. The total in the final column omits the 32.6 percent of the population that is under the age of 15, because it does not represent potential complainants to the Ombudsman. The sample total omits the 3 percent of the clients whose age was not ascertained and also the inapplicable category.

while those from middle-aged, working people have increased steadily. Even complaints from young people over such matters as university scholarships have increased, so that the age composition of those who complain to the Ombudsman has come closer to representing faithfully the general population.

An analysis of the complaints by age groups revealed that clients of retirement age were less likely than others (11 percent compared with 25 percent) to complain against unscheduled agencies, and their complaints usually were focused upon matters relating to their age. Half of their complaints as compared with only 28 percent for all other age groups were against client-serving departments, and retirement age clients were underrepresented among complainants against client-attending organizations. Furthermore, they were far more likely to make offensive complaints. Seventy-seven percent of the retirement age complaints were offensive compared with 52 percent for all other ages. Financial complaints also originated disproportionately from retirement age people, but by a lesser margin: 76 percent and 70 percent.

Educational Background

Unfortunately, there was no easy way to determine the client's educational background. It was sometimes evident from his occupation's educational prerequisites or from the nature of the complaint itself, but it often was necessary to rely upon internal evidence in the letters. Thus, fine discriminations were not attempted; in the absence of any definite evidence complainants were simply graded as average, and over 70 percent were thus categorized.

At least 15 percent had a university education or its equivalent, and the actual number is surely somewhat higher than that; for unless there was *specific* evidence of higher educational attainment, complainants were coded

ACCESS: CLIENTS

as average. In comparison, the 1966 census found that only 5.4 percent of New Zealand's adults had attended a university for one year or more, and that only 2.4 percent had obtained a degree or other university qualification.[15] Probably some of the Ombudsman's clients coded as having a degree had not actually completed theirs, however; so the 15 percent of the complainants who are listed as having a university education may not greatly overrepresent the percentage of such people in the country. As the most articulate group in society, one might expect them to take even more disproportionate advantage of the Ombudsman's services.

A low education ranking was ascribed only to those whose verbal skills were quite obviously deficient. This code was conservatively used and took such matters as spelling, punctuation, sentence structure, and word usage into account. A total of 12 percent of the sample was graded low, but when an historical analysis is employed, important changes are revealed. The number of low-education clients was large for the first three time periods, and it peaked at 44 percent in the second period. The percentages for the last five time periods fell, however, to 6, 0, 2, 0, and 0. This may indicate that at the Ombudsman's inception a number of society's relatively inarticulate, educationally marginal individuals saw him either as a generalized problem-solving mechanism or as a solution to a particular situation. Perhaps the pool of individuals who were psychologically capable of being mobilized to make an appeal to such an officer was quite a small one and was simply exhausted. Certainly, New Zealand's poorly educated group have come to be greatly underrepresented as complainants to the Ombudsman, but there are no data to indicate how many people in the

---

[15] *New Zealand Census of Population and Dwellings, 1966*, vol. 6 (Wellington: Department of Statistics, 1967).

general population are poorly educated according to the definition used here.[16]

One might predict that highly educated people seldom would complain against unscheduled agencies and that low-education clients would more often. Both assumptions were correct. Twenty-two percent of the entire sample complained about unscheduled agencies; the percentage for university-educated clients was 8, and for low-education complainants it was 32. Two other interesting findings about education and departmental targets were that university-trained clients complained disproportionately against client-serving agencies—53 percent compared with the total sample's 33 percent—and that, for reasons that remain mysterious, both university and low-education clients were less likely—24 and 26 percent, respectively—than the entire sample—32 percent—to lodge grievances against client-attending departments.

Despite the university-educated clients' predilection for client-serving agencies, they were not significantly more likely than the whole sample to make financial claims; and they were less likely to lodge offensive grievances (66 percent) than the total sample (72 percent). The low-education clients were more likely, however, to make both financial claims (68 percent) and offensive complaints (77 percent) than was the entire sample (56 and 72 percent, respectively).

Marital Status

In speculating about clients' marital status it might be postulated that proportionately more complainants would be "loners" than would exist in the population at

---

[16] According to the definition used by the United Nations, New Zealand is 98.5 percent literate. Thus she shares the first rank among nations with thirteen other countries. See Russett, *World Handbook,* p. 222.

ACCESS: CLIENTS

large. One could suppose that maritally marginal people, whether spinster, bachelor, widow, widower, or divorcé(e), might find the Ombudsman to be an attractive target upon which to focus the frustrations born of their loneliness. An examination of the data in Table 5-3, however, does not generally support this hypothesis.

TABLE 5-3
Marital Status of the Ombudsman's Clients Compared with the National Adult Population

Marital Status	Ombudsman's Clients %	n	National Adult Population[a] %
Married	52.7	(237)	76.0
Single	7.3	(33)	13.4
Widowed	6.7	(30)	1.0
Separated	2.7	(12)	1.3
Divorced	2.2	(10)	8.2
Other (Includes Not Ascertained and Inapplicable)	28.4	(128)	—
Total	100	(450)	100

[a] The national total equals 1.5 million.

Marital status could not be determined for over one-fourth of the complainants, and this fact complicates the analysis. The total percentage of clients confirmed as married is almost a quarter less than for the national total.[17] Certainly many of the "other" complainants are married—the normal condition of over three-quarters of New Zealand's adults. An historical analysis reveals that the married category has increased steadily from 34 percent in the first time period to 74 percent in the last; the

[17] The national totals are computed from data in *Summary Results*, p. 3. Those under twenty-one years of age and those whose marital status was unspecified were omitted in computing percentages. The base number used was 1,505,183.

"other" category also has shrunk, although not as steadily. Important contributors to both circumstances are the facts that more elderly people and more clients with low educational attainment complained at first; both groups may have tended to provide less information to the coder.

Relatively few single people complained. During no time period did the percentage equal the national percentage of 13.4. Thus, bachelors and spinsters seem not to have vented their frustrations upon the Ombudsman. Those widowed and separated, though, were overrepresented according to their proportions in the total population. Quite small numbers are involved, however, and this seems predictable considering the specific benefits and remedies that various government departments, such as Social Welfare, dispense for them—especially for women with dependent children. Presumably, since the government has relatively little to do with divorced people as such, there were few complaints from them. On balance, from what we know about the clients' marital status, they are not unreasonably unrepresentative of the national population when one considers various special justifications.

Although the hypothesis that maritally marginal people would complain disproportionately to the Ombudsman was rejected for the whole sample, after controlling for urban residence it was confirmed. Forty percent of the urban clients were maritally marginal as compared with only 17 percent for the nonurban. There were no statistically significant differences, however, between married clients and "loners" with regard to preferred types of targets of complaint or to the incidence of financial or defensive complaints.

Racial-Ethnic Background

New Zealand is a biracial society, but the Maori component is relatively small. The census determined that 4.5 percent of the population were full-blood Maoris; adding those who were at least one-quarter Maori brought the total to 7.5 percent.[18] The "European" majority is extremely homogeneous and almost uniformly from one of the British Isles. There are no census figures on this matter, but Robinson estimates that the size of the entire non-British element of the population (from Scandinavia, the Netherlands, Germany, China, and India) would total no more than 5 percent.[19]

Whereas, from their perspective as the principal racial minority group, one would expect that complaints from Maoris would overrepresent their numbers in society, they constituted only 1.3 percent of our sample's complainants to the Ombudsman, the smallest proportion of any racial-ethnic group. This figure probably somewhat understates the number of Maori complaints because of the difficulty of determining race. Since many Maoris have European names, names could not be used as a guide. Only when there was certain evidence of race were complainants so identified. At least it is clear that the Ombudsman seldom has been appealed to by Maoris on matters relating to their Maoridom. This is a reflection of two factors. First, racial problems in New Zealand arise infrequently and are by world standards very mild. Second, it is due to Maoris' close attachment to their traditional channels of redress: the Maori Land Courts, their four special Members of Parliament, and petitions to the Maori Affairs Committee of Parliament.[20]

Constituting 8 percent of the entire sample, the largest identifiable ethnic group were those complainants who were immigrants from the United Kingdom. An addi-

[18] Computed from data in *Summary Results*, p. 9.

[19] Alan D. Robinson, *Notes on New Zealand Politics* (Wellington: School of Political Science and Public Administration, Victoria University, 1970), p. 3.

[20] The fact that few Maoris utilized the Ombudsman's services was a principal impetus to Parliament's creation of a Race Relations Conciliator in 1970. For the first year and one-half of that office's existence, Sir Guy Powles was appointed Conciliator as well as Ombudsman.

tional 2 percent were immigrants from other Commonwealth countries, especially Australia, South Africa, and Canada; and 2 percent were from continental Europe. There are no national data with which to compare these, but the number of New Zealanders who were initially from another Commonwealth country—including Britain—surely would be higher than these figures. It seems that the popularly stereotyped "grizzling Pommies," who do nothing but complain once they arrive in New Zealand, do not constitute a larger percent of complainants to the Ombudsman than would be allotted according to their numbers or expected because of grievances over such matters as citizenship, entry of relatives into the country, reciprocal pensions, etc. The same is true of continental European immigrants. Because of language problems, one might expect them to have even more occasion to complain than the former groups. Perhaps their unfamiliarity with grievance procedures and their desire to avoid causing trouble may explain the paucity of complaints from them.

Finally, Polynesian Islanders, who constituted .98 percent of the population at the 1966 census, accounted for 1.8 percent of the complainants, so the Islanders are somewhat overrepresented.[21] But the small N's involved and the facts that they have peculiar problems with remaining in the country, repatriating funds, and bringing relatives to New Zealand seem to account for this.

Although no particular racial or ethnic group has by itself complained sufficiently to make much of a mark on the character of the Ombudsman office, when the complaints from minorities are combined it is clear that they represent a principal constituency: fully 15 percent of the total clientele. In comparing the "European" with the "non-European" complaints it comes as no surprise that the latter complain disproportionately about client-

[21] Computed from data in *Summary Results*, p. 9.

attending departments, for they often come into contact with such agencies as Justice, Labor (the immigration department), Customs, and Police. These departments were the targets of 42 percent of the non-European complaints compared with 32 percent of the whole sample. Also significantly more (38 percent) of their complaints were defensive than were the total sample's (28 percent), but non-European clients were not more likely to make financial claims.

Class-Occupational Background

Determining social class in New Zealand is complicated for the American who is accustomed to using income as a primary criterion, because income differentials are quite small.[22] The most reliable criterion for New Zealand is occupation, and the backgrounds of those clients whose vocation could be determined are arrayed in Table 5-4 and compared with the national percentages of those employed.[23] The occupations of nearly half of the clients in the sample could be determined from information in the file supplied by either the individual or the department.

[22] According to the 1966 census (*Summary Results*, p. 8.), only 5.5 percent of the population had an income that reached the range of 4,000–8,000 dollars (N.Z.). *The highest category used in the census was 8,000 dollars (N.Z.) and above; only 1.4 percent of the population was in it.* The New Zealand dollar's value was 1.39 dollars (U.S.) in 1966.

[23] The national totals are computed from the data in *Summary Results*, pp. 6–7. Percentages are based upon the 1,026,039 New Zealanders who were actively employed. Census categories and those used for the complainants are as comparable as possible, but they are not identical. The column is left blank if there is no closely comparable census category.

The total for the Ombudsman's complaints is 220 cases, or 49 percent of the total sample. The remaining cases were not identifiable on a class-occupational basis, but two-fifths of them can be classified into interesting categories that do not have definite class referents: retired, 17 percent; housewife, 17 percent; student, 5 percent; unemployed, 1 percent.

TABLE 5-4
Class-Occupational Backgrounds of the Ombudsman's Clients
Compared with the National Workforce

Class-Occupational Background	Ombudsman's Clients %	n	National Workforce[a] %
Total Professional	26.8	(59)	10.2
Top Professional	8.6	(19)	—
Lawyer	2.7	(6)	.2
Physician	2.7	(6)	.4
Clergy	.9	(2)	.4
Accountant	.9	(2)	—
University Teacher	1.4	(3)	—
Second-Level Professional	18.8	(40)	—
Teacher	10.5	(23)	3.4
Nurse	3.2	(7)	1.9
Scientist without Advanced Degree	1.8	(4)	—
All Other Professional	2.7	(6)	—
Executive-Administrative-Proprietorial	31.4	(69)	14.0
Top Executive-Administrative-Proprietorial	6.4	(14)	5.8
Business Owner, Director, Top Government Executive	2.3	(5)	—
Manager, Other	4.1	(9)	—
Second-Level Executive-Administrative-Proprietorial	25.0	(55)	9.2
Farm Owner or Manager	15.5	(34)	7.4
Working Proprietor and Other Self-Employed	7.7	(17)	.7
Other Lower Administrative	1.8	(4)	1.1

ACCESS: CLIENTS

TABLE 5-4—continued

Class-Occupational Background	Ombudsman's Clients %	n	National Workforce[a] %
Total White Collar	9.1	(20)	21.3
Sales	.5	(1)	7.5
Other Clerical	8.2	(18)	11.9
Typist, Secretary	.5	(1)	2.5
Total Manual Worker	31.8	(70)	53.6
Tradesmen—Skilled and Semiskilled	15.5	(34)	—
Laborer and Factory Worker—Unskilled and Semiskilled	12.7	(28)	—
Farm Workers, Fishermen, Hunters, Loggers	3.6	(8)	5.7
Armed Forces	.5	(2)	1.1
Grand Total	100	(220)	100

[a] The national total equals 1,000,000.

As one might hypothesize, the upper classes, described here as the professional and the executive-administrative-proprietorial, have expressed dissatisfaction more than have the lower classes. In fact, those two classes combined have been the source of two and one-half times more complaints than would be expected from their share of the population. The remaining three-quarters of the working population (the white collar and manual workers) have accounted for only two-fifths of the complaints. This disparity would seem to be explained by the upper classes' generally higher education and hence increased verbal skills, by the higher sense of political efficacy that would be occasioned by that fact, by their pattern of political socialization, and by the likelihood that their occupation would bring them into contact with the government to a greater degree than would be true of the lower classes.

Within general groupings, the top professionals complained less than did second-level professionals, and lawyers and physicians protested most often in the former group. It may seem surprising that the clergy seldom have complained on behalf of parishioners. Of the second-level professionals, nurses often have complained; but teachers have lodged more than three times more complaints than would be predicted from their proportion of the working population. In large measure this finding (as well as that for the nurses) can be explained by the fact that their employer is a government department; over four-fifths of the teachers' complaints were job-related.

Most of the complaints from the executive-administrative-proprietorial class came from its second stratum. As one might predict, based upon their presumed competence and feelings of efficacy, members of the top stratum evidently generally have continued to use their established appeals procedures rather than trying the Ombudsman. Within the second level, farmers, a traditionally efficacious voice in New Zealand politics, accounted for over twice their proportion of the working population. Small businessmen, too, contributed many more voices of dissatisfaction than would be expected from their numbers.

One could hypothesize that white collar workers might be a source of more complaints than their numbers would justify, because they could be articulate enough, possibly frustrated by unchallenging jobs, and—particularly in the case of government employees—well situated to observe complaint situations. This has not been the case, however; they have made less than half as many complaints as their number would warrant. Manual workers, who long have strongly expressed their political views through union activities and the Labor Party, also were somewhat underrepresented among the complainants. In total they did constitute nearly one-third of those whose occupation could be discerned, however; and it is probable that they account for a large number of those that could not be identified.

It would be interesting to know much more about the other half of the complainants. A cross-tabulation revealed that 8 percent of them had a university education, so they are not uniformly lower-class. This half of the sample did, however, account for 65 percent of the complaints against the Social Welfare Department. Thus the table's reported skewing toward the upper classes is exaggerated, but to an unknown extent. Those complaints that can be identified as coming from the manual workers were divided rather equally, about the same way that the total class divides,[24] between tradesmen and ordinary laborers.

Clients' class-occupational backgrounds were related to their complaints in some rather interesting ways. Fifty-one percent of the professional clients had grievances against client-serving departments (the total for the sample was 33 percent); but, despite what we might guess from this finding, they were insignificantly more likely to make financial claims. Also only 20 percent of their complaints were against client-attending agencies, and their level of defensive complaints did not exceed the sample's, 28 percent. Perhaps their backgrounds simply made them highly sensitive to the operations of the departments with which they most often came in contact. Also these are the same people as the university-

[24] This cannot be determined from the census, for it lumps together skilled and unskilled workers in a single industry. However, 38.8 percent of the Victoria University's urban sample's respondents were manual workers. Of these, 21.5 percent were skilled, and 17.3 percent were unskilled and semiskilled. Cited in Robinson, *Notes on New Zealand Politics*, p. 10.

educated clients, who also complained against the client-serving agencies in similar proportions. The executive-administrative-proprietorial class did complain more often (41 percent) than the whole sample (32 percent) against client-attending agencies, and more (35 percent) of their complaints were defensive than the total sample's (28 percent). This finding can be attributed to that class's—especially its second level's—working relationships with departments such as Inland Revenue, Labor, Customs, and Agriculture and Fisheries.

If one were to set up a hypothetical manual worker's complaint, it might be a demand that his Family Benefit be increased; this is an offensive, money claim against a client-serving department. But the data reveal that the stereotype is untrue. *Fewer* manual worker complaints (26 percent) than total complaints (33 percent) were against client-serving departments, and significantly more (43 percent as compared with 32 percent for the total) were against client-attending departments. Furthermore, somewhat *fewer* of the manual workers made a financial claim, and somewhat *fewer* of them were offensive (51 percent and 67 percent, respectively) than was the whole sample (56 percent and 72 percent, respectively). A satisfactory explanation for this pattern is not readily apparent.

Civil Service Employment

The Public Service Association was opposed to the transfer of the Ombudsman, whom they viewed as an intruder who would monitor their every action.[25] Once the Ombudsman was appointed, however, he became not only a watchdog over civil servants but also a channel for receiving complaints from them. Sixteen percent of the

[25] See Larry B. Hill, "The Role of Pressure Groups in the Policy Process: The New Zealand Public Service Association and the Adoption of the Ombudsman," *New Zealand Journal of Public Administration* 34 (March 1972), 46–58.

Ombudsman's clients were civil servants. For one-fourth of them, however, there was no apparent connection between that fact and the complaint itself. As of 1966, government employees constituted 11 percent of the work force,[26] so the number of complaints from them does not seem unduly high. An additional 3 percent of the grievances *were* related to their employment, but were *not* against their own department; examples of such complaints would be problems with the Government Superannuation Fund Board over pension rights or with the State Services Commission about the grading of their jobs.

A total of 9 percent of the clients disagreed with their own department over working conditions, salary, job conduct, etc. Those protests cover the entire gamut of labor problems. Hence, the Ombudsman has become in addition to his other functions a labor relations counselor. The incidence of this type of complaint has increased over the years, and it is one index of the degree of institutionalization of the Ombudsman. Primarily because of the State Services Commission, the service-connected complaints were levied disproportionately against client-attending agencies; and 86 percent of them were offensive. Service-connected complaints were not, however, more likely than others to be financial in nature.

Conclusions

This chapter has taken us further in our quest to determine what sort of institution an Ombudsman really is. Not only do we know what kinds of cases come to him, but also we now know who utilizes the Ombudsman's services. In drawing conclusions from these findings let us return to the two contending theories that were posed at the beginning of this chapter about the probable iden-

[26] Computed from the *New Zealand Official Yearbook—1966* (Wellington: Government Printer, 1967), p. 950.

tities of the clients: complaining is the act of a competent citizen, so that clients would be likely to constitute a reasonable popular cross section; and complaining is a deviant act, so that the Ombudsman would attract an unrepresentative clientele.

The data seem to provide some support for the second theory. Thus, clients originated disproportionately from the urban centers—particularly at the expense of the towns; women were greatly underrepresented, as they are generally in New Zealand public life; younger age groups were underrepresented and originally those of retirement age were overrepresented; those with a university education were overrepresented and the poorly educated were quite underrepresented; Maoris were underrepresented; and complaints came disproportionately from the professional and executive-administrative-proprietorial classes as opposed to the white collar and manual worker classes. Moreover, some additional unrepresentativeness is revealed when the complaints and clients are juxtaposed. For example, university-educated and professional clients complained quite disproportionately against client-serving departments.

Strictly speaking, these findings do reflect deviancy in the sense that the distribution among the Ombudsman's clients of certain sociological characteristics varied somewhat from their distribution in society. Much of this "deviancy" was of a particular sort, however. New Zealand's mainstream, or what we may call advantaged people, were overrepresented; and it is not hyperbolic to describe the Ombudsman's clients as increasingly supernormal.[27]

[27] From the institutionalization perspective, four noteworthy developments have occurred: fewer elderly people; more married clients; more government workers; and fewer people of low educational attainment have complained over time. The first two developments have increased the clients' representativeness, the effects of the third are not critical; and the fourth probably has slightly increased their "deviancy."

ACCESS: CLIENTS

But perhaps such judgments are premature; perhaps the clients are "deviant" in the sense that they are drawn from the least psychologically stable elements of the categories examined above. Some of the clients' lower-level psychological attributes will be explored in the following chapter, but it is appropriate to make some gross observations relative to that plausible hypothesis at this point. It is incorrect; most of the Ombudsman's customers revealed themselves to be rational and normal people. Only 1 percent of them could be proved to have been affected by mental illness. Evidence that was used included records indicating confinement in a mental institution or treatment for serious psychiactric disorder.

For all other cases internal evidence was used; stringent standards were applied before anyone was ascribed to the category "apparently psychotic," and only 2 percent were placed in it.[28] The mentally ill complainants evidently had been waiting for the appointment; for all of the validated psychotics complained during the sample's first two time periods, and all of the unvalidated ones did during the first five.

If this composite portrait of the clients reveals little deviancy of either a sociological or a psychological sort, what does this tell us about the Ombudsman's role in the political system? The implications are dual. On the one hand, the mainstream origin of the complaints has en-

[28] The most common characteristics of such complainants were sexual and other fantasies, paranoia, extreme incoherence, and irrelevance of the grievance to any function of the Ombudsman. Of course, many other letters contained irrelevant information and some alleged situations that seemed highly unlikely; but alternative explanations, such as a low level of intelligence or education, or senility, were plausible. The total of 3 percent that were coded as psychotic seemed qualitatively different from the others.

These figures somewhat understate the number of mentally ill people who have corresponded with the Ombudsman. Letters from some of the most obviously ill people are not considered to be complaints; they are dealt with separately and are kept on a cumulative file.

abled him to succeed as a rational-bureaucratic mechanism. Recall that a mere recommendation to Parliament is his most severe sanction. Because he wields such puny power, the Ombudsman is dependent upon the cooperation and respect of those whom he superintends. Those fragile resources would be compromised if departments became convinced that his clientele was unrepresentative of their own broader constituencies. He simply would not be taken seriously.

On the other hand, the implications are not so sanguine for those who have perceived of the Ombudsman as a combination social worker and community psychiatrist. According to their scenario, he would act as a magnet drawing complaints from the poor, the aged, the uneducated, the ethnic minorities, the alienated, and those who for various reasons are unable to cope with the stresses of modern, bureaucratized life. Our analysis has indicated that—apart from the Ombudsman's important services for urban clients—this role is a minor facet of his total job. Hence, some may feel that these findings compromise his legitimacy. From this viewpoint, the Ombudsman is merely a supernumerary access point to government for those who—through their educational, social, and other advantages—already were likely to be competent to deal with bureaucracy.[29] Furthermore, it can be alleged that the existence of barriers to access (especially the requirement that complaints be in writing) and the fact that, like the courts, the institution reacts to whatever complaints are presented rather than seeking them out, both act to discourage underprivileged clients.

Whether or not these findings do make the Ombudsman's legitimacy suspect, ultimately is a value judgment; but two observations should be mentioned in the institution's defense. First: from the whole system

[29] See G. Sjoberg, R. A. Brymer, and B. Farris, "Bureaucracy and the Lower Class," *Sociology and Social Research* 50 (April 1966), 325–37.

perspective, a complaint from a poor, uneducated Maori is not inherently more valuable than one from a university-trained, wealthy sheep farmer. In fact, if we hold aside moralistic judgments about such matters as the latter's probable higher motivation to defend and extend his economic self-interest, the level of complaints from society's successes is probably a better objective index of the bureaucracy's quality of administrative competence than is the level of complaints from disadvantaged people.

Second: the conception of the ombudsman as social worker is a recent image developed after the institution's "discovery" by professional social workers.[30] It was not important to those who were responsible for transferring it throughout Scandinavia and to New Zealand; they viewed the ombudsman as an aid to the undifferentiated, classical "citizen" in his encounters with the administrative state. In sum, it is this chapter's salient finding that the first theory offered in the introduction is supported: the great bulk of the clients are identified as competent, responsible, ordinary New Zealanders with very real problems. The classical citizen has been rediscovered as a complainant to the ombudsman.

[30] See F. M. Zweig, "The Social Worker as Legislative Ombudsman," *Social Work* 14 (January 1969), 25–33; and J. E. Payne, "Ombudsman Roles for Social Workers," *Social Work* 17 (January 1972), 94–100.

CHAPTER SIX

Exchange Processes: The Ombudsman and His Clients

Having determined what kinds of cases come to the Ombudsman and who uses his services, in this chapter we explore the relationship between the institution and that segment of the population who complain. Five aspects of this relationship are examined: the extensiveness of the interaction between the Ombudsman and clients; the clients' perceptions and images of the Ombudsman; their attitudes toward bureaucracy; the complaint strategies that clients employ; and other qualitative aspects of the Ombudsman-client relationship.

Extensiveness of Interaction

The quantity of interactions between the Ombudsman and his clients during the investigation of a complaint is not impressive, but these interactions are, of course, crucial to understanding the relationship. Complainants normally initiate the encounter through a letter. *For fully 45 percent of the sample, this first communication was both the beginning and the end of their submissions to the Ombudsman.*[1] An additional 25 percent communicated only once more with the Ombudsman, and 14 percent wrote three letters; the percentages fall off rapidly after that point. Because one might suspect that many inveterate correspondents would be attracted, it may be surprising that only 3 percent wrote nine or more letters. The mean number of communications to the Ombudsman per case was 2.3.

[1] In 3 percent of the cases this sole communication was not a letter but a personal interview or telephone call.

The Ombudsman's responses were only a little more numerous. *His initial reaction to the complaint was in two-fifths of the cases his sole communication.*[2] Twenty-two percent received two letters from him, 15 percent received three, and 9 percent received four. Although more than four letters were necessary in only 14 percent of the cases, it should be noted that these cases required a lot of work and that in 3 percent of the complaints the Ombudsman wrote nine or more letters. The mean number was 2.5 letters, only slightly higher than the mean number the clients sent to him. It might be hypothesized that eventually the Ombudsman would become so experienced in dealing with complaints that less and less correspondence per case would be required, and that fewer cases involving very extensive correspondence would arise. A longitudinal analysis confirmed only part of that supposition; it has become increasingly likely that the Ombudsman will write only one letter in response to the client.

For most complainants their letters were the only form of communication between them and the Ombudsman. According to the information on the files, a total of only 9 percent had a personal interview with the Ombudsman—almost always at the clients' request—at any time during the investigation, and an additional 1 percent were interviewed by his staff. Telephone conversations were even fewer, although records are not always kept. But Sir Guy is punctilious about such matters and has upbraided departments for just such omissions. It seems unlikely that the number found would very much underrate the actual frequency. According to the available information, only 3 percent of the clients telephoned the Ombudsman's office, and the Ombudsman initiated calls with 1 percent. Thus, although one of the purposes of the

[2] In the 2 percent of the cases in which the Ombudsman wrote no letters, the matter was quickly disposed of through an interview or telephone call.

Ombudsman was to bring some warmth and humanity into the administrative process, communication with citizens has been through relatively impersonal correspondence. Of course, there are valid reasons for this—especially cost, convenience, and the desire to maintain complete records. The finding that the Ombudsman-client relationship is not a very extensive one in a quantitative sense, highlights the importance of a qualitative analysis of it.

Perceptions of the Ombudsman

This section, which is based upon a careful analysis of the clients' original letters of complaint, begins an enterprise that the next two sections continue. Although no form is filled out in complaining to the Ombudsman, clients reveal many things about themselves in the course of their complaint; these data have been the basis of the two previous chapters. Now we begin to probe deeper and to extract from the letters some perceptions and attitudes that their writers hold and some strategies that they employ. These tasks were made easier by a curious phenomenon: clients tended to compensate for the lack of a complaint form by constructing one in their own minds and then providing any information that seemed relevant. Seldom was any facsimile bureaucratic form created, but, nevertheless, the existence of an ideal form in the writer's mind often was apparent. As a result, quite a lot of information usually was provided, and in the process clients revealed much about themselves—often unintentionally.

It would be fascinating to know what kinds of information about the Ombudsman and perceptions of his role clients possessed at the time of complaining. Although we cannot interview the clients, we can "interview" their letters about the images of the Ombudsman they reveal. The first matter to be considered is a fundamental one which also is related to the subjects of the next two sections (the complainants' attitudes to bureaucracy and the strategies they employ): Do the clients perceive of the Ombudsman in classical "universalistic," bureaucratic terms or do they view him as a particularistic "fixer"? Studies of American Congressmen indicate that a large proportion of their constituents' pleas for assistance actually are requests for *preferment*.[3] Although the Ombudsman is supposed to help clients, his operating norms are *universalistic*. Would clients perceive this subtle distinction? Ninety percent of them did; in proferring their cases, they did not ask to be made an exception to a rule. Only 10 percent of them asked for preferment, and even this low percentage declined after the first three time periods.

Thus, clients usually correctly perceived the Ombudsman as an impartial, neutral, bureaucratic mechanism. Furthermore, they seldom revealed that they were ignorant of his formal powers. Only 14 percent of them indicated at some point in their letters that they were under the inaccurate impression that the Ombudsman had the power actually to *change* administrative decisions.

The complainants' perceptions of the Ombudsman next are explored through an examination of what they said they wanted him to do to solve their problem. The two major roles, which were chosen by about equal numbers of clients (29 and 28 percent, respectively), were investigator and intercessor. That is, the Ombudsman was asked to *investigate* or review the problem; or he

[3] See Walter Gellhorn, *When Americans Complain: Governmental Grievance Procedures* (Cambridge, Mass.: Harvard University Press, 1966), pp. 58–73. Gellhorn (pp. 61–62) quotes an urban Congressman as saying that "most of his rather exceptionally large casework docket consists of requests for preferment—being assigned a bed in a Veterans Hospital ahead of others already on a waiting list, or quickly obtaining an entry visa for a relative, or procuring a passport overnight; no more than 2 or 3 percent, he estimates, could be regarded as grievances or complaints about administration."

was requested to *intercede*, help, or mediate their disagreement with the bureaucracy. Twelve percent viewed the Ombudsman as *advisor* and merely solicited his guidance in dealing with their problem. Half that many presented their complaint so diffidently that they only asked whether or not it lay in his jurisdiction. A surprisingly large number, 14 percent, said nothing whatever about how they wanted the Ombudsman to solve their complaint; often in stream-of-consciousness style they poured out their grievance and then simply signed it.

In total, almost 90 percent of the clients proposed either an indirect solution to their problem or none at all. Only one-tenth of them proposed a direct solution; e.g., they asked the Ombudsman to take a particular action— to obtain a document, to protect their rights, etc. It developed that most clients tended to have a rather vague but confident view of the Ombudsman as an officer to whom they should merely present their grievance, an officer who would proceed from there if action were warranted.

Knowledge is the basis of perception; a longitudinal analysis of how the Ombudsman is addressed in the clients' first letters provides one measure of the depth of their familiarity with the institution (in subsequent letters they could reply in terms of the Ombudsman's letterhead). A total of 73 percent of the sample's letters used the word *Ombudsman* in their salutation. This seems to be quite a high percentage, considering the entirely foreign character of the word. Just "Dear Ombudsman" appeared in almost half, 48 percent. Over one-fifth began "Sir Guy Powles, Ombudsman," but in 2 percent of the total, one or both of them were misspelled. Almost one-third of the complaints specifically referred to Sir Guy Powles, so it was evident that the institution's incumbent also was relatively well known. "Parliamentary Commissioner," the Ombudsman's alternative legal name, has not found favor; less than one-tenth have used it. Despite a plausible hypothesis that the usage of the term *Ombudsman* and of Sir Guy Powles' name would increase dramatically over time as both became better known, this has not happened. There is a tendency for *Ombudsman* to be used somewhat more frequently, but the use of Sir Guy's name actually has decreased slightly.

CLIENT ATTITUDES

Alas, severe limitations hamper the would-be psychoanalyst of pieces of paper, but we have determined already that few clients were mentally ill. Nevertheless, they may have been angry, scheming, etc.; and here we note whatever psychological material was available about their attitudes—particularly bureaucratic attitudes. All of them labored under a sense of being wronged; in what terms would they represent this injury? In the preliminary coding it was noticed that frequent mention was made of the perpetration of "injustice" or that "justice" was invoked as a principle. Apparently, many clients felt that no other concept could express accurately their feelings. The analysis revealed that one or the other term was employed by a majority, 53 percent, of the Ombudsman's clients; but most used either term only once. Few were preoccupied with them; only 11 percent used them more than five times, and 3 percent invoked them nine or more times. The mean mentions of justice or injustice for those who used the terms was 1.6.

Although clients tended to allude to the traditional concept, justice, often it was invoked as an abstract principle. And well over half (55 percent) said nothing critical of either the department or its officers. This fact is highly significant in understanding how complainants perceive the public service. They were willing to take the unusual step of complaining to this new grievance man, but the preponderance of their complaints were expressed in rational-bureaucratic language. Over one-third (36 percent), however, characterized either the department or its officer as hostile to them. It is noteworthy that all but 6 percent viewed this hostility as originating from the vague entity of a department rather than from a particular officer. Even hostility usually was expressed with some diffidence; few clients were really vitriolic. Complaints also were increasingly neutral and less hostile over time.

Furthermore, complaints were expressed impersonally; specific departmental officers seldom were mentioned. Only 26 percent referred to an official's title and 9 percent cited one's name. Local departmental officials accounted for the preponderance of both percentages. For example, an officer, such as the District Registrar of Social Security, was mentioned by title in 17 percent of the cases, but by name in only 5 percent. Ministers, department heads, and other officials in the Wellington office then were named in that order. These data indicate that the bureaucracy is viewed as a single, impersonal entity by those New Zealanders who protest its actions. All of the complainants had dealt with some individual official either personally or by correspondence, yet most perceived their quarrel to be with "the department." This fact is probably a good insulating device for the bureaucracy, but the lack of personalization indicated in the letters may help to explain why New Zealand was receptive to the Ombudsman.

Additional inferences as to the psychological state of the complainants at the time of writing can be made from the following data: fewer than 3 percent marked their letters "confidential" or asked that the matter be kept confidential. This seems surprisingly low, for it could be expected that many individuals might have become somewhat obsessed with the necessity to keep their complaint secret. Also, the practice of stamping documents "confidential" is widespread in the New Zealand public service.

Many more complaints, just over one-fifth of the total,

were described as "urgent," or there was a high degree of tension expressed about a time factor. This incidence probably is not unexpected if one takes into account the manifold circumstances, such as court appearances, deadlines for payment of taxes or for applications for benefits, departures of ships, etc. This finding is indicative of the considerable personal psychological investment that many clients had in the subject of their complaint. Of course, both confidentiality and urgency also can be interpreted as complaints strategies which were designed to convince the Ombudsman to treat their problem seriously.

It is interesting to speculate about the age of the clients' grievances. Is complaining to the Ombudsman an action one takes immediately after an unacceptable bureaucratic encounter, or are complaints distilled out of ancient history? The findings, which cast further light on the clients' state of mind, were distributed as follows: less than 1 month between occurrence of alleged grievance and complaint, 10 percent; 1–4 months, 19 percent; 5–7 months, 17 percent; 8–13 months, 10 percent; 14–19 months, 3 percent; 20–32 months, 5 percent; 33–47 months, 5 percent; more than 48 months, 15 percent; general–no apparent time, 8 percent; and unascertainable, 8 percent. This array reveals that complaints are reasonably evenly distributed over the various time periods. Thus, complaining to the Ombudsman probably plays a number of separate functions in the internal dynamics of different clients. It is noteworthy that many did complain soon after the occurrence of the alleged injustice while it still rankled sharply, that in total well over half were no more than about a year old, and that so many brought grievances that were more than four years old. Some of the latter, particularly those involving land disputes, had been nurtured and brooded over for more than a generation. A striking finding of a longitudinal analysis and one difficult to interpret is that there is very little tendency for complaints to become more current over time.

Reflecting the amount of time if not emotion invested in them, letters to the Ombudsman varied considerably in length. Over 16 percent were quite short, less than 100 words, and some of those were cryptic (but the enclosure of some document may have rendered their complaint quite intelligible). Roughly one-fifth of the letters fell into each of four other categories: 101–200 words, 201–300 words, 301–500 words, and over 500 words. Some were very long, well over 500 words; and this final category of long letters is the only one whose proportion of the complaints has substantially changed over time. Three times more long letters were written during the first period than during the last. Thus, when the Ombudsman was first established, more clients were of the psychological disposition—for reasons discussed above and for others discussed below—to fill page after page with their description and evaluation of their situation.

Client Strategies

Several of the items treated above as pertaining to perceptions of the Ombudsman or to bureaucratic attitudes also have strategic relevance. For example, approaching the Ombudsman with a demand for preferment, invoking justice, marking complaints urgent or confidential, and writing a short or long letter all reflect strategic—but not necessarily consciously made—decisions. Many other decisions relating to the structuring of the act of complaining are implicit in each complaint, and this section examines them.

Fully 53 percent of the letters to the Ombudsman were typed. Although no statistics are available, this figure surely is far greater than the incidence of private ownership of typewriters in New Zealand, where they are much rarer than in the United States. It suggests that many individuals believed that the act of complaining to the Ombudsman was important enough for them to go to what must often have been considerable trouble, either to borrow a typewriter or pay or cajole a friendly secretary to type for them. Even 36 percent of the complaints from manual workers were typed.

Most of the typed letters were on ordinary white paper, but 10 percent of the complaints were typed on personal letterhead stationery. This could be viewed as an indication of comparative wealth and an attempt to impress the Ombudsman and other correspondents with the writer's social position. Only 2 percent were typed on the letterheads of various businesses, organizations, etc.; and few of these seemed to be using the stationery in such a way that its use could be considered "illegitimate." Only one letter seemed to misuse the stationery of a government department. It might be supposed that using letterheads as a means of attempting to increase status would be quite a common tactic.

One of the strategic decisions a complainant has to make in trying to convince the Ombudsman of the justice of his case is what evidence he shall use. Over 60 percent of them relied solely upon the force of their own letters. The majority—an increasing one—of those who did buttress their arguments with documentary evidence, 23 percent of the total sample, included previous correspondence with the department complained against. Five percent of the sample included some correspondence with other appeals agents that previously had dealt with the case;[4] a similar number sent documents, such as

[4] Before trying the Ombudsman, clients had invoked the assistance of other appeals agents as follows: local department office, 60 percent; department head office, 37 percent; solicitor, 21 percent; Minister, 17 percent; Member of Parliament, 10 percent; court, 9 percent; pressure group, 7 percent; the Prime Minister, 3 percent; an administrative tribunal, 3 percent; a newspaper, 2 percent.

photographs, maps, deeds, references, forms, etc. Three percent included two or even all three types of enclosures; an additional 2 percent sent with their complaint a position paper or brief of their case. Usually these were not as well prepared as lawyers' briefs, but it was of interest that some chose this method of structuring their complaint.

In the preliminary coding it became apparent that many clients were unwilling to rely upon a recountal of the mere facts of their case to win the day. They also invoked various "authorities" to support their claims. The analysis revealed that almost half, 48 percent, did indeed choose to align themselves with a long list of authorities. That list was widely scattered; no more than 8 percent explicitly claimed support from any one of the following (arrayed in descending order from 8 to 1 percent): a precedent decision; the principles of humanity, honesty, integrity, reason, morality, or fairness; a detailed logical argument—analogies; an "expert"; a documentary source; a friend or relative; a Member of Parliament; "everybody"; a special group; a particular law; law in general; various public figures; a lawyer; an employer. As exhaustive as these may appear, the entire list was even more widely scattered. Less than 1 percent allied themselves with such other figures as God, a clergyman, a physician, or with the Ombudsman himself.

It is the client's mission to convince the Ombudsman to investigate and resolve his complaint. The Ombudsman's assistance never is automatic; always he must be convinced to help. Thus it is expected behavior for the client to construct a compelling persuasive appeal. Since complaints affect the client personally, often he cannot communicate his problem to the Ombudsman without referring to his personal circumstances in specific terms. The sociological circumstances listed in Table 6-1 are arrayed according to the frequency of mention of the cir-

EXCHANGE PROCESSES: CLIENTS

TABLE 6-1
Types of Appeals Invoked by the Ombudsman's Clients

Basis of Appeal	Percent Mentioning Circumstance	Percent Irrelevant Appeals of Total Complaints	Percent Irrelevant Appeals of Total Mentions of Circumstance
Finances	68	3	4
Occupation	47	15	32
Marital Status	40	20	51
Other Family Status	36	20	56
Expertise	35	13	32
Age	26	16	62
Health	26	15	59
War Service	14	7	54
Migrant Status	14	5	34
Unemployment	9	2	21

cumstance, and it is interesting to note how often clients refer to particular aspects of their status.[5]

On the basis of what we have learned about the Ombudsman's function thus far, it is not surprising that by a considerable margin *financial appeals* occur most frequently. But our interest in the appeals employed goes deeper than their frequency. In what context are the appeals made? For example, the statement "I am a poor person" has to be interpreted quite differently depending upon whether the context is that the author is seeking a welfare benefit, or that he is trying to avoid the payment of taxes. In the first case, the client challenges a bureaucratic decision and claims that his financial position should in objective terms qualify him for a benefit. In the second,

[5] Categorizations of clients' appeals were developed in collaboration with Laurie Brown, formerly Professor of Psychology at the Victoria University of Wellington.

his financial appeal is irrelevant to his obligations under the law. In the latter context, his appeal is a violation of the bureaucratic norm of universalism, and it can be considered illegitimate. To be sure, clients' motives were not always so transparent. Sometimes their arguments included mentions of extraneous personal circumstances, but it was not clear that the intent was to assert particularistic over universalistic criteria. As indicated above, many clients included additional information about themselves because they seemed to feel that their letter should serve as a complaint form. Of course, they are likely to choose such information selectively, so noting the incidence of its provision is pertinent to this inquiry. Nevertheless, I prefer to characterize such appeals as irrelevant rather than illegitimate.

Although financial circumstances were most often discussed, it is interesting that irrelevant financial appeals were very seldom made. This is apparently related to the earlier finding that money was so often the complaint's actual subject matter. Nonetheless, reflecting the clients' income levels, 58 percent of the relevant financial appeals did not claim any poverty; they merely felt they were due whatever amount of money was at contest. Precisely why the number of irrelevant financial appeals should be so miniscule both as a percentage of total complaints and as a proportion of total mentions of the appeal is unclear. Indeed, this is the table's most surprising revelation. Perhaps it is an index of the clients' sophistication that those who were inclined to use irrelevant appeals perceived—probably accurately—that crass financial appeals were less likely to promote sympathy than were other available claims, such as sickness, age, status as a parent, etc.

The clients' *occupational status* also was mentioned frequently, because it often was related in some fashion to the complaint; and most references to that circumstance were relevant. When the appeals are ranked according to percent irrelevant of total mentions, only two other appeals are lower than occupation. In total, more clients were likely to mention their *marital* or *other family status* when this was an irrelevant consideration than any other appeals. That is, they would comment: "I wouldn't be so interested in this matter if I didn't have my wife to think of," or "as a father I think I should battle this out for my children's sakes." *Expertise* or some other social status also was invoked frequently. Clients would say, "as a lawyer [or businessman or accountant], I know about such matters, and it is my recommendation . . . ." But only about one-third of the citations of special expertise were irrelevant to the complaint.

Seldom were appeals on the basis of *age* made by young people (but apprentice teachers have argued that they were too young to know what they were doing when they bonded themselves to teach for a certain number of years in exchange for free education). Usually it was elderly people who mentioned their ages, and over sixtenths of the time, more than for any other appeal, the mentioning of age was an irrelevant consideration. A typical client might implore: "Why can't the bureaucracy leave two elderly people alone to enjoy what they can of their declining years?" The usage of the clients' state of *health* as an appeal was very similar to age; and, as with age, nearly all of the irrelevant usages clearly were illegitimate appeals. The client who moans, "Since I've been crippled by arthritis for the past decade, everything has been going wrong; now the government wants . . . ," clearly is appealing to criteria other than universal norms.

Fewer clients mentioned their *war experiences*, which often are relevant to those seeking disability pensions and other veterans' benefits; but the majority of those who referred to them did so in an irrelevant context, saying such things as "I came back from North Africa full of shrapnel, and now we see how the bloody bureaucrats treat those who risked their lives." Similar numbers referred to their *migrant status,* but it was much less often done when it was irrelevant to the complaint. Fewest of all invoked their status as an *unemployed* person, and such appeals were raised in an irrelevant context less often than any other except financial appeals. This finding surely is accounted for by the fact that New Zealand has enjoyed what economists call a situation of overfull employment during the Ombudsman's existence.

Precisely how to interpret these findings about the usage of situational appeals—especially irrelevant appeals—is not clear. There are no comparative data from complaints to other ombudsmen or other public officials.[6] On the face of it, however, it seems surprising that no more than 20 percent of the clients invoked any one of the situational appeals in an irrelevant context.

In the course of their letters many clients, 43 percent of the total, revealed that they had undergone some recent social change. Of those who had, 42 percent of their personal upheavals were connected with one of those situations discussed above (e.g., a financial catastrophe, a disabling illness, a divorce, a runaway child, retirement, etc.). The remaining personal traumas covered a wide gamut of circumstances. It is highly significant to observe that the preponderance, 87 percent, of the social changes that were detailed to the Ombudsman were relevant to the complaint. Thus, these clients were asking for the Ombudsman's help with legitimate matters that vitally concerned them.

[6] The research closest to mine is that inspired by Elihu Katz and now carried on by his former students. Elihu Katz and Brenda Danet, "Petitions and Persuasive Appeals: A Study of Official-Client Relations," *American Sociological Review* 31 (December 1966), 811–22; Brenda Danet, "The Language of Persuasion in Bureaucracy: 'Modern' and 'Traditional' Appeals to the Israel Customs Authorities," *American Sociological Review* 36 (October 1971), 849–59; and Brenda Danet and Harriet Hartman, "Coping With Bureaucracy: The Israeli Case," *Social Forces* 51 (September 1972), 7–22.

EXCHANGE PROCESSES: CLIENTS

Nature of Relationship

At the beginning of this chapter we learned that the total amount of communication between the Ombudsman and his clients was not very great, and subsequently we have examined several aspects of the approaches clients have employed in their initial complaints. Now let us explore the character of the subsequent Ombudsman-client relationship.

A variety of options are open to the Ombudsman when he receives a letter of complaint. *The action taken more often than any other single action—in 45 percent of the sample cases—was to reject immediately the complaint for lack of jurisdiction or for various other reasons.* (The Ombudsman's decisions and their impact are considered in Chapter 8.) This action was taken somewhat more often as his experience increased. Thus, the remaining 55 percent of the clients have had the good fortune, or the wisdom, to complain about matters that were not on their face outside of the Ombudsman's purview. One-tenth of those rejections were only tentative. In such cases the reply said that the facts provided were somewhat scanty or vague, but that for the following reasons a preliminary analysis indicated that there was no real basis for an investigation; the complainant was told that if he had further information or if the circumstances were different than they appeared, then he should respond and the Ombudsman would reconsider. Clients replied in 28 percent of those tentatively rejected cases, and further investigation occurred. We conclude that, for over half of the total cases, the Ombudsman's first action was the final one: either rejecting the case or sending a letter that was never answered.

Upon receiving a complaint, the Ombudsman took four other types of immediate action: the second most frequent action, which was taken in 29 percent of the total, was to begin immediately the investigation without further consultation with the complainant. Normally he would be notified of this action. Thus, nearly a third of the clients not only complained about matters that were within the Ombudsman's jurisdiction, but they also were skillful in presenting their complaint so that the Ombudsman was adequately informed and could begin an investigation. Furthermore, they succeeded in piquing his interest. It is not surprising that more immediate investigations occurred in the first time period, while the Ombudsman was gaining experience, than in any other. Third, in a further 11 percent of the cases the Ombudsman felt that the information supplied by the client was insufficient to make a determination as to whether or not to begin investigation. For various reasons, probably including the lack of a firm foundation for the complaint, the inability to provide the detailed information requested, and the fear of becoming further implicated in an investigation, 39 percent of those complainants never responded.

Fourth, the Ombudsman's immediate action to an additional 9 percent was to send Form Letter B or its variation, which either simply reminded the client that under the terms of his Act a two-dollar fee was required or also asked if there were any particular urgency involved. Sometimes, in the case of matters that appeared not really to be complaints or that seemed on their face to be invalid, this seemed to be used as a maneuver to discourage the complainant. Whether or not this was the intent, and whether or not it was the cause, 29 percent of them never replied and the case was dropped. Fifth, a further 6 percent were sent Form Letter A, which informed them of the Ombudsman's heavy workload and inquired whether there were any special circumstances of urgency (but did not mention the fee). This usually was not intended to discourage complaints, but in 19 percent of those cases there was no further investigation.

A question very important to the clients is, how responsive is the Ombudsman? We have seen that many have a substantial psychological investment in their complaint, so they will anxiously await a reply from this official with the foreign name whom they have never dealt with before and whose function they may understand only dimly. Clearly, an Ombudsman who is attentive to his clients has a higher social value than one who is not.

This Ombudsman's own internal administrative procedures are quite efficient. On almost one-fourth of the complaints (23 percent) definitive action was taken on the first day (on some of those cases the typing and mailing of the letter would not be completed until the next day). Since four-fifths of New Zealand's mail is delivered within one day of posting,[7] this would mean that many would receive a reply from the Ombudsman within three days after they mailed their letter (the percentages for which this was true climbed from 12 in the first time period to 42 in the last). An additional 40 percent were handled in one to three days; so that in total, *probably over half of the clients would have heard from the Ombudsman within one week.* Twenty percent more were taken care of in four to six days. Considering the extreme complexity of many of the issues raised, the fact that the Ombudsman's decision on a course of action was made within a week for over four-fifths of the cases seems to be quite an accomplishment. A further 8 percent required seven to twelve days for processing, and thirteen or more days were required for 9 percent.

Until 1975, one of the most confining structural restrictions upon access to the Ombudsman was his fee, which the original Act established at two dollars and gave him discretion in collecting. How did he exercise this discretion, and what part did the fee play in the Ombudsman-

[7] Cited in "Submission by the Post Office, National Development Conference," mimeographed (Wellington: Post Office Department, 1968), p. 6.

client relationship? The analysis revealed that the total incidence of the fee being paid in the original letter of complaint was 22 percent, but this decreased from 56 percent during the first time period to 14 percent at the last.

In a further 26 percent of the cases the Ombudsman sent the client a letter (often simply appended to a substantive letter) reminding him of the fee's existence and asking that it be remitted. This was successful in fully 87 percent of those cases, and in only 3 percent was the complainant never heard from again. After collecting the fee, the Ombudsman refunded it in 7 percent of the cases; this was done on the grounds of the client's insolvency in only about one-fifth of such cases. Usually it happened because the case was discontinued before proceeding very far.

The largest single group of complainants, 45 percent, did not pay the fee either in the first instance or subsequently. In 5 percent of these cases the Ombudsman waived the fee because of the client's financial circumstances. But in almost all of the others it was apparent immediately that the complaint was not investigable. Sending them a letter asking for a fee in those circumstances was costly and had little hope of success. The incidence of unpaid fees rose over time from 20 to 50 percent or over for the last five periods. Perhaps those who complained at the very beginning had been more carefully attuned to detailed descriptions of the office, and later the remembrance of the existence of his fee dimmed. On the other hand, it may be that more people somehow realized that it might be possible to get a preliminary judgment of the soundness of one's complaint without risking two dollars. This history of experience with the fee indicates that although its formal existence surely deterred some people from complaining, once a complaint was lodged the fee was not actually a very formidable obstacle.

It would be most interesting to know how clients

evaluate the Ombudsman's service, but unfortunately we have no direct data. (The only substantial research limitation the Ombudsman placed upon my activities was that I not contact clients.) Nevertheless, the following findings provide some indirect information about clients' affect for the Ombudsman: seldom was there any reaction from them after the Ombudsman made his decision about their case. In nearly three-fourths of the cases, the Ombudsman heard nothing from the clients after rendering his decision. This was true even in cases in which he helped them—perhaps by providing a continuing income supplement—and in others in which there had been long and detailed correspondence. In only 12 percent of the complaints did the Ombudsman receive a "thank-you" message at the conclusion of the case. Instead of expressing gratitude, 6 percent seized the occasion of the Ombudsman's judgment to denounce the "bureaucrats," and 2 percent also served notice that they were going to take their case to another appeals agent. A total of 7 percent replied that they were dissatisfied, and 4 percent asked that their case be reopened. The fact that complainants have so seldom responded to the Ombudsman's decisions probably indicates that he is regarded as simply another faceless bureaucratic channel to whom no personal debt is due, or it may relate to some undetermined cultural characteristics.

Conclusions

This chapter has begun to analyze the Ombudsman as a client-serving institution. The task will be completed in Chapter 8. What do the findings thus far tell us about his performance in this role? In drawing conclusions, it is important to recall that the Ombudsman-client relationship is not very extensive. The mean number of client-to-Ombudsman communications per case has been 2.3, and the mean Ombudsman-to-client communications has been 2.5. Nearly all interactions occur through correspondence rather than individual contact. In theoretical terms, I have thought of the Ombudsman and his clients as members of a system; our findings indicate that the relationships in the system are not very tightly integrated.

In addition to their paucity of contacts with the Ombudsman, complainants never meet each other (it would be very rare for more than one client to be in the Ombudsman's office at the same time), and their contacts with the Ombudsman are segmental—that is, being a client is one of many relationships they have with other people and organizations and does not involve them as a "whole" person. Nevertheless, clients may become intensely involved with the Ombudsman, and the subject matter of their complaint may have a wide scope of interest for them, i.e., their complaint may be that their livelihood—a welfare benefit—has been cut off. Talcott Parsons conceives of the agency and its clients as fellow members of a collectivity; schools and hospitals are prototypical organizations in which "collectivity membership" exists.[8] Whether or not the relationship between the Ombudsman and his clients has enough solidarity to qualify as one involving collectivity membership is problematical; at best it would be a marginal case.

It is significant that clients tended to hold relatively accurate perceptions of the Ombudsman's proper role as an impartial, neutral, bureaucratic mechanism. Since they generally understood what the institution was about, the matters they brought to the Ombudsman usually were reasonably on target.

That clients were in various states of mind at the time of complaining was obvious from their letters. Although

[8] Talcott Parsons, "How Are Clients Integrated into Service Organizations?" in William R. Rosengren and Mark Lefton, eds., *Organizations and Clients: Essays in the Sociology of Service* (Columbus: Charles E. Merrill, 1970), pp. 1–16.

many labored under a sense of injustice, most tended to express their grievance impersonally, in rational-bureaucratic language. "Confidentiality," which could indicate paranoia, very seldom was invoked, but "urgency," indicating the clients' psychological investment in the complaint, was not uncommon. The extreme variability of the complaints' ages and of the length of clients' letters seems to indicate that complaining performed very different roles for different people.

Clients employed various kinds of strategies, such as typing their letters, enclosing documents, and invoking various authorities, to convince the Ombudsman seriously to investigate their cases. But no one of the situational appeals, based upon finances, age, health, etc., was raised in an irrelevant context by more than one-fifth of the clients. As a further indicator of the personal significance of the grievances, over two-fifths of the clients revealed that a recent important social change, which almost always was relevant to their complaint, had occurred in their lives.

Because the Ombudsman's jurisdiction is limited as to both the organizations and the types of matters included, he must decline to investigate nearly half of the complaints received. The rapidity with which clients get replies indicates that he is highly responsive. Before the fee was abolished, it was increasingly unlikely to be collected; normally it was not used as a barrier to fend off clients. The Ombudsman carefully constructs his letters so as to indicate his interest in clients' problems and tries to create feelings of warmth and humanity; normally all letters to clients are signed by him personally. But clients seldom are responsive. Some are, of course, but—even though it is always open to the client to continue the correspondence—few clients send him a thank-you note.

The fact that the Ombudsman's relations with clients are not extensive and intimate is a reflection of the institution's structure, but this does not mean that it is unimportant as a client-serving agency. The Ombudsman's substantive assistance to clients is explored in Chapter 8, but he also is important in a psychological sense. The act of complaining and the knowledge that a sympathetic person has responded may have important therapeutic value for ordinary citizens. George H. Wolkon and Sharon Moriwaki have made this point cogently:

> In the language of mental health and social science, the ombudsman functions to reduce alienation, anomie and frustration by involving the individual in the reduction of his own external stresses. The ombudsman, as a programme for the primary prevention of psychological disorders, offers appropriate resources (be it information, communication channels, or psychological support) to the individual for resolving the immediate stress situation, thereby preventing maladaptive coping patterns and ultimately, psychiatric hospitalization.[9]

In considering the usefulness of an ombudsman, the value of this prophylactic function cannot be measured with precision, but it should not be ignored. Furthermore, the ombudsman's mental health role is even larger; it goes beyond his actual clients. The knowledge that the ombudsman is "there" if a problem should arise is diffused throughout society, and this knowledge provides a certain psychological reassurance.

[9] George H. Wolkon and Sharon Moriwaki, "The Ombudsman Programme: Primary Prevention of Psychological Disorders," *International Journal of Social Psychiatry* 19 (Autumn/Winter 1973), 221.

CHAPTER SEVEN

Exchange Processes: The Bureaucracy and the Ombudsman

THIS chapter's focus is different from its three predecessors. In examining complaints, clients, and ombudsman-clientele relations, those chapters analyzed the ombudsman's role as a client-serving agency. Such a focus has become popular as increasing numbers of sociologists, social workers, and mental health professionals have come to perceive the ombudsman's virtues as a "helping" institution. Helping individual citizens always has been a component of the ombudsman's role, but one searches the early literature for studies from this perspective in vain. It is principally as an institution of public administration that the ombudsman first gained the attention of students of governmental affairs, and this chapter focuses upon the Ombudsman as governmental institution. What sorts of relationships does an ombudsman develop with bureaucrats? Does he improve administration, bog it down, or is he inconsequential?

Despite the long history of interest in these matters little research beyond the descriptive level has been done, and most of the attention paid to them has been speculative. The administrative implications of ombudsmen remain obscure. His supporters allege that an ombudsman can correct individual mistakes, utilize his broad perspective to stimulate general reforms, act as a "cop on the beat" to prevent bureaucratic malfeasance, and remove some public pressure from administrators by demonstrating that most complaints are unfounded. According to his critics, on the other hand, an ombudsman's importance is overblown by romantic reformers; and he may have some of the following deleterious administrative consequences: he may cause civil servants to be too timid to make decisions; administrators may be encouraged to "cover" themselves by creating extensive "red tape"; as an amateur, he often is unqualified to judge the actions of departmental professionals; he becomes a departmental adversary and cannot get needed cooperation; he wastes the time of busy administrators with unimportant claims; and he may coerce departments into making individual exceptions to policy against the public interest.

Unfortunately, the scholar or public official who wishes to evaluate the institution as a bureaucratic control mechanism, presently has little guidance in choosing between the often unqualified praise of the ombudsman's proponents and the usually uninformed invective of his critics.[1] Sketching a portrait of the patterned relationships between the New Zealand Ombudsman and the bureaucracy, this chapter begins to address these competing allegations, which are explored more fully in the two succeeding chapters.

Each government department performs different functions, operates under different statutes, and has different relationships with its Minister and with other control agencies—such as administrative tribunals. Nevertheless, the departments usually are only shadowy opponents of the Ombudsman in most accounts. This chapter begins with some brief case studies which attempt to place the Ombudsman's complaints and his subsequent investigations in the context of the departments' broader activities and responsibilities. In comparison with the agency's vulnerability to complaint and to Ombudsman investigations, this exploration inquires: How significant is it that during twelve and one-half years the Om-

[1] Most of these alleged virtues and defects may be found in William B. Gwyn, "Transferring the Ombudsman," in Stanley V. Anderson, ed., *Ombudsmen for American Government?* (Englewood Cliffs, N.J.: Prentice-Hall, 1968), pp. 43–45.

budsman has investigated X number of complaints against it?

Following this important preliminary, the Ombudsman-bureaucratic relationship is explored through pursuing four questions: How extensive is the Ombudsman's interaction with the bureaucracy? How consequential for the government department is the threat posed by complaints? What demands does the Ombudsman make upon the agency? How cooperative is the department in responding? Their answers also will illuminate the public policy question of what kind of governmental device an Ombudsman actually is.

Investigations and Targets

Because a common objection to the Ombudsman institution is that it would create a large additional workload for already overburdened agencies, a preliminary step in interpreting the relationship between the Ombudsman and the agencies was to measure the frequency and mode of their interaction. After receiving a complaint, the initiative lies with the Ombudsman. He can have no impact upon the bureaucracy unless he decides to investigate; thereupon he must make important strategic decisions about how to conduct the investigation and about whom to involve.

Incidence of investigations. According to Table 7-1, the Ombudsman has investigated nearly three-fifths of the complaints that were within his jurisdiction. One might speculate that as he gained experience he would investigate fewer and fewer complaints, but according to the data in his reports, this has not occurred. Although there have been some fluctuations in the annual proportions of cases investigated, the deviations are minor and there is no secular trend.

When investigation is defined slightly differently as I do in the sample of cases, however, the incidence of investigation *has* fallen somewhat from 72 percent in the first time period to 56, 50, 58, 32, 38, 44, 46, and for the last period 46. This definition is a behavioral one: if the Ombudsman queried the department about the case, then it was investigated. He sometimes tentatively began an investigation and then discontinued it for various reasons, but nevertheless labeled the case "not investigated." It is because my definition of investigation and the Ombudsman's are not exactly the same that comparisons of the actual complaints with the sample are not made in Table 7-1. The definitions, however, are quite similar, and 63 percent (N = 221) of the sample cases were investigated compared with 60 percent for the actual cases as of 1969—the reporting period closest to that encompassed by the sample. Since interaction with departments took place only on those cases that were investigated, 221 becomes the N for subsequent discussion of the findings from the sample.

Targets of complaint. Table 7-1 indicates that nearly four-fifths of the Ombudsman's complaints processed were against fourteen major agencies of government. Only five departments (Treasury, External Affairs, Defense, Internal Affairs, and Agriculture and Fisheries) that traditionally are considered major are missing from that list. However important the functions performed by them are, they do not regularly come into contact with large numbers of individual citizens. The major targets of complaint are the primary institutions of New Zealand's highly developed welfare state, the institutions that most often interact with citizens.

The table's fourteen "major investigative targets" are the same as the "major complaint organizations" of Table 4-1, except that Transport, Lands and Survey, State Insurance Office, and Defense have been dropped because

EXCHANGE PROCESSES: THE BUREAUCRACY

TABLE 7-1
Departmental Targets of Complaint and Investigation
1 October 1962 to 31 March 1975

Department	Complaints Processed n	%[b]	Complaints Investigated n	%[c]	Target's Percent of Processed Complaints Investigated
Total Major Investigative Targets	6,582	78	3,827	80	58
Social Welfare	1,363	16	954	20	70
Justice	776	9	385	8	50
Education	689	8	389	8	56
Inland Revenue	524	6	193	4	37
State Services Commission	421	5	292	6	69
Police	397	5	199	4	50
Post Office	383	5	230	5	60
Labor	356	4	188	4	53
Health	341	4	201	4	59
Housing Corporation	331	4	203	4	61
Customs	312	4	194	4	62
Works and Development	293	3	148	3	51
Railways	201	2	123	3	61
Government Superannuation Fund Board	195	2	128	3	66
Total Other Targets	1,876	22	946	20	50
Grand Total	8,458[a]	100	4,773	100	56

Compiled from *Report of the Ombudsman* (Wellington: Government Printer, 1975), Appendix B.

[a] One hundred eighty-nine complaints still under investigation at the end of the year and 2,129 complaints against agencies outside of the Ombudsman's jurisdiction are excluded from this total.

[b] Means target's percent of total complaints processed.

[c] Means target's percent of total complaints investigated.

less than one hundred of their complaints have been investigated. Five of the major investigative targets (Social Welfare, Education, Health, Housing Corporation, and Superannuation) are client-serving agencies; eight (Justice, Inland Revenue, State Services Commission, Police, Post Office, Labor, Customs, and Railways) are client-attending agencies; and one (Works and Development) is non-client-oriented.

Social Welfare's incidence of complaints investigated is artificially high because it had no separate appeal agency until 1972, whereas Inland Revenue's is low because of the Tax Court's displacement of the Ombudsman's jurisdiction. Otherwise there are no particular surprises in the departmental percentages of complaints which the Ombudsman has deemed worthy of investigation. Certainly, the fact that—excepting Social Welfare's special circumstances—during the Ombudsman's entire existence the office has investigated fewer than four hundred cases against any one department indicates in a gross quantitative sense that the burden of the complaints has not been overpowering.

These observations are, however, only provisional until we put the number of investigated Ombudsman complaints into the departments' broader contexts. In seeking to determine what kinds of targets they presented for Ombudsman investigation, I went to each of the major investigative targets—and to several additional ones as well—and sought their cooperation. Informal interviews were held with officials, particularly with those who processed the Ombudsman's complaints. Reports, memoranda, etc., were collected, and relevant files were perused. In all cases the department head was given the structured interview schedule whose results are reported in Chapter 9. Because of space considerations, sketches of only three client-serving agencies, of three client-attending departments, and of the lone non-client-oriented agency are presented. These sketches are only illustrative of the enormous gamut of contact between New Zealand government and its citizens.[2]

Client-Serving Major Investigative Targets

As we would have predicted, the Ombudsman investigates a large proportion of the client-serving agencies' complaints, 64 percent. This is somewhat greater than the proportion for the other two types. We shall examine his relationships with Social Welfare, the chief investigative target; with Education, the second-ranking target; and with Health, which ranks seventh.

Social Welfare. As would be expected in a welfare state, Social Welfare is one of the largest and most important government agencies. Among its major responsibilities are the administration of the following: Superannuation Benefits, Age Benefits, Widows' Benefits, Special Benefits, Orphans' Benefits, Unemployment Benefits, Sickness Benefits, Emergency Benefits, Special Annuities, Supplementary Assistance, Capitalization of Family Benefits for Housing Purposes, Advances for Repairs to and Maintenance of Homes, Special Christmas Payments, Legal Aid, and Training and Rehabilitation of Disabled Civilians. Nearly one-half of the New Zealand population receives some kind of a benefit from the department, and over a half-billion dollars (N.Z.) are paid out to beneficiaries each year.

The efficient administration of such a complex and extensive system demands that many thousands of discretionary decisions be made each year on such matters as who shall or shall not be given a benefit. Most of this

[2] No comprehensive, descriptive treatment of New Zealand government departments exists, and the following accounts are pieced together from scattered sources. The principal sources are internal departmental documents, the agencies' annual reports to Parliament, and the *New Zealand Official Yearbook*.

work is delegated to one of the forty-nine district and suboffices where the preponderance of the department's employees are stationed.

An administratively interesting artifact, the Social Security Commission, is at the apex of the social security system; the Commission's peculiar structure has brought the department into a special relationship with the Ombudsman. The three ranking officials of the department constitute the Commission; in this position they are asked to transcend their function as departmental officials and to assume a most interesting quasi-judicial, quasi-administrative role.

In addition to supervising some decisions that must be made in Head Office, the Commission acts as an internal check in that it reviews cases on its own initiative. Within three months of the receipt of an unfavorable ruling from a district, an appellant may demand that the Commission review his case; also, single members of the Commission may make a limited range of decisions, which can later be reviewed by the whole Commission. To continue the Commission's and the department's anomalous situation, the Commission is responsible to the Minister of Social Welfare in the same way that other agencies relate to a Minister. Until 1972, unlike the situation in most other similar departments, no administrative tribunal existed that had the authority to review the Commission's decisions; thus, the Minister and the Ombudsman were the only realistic appeals channels, and this explains, in large measure, the high number of complaints lodged against Social Welfare.[3]

---

[3] In 1972, a Social Welfare Appeal Authority was created, and the Ombudsman was barred from reviewing its decisions. The absolute bar was replaced in the revised Ombudsman statute by a discretion that may be exercised by the Ombudsman in special circumstances. Additionally, a War Pensions Tribunal, whose name reflects its function and whose decisions are not appealable to the Ombudsman, has existed from the Ombudsman's inception. For a more extended, general ac-

EXCHANGE PROCESSES: THE BUREAUCRACY

Social Welfare was created in 1972 by amalgamating the Social Security Department with the Child Welfare Division of the Department of Education. Under the new arrangement social work responsibilities for certain classes of adults—the mentally and physically disabled, solo parents, and the aged—have been assumed, but attention remains focused upon children's problems. The extensive and highly sensitive duties undertaken by the department's social workers include such matters as investigating and reporting for the Children's Court, placement in foster homes and institutions, adoption and illegitimate birth inquiry work, and the inspection and registration of child care centers. These activities involve social workers in many thousands of child-parent contacts; some 16,000 children are placed under the division's control and supervision each year. Because Social Welfare is such a vulnerable target, it is not unexpected that it leads all others in investigated complaints to the Ombudsman with a total of 954.

Education. Power over most of the public education system centers in the Education Department. Curricula, examinations, inspections, teacher training, staffing, and allocation of money, all are its responsibility. Locally elected education boards and school committees have limited administrative and budgetary functions, but they are dependent upon the department for grants since they have no independent tax base. The department's annual appropriations total about 400 million dollars (N.Z.), and it is useful to explore some of the functions performed in spending that large amount—functions that could give

---

count of the relationship between the department and the Ombudsman, see Larry B. Hill, *Monitoring Social Administration: Social Welfare and the Ombudsman in New Zealand,* Sage Professional Papers in Administrative and Policy Studies (Beverly Hills and London: Sage Publications, forthcoming).

rise to a considerable number of complaints to the Ombudsman. There are over 2,500 primary and secondary schools in New Zealand—all under the general guidance of the department, but not as far as day-to-day operations are concerned.[4] In all of them, the syllabus is set by the department, which even produces and publishes many texts.

Education also manages nine teacher training colleges, which enroll over 8,000 students. The students usually are supported through various bonding arrangements in which they agree to teach for a certain number of years after finishing. Later, these teachers (there are about 30,000 of them) become employees and the souce of complaints against such matters as the payment of a "married allowance," retirement allowance, living accommodations, salary, promotion, and departmental attempts at discipline.

Furthermore, Education performs very extensive functions as an examiner. Each year thousands of students take one of the following exams: Teacher's Certificate, School Certificate, Technological, Samoan Public Service, Engineers' and Surveyors' Assistants, Certificate in Engineering, Technical Teacher's Certificate, Diploma in Teaching, or Trades Certification. Just the fact that more than 10,000 students per year fail School Certificate, the major secondary school examination, certainly opens up a fertile field of complaint on matters such as content of the exam and grading. Taken as a whole, the multiple activities of the Education Department offer an inviting target for complaint to the Ombudsman and then for his investigations.[5] It is surprising that the Ombudsman has investigated only 389 cases against Education.

[4] Decisions of local education boards were included in the Ombudsman's jurisdiction from December 1968. Special schools, such as the Maori Schools, the Correspondence Schools, schools for the blind and deaf, and speech clinics, also are operated by Education.
[5] Complaints against Child Welfare, which formerly was—as indi-

EXCHANGE PROCESSES: THE BUREAUCRACY

Health. The Department of Health is charged with administering a comprehensive health program. It has broad responsibilities in the environmental health field. Health approves and tests water supply systems (and the fluoridation of water) and sewage disposal systems, tests for water and air pollution, gives licenses for all poisons, and supervises swimming pools. Also, a team of inspectors tests food hygiene, and citizens annually lodge over 1,000 complaints with the department about bad food. Additionally, Health is responsible for disease control and operates such programs as tuberculosis x-ray units and venereal disease clinics. And it administers various maternal and child health programs—such as pre- and postnatal advice and treatment, the medical examination and immunization of school children, and the School Dental Service. An Occupational Health Unit provides a broad preventive and treatment service in industry, and the department operates various laboratories, such as the national Radiation Laboratory.

The Bureau of Medical Services and Drug Control has responsibility over the remainder of the health program. Local hospital boards, which were added to the Ombudsman's jurisdiction in 1968, operate the hospitals on a day-to-day basis; but the department has general control over policy and allocates funds for building and operations. Furthermore, Health is responsible for paying for two major boons of the welfare state: Medical and Pharmaceutical Benefits. They are collected by physicians and pharmacists, and the department does not normally

---

cated above—a division of Education, also were lodged against this department until 1972.

The university councils, governing bodies of secondary schools, and teacher training college councils are largely autonomous of the Education Department, however; and they have been outside of the Ombudsman's jurisdiction. Under the revised Ombudsman Act, the two last named agencies will be brought within the jurisdiction in 1976.

come into direct contact with citizens in the administration of the benefits; both services are heavily used.[6]

Finally, Health is a large employer, having a staff—including doctors, dentists, nurses, social workers, technicians, etc.—of over 8,000. Thus, such matters as the registration of nurses, eligibility for postdoctoral grants, and general employee conflicts could be the stimulus of many complaints to the Ombudsman. Considering the wide scope of Health's responsibilities and functions, the total number of complaints that the Ombudsman has deemed worthy of investigation (201) seems small.

Client-Attending Major Investigative Targets

Nearly as many of the client-attending complaints (58 percent) as of the client-serving complaints (64 percent) have been investigated. Brief sketches of three of the eight client-attending agencies that are major investigative targets are presented here: Justice, Labor, and Police.

Justice. The Justice Department is the third-ranking major investigative target with 385 investigated complaints. Indications of its vulnerability are that it has six major divisions: Penal, Courts, Registrar-General, Lands and Deeds, Commercial Affairs, and Patents.

The Penal Division has as its involuntary guests a large number of prisoners, who seldom are satisfied with their

[6] Until 1971, New Zealand's mental hospitals were operated or supervised by the Bureau's Mental Health Division, so complaints from patients up to then (when mental hospitals were transferred to local hospital boards) are charged against the Health Department. Most patients are voluntarily (or "informally") admitted, but others are formally committed under the terms of statutes which prescribe strict conditions—including a certification by two physicians and a hearing by a magistrate—for committal. Inmates may appeal against their confinement to a Judge of the Supreme Court in addition to complaining to the Ombudsman.

lot. Although the total population of New Zealand's twenty-four prisons remains relatively stable at the remarkably low (in international terms) figure of about 2,500 inmates, the flow through the prisons is much greater—as many as 10,000 receptions may occur during the year. Since many of these people were found "not guilty," it could be expected that they would be highly likely to complain. Also, Justice's officers supervise about 5,000 offenders on probation and about 4,000 paroles. Furthermore, three special programs are operated: the Periodic Detention Program, the Release-to-Work Parole, and Home Leave for First Offenders. Because of their attractiveness, it might be expected that a number of complaints from prisoners and their families would arise on such matters as eligibility. From the other side of the wall, one would predict complaints from the public about prison escapes (which usually exceed 150 per year) and about other matters—such as the department's administration of the Criminal Injuries Compensation Act.

The judicial system's administrative duties are performed by the Courts Division. These duties are extensive: around 200,000 trials, hearings, and other types of proceedings are filed before the Supreme Court and the Magistrates' Courts annually. Manifold possibilities exist for errors and disputes concerning records, transcripts, jury duty, witness expenses, fees, assessments of court costs, etc.[7] This division also is in charge of bankruptcy actions and company liquidations. Too, the Marriage Guidance Program is administered by the division, and its counselors conduct more than 15,000 interviews per year.

The Registrar-General's Division is responsible for two matters. The first is administering election processes. The department sets up the actual mechanics of voting for

[7] Precisely where the Courts Division's administrative responsibilities leave off and where those of the courts themselves (which are outside of the Ombudsman's jurisdiction) begin, may often be unclear.

parliamentary elections, by-elections, and for referenda. (New Zealand has very extensive "special voting," or absentee balloting procedures.) Second, the division registers births, deaths, marriages, adoptions, legitimations, and name changes. More than 100,000 such over-the-counter contacts with the public—including the collection of the requisite fees—take place each year.

The duties of the Land and Deeds Division likewise are straightforward but extensive. Nearly a half-million instruments relating to various types of land registration are completed annually; the division also is responsible for maintaining and allowing searches of the records of all land transactions since 1870. In a candid discussion of the division's problems, the Secretary for Justice commented in the 1973 *Report:* "One defect that I am anxious to see remedied speedily is the disparity of practice between different offices. . . . A document that is accepted for registration . . . in one office may be summarily rejected in another. This situation has long since ceased to make any sort of sense."

The Commercial Affairs Division was created in 1972 in order to consolidate Justice's administration of several statutes regulating business affairs. In addition to its general responsibilities to insure fair dealing among investors, borrowers, buyers, and lenders, the division registers companies and collects annual license fees. Over 200,000 documents have been registered annually in recent years.

Patents is the final division. Around 7,000 applications for patents, designs, and trademarks are received each year, and most of those processed are granted. A six-month delay in approval, because of a shortage of staff, is common, however. Obviously, in most of the six divisions, Justice's vulnerability to complaint is acute.

Labor. In addition to matters related to industry and employment, the Labor Department performs other

EXCHANGE PROCESSES: THE BUREAUCRACY

major functions. With 188 investigated complaints lodged against it, the department ranks eleventh as a major investigative target. Labor has responsibility over a wide range of industrial matters. Under the authority of eleven separate laws (such as the Machinery Act, the Factories Act, the Workers' Compensation Act, the Minimum Wage Act, the Industrial Conciliation and Arbitration Act, and the Weights and Measures Act), the department's corps of inspectors conducts annually more than 150,000 separate inspections. Almost all of the breaches discovered are uncovered by the inspectors; few originate from complaints by workers or the public. Most of the breaches are settled by negotiation, but as many as 700 prosecutions may be taken yearly. The department has a full range of contacts with employees and employers. It maintains an employment service, and about 25,000 applicants are placed in jobs annually. Obviously, many opportunities for complaint arise over such matters as the matching of a worker with a job for which he is qualified—or thinks he is qualified.[8] Other complaint occasions arise over the dispensation of the Unemployment Benefit, which is granted in conjunction with the Social Welfare Department. Labor also has a general responsibility for nearly 28,000 apprentices, who may be given a lodging allowance if their training forces them to live away from home. Nine hostels having a total capacity of about 1,400 are also operated for apprentices, workers, and immigrants.

Finally, Labor serves as the department of immigration. For public relations purposes, New Zealand's gen-

---

[8] Administering the Tenancy Act 1955 is a further responsibility. Under it the department assesses fair rents and settles disputes about rents, but such matters as effecting repairs also are included; the largest single category of matters dealt with is applications for increase in fair rent, most of which are granted. It should be mentioned that the exercise of this responsibility, along with many aspects of the other Labor activities discussed thus far, is appealable to a court or administrative tribunal and hence outside of the Ombudsman's jurisdiction.

eral policy (which has been relaxed somewhat in recent years) of excluding all but those of Western European ethnic origin—with certain exceptions—is not legally formalized. Instead, discretion as to a potential immigrant's suitability is exercised, at least theoretically and often actually, by the Minister. No immigration statistics are presented in Labor's annual *Report* about such matters as entry permits denied, although there are hundreds of these each year. Many exceptions are made for those from neighboring Polynesian islands; particularly, many Samoans are admitted. Problems sometimes arise when a worker applies to bring his often numerous dependents—who might become a burden on the welfare system—into the county. Other disputes concern deportation and the attempt to make a temporary entry permit permanent.

The only immigration matter mentioned in detail in Labor's annual report is the assisted passage scheme through which immigrants who meet various age, familial, and occupational criteria may qualify for free passage to New Zealand. Since 1946 about 100,000 people, mostly from Britain, have participated in this scheme. Problems arise because some immigrants do not like the country or, more often, the area where their job is. Many claim that the job or the accommodation provided was not as promised by their sponsor, etc., whereupon the department attempts to enforce the agreement by demanding repayment of the amount of passage. Clearly, the Labor Department is wide open for complaints, and the number investigated by the Ombudsman seems quite low.[9]

Police. In a free society the activities of the Police are a tempting focus of complaint, and it might be expected

[9] A further highly sensitive function performed by the department, until the Labor Party's government ended compulsory national military service in 1972, was the procurement of soldiers.

that the department would be a leading major investigative target. In fact, it is eighth. Since New Zealand has one of the world's few truly national Police Departments, every police-citizen exchange is a potential complaint to the Ombudsman.

Due to the nature of Police activities, interactions with citizens are innumerable; the "cop on the beat" is omnipresent. According to departmental statistics, over 200,000 offenses are formally investigated annually. Of these, about two-fifths are prosecuted, and the others are dropped after investigation, or dealt with in some other way. Additionally, over 40,000 juvenile cases are handled yearly. The most frequent types of offenses reported are theft, burglary, violations of traffic laws, willful damage, drunkenness, violations of liquor laws, and different classes of assaults. Officers' discretionary decisions about whether or not to press charges on matters such as these leave the department vulnerable to immense numbers of complaints. This is even true in the case of some minor offenses; for example, well over 1,000 New Zealanders annually are prosecuted for using obscene language; considering the huge public volume of such language, to decide to prosecute a particular case would involve delicate considerations.

The Police may be criticized from both directions, either offensively for failure to prosecute or defensively for the act of prosecution on any given case. Complaints can be made about wrongful arrest, invasion of privacy, harassment, violations of personal rights, discourtesy, and failure to follow various legal formulae. Of course, criticism also can arise over such administrative matters as incorrect records and inadequate communication between the district offices, where most actions are handled, and the head office. In addition to the usual departmental and ministerial channels of appeal, Police complainants often have taken the offending officer to court—most commonly in a suit for wrongful arrest. A perusal of departmental records for 1966 uncovered 20 such prosecutions, and departmental officers believed this to be a fairly steady number. The Ombudsman's mean number of annual investigated cases, 16, is fewer.[10] Taking all factors into consideration, the Police's 199 total investigated complaints from the Ombudsman seems small.

A Non-Client-Oriented Major Investigative Target

The Ombudsman chooses to investigate nearly as large a proportion of the non-client-oriented complaints (56 percent) as he does of those against the other two types of departments. Only one such department, however, the mammoth Ministry of Works and Development ("Development" was added to the Ministry's name in 1974), qualified as a major investigative target and earned the twelfth rank among those agencies. The Ministry's major function is to act as a coordinating and servicing authority for all government building projects whether they are actually constructed by Works and Development, by private companies under contract, or by a local body. As an indicator of its conglomerate character, the following eight divisional reports are appended to the Ministry's annual *Reports:* Architectural, Civil Engineering, Power Engineering, Mechanical and Electrical Engineering, Roading, Housing, Water and Soil, and Town and Country Planning.

These divisions undertake the architectural and various engineering designs for proposed building projects and construct many themselves. Post offices, prisons, hospitals, courts, departmental offices, airports, defense installations, school and university buildings, state houses for private use, harbor improvement, tunnels,

---

[10] It is likely that the Police's number of complaints investigated will be reduced in the future, for the Ombudsmen Act 1975 (Section 7 [d]; see Appendix B) provides that before complaining to the Ombudsman a client must have exhausted internal Police Department appeals.

highways, sewerage treatment plants, water systems, and irrigation and land reclamation projects all fall within the Ministry's compass. Special projects, such as the huge Tongariro and Manapuri power stations, the production of geothermal power, and work on two stations for the production of nuclear power, also are noteworthy. The coordination of these activities with independent local government units and with private contracting firms (with whom about 900 contracts are let each year) and the employment of 15,000–20,000 workers of diverse classes in all sections of the country, certainly open the department to complaints.

Furthermore, the Ministry is responsible for the acquisition of land. Although the Land Valuation Court has jurisdiction over part of this field, the basic decision of whether or not to exercise eminent domain is a contestable ministerial decision delegated to the department. In pursuing these various functions, the department's annual expenditures are over 300 million dollars (N.Z.). Additionally, beginning in 1965 the Ministry was assigned to administer the Economic Stabilization (Building Construction) Regulations which introduced building programming—a system for the control of all construction projects over 60,000 dollars (N.Z.).

Because of its size, organizational complexity, and diverse functions, Works and Development long has been regarded as an administrator's nightmare. But in the mid-1960s, accepting the advice of a management consulting organization, the Ministry took several actions to streamline its operations and embarked on a public relations campaign that attempted to improve its popular image. From this description it should be apparent that Works and Development is far different in character from such a department as Social Welfare. After a general policy is established, the latter department's main task is to administer it as uniformly as possible; complaints generally are limited to how the policy was implemented in a given case. The Ministry has no such protection, and—even though it does not come into contact with masses of individual citizens—its situation as a department of variegated action places it in a vulnerable position for Ombudsman investigations.

Extensiveness of Interaction

If the Ombudsman's number of cases investigated does not appear to be very burdensome even for the major investigative targets, how extensive have the investigations of the individual cases been?

Interaction through correspondence. Nearly all of his interactions with departments on particular cases have been through correspondence that he initiated. There was a long-range tendency for him to write more than a single letter, which was all he wrote in 21 percent of the investigations; but the most common situation (36 percent), one that remained relatively stable over time, was that in which he wrote two letters. The mean was 2.8 letters. In only 13 percent of the cases were five or more letters sent, so the instances of a heavy input from the Ombudsman were few. But such cases (nine or more Ombudsman-letters were sent in 3 percent of the investigations) could be expected to have a considerable impact upon the departments.

Although letters do vary greatly in length and in the effort that goes into them, the fact that in nearly half (48 percent) of the cases the department wrote only a single letter in response to the Ombudsman indicates that agencies may not regard responding to him as onerous. The mean number of departmental replies was 2.1 letters to the Ombudsman. Truly extensive correspondence involving five or more letters from the departments was required in only 7 percent of the investigations, and departmental responses per case exceeded nine only 1 percent of the time. These facts confirm that departments have not been heavily burdened by the Ombudsman's investigations. Also, they support an impression gained from reading the letters that departments have prepared carefully their initial response so as to preclude a request for fuller information. No secular shifts in the number of departmental responses have occurred.

Other interaction. The Ombudsman held personal interviews—all initiated by his office—with departmental officers in just 7 percent of the cases. Most of them were with permanent heads, and all but one conference was held at the Ombudsman's office. In only 13 percent of the investigations did the Ombudsman's office telephone the department. Most calls were by the Ombudsman himself, primarily to department heads. There are notes of telephone conversations that were initiated by the department in 6 percent of the cases; the real figure is probably somewhat higher.

Furthermore, despite the Ombudsman's very extensive power to investigate departmental premises, in only 3 percent of the cases did he exercise it. The circumstances then at issue usually were a construction site or disputed piece of property. Knowing of the Ombudsman's legal powers, some administrators have held a fearful image of him as a crusading figure who barges into agencies looking for secret files; this image is incorrect. Although it is clear that the Ombudsman's communications with the departments by means other than correspondence have been quantitatively infrequent, this is not to say that they are necessarily unimportant.

Not only was the interaction initiated by the department with the Ombudsman limited, but also interaction with other actors in the course of dealing with a complaint was rare. Perhaps surprisingly, governmental officials other than the Ombudsman and departments very seldom participated. Cabinet Ministers played some role in the investigation of only 5 percent of the cases; Members of Parliament were implicated in 8 percent. Other government departments seldom participated in investigations, and there was no pattern of departments consistently being jointly involved in cases; in fact, four was the most times any given department interacted with any other. Two departments became involved in 16 percent of the investigations; three agencies participated in 4 percent of the cases; and four were concerned with a single case in only 1 percent of the investigations.

Pervasiveness of Complaint's Threat

Writers sometimes have provided examples of the kinds of complaints that Ombudsmen investigate, but these usually rather dramatic stories may be quite unrepresentative of the general run of cases. Determining how great a threat is posed to agencies by those complaints the Ombudsman decides to investigate is central to an understanding of their experience with him.

Extent of departmental discretion. One matter vital to an assessment of the Ombudsman-departmental relationship is whether or not the agency had been free to make a contrary decision. It emerged from the analysis that 4 percent of the complaints were really not against a decision of a government department. An additional 1 percent pertained to a decision made by a Minister rather than a department (New Zealand does not work very hard at maintaining the British convention that all decisions are made by Ministers). Eight percent concerned the department's duty to enforce a law or regulation; many statutes allow hardly any discretion—as in the computation of several taxes. Slightly more complaints really were against government policies, which the departments were forced to implement; except as they may have convinced Cabinet to adopt the policies, they cannot be held responsible. An additional 16 percent fell into the less formal category of departmental procedures or policies, which normally were at least tacitly approved by government. The complaints arose over their content, their justice, etc.; whether or not the complainant met the established criteria was not at issue.

Only about one-third of the complaints investigated concerned matters on which the department had made discretionary decisions. The administration of any welfare state requires that huge numbers of such decisions be made—about matters such as whether Applicant X meets the qualification rules for Benefit Y—and it is not surprising that they should be the largest single occasion for complaint. Almost another third of the complaints were lumped into a miscellaneous category; often a departmental omission or failure to act was alleged. In perhaps a majority of that category of cases it was not within the province of the department to have acted differently. The finding that emerges from this analysis of the extent of the departments' discretion is that—either because they did not make the decision or for various legal or procedural reasons—in probably no more than *half* of the total complaints investigated could the department reasonably have acted to forestall the complaint. Knowing this, departments would not have been particularly concerned about the other half of the cases.

Depth of threat. The complaints that the Ombudsman forwarded did not often seriously threaten departments; in 74 percent of the total sample only an individual case was involved. For example, questions about such matters as the interpretation of a citizen's qualifications to receive a benefit would be at issue. Even these mundane matters, however, were potentially costly; 53 percent of them made some financial claim upon the department. Broader matters were raised by the remaining 26 percent. These included issues such as whether or not, according to a proper interpretation of the Act, a particular subclass of people should be entitled to a benefit; in about one-third of these cases the Ombudsman added importance to the investigation to the extent of asking the department for an explanation of its policy. Some of these cases raised for the department the specter of being forced to amend an Act or of reallocating resources. Indeed, 58 percent of these cases involved financial claims. It was obvious from a reading of the departmental responses that such possibilities—especially prospective Treasury raids—evoked feelings of trepidation and even indignation. Although the Ombudsman's complaints did not usually threaten departments beyond a single case, they have raised more far-reaching matters often enough to keep agencies acutely aware of his existence.

Locus of decision making. Fifty-three percent of the complaints investigated concerned decisions originally made at the across-the-counter level. Since the Ombudsman's complaint is routed to the department head, this meant that it often was necessary for a local branch office of the department to become involved in the internal investigation. Sometimes files were sent to the head office, sometimes reports were sent, and sometimes conferences were held. A dramatic increase has occurred in the complaints made against local office decisions, while those made by the head office have decreased. This has been due to complainants deciding to skip an internal appeal to the head office as the Ombudsman's existence as an alternative appeals agent became more widely known.

Despite increased work in communication, the fact that complaints were increasingly against a local office rather than headquarters actually may have tended to reduce the level of Ombudsman-departmental conflict, for less threat was involved. It is easier for an agency's chief pol-

EXCHANGE PROCESSES: THE BUREAUCRACY

icy makers to consider reversing a subordinate's decision than one of their own.

Focus of responsibility. Although the Ombudsman sometimes has been depicted as the scourge of civil servants, the complainants normally conceived of the department as a corporate body and focused their ire upon it. Individual employees were accused or challenged for mistakes, misbehavior, etc. in only 7 percent of the investigations. In none of them was the matter ever carried far enough for the accused civil servant to ask to state his defense to the Ombudsman as the Act provides (Section 18 [3]). What usually happened in those cases was that the department pointed out to both the complainant and the Ombudsman that what had been interpreted as the capricious action of an individual civil servant was actually an action in pursuance of the law or government policy, etc., so that the focus of the complaint was shifted to the department as an impersonal entity. Since the Ombudsman's complaints usually are potential threats to the agency as a whole rather than to individual civil servants, agencies must be quite sensitive to them.

Nature of the Ombudsman's Demands

Of course, it is the Ombudsman's own actions that are crucial in this relationship. That he has little coercive ability is clearly established, but he does have discretionary power about how he shall allocate his energies and define his role. Is he, as some have supposed, a modern Don Quixote with his lance ever poised for tilts at bureaucratic windmills?

Amount of information provided. In nearly half of the cases the Ombudsman began the investigation by writing to the department giving an extensive précis of the complainant's allegations, including long quotations from his letter, and the Ombudsman's preliminary legal investigations. This practice has remained stable, but that of sending the department a copy of the client's letter, which was done in about one-third of the cases, has greatly increased. It may be that complainants have come to make fewer contentious—and potentially legally actionable—statements in their letters, so that the Ombudsman has felt less hesitation in sending copies to departments; or it may be that he has decided more often than previously that it is sounder strategy or administration to send a copy. (The office had no copying machine, so copies had to be individually typed.) In the remaining cases the Ombudsman forwarded only a bare sketch of the complaint; that procedure virtually has stopped. It was becoming usual for the department complained against to be given nearly as much information about the complaint as the Ombudsman possessed. Under such circumstances, departments would have no fear that the Ombudsman could be holding out information on the complaint in an attempt to trap them.

Action demanded. Aside from the ultimate power of recommendations to Parliament, the Ombudsman's most important potential threat over government departments is that he may examine any of their files. He exercised this option, however, in only one-fifth of the investigations. The Ombudsman asked for the files *alone* in about half of those cases (but sometimes the files were accompanied with an unsolicited report). Ordinarily, these were cases in which he was only interested in determining a factual matter that could be found easily in the file, and the practice usually should be interpreted as an attempt to relieve the department of the burden of preparing a report on a simple matter. In the other half of the cases in which the Ombudsman demanded the department's files, he also required them to submit a report. Only twice did he originally ask for a report and then subsequently also ask for the files.

In more than three-quarters of the cases investigated the Ombudsman was satisfied merely to demand a report from the department concerned. Even though they were not requested to do so, in 4 percent of the cases the departments sent the relevant files in addition. Thus, he generally has been satisfied with the quality of the reports received. It could have been predicted that in a first flush of crusading zeal the Ombudsman might often have demanded to see the files, and that as he gained confidence in the departments' dependability, he would then tend to rely more heavily on their reports. This has not been the case, and the only trend discernible over time is that a miscellaneous category composed of situations in which interviews and telephone calls were requested, has vanished.

Finally, it is the Ombudsman's style to promote conciliation. If a preliminary investigation convinces him that his client's complaint has foundation, then he tries to bring the agency to see the case through the same lenses he has used. He usually does this by setting out his reasoning in step-by-step detail. After the agency has been convinced that this analysis is correct, the Ombudsman hopes that they will volunteer to set the matter straight. Preferring gentle persuasion to coercion whenever possible, the Ombudsman has used his legal powers to make a formal "recommendation" in only 5 percent of the sample's investigated cases. Even in those cases, he generally took this action as a last resort only after several attempts to gain compliance had failed. Rather than tilting at windmills, he has proceeded with caution.

Departmental Reaction

The nature of the Ombudsman institution makes it more probable that government departments will be acted *upon* than that they will initiate action. This does not, however, mean that they are passive. The bureaucracy might use "sandbagging" or other obstructure strategies to increase the difficulty of the Ombudsman's job; thus, an analysis of the departments' reactions to the Ombudsman's investigations is essential to an understanding of their relationship.

Speed of reply. Departments generally have accorded the Ombudsman's complaints high priority. *On almost one-third of them the Ombudsman received a substantive reply within one week.* (Interim replies merely acknowledging receipt of the complaint were not counted.) Nearly as many more were received in the second week, and less than one-tenth took more than a month. Taking into account the large volume of paper work that government departments must process, the common occurrence of crises, the fact that reports from subsidiary offices were so often required, and the complex nature of many complaints, the replies seem quite prompt. Also, there is a trend for complaints to be dealt with more quickly over time. As further evidence of the alacrity of departmental response, in only 7 percent of the complaints did the Ombudsman send a reminder to the department; and in only one sample case was it necessary to send a second reminder.

Contested jurisdiction. There is a high rate of agreement between the Ombudsman and the departments upon his jurisdictional boundaries. In only three cases did the department contest his jurisdiction. In two of them the department convinced the Ombudsman that he had no jurisdiction, and in the other he convinced them that he did. But in none of them did the department carry its disagreement to the Crown Law Office for a legal opinion to buttress its claim as the Act provides that it may. Measured by this important criterion, the relations between the Ombudsman and departments generally have been amicable. Another obstacle that departments could raise would be an attempt to hide behind their Minister's authority. In only one case in the sample, however, did they involve their Minister in a case when neither the Ombudsman nor the complainant previously had done so. This is further evidence that the departments did not view the Ombudsman as a dangerous enemy who should be opposed at every turn.

Disputed facts. An important insight into the departments' perceptions of the Ombudsman's complainants can be gained from another finding. In only 19 percent of the investigations did they dispute a fact given to the Ombudsman by the complainant. It is interesting that essential facts were at issue in half of the cases in the first time period, so that the initial conclusions of some agencies about the Ombudsman's complainants were that they were often not truthful. Of course, it might be that the department was wrong and that it was defending its position by attacking the complainant's integrity. Its contentions usually were substantiated, however, with documentary evidence that convinced the Ombudsman and the coder. Some of the facts in contention were easily verifiable, such as a date of application, but others were less so, such as a verbal promise from an officer. Thus, in four-fifths of the cases, disputes between the department and the Ombudsman were on grounds other than the facts of the complaint.

Conciliation. Just as it is the Ombudsman's style to avoid using coercion if possible, so also it is the preference of government departments to avoid confrontations with him. As we shall see in the following chapter, which treats the outcomes of the investigations, agencies commonly comply with his wishes and rectify a large proportion of the complaints—usually voluntarily.

Conclusions

The impressionistic portraits, which were unveiled at the beginning of this chapter, of six of the major investigative targets, indicated that the number of Ombudsman complaints that could be reasonably expected to be generated against them is very large indeed. Most of the other major investigative targets and many of the other scheduled departments, too, are so highly vulnerable to Ombudsman investigations that the total number actually investigated during twelve and one-half years, 4,773, seems very small. In fact, on the basis of our review, it would not seem untoward if the total of the complaints investigated had been lodged against a single department.[11] If we assume that New Zealand citizens are not so servile as to be incapable of complaint, the small number of grievances lodged against these acutely vulnerable targets seems to be a tribute to the quality of administration.

The Ombudsman-departmental relationship is a theoretically interesting one; no English concept accurately describes it. The departments are not his clients, his customers, or his subordinates; nor are they necessarily his victims. The Ombudsman does not have "normal" transactions with agencies; for, except over complaints, there usually is no reason to interact. Many bureaucratic

[11] I should mention, however, that the Ombudsman believes this assessment to be somewhat exaggerated. In reacting to a draft of the descriptions of the six major investigative targets presented above, he commented as follows: "I think you have over-stated the scope and monolithic structure of the big departments such as Social Welfare, Education, Health, and Works, together with the number of decisions that they have to make, and contrasted them with the very small number of complaints received by the Ombudsman. I think the limitations on the Ombudsman's jurisdiction must be considered in this context—particularly the existence of appeal and review mechanisms and structures in the departmental organizations." (Personal communication from Sir Guy Powles to the author, 22 October 1975.)

officials may be aware of the Ombudsman's legal authority, but he cannot build an actual authority relationship with them without interaction. On the other hand, the decision of whether to involve a department in the investigation of a case must be considered carefully, for the Ombudsman's credibility is at stake in each investigation. A review of our findings on the policy questions posed at the start of this chapter will assist in evaluating the Ombudsman's institutionalization vis-à-vis the bureaucracy.

First, this analysis clearly revealed that the volume of complaints that the Ombudsman investigates does not create a consequential burden for administrative agencies; few departments would receive more than one complaint per month. The investigations, which almost always are limited to exchanges of correspondence, seldom are very extensive; and political actors other than the department and the Ombudsman almost never are involved. In no case are departments inundated by work from the Ombudsman; and in comparison with the tasks they must complete to perform their missions, the Ombudsman would loom large on the horizons of few administrators.

Second, the Ombudsman's complaints seldom are fundamentally threatening to departments. The bureaucracy would have had the option of deciding in favor of the citizen in only about half of the cases investigated. Also, complaints seldom have repercussions beyond a single, individual case, but the focus of complaints is almost always the department and not an individual civil servant. Consequential, if not vital, matters are raised often enough to keep top administrators acutely aware of the Ombudsman's existence. The finding that the Ombudsman's investigations are unlikely to pose a serious threat is positive for his authority, because a perception of threat would be likely to produce attempts at cover-up rather than cooperation.

Third, the Ombudsman normally is punctilious to avoid the disruption of the administrative process; he treads softly and usually fully informs departments as to the complaint's details. The Ombudsman has found that he can depend upon the administrators to such an extent that his option of calling for documents seldom is exercised. The Ombudsman's demands usually are undramatic; coercion is avoided. The office has little real power, and the judicious use of this limited resource has been important to its institutionalization.

Fourth, bureaucrats do not obstruct the Ombudsman; cooperation is the norm. Even though the Ombudsman's jurisdiction often is debatable, it is almost never contested. Willing rectification of clear mistakes is also normative for the Ombudsman-departmental relationship; such cooperation is an important index of the Ombudsman's institutionalization.

Probably the congruence between the norms of the New Zealand political-administrative environment and the Ombudsman's putative norms goes far to explain a salient finding: there were few changes over time in Ombudsman-environmental relationships. Although the relationships have not changed in critical ways, time may yet be an important variable. The sharing of stable interaction patterns, which—based upon behavioral evidence—seem to have been reasonably mutually satisfactory, probably has tended to create expectations of further similar experiences. Presumably the creation of such expectations enhances the Ombudsman's authority. At least, this chapter has established that the truth lies somewhere in between those who perceive the Ombudsman as a panacea for bureaucracy's ills and those who view him as an administrative ogre.

CHAPTER EIGHT

Outcomes: The Ombudsman's Impact

Focusing upon the Ombudsman's complaints, his clients, and the pattern of Ombudsman-client and bureaucracy-Ombudsman interaction, this Part's previous four chapters have contributed much to our understanding of the nature of the institution under study. That understanding is, however, incomplete in a major respect: we have not yet analyzed the *consequences* of having an Ombudsman. How can the impact upon the New Zealand political system of establishing an Ombudsman be measured, and what has the impact been?

Certain of the findings thus far presented may have aroused suspicions among some readers that the Ombudsman accomplishes little. As examples: he has hardly been deluged with complaints; those who have complained have been—in the main—a cross section of society seeking benefits from the state rather than society's unfortunates trying to escape from the clutches of a grasping bureaucracy; the Ombudsman's relationships with his clients are neither extensive nor deep; and his bureaucratic interactions are low-keyed, nonthreatening, and conciliatory. Even some of the Ombudsman's sympathizers may have concluded, with regret, that the institution seems to be a well-meant but an unnecessary and not very effective democratic luxury. Perhaps critics of the Ombudsman will believe, less charitably, that the data vindicate their distrust of the institution. Especially, they may look askance at what has been revealed about his generally good working relationships with the bureaucracy: Does this not indicate, they may ask, that the Ombudsman has been coopted by and has become an apologist for the political system's power elites? It is easy to understand the reasoning behind such conclusions, but they are premature. As will be seen, it is my contention in this chapter that the New Zealand Ombudsman's impact upon the political system has been a substantial one.

Several terms—such as *output, outcome,* and *impact*—commonly are employed in policy analysis. Too often, they are used in confusing and contradictory ways. No esoteric theories are offered here. Our overall goal can be stated simply: it is to investigate what effects the Ombudsman has had on political life in New Zealand. We shall begin with an analysis of the Ombudsman's case decisions, or outputs; then we shall note their consequences, or outcomes, and attempt to deduce the apparent political repercussions, or general impact. Although we want to assess the Ombudsman's impact upon the political system, broadly conceived, we shall do so by measuring his specific consequences for the two principal protagonists in his authority system—the clients and the government agencies. How often does he help complainants, and how often does he successfully initiate administrative reform?

The Meaning of the Ombudsman's Decisions

Between his inception and 31 March 1975, the Ombudsman received 10,776 complaints. After the office finishes whatever investigation is conducted into each case, the case is assigned one of the seven labels indicated in Table 8-1, which summarizes for the entire period the Ombudsman's classification of his complaints.[1] Recall

---

[1] Table 8-1 offers a useful opportunity for a statistical test of the sample (the sample figures are best compared with the cumulative figures for 1969 in parentheses in the table). When the frequencies for each classification that were observed in the sample are compared with the frequencies expected—because they represent the actual classifications—and the standard one-sample (or 1 × n) chi-square was applied, it was determined that the differences were not significant. According to the .05 criterion, the sample is representative of the universe (one-sample X^2 = 3.98, d.f. = 5, >.50).

OUTCOMES: IMPACT

TABLE 8-1
Classification of the Ombudsman's Decisions
1 October 1962 to 31 March 1975

Classification	Percent of Actual Complaints $n = 10{,}587$[a]	$(n = 4{,}414)$[b]	Percent of Complaints in Sample $n = 450$	Percent of Sample Complaints Investigated $n = 221$
Not Justified	35	(38)	39	61
Declined	32	(36)	34	6
Discontinued	15	(9)	8	13
Withdrawn	8	(9)	11	4
Justified—Rectified	8	(6)	5	11
Justified—Recommendation Made	2	(2)	2	5
Justified—No Recommendation	1	(—)[c]	—	—
Total	101[d]	(100)	99[d]	100

Compiled from *Report of the Ombudsman* (Wellington: Government Printer, 1975), Appendices B and C; and from Appendix C of the annual *Reports* for the earlier years.

[a] One hundred eighty-nine complaints still under investigation at the end of the year are excluded from this total and from the computations reported in the text.

[b] This column reports cumulative figures as of the 1969 *Report*, which is the reporting period closest to the one covered in the sample.

[c] At the time of the 1969 *Report* this classification had been used a total of only twelve times.

[d] Percent is more or less than 100 because of rounding.

that these decisions are the Ombudsman's *outputs;* they are not necessarily indicative of the *outcomes* for complainants or agencies. An analysis of these decisions is, however, prerequisite for further studies of the institution's impact. The table's dispositional categories require some interpretation:

Not justified. Constituting some one-third of the total complaints but about three-fifths of those investigated, are the cases determined to be "not justified." More complaints were given this label than any other, and, of course, the reasons for awarding it were manifold. In essence, the Ombudsman found no grounds under his Act for criticizing any action of a government agency. Although a few of these complaints obviously were quarrelsome in nature, most were not. Misinformation and misunderstanding, however, were common. Often an agency appeared to the complainant to act unjustly, but the Ombudsman's investigation revealed that its discretion was bound by law or government policy. The Ombudsman's expertise enables him to dispose rather quickly of complaints that obviously have no substance, so the finding that he conducted an investigation that entailed consultation with the agency complained against in over three-quarters of the sample's "not justified" complaints indicates that they often have raised complex matters. Thus, the term "not justified" is not a synonym for insignificant or worthless.

Declined. Usually it is apparent on its face if a complaint should be "declined," as nearly one-third of the complaints received have been designated; and these cases seldom require a departmental investigation. Complaints are "declined" on the following four legal grounds.

First: Section 13 (1)[2] of the statute specifies that an Ombudsman may "investigate any decision or recommendation made, or any act done or omitted . . . relating to a matter of administration and affecting any person or body of persons in his or its personal capacity, in or by any of the departments or organizations [or individuals within the institution's jurisdiction]." From Appendix B of the 1975 *Report,* we can determine that 78 percent of

---

[2] This section number and others cited below refer to the new numbers of the revised Act, which is printed in Appendix B.

OUTCOMES: IMPACT

the total "declined" cases have fallen afoul of this section. Three-quarters of those complaints were against organizations (as detailed in Table 4-2) that were outside of the Ombudsman's jurisdiction. The remainder were excluded because they really were complaints against a law or established government policy (whose fairness, legality, reasonableness, etc., the Ombudsman did not question) rather than against a "matter of administration." Even though the section quoted above allows the Ombudsman to require that complainants have "standing," as administrative lawyers use the term, this is almost never done.

Second: 15 percent of the "declined" cases were so disposed of because of the statute's Section 13 (7) which excludes from the Ombudsman's jurisdiction cases in which a legal "right of appeal or objection, or a right to apply for a review, [was] available to the complainant, on the merits of the case, to any Court or to any tribunal . . . , whether or not that right of appeal or objection or application has been exercised in the particular case." Furthermore, complaints against actions of "any person in his capacity as a trustee within the meaning of the Trustee Act," and against actions of government legal advisers, were excluded. And when in 1968 the Ombudsman's jurisdiction was extended, complaints "in respect of the medical, surgical, or dental treatment of a particular patient" by medical practitioners and dentists who were employees of hospital boards were excepted, as were the teaching activities of employees of local education boards.[3] An analysis of the sample's cases "declined" because of Section 13 (7) indicated that for four-fifths of them a legal appeal was found to exist. Of those

---

[3] The exemption of these actions of employees of hospital and education boards was omitted from the 1975 revision of the Ombudsman Act. The revision includes one pertinent further requirement: complaints against the Police must in future be processed through internal departmental channels before they can be brought to the Ombudsman.

cases the right of adjudication had been exercised at the time of complaint by only one-fourth of the clients, and in most instances (three-fifths) an appeal lay to an administrative tribunal rather than the ordinary courts. Thus, the Ombudsman often provided clients with legal advice describing an inexpensive (usually free), specialized, and simple administrative remedy. According to the 1975 *Report*, four-fifths of the 114 complaints against the Public Trust Office that were processed during the entire period were "declined" under Section 13 (7); the single complaint laid against the Crown Law Office was "declined" on this basis; none of the 92 complaints against hospital boards, but 4 percent of the 108 against education boards, were so "declined."

Third: 3 percent of the total cases "declined" earned this label because they infringed upon the Act's prohibition against allowing the Ombudsman to investigate a complaint from a member of the military relating to the "terms and conditions of his service . . . ; or any order, command, decision, penalty, or punishment given to or affecting him."[4]

And fourth: the Ombudsman chose to "decline" 4 percent of the total complaints so designated on the basis of Section 17 (2) of his statute, which allows him to do so at his discretion if the action complained of occurred more than twelve months before the complaint was filed; or if the "subject-matter of the complaint is trivial; or the complaint is frivolous or vexatious or is not made in good faith; or the complainant has not a sufficient personal interest in the subject-matter of the complaint." The small number of complaints rejected on these bases (which actually allow the Ombudsman to conclude that the cases are inconsequential) is indicative of the Om-

---

[4] Under the original Ombudsman Act, out-of-jurisdiction military complaints were listed under a separate section; the new Act places them under the same section, 13 (7), as the "declined" complaints which are discussed in the previous paragraph.

OUTCOMES: IMPACT

budsman's belief that the vast majority of his clients raise issues that are worth taking seriously.

Discontinued. The Ombudsman's authority for labeling 15 percent of his cases as "discontinued" derives from the Act's Section 17 (1), which gives him a broad discretion to refuse to investigate a complaint further if he finds "that under the law or existing administrative practice there is an adequate remedy or right of appeal, other than the right to petition Parliament, to which it would have been reasonable for the complainant to resort; or . . . that, having regard to all the circumstances of the case, any further investigation is unnecessary." About all that can be said for certain about complaints given this designation is that they were not immediately recognized as unactionable and classified as "declined," and they were not investigated thoroughly enough to be classified as "not justified." An analysis of the sample revealed that about one-fifth of these complaints were "discontinued" because the Ombudsman found that the client had available an adequate appeal to another complaint mechanism. The majority of the remainder were found really to be not justified after a very quick investigation, but in almost as many cases the Ombudsman halted his investigation after he found from his initial approach that the agency was already in the process of rectifying the complaint.

Withdrawn. Although 8 percent of the Ombudsman's intake was designated as "withdrawn," complainants actually asked that their case be "withdrawn"—either because the complaint was being settled independently of the Ombudsman or because they had come to believe that their case was hopeless—in only about half of those cases in the sample. After an inquiry for more information and/or his fee, the Ombudsman simply never heard again from nearly one-third of those whose cases he classified as

191

"withdrawn." Likewise, he assumed that the remainder intended to "withdraw" their complaint when he received no response to his tentative rejection of their claims.

e) *Justified*. In his "Statistical Summary of Complaints" contained in Appendix B of the annual *Report*, the Ombudsman lumps together the final three classifications of Table 8-1 and calls those complaints "justified." Over the years 1,086 cases, about one-tenth of the total complaints processed, have been "justified." A detailed analysis of the *Reports'* Appendix C reveals that the vast preponderance of these complaints (79 percent) have been individually labeled as *rectified*. "Rectified" generally is used to mean that the department has agreed to comply with the Ombudsman's interpretation of the situation and probably also to take corrective action if appropriate. In only one-quarter of the sample's "rectified" cases did the Ombudsman have to use pressure or any element of coercion to get the agency to agree to comply. In the remaining cases the agency voluntarily set the matter straight. It was even found that the agency was itself in the process of "rectifying" the citizen's complaint (or had already done so) when the Ombudsman forwarded it in about one-third of the "rectified" cases.

In only 2 percent of the total complaints processed (14 percent of the "rectified" cases) did the Ombudsman label his decision *recommendation made*. These were situations in which the agency refused to comply with his wishes until he wrote them a letter formally "recommending" that they do so. Even then, they may have asked their Minister to overrule him. But, having regard either to the Ombudsman's rational arguments or to the political embarrassment that would follow if the Ombudsman made a public report to Parliament, Ministers generally have complied with the Ombudsman. Only once among the sample cases was the Ombudsman's "recommendation" not implemented, and I am aware of only two cases in all among the total actual cases in which this occurred.[5]

Some cases appeared to have merit, but—perhaps because the complaint was too long after the event—nothing could be done to help the situation, and no general reform was indicated. Thus the Ombudsman has begun to use the categorization of *justified–no recommendation*. For the first seven years of his existence it was used a total of only twelve times, but since then it has been used frequently enough to account for a total of 6 percent of the "justified" complaints.

Time and case classifications. The classification pattern has remained rather stable over the years, but three shifts can be noted. Somewhat fewer complaints have been "declined" in recent years, perhaps because potential complainants have become more sophisticated about the office's jurisdiction. Furthermore, the level of "discontinued" complaints has risen. This may be attributable to the Ombudsman's increased experience, which could cause him quickly to dispose of certain types of complaints without becoming involved in a full investigation; it also may help to account for the slight fall in "not justified" complaints.

Finally, the changing relationship of the "rectified" to the "recommendation made" complaints is a significant index of the Ombudsman's institutionalization. Although these are output categories and do not necessarily indicate that there has been an impact upon either client or

[5] My assessment is confirmed by the Ombudsman's scorekeeping (personal communication to the author from Sir Guy Powles, 26 March 1975). This is not to imply that the Ombudsman is nearly always victorious. He often has considerable latitude about whether or not to provoke a confrontation, and he uses his political skill to avoid unnecessary clashes. For examples, see Walter Gellhorn, *Ombudsmen and Others: Citizens' Protectors in Nine Countries* (Cambridge, Mass.: Harvard University Press, 1966), pp. 120–21.

agency, the complaints given these labels are in most cases those in which the Ombudsman has tried to obtain voluntary or involuntary compliance with his demands. For the first four and one-half years of the Ombudsman's existence, 68 percent of the total of the "rectified" and the "recommendation made" cases were "rectified." That percent climbed to 88 for the second four years, and for the last four years willing—if not necessarily cheerful—compliance had become the norm: 92 percent of those cases were "rectified," and formal "recommendations" were very seldom issued.

Helping and Its Correlates

Probably the odd case has arisen in which the Ombudsman's investigation has revealed that a client was illegitimately receiving a government benefit or that he or she should pay higher rather than lower taxes. But in virtually all cases, the outcome of complaining to the Ombudsman is being helped or not helped—in the latter circumstance the result is simply no change. Thus, our index of the Ombudsman's impact upon his clients is a measurement of his frequency of helping them. If one defines helping in a loose fashion, the Ombudsman obviously is quite helpful to his clients. As discussed in Chapter 6, the Ombudsman's mere existence as a wailing wall for the expression of grievances is therapeutic for citizens. Furthermore, his provision of complainants with a compassionate response, which may explain away their grievance or only detail why he cannot assist them, surely is psychologically beneficial for many.

But for the present purpose of assessing the Ombudsman's impact, we shall adopt a more stringent definition of helping: *clients are said to be helped only if as a result of their complaint some material circumstance has been altered in their favor.* Perhaps the Ombudsman believed that the client was eligible for a Widow's Pension and succeeded in convincing Social Welfare to grant it, or perhaps he found that someone was being taxed at too high a rate and got Inland Revenue to comply with his recommendation that a lower rate be assessed. In such circumstances in which people were demonstrably better off as a result of their complaint to the Ombudsman, the case was coded as "client helped."

No previous investigations have attempted to go behind the annual *Reports* and measure quantitatively an Ombudsman's actual performance as a social service delivery system. But those who have been curious have assumed that the Ombudsman would be likely to help only the one-tenth or so of the clients whose cases he has classified as "justified." Moreover, since it can be deduced from a reading of case notes published in the *Reports* that many of those whose complaints were designated as "justified" were not materially helped, some scholars have concluded that the Ombudsman's actual impact upon his clients is minimal. The results of our investigation indicated, however, that the office's capabilities as a helping institution have been underestimated.

According to our stringent definition, the Ombudsman managed to help 13 percent of the sample's 450 complainants. Since we are, however, making calculations that reflect upon an important aspect of the Ombudsman's social usefulness, it is unfair to the institution to base the proportion of clients helped upon the total of all complaints received. The Ombudsman should not be expected to help those who complained about the activities of organizations that were outside of the office's jurisdiction (one such complainant was, nevertheless, helped). A reanalysis indicated that on this basis—helping as a percent of the total complaints against agencies on the Ombudsman's schedule (N = 352)—a higher proportion of the clients was helped: 16 percent (N = 52).[6] No important trends developed over time.

In the remainder of this section we shall first briefly relate the Ombudsman's helping behavior to the discussion just completed of the classification of his decisions. Then three questions will be explored: Who are the successful clients? What are the characteristics of successful complaints? Which agencies are the targets of successful complaints?

Case classifications and helping. In our earlier treatment of the Ombudsman's disposition of the complaints, a caveat was entered against assuming a close relationship between particular categorizations and outcomes for clients. That this was sound advice can be determined from the following results. The complaints of nearly half (48 percent) of the clients helped by the Ombudsman were given labels *other than* "justified." Most of that half were "discontinued," but about one-fifth each were listed as "not justified" and "withdrawn." In toto, 43 percent of the "discontinued" complainants were helped; none of those that were "declined" for various reasons had any positive outcome for the writer.

An analysis of the half of the helped clients whose cases were "justified" revealed that the complaints of most, 69 percent, were classified as "rectified." The originators of over four-fifths of the total complaints "justified" (87 percent of the cases "rectified," and 82 percent

[6] Of course, the Ombudsman's success in helping clients was principally limited to those cases in which he consulted with the accused agency, or investigated; and it might be argued that our analysis of his helping performance should be limited to the complaints *investigated* against scheduled organizations. Figured on this basis, he helped an even greater proportion of his clients: 21 percent. Adopting this standard would, however, be unwise, for the Ombudsman often has considerable discretion about whether to investigate a case. Too, he did manage to help 7 percent of the clients whose cases he did not "investigate."

OUTCOMES: IMPACT

of the "recommendation made" cases) were helped by the Ombudsman.

Clients' identities and helping. In Chapter 5 we inquired: Who complains? We now ask: Which clients, in a sociological sense, are most likely to be successful? Clients' *demographic origins* matter to a certain degree. Whereas more than three-fifths of the total clients helped lived in urban areas—a function of the fact that most of the total complaints had urban origins—urban clients were less likely than nonurban ones to be helped. Twenty-one percent of the nonurban (composed of small-town and rural) clients were helped, but only 14 percent of the urban ones were. Just why the nonurban clients should be more successful is unclear. Perhaps because the complaints of rural clients, especially, often concern land, taxation, and other related matters about which they must have much detailed knowledge in order to pursue their livelihoods, they are more likely than urban clients to present complaints that are actionable by the Ombudsman.

The clients' *sex* has not been related to helping to any important degree; 16 percent of the male clients have been assisted, and nearly as great a proportion, 14 percent, of the females have benefited from their complaints. *Age*, however, has had more salience. Clients of retirement age have been less successful (15 percent as compared with 21 percent) than the other age groups combined in obtaining assistance from the Ombudsman. The principal explanation seems to be that people of retirement age tend to complain about various government pension schemes, and, because many of their provisions leave agencies with little discretion, complainants are likely to be disappointed. Also, senility appeared to be a factor in a few complaints from aged people; one would expect such complaints to be more "expressive," hence less rational.

An analysis of the *educational levels* of the helped clients proved interesting. Whereas only 13 percent of those who had a university education were helped, 19 percent of the low-education clients were helped. It appears that the small number of low-education clients who were mobilized to complain, out of the large potential pool of such clients, were those who were unusually perceptive in knowing the kinds of matters on which the Ombudsman could provide assistance.

How might clients' *marital status* be related to their success with the Ombudsman? According to one possible hypothesis, married clients would be helped more often than unmarried ones because the former's complaints would tend to be based upon objective circumstances; and there would be a greater likelihood that those from the latter would be "expressive" in the sense that complaining to the Ombudsman was a way of venting generalized frustrations that were engendered by loneliness. This hypothesis seems plausible, and it is confirmed in some measure by the data: only 10 percent of the nonmarried complainants (they were single, separated, divorced, widowed, or deserted) were helped; but the Ombudsman assisted 21 percent of all those who were married.

When the relationship of helping to the client's *racial-ethnic backgrounds* is investigated, it develops that the Ombudsman has not been able to help internal minority group clients, such as the Maoris, disproportionately. He has been, however, moderately more likely to assist immigrants (22 percent helped) than nonimmigrants (15 percent helped). Decisions concerning the tenure of immigrants in the country, allowing relatives to enter, etc., are highly discretionary. It is not surprising that the Ombudsman—following a thorough and compassionate review in which he may have drawn out relevant information of which the agency may have been unaware, perhaps because of linguistic difficulties—often was able

OUTCOMES: IMPACT

to convince the department and its Minister that there were grounds for altering their original decision.

Many observers probably would predict that those who are most successful in life—as measured by their *class-occupational backgrounds*—also would be most successful as complainants to the Ombudsman. This prediction is borne out to a certain degree by our findings: one-quarter each of the top- and the second-level professionals were helped; the percentages helped for both the executive-administrative-proprietorial and the white collar classes were about the same as the one for the entire sample, 17 percent; but only 11 percent of those who could be identified as manual workers were assisted.[7]

It seems reasonable to assume that *civil servants* would be highly knowledgeable about the subjects of their complaints and about how capable the Ombudsman might be of resolving them. Hence, one would expect them to be disproportionately successful. That assumption, however, is incorrect. Only 13 percent of the civil servants who made service-connected complaints were helped, but 16 percent of all other clients were benefited. Perhaps civil servants' complaints are slightly more quarrelsome than others.

Finally, we shall examine the Ombudsman's ability to assist the two-fifths of his clients who recently had undergone significant *social change*. According to our data, he is somewhat more likely to help those who have not experienced social change than those who have; the respective percents helped are 17 and 14. Social changes—usually having to do with personal health, job changes, or

---

[7] Recall from Table 5-4 that the class-occupational backgrounds of about half of the clients could be determined. Equal percentages, 17 percent each, of those who could not and those who could be categorized were helped by the Ombudsman. It is probable that many, perhaps a majority, of those who could not be classed were manual workers, so the figure of 11 percent helped, which was given in the text, is to some extent an underreport for the manual clients.

family matters—seldom were mentioned frivolously; only 10 percent of those mentioned were irrelevant to the complaint. Nevertheless, a reason why the Ombudsman was not especially able to help clients who had experienced personal crisis is that their complaints sometimes were expressive in character: in some cases their recent experience was related to—even the source of—their complaint, but they had been affected so deeply that their judgment about the kinds of matters on which the Ombudsman could assist was impaired.

Complaint characteristics and helping. Having learned the identities of the clients who have been helped, let us turn our attention to four selected characteristics of the victorious complaints.

First: How old were the successful grievances? As we might expect, the Ombudsman was rather more able to help those which had occurred recently. His rate of success was 20 percent for complaints less than five months old and only 14 percent for those that had rankled for from five months to more than four years. These findings suggest that the newer complaints were more likely to be valid, and the major purpose of many later ones may have been to serve the psychological needs of the complainant. This interpretation is mitigated, however, by the facts that memories blur, and people and records become difficult to locate as time passes. Although it was best to raise a relatively recent matter, raking up grievances long past was not necessarily a waste of time; 12 percent of even those that arose more than four years previous to the complaint were helped, as were 17 percent of the complaints whose age could not be determined.

Second: Was the Ombudsman more likely to help the 72 percent of the total complaints that we identified as assuming an "offensive" perspective or the other 28 percent that were "defensive"? The data indicate that offensive complaints were helped somewhat more often; 17

percent as compared with 13 percent helped among the defensive complaints. This finding seems generally consistent with our understanding of the basis of the decisions upon which the two types of complaints are likely to be grounded. Whereas policies and statutes which are the basis of actions that caused offensive complaints sometimes leave wide avenues open for the exercise of discretion and hence for varying decisions, those upon which defensive complaints are based often have been tightly constructed so as to narrow the field for discretionary judgments.

Third: Were those who made a financial claim against the government, 56 percent of the total, more likely to be helped by the Ombudsman than the remainder who did not? The answer is negative, but a substantial portion of the financial claims were granted. Fourteen percent of those making a financial demand were helped, usually by having their demand granted, whereas a bit more of the remainder (19 percent) were assisted. Perhaps it is not surprising that complaints having nonmonetary costs for an agency are more likely to be allowed than those that would make incursions into its budgetary allocation.

And fourth: How successful were those complaints that already had been appealed to the department as compared with those that had not? A plausible hypothesis—one that was voluntarily mentioned several times in interviews with civil servants—is that the Ombudsman often could achieve something for the "virgin" complaints, i.e., those that previously had not been appealed to the agency. The assertion was that if it had the chance, the agency itself would have fixed up what were often referred to as genuine complaints, and the Ombudsman was artificially running up his score by counting among his "justified" complaints those that had not yet been brought to the department's attention. Our findings do not support this contention, although the differences are small: 15 percent of both the complaints that *had not* been appealed to the department's local office and those that *had not* been appealed to its head office were helped, but somewhat more—16 percent and 17 percent, respectively—of those that *had* been appealed to one level or the other were helped. The implication seems to be that those who had not bothered to follow the traditional channels of appeal were very slightly less knowledgeable than those who had about what constituted a potentially actionable complaint to the Ombudsman.

Complaint targets and helping. In order to understand fully the Ombudsman's role as a helping institution, not only must we learn the identities of those clients whom he helped and the properties of the successful complaints, but also we must examine the *targets* of these complaints. Are there some agencies against which complaints are especially likely to be successful or unsuccessful?

The numbers of those helped become too small to warrant extensive analyses of particular agencies,[8] but an aggregate study of the complaints helped reveals that it is through repeated dealings with those agencies that are his regular targets that the Ombudsman is most often able to assist his clients. Eighteen percent of the complaints against the eighteen "major complaint organizations" of Table 4-1 were helped, but somewhat fewer—10 percent—of the complaints against all of the other government departments on the Ombudsman's schedule were helped. Whether the explanation is that for some reason more "valid" complaints are lodged against these major targets or that the Ombudsman is better able to resolve complaints against these agencies because of his

---

[8] The percents helped of the four departments in our sample that had five or more helped complaints follow: Health, 38 percent; Social Welfare, 20 percent; Education, 17 percent; and Inland Revenue, 16 percent.

OUTCOMES: IMPACT

regularized pattern of relationships with them is unknown.

In Chapter 4 the nature of the agencies' relationships with their public-in-contact was used as the basis for classifying them into three types: "client-serving," "client-attending," and "non-client-oriented" organizations. Which of these types would we expect to have more successful complaints charged against them? No clear answer is apparent, although rationales quickly come to mind for believing that complaints against both of the client-oriented types often might be successful. Generally reflecting their proportions of the total complaints investigated, we find that 48 percent of the Ombudsman's customers who were helped had complained against client-serving organizations, that 32 percent were against client-attending organizations, and that 20 percent were against non-client-oriented organizations.

But when we examine *relative* rates of success among the types of organizations we find that those who have complained against non-client-oriented agencies were slightly more often helped than the others; 19 percent of them were helped. Perhaps because most of these agencies come into contact and thus into conflict with individual members of the public less often than the other two types of agencies, they regard a complaint forwarded by the Ombudsman as an interesting rarity and make a strong attempt to satisfy him and his client. As might be expected, about as large a proportion (18 percent) of the complaints against client-serving agencies were helped. But some fewer (12 percent) of those credited to client-attending agencies were helped. Perhaps many policies of such client-attending agencies as Inland Revenue or Justice have been deliberately refined in statutes so that their area of discretion may be narrower than that of other types of agencies; such decisions could be less reversible. Alternatively, these client-attending agencies may be somewhat more repressive or stubborn than others.

THE OMBUDSMAN AND ADMINISTRATIVE REFORM

Thus far, we have found that the Ombudsman has had a beneficial impact upon a substantial group of his clients. But what are the consequences for the agencies complained against and for society as a whole?

Often a dispute between an agency and a member of its public-in-contact who later becomes the Ombudsman's client is a zero-sum confrontation. If the client is rewarded—i.e., given a welfare benefit, taxed at a lower rate, allowed to purchase government land, then the agency is deprived. Sometimes the result is that the department has a smaller quantity of material resources under its control than if the Ombudsman had not interfered. In other cases, as when a prisoner is released or an apology is made for a delay in providing services, the tangible costs to the agency may be so minimal as hardly to be calculable. This is not to say that there are no repercussions; intangible costs may be high. Departments may value greatly their reputations for fairness, justice, etc., and may feel that the Ombudsman's labeling of a complaint against them as "justified," for example, is a severe deprivation.

Whether the costs are material or symbolic, whenever the Ombudsman helps a client the agency complained against incurs some costs. And since we have found that relief is granted to 16 percent of the clients, the Ombudsman's total impact upon the departments appears to be a considerable one when impact is measured in this fashion. There is reason for contending, however, that the Ombudsman's success in resolving grievances of individual clients in their favor is insufficient as an index of the institution's impact upon government agencies. The mere fact that a client was helped does not necessarily mean that the agency was affected in any important way; adding one more client to Social Welfare's rolls at the Ombudsman's insistence, for example, may not cause much concern at that agency. And just as we decided in the previous section that the Ombudsman's provision of psychological assurance to citizens was an inadequate gauge of his helping behavior, so too, interpreting agencies' symbolic costs as a principal measure of his impact upon them would be an inadequate basis for judging the Ombudsman's administrative impact.

Rather than considering the Ombudsman's bureaucratic impact to be the sum of the cases in which he has obtained a successful outcome for his clients, a much more demanding definition will be adopted: *we shall reserve the term "impact" for those situations in which, as a result of the Ombudsman's investigation, government departments make policy changes that have consequences reaching into the future beyond the particular decision complained against.* That the Ombudsman's investigation might have administrative effects even though the client was not helped is an obvious possibility, which the definition takes into account.

In normative terms, this study of the Ombudsman's impact will be an analysis of his role as an administrative reformer, and the concepts *impact* and *reform* are used synonymously below.[9] From the beginning, it was expected that the office would be involved with reform. Section 22 of the statute provided that the Ombudsman might take further action if after an investigation of a complaint he formed the opinion that the agency's behavior was not only subject to criticism in a particular instance but also that it "was in accordance with a rule of law or a provision of any Act, regulation, or bylaw or a practice that is or may be unreasonable, unjust, oppressive, or improperly discriminatory." If upon further reflection the Ombudsman should conclude "that any

---

[9] Compare my conception of impact with Gerald E. Caiden's definition of administrative reform as *"the artificial inducement of administrative transformation against resistance."* Administrative Reform (Chicago: Aldine, 1969), p. 8 (Caiden's italics).

practice on which the decision, recommendation, act, or omission was based should be altered; or that any law on which . . . [it] was based should be reconsidered," then he was charged as follows:

> The Ombudsman shall report his opinion, and his reasons therefor, to the appropriate Department or organization, and may make such recommendations as he thinks fit. In any such case he may request the Department or organization to notify him, within a specified time, of the steps (if any) that it proposes to take to give effect to his recommendations. The Commissioner shall also . . . send a copy of his report or recommendations to the Minister . . . [or] to the Mayor or Chairman of the organization concerned.

Let us see how active and how successful the Ombudsman has been in fulfilling these reformist expectations.

Administrative reform in the annual Report. Each year the Ombudsman selects from his total intake a number of cases that he believes have general interest and writes a short, one- to two-page account of them for inclusion in his *Report.* Called case notes and arranged by department, 863 of these vignettes—a figure that constitutes one-tenth of the total complaints received against scheduled agencies—have been published over the years. The criteria employed in selecting cases to be accorded this treatment are nowhere clearly articulated, but it is certain that they are not randomly chosen. Because the annual *Report* is the Ombudsman's major opportunity to capture the attention of the bureaucracy, of Parliament, and of the general public through the news media, it is very carefully crafted to appeal to readers. Instead of being dry and technical as are the reports of most government agencies, the Ombudsman's notes usually feature human dramas recounted in an interesting fashion.

OUTCOMES: IMPACT

Of course, the Ombudsman wants to put his best foot forward, but he does not bother to write up every case in which he succeeded in helping the client.[10] And in many of the cases recounted he was not able to get satisfaction for his complainant. Often it appears that cases were chosen to be excerpted merely because they raised interesting issues or involved unusual interaction patterns.

The major significance of the case notes for our present purpose of assessing the Ombudsman's impact is that they include descriptions of the vast majority of the instances in which he has had a significant impact upon an agency. Through a detailed study of these documents, which is undertaken in the remainder of this chapter, it is possible to trace the Ombudsman's actual impact upon the departments under his jurisdiction without relying upon a limited sample of the cases.

Before attempting an aggregate analysis of those cases in which the Ombudsman had administrative impact, let us closely examine one case: The following chronicle of a housewife's complaint is written in the style of the Ombudsman's case notes. Through a rare administrative error, however, no note of it was written for the 1967 *Report*. This case provides a concrete illustration of the sorts of consequences the Ombudsman can have for public administration, and a discussion of the case will allow us to begin to define more precisely what we mean when we talk of the institution's policy impact.

The complainant protested that the Social Welfare Department had canceled benefits to which she believed she remained entitled while on an extended visit to the United Kingdom. Since her ineligibility was not immediately apparent, the department had continued the normal procedure of paying the benefits into her Post

---

[10] If the Ombudsman managed to help the same proportion of the total actual clients as he did of those in the sample, 13 percent, then 1,400 case notes would have been required just to tell the stories of those whom he helped.

Office Savings Bank account. Social Welfare had an arrangement with the Post Office under which the Post Office would withdraw from the beneficiary's POSB account money paid into it to which the beneficiary was not entitled and would return the funds to Social Welfare. Accordingly, at Social Welfare's request, the Post Office withdrew the amount of the alleged overpayment from the complainant's account without consulting or notifying her. Disagreeing with Social Welfare's ruling as to her eligibility and seeking restitution of the amount of the confiscated benefit, the complainant appealed to the Ombudsman.

After an investigation, which required only one exchange of correspondence with Social Welfare, the Ombudsman concluded that he could not fault the department's decision. The client was, indeed, ineligible to receive the benefit while she was out of the country, so that the complaint was classified as "not justified." The Ombudsman was not satisfied, however, that the procedure used to secure repayment from the complainant's POSB account was just or proper; and he decided on his own initiative to pursue this matter with the Post Office by asking them for their authority for withdrawing the funds from the complainant's account without her knowledge or consent.

The Post Office defended its case in two ways. First, it sent the Ombudsman copies of the relevant application forms and contended that in signing them, beneficiaries, in effect, appointed the Social Welfare Department as their agent and that the Post Office's policy of dealing with Social Welfare rather than the beneficiary in such cases was therefore justifiable. Second, the Post Office contended that Social Welfare, as the beneficiary's agent, was competent to decide whether the deposit was "made in error" (Regulation 60 of the POSB Regulations) and that the Post Office was obliged to accept this agent's direction regarding the disbursement of such benefits.

OUTCOMES: IMPACT

After examining the application forms, the Ombudsman was of the opinion that beneficiaries, by signing them, did not appoint Social Welfare as their agent as contended by the Post Office. Furthermore, he doubted whether the funds had been deposited as a result of the kind of genuine mistake, or "error" he thought Regulation 60 envisaged. He suggested that the department should seek a Crown Law Office opinion on both issues. The subsequent opinion confirmed the Ombudsman's contentions and was accepted by the department.

Henceforth, Social Welfare's methods of recovering funds are limited to those described in Section 86 of the Social Security Act, which provides that the rate of any future benefits may be accordingly adjusted or alternatively that legal action may be taken to effect recovery as a debt due to the Crown.

From what we have learned thus far about the Ombudsman's functioning, much of this case has a familiar ring. But some atypical aspects should be mentioned. The involvement of a second government department in the investigation is, as we have seen, very unusual as is the participation of a boundary-maintaining agent: the Crown Law Office. Equally unusual are the Ombudsman's own activities. He was the author of the complaint to the Post Office. Whereas he could have simply commiserated with the client once he determined that Social Welfare's actions followed established guidelines, he took the initiative and managed to get changed a policy he considered unjust.

The dimensions of reform. As noted above, Section 13 of the Ombudsman Act limits the office's jurisdiction to departmental actions "relating to a matter of administration." Presumably, such matters are to be distinguished from political matters, although this is never specified.

Even though many political scientists would argue that the old politics-administration dichotomy has no intellectual validity, the Ombudsman has been forced to operationalize it. And, as we shall see, he seldom has gotten into trouble with his political overseers for allegedly violating his bounds and intruding into the political sphere. The term *policy* is used in many different ways. Here I shall classify as policies those decisions which agencies make that will affect how some of their activities—particularly those having to do with their public-in-contact—will be handled in the future.

Journalists occasionally feature a case in which an ombudsman has slain an administrative dragon, and academicians—especially lawyers—have written about a few instances in which an ombudsman has effected some reform. But the accounts describe in detail matters that usually seem in themselves rather minor, and I believe that even most of the ombudsman's supporters have been led to underestimate the office's impact upon public administration. What is easily forgotten is that policy changes that are individually small may over time amount to quite a large body of administrative reform, and the following cumulative analysis of the New Zealand Ombudsman's policy impact indicates that it has been considerable.

An analysis of the case notes shows that between 1 October 1962 and 31 March 1975 *the Ombudsman was responsible for at least 177 separate reforms of the administrative process*. The fact that this figure constitutes 2 percent of the total complaints made against scheduled departments is of only marginal relevance to our present concern; the total number of reforms initiated is of more importance. We have no definite criteria for determining how many reforms represent a high or low number, but the total accomplished seems on its face to be respectably high. The reforms have been reasonably spaced out over the years, except that 38 were initiated in the first year

OUTCOMES: IMPACT

and a half and 23 in the second year, as the Ombudsman rid the bureaucracy of a number of practices that seemed to him glaringly improper. Since then, the average has been a rather steady 11 per year.

Our research design considerably underestimates the Ombudsman's impact in the following respects. First: I am aware of a few cases in addition to the Social Welfare–Post Office one recounted above in which a lasting impact upon the agency was achieved, but, inadvertently, a case note was never written for the *Reports*. Second: reforms surely occurred in many instances in which we could not be certain that an impact resulted, either because the case notes were too cryptic or because the investigation was not complete at the time the *Report* went to press; the Ombudsman did not always pick up reforms resulting from the latter situation in his next *Report*. Third: the Ombudsman often made a suggestion— rather than a recommendation—that a particular change in policy should be discussed with the Minister or considered when a law or regulation was next given a general revision; to be sure, many of these suggestions fell on fertile ground.[11] Fourth: many cases set precedents without necessarily altering policy to any substantial degree, e.g., the Ombudsman may have convinced the agency that, according to their existing criteria but contrary to their initial interpretation, the complainant's circumstances really did qualify him for a favorable ruling; although the policy was not changed, future clients in a position similar to that of the original complainant should

[11] In 1975, for example, while examining a complaint against an officer of the Valuation Department, the Ombudsman discovered that a large number of legislative provisions gave authority to various government officials to enter private property without the owner's knowledge or consent. He believed that the terms of these provisions were quite diverse and unclear and reported that he was undertaking a survey of them with a view toward making them more uniform and limiting their scope. When the survey is completed, it is likely that a number of amendments to law will occur over a period of several years.

be treated according to the precedent set with that case. Fifth: the Ombudsman has a further administrative impact upon agencies as a teacher; he points out the path of righteousness both indirectly, through the sorts of answers he demands during an investigation, and directly, through admonitions in letters and published case notes.

Finally: it appears that some episodes involving a minor administrative impact are being excluded from the *Reports* by design. Although, as we have observed, the number of complaints actually received has increased substantially over the years, the number of administrative impacts recorded has remained steady; 11, the average for the entire period, were recorded for 1975. The proportion of "justified" cases has not dropped following the bulge of complaints, and there are no data that suggest that the incidence of the Ombudsman having an impact upon agencies has declined. Instead, the Ombudsman apparently has begun to feel that not every minor victory for administrative reform needs to be documented, just as not every instance of helping clients is reported.[12] Thus, the Ombudsman's actual impact upon the New Zealand bureaucracy has been greater (but to an indeterminate degree) than the following description will indicate.

Much of the analysis in the remainder of this chapter will focus upon two types of policy impacts: those concerning *substantive* policy and those about *procedural* policy. Substantive policies are normative statements about objectives—about what should be done in a given

---

[12] Sir Guy Powles agrees with this interpretation and also refers to the Government Printer's recent space restrictions in compiling the *Reports* (personal communication to the author, 26 March 1975). A mean of 67 case notes have appeared each year, but the numbers have declined from a high of 145 in 1964 to a low of 29 in 1975. It is, of course, logically possible that the Ombudsman has recorded proportionally fewer administrative impacts because fewer have occurred, either because he has by now solved most problems or because the office suffers from goal displacement.

situation. In the present context, substantive policies are likely to affect citizens directly. The policy change that the Ombudsman brought about in the above case note was a substantive one: because of his intervention, Social Welfare and the Post Office changed their attitudes toward citizens' bank accounts, which will be dealt with differently in the future. In contrast, procedural policies are instrumental in character; they are likely to be intermediary and to affect the implementation of substantive policies—e.g., improving record keeping or eliminating delay. Such changes are often minor, and their principal immediate impact is internal to the agency. Yet—as we shall see—they are not inconsequential; in the future they may have important impacts upon the fortunes of individual citizens.

Because the costs to the agencies of procedural reforms are likely to be low and because such technical problems would seem especially likely to be uncovered by the Ombudsman, one might suspect that procedural reforms would predominate over substantive ones. Our findings, however, belied this suspicion: *54 percent of the impacts were substantive in nature, and 46 percent were procedural.* During only four years (1966, 1967, 1972, and 1973) has the number of procedural reforms exceeded substantive ones. Principal explanations for these findings may be that New Zealand government departments were before the Ombudsman's coming already well organized in a procedural sense, and, because there is always room for argument about the direction of policy, we should not be surprised that the Ombudsman has more frequently disagreed with departments' choices and has convinced them to go along with his wishes.

The targets of reform. Has the Ombudsman's bureaucratic impact been widespread or concentrated upon certain agencies or types of agencies? In the previous section we found that about half of the complainants who were helped had objected to the actions of a client-serving agency, but our impact analysis reveals that this type of agency accounted for only 35 percent of the Ombudsman's total reforms. Conversely, whereas the client-attending complaints represented less than one-third of the total helped, they accounted for 56 percent of the administrative reforms. Nineteen percent of the impact cases were found to be lodged against non-client-oriented agencies, and 20 percent of the complainants helped had grievances against agencies of this type.

Although the first two findings are not startling, they require some interpretation: because of the nature and quantity of their public contacts, it is not surprising that the result of many complaints to the Ombudsman against client-serving organizations is the correction of a mistake, so that an individual is helped but no impact beyond that case is felt by the agency. And because the discretion of many of those agencies that we have labeled client-attending typically is more tightly constrained than that of client-serving agencies, the former's clients are less likely to be dealt with wrongly so that the Ombudsman could help them on appeal. At the same time, the tightness of the rules and practices of client-attending organizations may increase the possibility that the Ombudsman will spot an injustice or inconsistency and cause an impact upon them. This interpretation is reinforced somewhat by the further finding that 53 percent of the client-attending reforms were procedural in character as compared with only 40 percent for client-serving agencies.

Our analysis by department of the institution's initiation of administrative reform reveals that *the Ombudsman has had no policy impact upon two-fifths of the agencies under his jurisdiction.* Six of these twenty-one agencies are relatively small-scale, client-serving organizations—the Public Trust Office, Maori and Island Affairs, the Rehabilitation Board, the Government Life

OUTCOMES: IMPACT

Insurance Office, the Maori Trust Office, and the Maori Affairs Board. Only three client-attending agencies experienced no impact—the Decimal Currency Board, the Tourist and Publicity Department, and local education boards. But the majority of the departments upon which the Ombudsman had no impact were technical, non-client-oriented agencies—including Marine, Trade and Industry, Valuation, Mines, the Soil Conservation and Rivers Control Council, Audit, Scientific and Industrial Research, Legislative, Statistics, the Government Printing Office, the Prime Minister's Department, and the Crown Law Office. Virtually all of these organizations have a myriad of functions, but in the performance of their missions they do not usually come into contact with large numbers of clients. And the ones that do experience many such contacts tend to have highly routinized, limited scope operations—e.g., the Government Life Insurance Office.

According to Table 8-2, four-fifths of the Ombudsman's administrative reforms have been concentrated upon fourteen actors in his authority system. Agencies registering six or more impacts were arbitrarily designated as "major impact targets"—although such a quantitative measure of impact might be fallacious: the Ombudsman's consequences for an agency upon which he had six procedural impacts could, nevertheless, be mini- whereas through only one substantive reform, he could have a profound impact. The table's third column, which indicates the percent of each principal target's impacts that were substantive, puts this matter into quantitative perspective. Finally, the table provides an opportunity to compare our policy impact findings with the Ombudsman's publicly reported scorekeeping index, the agencies' numbers of "justified" complaints.

There is some reordering but the "major impact targets" are the same as the "major investigative targets" of Table 7-1, except that the Housing Corporation and the

215

TABLE 8-2
Departmental Targets of Administrative Reform
1 October 1962 to 31 March 1975

Department	Administrative Impacts n	Administrative Impacts %	Percent of Substantive Impacts	Complaints "Justified" n	Complaints "Justified" %
Total Major Impact Targets	144	81	53	837	77
Education	26	15	73	76	7
Justice	19	11	53	88	8
Social Welfare	12	7	33	201	19
Health	11	6	64	31	3
State Services Commission	11	6	27	76	7
Post Office	10	6	40	84	8
Internal Affairs	8	5	75	17	2
Works and Development	8	5	63	46	4
Customs	7	4	57	38	4
Inland Revenue	7	4	43	53	5
Transport	7	4	43	12	1
Labor	6	3	67	51	5
Railways	6	3	33	33	3
Police	6	3	33	31	3
Total Other Targets	33	19	58	249	23
Grand Total	177	100	54	1,086	100

Compiled from *Report of the Ombudsman* (Wellington: Government Printer, 1964–1975), Appendices B and C.

Government Superannuation Fund Board have dropped out and Internal Affairs and Transport have been added. Just as we learned in the previous section that the Ombudsman was somewhat more likely to assist those clients who complained against his most regular targets, we now find that the lion's share of his administrative impacts has been suffered by these agencies with which he has a well-established relationship.

The association between those departments upon which the Ombudsman has had the most policy impacts and those which have the most "justified" complaints charged against them is in general a close one.[13] The most striking disparities belong to Social Welfare and Health. Although Social Welfare is far ahead of all others in the number of "justified" complaints, it merits only a low third ranking in terms of administrative impact. Conversely, Health is tied for eleventh according to the cases "justified" criterion but is tied for fourth in policy impact. As we might have suspected, instances of malfeasance by Social Welfare are usually only individual mistakes, but those by Health are more likely to expose general problems.[14]

The content of substantive reform. A warning was entered above concerning the possible dangers of judging the Ombudsman's impact upon administrative agencies by merely counting the number of reforms he had successfully urged against them. Counting is permissible to provide an overview, but it masks crucial qualitative differences, which involve the actual reform implications for agencies, among the impacts.

[13] The correlation coefficient (Spearman's rho) is 2.45, which is significant at the .05 level.

[14] The "other targets" upon which the office has had some impact number only seventeen. Four impacts were registered against the Housing Corporation, Agriculture and Fisheries, and Defense; the Government Superannuation Fund Board and Lands and Survey were the objects of three Ombudsman impacts; the National Provident Fund Board, the National Roads Board, and the Earthquake and War Damage Commission each logged two reforms; and one impact was recorded by the following agencies: the State Insurance Office, Foreign Affairs, the Treasury, local hospital boards, the Land Settlement Board, Electricity, the Forest Service, the National Parks Authority, and the Government Stores Board.

Malinowski was quoted above (epigraph, p. 35) as advocating the analysis of each phenomenon "through the broadest range possible of its concrete manifestations; each studied by an exhaustive survey of detailed examples." "If possible," he suggested, "the results ought to be tabulated into some sort of synoptic chart." I believe that most of this book's tables follow Malinowski's recommendation in spirit, but Table 8-3 is an example of precisely what he appears to have meant by a synoptic chart:

TABLE 8-3[*]
Synoptic Chart of the Ombudsman's Substantive Policy Impacts upon Selected Major Impact Targets
1 October 1962 to 31 March 1975

EDUCATION Total Impacts = 26 Number of Substantive Impacts = 19
1. A regulation recognized foreign secondary schooling for the purpose of awarding university bursaries (scholarships) only if the student's parent had been transferred in the course of employment. The Ombudsman recommended that recognition be based instead upon the standard of education received. 1963
2. The Ombudsman objected to the practice of the Child Welfare Division whereby case workers' evaluations of the suitability of couples who wished to adopt children were made known to natural mothers. The division agreed to prohibit such possibly prejudicial reports and guaranteed that proposed adoptive parents were allowed to have their application heard by the courts. 1964[a]

---

[*] Compiled from *Report of the Ombudsman* (Wellington: Government Printer, 1964–1975), Appendix A.

[a] The functions of the Child Welfare Division were transferred to the Department of Social Welfare in 1972.

TABLE 8-3—continued

3. The Ombudsman concluded that the nonteaching staff of local education boards had insufficient avenues of redress against possible unjustified disciplinary actions and recommended that in serious cases alleged offenders be given written charges and be granted an impartial hearing. 1964
4. As a result of the Ombudsman's investigation of a complaint about the abolition of a scholarship program which had allowed students to pursue a diploma in both dairy farming and sheep farming, the department was persuaded to change its policy and reinstitute a conjoint bursary. 1965
5. When the Ombudsman found that the salaries of teachers whose schools were downgraded because the enrollment dropped, were *automatically* lowered if the teacher did not move within two years to another school having the grading their school originally merited, he objected. The department changed the legislation to allow discretion in circumstances such as the complainant's when no similar position became available. 1965
6. The Ombudsman recommended that the criteria should be reviewed and a coherent policy formulated concerning whether students who had bonded themselves to become teachers when they completed their departmentally financed university educations could have their obligations suspended to undertake postgraduate study. 1965
7. The Ombudsman expressed the view that Education's policy of paying a boarding allowance to married bursars on the ground of hardship if they had received the allowance at the time of their marriage, took into account a condition that was, in terms of the governing regulations, irrelevant. The department

TABLE 8-3—continued

concurred and decided that future hardship cases would be dealt with out of a special fund.   1965

8. A regulation outlining the conditions under which a bursary could be reinstated after its suspension, specified that students first had to complete successfully a year of study at a New Zealand university. The Ombudsman believed that the regulation's intent that students demonstrate their ability to attain a prescribed academic standard would be met wherever the study was undertaken, and he convinced Education that the regulation should be amended to include non–New Zealand universities.   1968

9. The Child Care Center Regulations, which provided for two classes of license—an A license where the center had an employee holding a recognized training qualification and a B license where there was no such employee—did not contain the usual transitory provisions protecting competent practitioners who were already in business but did not possess the prescribed qualifications. At the Ombudsman's urging, the regulation was amended so as to allow A licenses to be granted to those in such circumstances who could satisfy the department as to their competence.   1969

10. During his investigation of a dispute about what proportion, if any, of his legal costs a teacher vindicated of a disciplinary charge should bear, the Ombudsman advised—and the department concurred—that the law be amended to require the tribunal hearing the charge to make a recommendation to the Minister regarding legal costs.   1969

11. The department agreed that teachers who were appointed to new positions that were, before the appointees commenced work, regraded to a higher

OUTCOMES: IMPACT

TABLE 8-3—continued

level with the result that the teacher no longer qualified for the position, sometimes suffered injustice. Consequently, Education gave such teachers full transfer rights, including moving expenses, to another position anywhere in the country.   1970

12. The Ombudsman discovered that the department was incorrectly equating the terms "permanent residence" and "domicile" in their interpretation of the University Bursaries Regulations, with the consequence that some students whose parents resided outside of New Zealand but who retained their domicile there were refused a boarding allowance. Education changed their policy to comply with the regulation.   1970

13. The Education Regulations specified how primary teachers were to be evaluated, but the Ombudsman found that the department had in fact instituted a different system without bothering to have the regulations changed. He recommended that either the policy be changed to comply with the regulation or the regulation be changed to allow the new policy. The latter course eventually was taken.   1971

14. An anomaly came to light in the Salaries and Staffing Regulations which allowed moving expenses for new employees, for those promoted within either the public service or the teaching service, and for those transferring from the education service to the Department of Education; but those promoted from the department to the locally based education service were not similarly compensated. The regulations were appropriately amended.   1971

15. The regulations conferred a wide discretion upon the Director-General of Education with regard to the number of years a bursary could be held, and seventy

TABLE 8-3—continued

medical students complained that he should be more liberal in its exercise. At the Ombudsman's urging, the Director-General agreed to some specific liberalizations of the principles he had applied and agreed to notify the universities whenever new principles for the exercise of his discretion were established. 1970

16. The Ombudsman found that inconsistencies and much confusion arose between the department and local education authorities about eligibility for boarding allowances. He persuaded the department to clarify their policy and to draft regulations that embodied it. 1971
17. The regulations required that in order to qualify for bursaries, students proceeding from one degree or diploma program to another should do so in the year immediately following the completion of the first, except in "special circumstances," The Ombudsman convinced the Director-General that the unavailability of a particular program at that time should be regarded as such a circumstance. 1972
18. Probationary teachers are classified as "mobile"—available for transfer anywhere in the country—or "immobile"—required to stay in a given district, and the Ombudsman objected to one criterion of immobility: "husband's employment in the case of a married woman, but not vice versa." The department would not agree to full sexual equality, but did cover cases in which the wife was employed as a teacher or was undertaking study or was in employment involving formal contractual obligations. 1974
19. Education offered teachers a study leave on full pay to complete their degrees; one qualification was that applicants must satisfy the criteria set for a full-time university course. A teacher who had nearly com-

OUTCOMES: IMPACT

TABLE 8-3—continued

pleted a degree during nine years of extramural study complained that his application for leave, in order to complete a Stage III unit which could not be taken extramurally, had been rejected on the basis that his degree was too nearly finished for him to be a full-time student. The Ombudsman convinced the department that such students should be allowed to take enough approved courses beyond the B.A. to constitute a full load. 1975

JUSTICE   Total Impacts = 19   Number of Substantive Impacts = 10
1. Licenses allowing hotelkeepers to sell liquor could be purchased for a portion of a year, but the converse did not apply; those who gave up their business during the licensing year were not allowed to have the fee reduced. The statute was amended appropriately at the Ombudsman's request. 1964
2. After finding considerable truth in a furniture manufacturer's allegations that the Prisons Administration was producing chairs which had been altered from one of his registered designs only enough to prevent legal action for design infringement and that Prisons was competing with him for sales, the Ombudsman intervened. According to a new policy, sales were restricted almost exclusively to government-financed agencies. 1964
3. As Justice interpreted the law, the clients of an insolvent automobile dealer whose license expired *before* their car was sold could not be reimbursed from the dealer's fidelity bond. After a reexamination inspired by the Ombudsman, the department allowed the complainant's claim—along with some others—and altered the Act to cover clearly such situations. 1965
4. In investigating a complaint about duplicate trade

TABLE 8-3—continued

names, the Ombudsman found that Justice did not systematically consult their company registers and notify those who might wish to object about a pending application. His recommendation that such a policy be adopted for both companies and trademarks was implemented. 1965

5. After learning that a judge had awarded to a man who had been acquitted of a criminal charge an amount as defense costs that turned out to be only a small portion of his actual legal bills, the Ombudsman suggested and Justice agreed that an amendment be drafted providing in such cases for the disclosure to the court of the actual legal costs for which the defendant was liable. 1970

6. A salesman of boats and marine business who discovered that a recent law required him to have a real estate agent's license complained that because the act had intruded upon his activities he should be licensed without examination, or other special provisions should be made for people in his situation. At the Ombudsman's suggestion, Justice agreed to establish a Real Estate Board, which could grant a limited license in such circumstances. 1972

7. The department sometimes transported work parties of prisoners in an open truck—a practice that a complainant pointed out was illegal, as the truck had no passenger-loading certificate and the driver had no passenger license. Justice agreed henceforth to use methods of moving inmates that were approved by the Ministry of Transport. 1973

8. The investigation of a further complaint on the same subject revealed, however, that the policy change evidently did not go far enough or it was not understood by subordinates, so it was extended and

TABLE 8-3—continued

    clarified. The Secretary directed that "inmates were at no time to be carried on the back of any open truck." 1973

9. Without consulting his medical officer, a prison superintendent instructed that in order to prevent the possible hoarding of pills, all medication for prisoners must be dissolved in water. When the Ombudsman questioned the policy, medical advice was taken with the result that the instruction was rescinded. 1973

10. A prisoner who was in restricted confinement (on "penal grade") complained that because of a further instance of "hostile and uncooperative behavior," he had been kept in this condition for more than three months—the maximum period he thought the law permitted. The Ombudsman agreed that under the statute, convictions for three additional legally defined disciplinary infractions were necessary to extend the time spent on penal grade; and Justice agreed to change their policy to comply with this interpretation. 1974

SOCIAL WELFARE Total Impacts = 12 Number of Substantive Impacts = 4

1. Having learned that the department had adopted the policy of declining to allow the family benefit to be capitalized to finance home building on working farms—despite the absence of statutory authority—the Ombudsman recommended that the policy be abandoned. Instead, the government affirmed it legally and extended it to exclude buildings to be used for "any business, profession, or undertaking." 1964

2. Citizens whose application for an invalid's benefit was rejected on medical grounds had the legal right to appeal within three months to a three-member

TABLE 8-3—continued

medical board, but the Ombudsman learned that applicants were not normally notified of the appeal's existence. He believed that they should be, and the department issued instructions that all such applicants be formally advised of their appeal rights. 1969

3. When the department altered a long-standing policy and prohibited the receipt of duplicate New Zealand and United Kingdom pensions, the Ombudsman felt that it was unjust to apply the policy change to those who had made their financial preparations for retirement in dependence upon the previous policy. Consequently, he persuaded the department—with great difficulty—to amend the law so that a British pension would be treated as income rather than as a direct deduction from the New Zealand age or superannuation benefit; furthermore, negotiations were completed between the authorities of the two countries to reinstate those who had followed the department's advice to withdraw from the British scheme. 1970

4. The department paid the boarding costs of state wards who had entered the work force but became unemployed before reaching their sixteenth birthday—hence they were ineligible for the unemployment benefit. The payment was, however, established as a debt against the ward's future earnings. The Ombudsman demurred, and the department agreed not to attempt to recover such payments in the future. 1974

HEALTH Total Impacts = 11 Number of Substantive Impacts = 7

1. As a result of several investigations, the Ombudsman made three general recommendations: that practices

OUTCOMES: IMPACT

TABLE 8-3—continued

for informing gynaecological patients of the full consequences of certain operations be strengthened; that the forms used by some hospital boards to allow consent for surgery be clarified and the implications of consent explained to patients; and that potentially defamatory documents that were sent to the department not be forwarded to others.   1963

2. Government policy allowed local authorities to hold a referendum on whether to fluoridate the water supply, and Health mounted an extensive propaganda campaign in favor of fluoridation in a particular locality. The Ombudsman concluded that partisan intervention went far beyond the department's legitimate health education activities, and he made a recommendation, which was accepted, that such activities cease.   1964

3. The Association of Part-time Hospital Staff complained that their members, who worked for local hospital boards, were forced to retire at age 60. The Ombudsman found that although the principal arguments favoring the policy were directed to the inefficiencies of aging surgeons, the 60-year-old limitation actually seemed to be an anomaly, because the permanent staff was allowed to work until 65 as were part-time staff employed directly by Health. He recommended that the anomaly be corrected.   1965

4. The Ombudsman recommended that Health's practices for evaluating applications for government loans to private hospitals be revised so as to increase the role of the local medical officer of Health (who could advise about the need for expansion of hospital facilities) in decision making. Health agreed to the change.   1965

5. The Ombudsman found that Health and the Police

TABLE 8-3—continued

did not always follow the dictates of the Mental Health Amendment Act, which governed admissions to mental hospitals. The act's simplified, informal procedure was to be used only if patients entered voluntarily; if they opposed entering the hospital, a full magisterial inquiry had to be held. Both departments agreed to change their policies to comply with the act in the future. 1965

6. The Ombudsman noticed a departmental announcement that an amendment to the Poison Regulations which had been approved by the Minister could be anticipated and put into effect immediately. Health defended the policy of using relaxing provisions as a convenient means of dealing with complex problems, but the Ombudsman convinced them that such anticipantions were illegal and should be halted. 1965

7. An investigation revealed that, at the doctor's request, psychiatric patients were photographed without their consent as a supposed aid to diagnosis and treatment. Health agreed that such photography was both medically and ethically unjustified; in the future it would be undertaken only if patients signed a consent form. 1972

WORKS AND DEVELOPMENT Total Impacts = 8
Substantive Impacts = 5

1. Land owners in an area which for the past three years had been designated as a proposed reserve for public works complained that they were denied the full enjoyment of their property rights and objected against the government's unpublished development scheme. Because the plans had not been publicly disclosed, no appeal lay to the Town and Country Planning Ap-

OUTCOMES: IMPACT

TABLE 8-3—continued

peal Board, and the Ombudsman recommended that appeal provisions be established to cover such circumstances. 1965

2. Following the bankruptcy of the main contractor of a building being erected for the Ministry, a subcontractor complained that its interests were not being as fully protected as if the Crown were bound by the Wages Protection and Contractors Liens Act. Government subsequently agreed in principle to amend the act to include the Crown, and the Ombudsman's suggestion was influential—whether it was decisive is unclear. 1965

3. A complaint arose from a firm of suppliers of materials to a company then in receivership which stated that they were treated less generously by the Ministry than if they had been subcontractors. The Ombudsman felt that a policy change to treat them equally was in order and recommended that the drafting of the above-discussed amendment to the Wages Protection and Contractors Liens Act, which would eliminate this anomaly, be hastened. 1966

4. As a result of the Ombudsman's investigation, the Ministry agreed in the future to pay the normal wage scale, as specified by the State Services Commission, to students who were employed during vacations in nonclerical jobs that would normally be performed by wage workers. 1973

5. After receiving a complaint from conservationists that they were forced to pay a deposit ("against expenses and costs") for registering their formal objections to development proposals before local water and catchment boards, the Ombudsman informed Works and Development—which administers the relevant Act—that he believed the requirement to be

TABLE 8-3—continued

unlawful. The Ministry agreed but had the Act amended to remove any ambiguity. 1975

LABOR Total Impacts = 6 Number of Substantive Impacts = 4

1. A worker and his union complained to the Ombudsman that Labor did not always consult the claimant when it investigated allegations that employers were breaching contracts. After a review, Labor agreed in the future to interview both of the parties before reaching a decision. 1965
2. The Ombudsman learned that there was a lamentable lack of coordination between the immigration authorities and universities concerning the responsibility for canceling, because of poor academic performance, a foreign student's permit to remain in the country. Labor agreed in the future to consult with the universities on each case and to establish a formal appeals process. 1969
3. In considering paroles for prisoners who were subject to deportation, the Parole Board did not know if Labor planned to deport them; the department wanted a recommendation from the board before making a decision. After the Ombudsman's investigation it was agreed that in the future, Labor's intentions would be given to the board in advance of the hearing, because knowledge of plans for deportation might incline them toward early release. 1972
4. Chinese nationals who entered the country and their New Zealand relatives were required to affirm that no request would be made for an extension of the visitor's permit. Because the Immigration Act expressly conferred the right to apply for an extension,

OUTCOMES: IMPACT

TABLE 8-3—continued

the Ombudsman believed the practice to be illegal. Labor's legal advice confirmed his belief, and the discriminatory policy was discontinued. 1974

POLICE   Total Impacts = 6   Substantive Impacts = 2
1. See Substantive Impact Number 5 listed under Health. 1965
2. The Ombudsman refused to reveal the name of the person who applied for the court order which committed the complainant to a mental hospital, because the Police and hospital authorities feared that the person—the man's wife—would be subject to a physical assault. When the complainant later obtained the information from a magistrate pursuant to the Mental Health Act's provisions, the Ombudsman became concerned. While awaiting revision of the Act, the Police General Instructions were amended so that, when the Police believed revealing the applicants' identities could be dangerous for them, a warning would be placed on the court file that magistrates should consult the Police before allowing the file to be inspected. 1975

Closely following Malinowski's "method of statistic documentation by concrete evidence," the table offers a compendium of the Ombudsman's substantive policy impacts upon the seven departments—Education, Justice, Social Welfare, Health, Works and Development, Labor, and Police—whose vulnerability to complaint was discussed at some length in the previous chapter. These major investigative targets, which are also major impact targets, are ordered according to the total number of impacts. A composite portrait of the Ombudsman as administrative reformer is presented in the table; the likeness is broadly brushed, yet it contains sufficient detail to delineate clearly the scope of the office's substantive policy impacts.

A variety of conclusions can be drawn from a perusal of this synoptic chart of the Ombudsman's reforms, but three stand out.

First: This investigation has corroborated assertions made earlier about the generally high standards of public administration in New Zealand. Despite prodigious digging over twelve and one-half years, the Ombudsman has uncovered little that was objectionable and nothing really horrendous. In the previous chapter we charted the great variety and number of citizen contacts experienced by the agencies included in the table and decided that their missions left them all highly vulnerable to complaint. If we assume that the complaints made to the Ombudsman reasonably reflect the range of agencies' dissatisfied clients and that the Ombudsman aggressively investigated complaints received—impressionistically, both assumptions seem to this observer to be warranted—then the fact that the Ombudsman found so few substantive reforms to sponsor seems remarkable. In most instances, agencies' policies were reasonably clear, comprehensive, and just.

Second: It is apparent that the Ombudsman's impact upon none of these departments has been profound. Nearly all of the impacts have involved second-order, or lower, policies; in no case have central aspects of the agencies' general functioning or even of their relationships with clients been altered. Usually, the Ombudsman found that the existing guidelines for action did not go quite far enough to insure against injustice, an anomaly was discovered, or a factor was insufficiently weighed in making decisions.

Third: Observing that the Ombudsman's substantive administrative impact has not been drastic is not, however, the same as saying that he has been inconsequen-

OUTCOMES: IMPACT

tial. A reading of these cases reveals that he has pushed the already high levels of administrative performance to even higher plateaus. Through his dealing with the three targets upon which he has had the most substantive impacts (Education; Justice, and Health), for example, it is quite clear that their policies having to do with students, teachers, prisoners, and hospital patients have been rationalized and made more humane in significant respects.

The content of procedural reform. Table 8-4 indicates that the sorts of procedural reforms prompted by the Ombudsman fall into two nearly equally occurring basic types: those that principally concern agencies' external relationships; and those that principally concern their internal processes.

Most of the *external* reforms have affected agencies' relationships with their clients or potential clients. An exemplar of each of the table's four kinds of client-related external reforms follows: 1) Social Welfare withdrew from circulation a leaflet containing an ambiguous discussion of the process of capitalizing the Family Benefit, 1964; 2) Labor revised the wording of the registration form, which the Ombudsman believed was confusing, that one filled in to obtain conscientious objector status, 1964; 3) Inland Revenue agreed to warn taxpayers that the answers given in interviews with the department's investigators could be used in court against them, 1964; and 4) Inland Revenue arranged to have the stamping of documents and the processing of estates for the Rotorura area carried out in Hamilton, which was more convenient than Tauranga, the then existing center of those operations, 1964. The remaining ten external reforms, in which an agency agreed to improve its linkages with others, covered a wide range of circumstances; a typical one was the agreement of Works and Development that District Commissioners should be made fully aware of the re-

TABLE 8-4
The Content of Procedural Reforms
1 October 1962 to 31 March 1975

Type of Reform	n	%
Total External Reforms	43	52
1. Improvement of general publicity about rights, benefits, etc.	7	9
2. Replacement of misleading or inaccurate forms	10	12
3. Improvement of communication with agency's clients	10	12
4. Better quality of service for clients	6	7
5. Increased cooperation with other administrative actors	10	12
Total Internal Reforms	39	48
6. General improvement of agency's internal functioning	18	22
7. Elimination of delay	8	10
8. Keeping of better records	4	5
9. Strengthening, reexamination, or clarification of specific procedural policies	9	11
Grand Total	82	100

Compiled from *Report of the Ombudsman* (Wellington: Government Printer, 1964–1974), Appendix A.

quirements for authorizing *ex gratia* payments to contractors and that all relevant information about claims for such payments should be made available in writing to the National Roads Board, which made the final decisions, 1964.

Reflecting the complexity of bureaucracies, the procedural reforms through which the Ombudsman has affected agencies' *internal* operations are highly varied. Category 6 contains a miscellany of cases in which departments agreed to eliminate administrative defects, improve communication, or otherwise reduce muddle. Illustrations of the table's three specific categories of internal procedural reforms follow: 7) The Commissioner of Police undertook to reduce delays in allowing citizens to repossess property that had been stolen and that the Police had recovered, 1964; 8) The Post Office initiated extensive changes in their system of keeping records of the training of apprentices, 1967; and 9) Health clarified its procedures employed in enforcing the Food and Drug Regulations to insure that competing manufacturers were treated equally, 1967.

The conclusions drawn above about the significance of the Ombudsman's substantive impacts upon the bureaucracy also appear to be applicable to an evaluation of his procedural impacts.

Reform and the costs of compliance. Learning that agencies are somewhat more likely to sustain substantive than procedural reforms is, of course, one indicator of the costs incurred in complying with the Ombudsman's demands. But costs can be measured in other ways, too.

Assenting to the Ombudsman's reform demands does not usually cause the departments great inconvenience or political embarrassment. In over four-fifths of the cases occasioning administrative reform, the changes could most likely be carried out internally—although the responsible Minister usually would have been consulted or advised. But in 18 percent of the impact cases the costs were higher: complying with the Ombudsman's wishes required that a law or regulation be changed. Thus, the policy change had to be approved by the Minister, by Cabinet, and by the whole of Parliament. Nearly all of these reforms were, of course, substantive rather than procedural.

Any assessment of the costs of the Ombudsman's bureaucratic impact must, of course, include monetary

THE OMBUDSMAN CRUCIBLE

costs. Our analysis indicated that it was unusual for departments to incur monetary costs by complying with the Ombudsman's reform demands. The outcome of only one-quarter of the cases resulting in impact upon agencies included payment to the Ombudsman's clients of a sum of money that had been at issue. The mere incidence of such monetary costs is, however, an inadequate measurement; for these cases involved policy changes that sometimes required that whole classes of the department's clients be treated differently in the future—usually more generously. In such circumstances, the bureaucratic costs of reform might be very high indeed. The probability that the type of reform effected would be substantive in nature was greater in those cases that required a pay-out to clients (percent = 63) than in those that did not (percent = 51).

Findings on a related matter inflate our assessment of the bureaucratic costs of complying with the Ombudsman. In addition to the one-quarter of the impact cases that involved a payment to clients, another 35 percent of the total had as a major issue a *claim* for such a payment. Although the agency agreed to the Ombudsman's reform demands, no money was delivered to the complainant—perhaps because his or her circumstances had changed. But the consequence sometimes was that a department's eventual costs might be increased considerably, even though no money changed hands as a result of the particular complaint.

Reform and case disposition. How are those cases labeled by the Ombudsman which have as their outcome a policy change for the agency? It should come as no surprise that over three-fifths of them, 64 percent, were "justified." And just as we found that about equal proportions of the "justified" complaints that were helped were further designated as "rectified" and "recommendation made," so too, nearly equal percents (32 and 30, respectively) of those cases resulting in administrative reform were thus designated. The finding that when the Ombudsman considered the complaint to be well founded and also advised reform, the agency was slightly more likely to rectify the situation voluntarily than it was to wait for him to apply his most powerful sanction, is an important one. It reinforces the other evidences we have of the muted nature of Ombudsman-departmental conflict.

The remaining three-eighths of the impact cases that were given designations other than "justified" were principally "not justified"—24 percent of the total was so labeled—or "discontinued"—10 percent. Only 1 percent were "declined" or "withdrawn." These findings lend support to the previous section's determination that the labels "not justified" and "discontinued," especially, have misled us if we believe that these cases were inconsequential. Not only do they often mask the Ombudsman's ability to deliver services to clients, but also they may obfuscate his potential for administrative reform.

A comparison of the Ombudsman's formal disposition of the cases with the type of impact caused, revealed an interesting difference: a large majority, 58 percent, of the "justified" cases resulted in substantive reform. Conversely, the "not justified" cases were disproportionately likely to be the cause of procedural reform; only 42 percent of them occasioned substantive reform. Even though we rehabilitated the latter designation in the previous paragraph, if we believe that substantive reforms have a higher social value than procedural ones, then the "justified" complaints retain their preeminence.

Reform and clients. What is the relationship between administrative reform and the welfare of clients? The data reveal that the office managed to help 44 percent of those whose complaints resulted in the Ombudsman having an impact upon the agency's policy, so the correlation between helping and reform is not necessarily close. Fifty-six percent of those helped received monetary assistance.

Perhaps surprisingly, about one-half of the clients were helped when substantive reforms were achieved, but only about one-third of those who caused procedural reforms were helped. The apparent explanation for what may seem an anomaly is that the flaws that are revealed in procedural policies often have determined how a client's problem was dealt with rather than the case's outcome. But substantive changes are more likely to affect outcomes, e.g., make a client eligible for a benefit.

Would we predict that the Ombudsman's ability to have an impact upon agencies would be related in any particular way to the offensive or defensive posture of the client? At least two possibilities come to mind. On the one hand, it could be that impacts would flow disproportionately from offensive complaints because they often concern welfare benefits whose administration is highly complex and which, one would suppose, could always stand improvement. On the other hand, perhaps the Ombudsman might cause reform more often after investigating defensive cases, which typically involve civil liberties matters, because many agencies could be so interested in performing their basic mission that their practices for protecting the rights of citizens would be sloppy. Neither possibility was fulfilled. Seventy-two percent of the cases in which the Ombudsman had an impact were offensive, and 28 percent were defensive. Remarkably, these figures are precisely the same as the distribution of the two perspectives for our sample of cases, which was reported in an earlier chapter. Furthermore, almost equal proportions of the complaints that held the two perspectives occasioned substantive reforms, 54 and 53 percent, respectively.

Conclusions

This chapter has probed the Ombudsman's consequences for two populations—the office's clients and public administrative agencies. The two, which are of course the protagonists of the Ombudsman's investigations, are so closely interrelated that any impact the office may have upon one ultimately will have implications for the other.

Our most salient client-related finding is that the Ombudsman actually has helped a substantial portion of his appellants: 16 percent of those who complained against agencies under his jurisdiction. During our investigation of the office's capabilities as a social service delivery system, we discovered that the Ombudsman's impact is not—as has been generally assumed—confined to those clients whose cases were "justified"; more than four-fifths of them were helped. But in addition, the complaints of almost half of those who were helped were labeled "discontinued," "not justified," and "withdrawn." It would be difficult, if not impossible, to establish scientifically valid standards for comparison; but based upon impressionistic evaluations, the Ombudsman's record of achievement probably compares favorably with the success ratios of social work agencies and others involved in the "helping professions."

We found that certain categories of clients were somewhat more likely to be helped than the mean of 16 percent. The Ombudsman helped one-fifth to one-fourth of the clients falling into the following major categories: nonurban origins; ages other than retirement age; married; immigrant; professional occupational background; and more recent confrontation with bureaucracy than five months before the complaint. The investigation of the Ombudsman's ability to help particular categories of clients, specific types of complaints, and grievances against certain administrative targets revealed that the institution is moderately more likely to be helpful in some circumstances than in others. But the qualifying adjectives that were used throughout the anlysis (such as *moderately, somewhat, rather, to a certain degree, slightly*) were chosen advisedly, for the differentials in the Ombudsman's ability to help were small. None of those reported was large enough to be statistically significant at the .01 level. What this means is, of course, that the Ombudsman has been able to help a remarkably wide cross section of his clients.

The term *compliance* has considerable usefulness in political analysis, alongside other related terms—including *power, authority,* and *legitimacy*. It is self-evident that the Ombudsman has been able to help clients, or to achieve any other goals, only because government agencies have complied with his wishes. And it is an indicator of the office's institutionalization that compliance is increasingly voluntary. The extent to which agencies comply is all the more remarkable considering the Ombudsman's low power quotient. This subject is explored through interviews with administrators in the next chapter.

In evaluating the Ombudsman's degree of institutionalization, agencies' compliance with certain of the Ombudsman's demands is more significant than with others. I refer to those in which he had some lasting impact, or initiated what is generally called an administrative reform. The ability to achieve such impacts is the severest test of an organization's offensive capability. Calling this criterion of institutionalization "spread effect," Milton Esman has described it as "the degree to which the innovative technologies, norms, or behavior patterns for which the institution stands have been taken up and

OUTCOMES: IMPACT

integrated into the ongoing activities of other organizations."[15] Similarly, Ralph Braibanti has advocated a focus upon the institution's "penetrative dynamic," which involves "the propelled redifussion of norms from one institution to others."[16]

In addition to whatever psychological impact the Ombudsman may have upon citizens in general, upon his clients, and upon bureaucrats, and in addition to his ability to help particular clients; he has been the instigator of at least 177 administrative reforms. He has succeeded in propelling into agencies his normative concepts of how public administrators should perform their jobs often enough to be taken seriously as an authority figure. Although a majority of the reforms initiated have required substantive changes in policy rather than procedural changes, this is not to claim that the reforms have been drastic. We have not distinguished between "political" and "administrative" types of reform, but it is clear that few of those accomplished by the Ombudsman would excite the sensibilities of politicians of any ideological persuasion. Nevertheless, in the aggregate these impacts amount to a not inconsiderable body of administrative reform. As a result of the Ombudsman's interventions, citizens have been placed in a more favorable position vis-à-vis the government in several noteworthy respects. The existence in most cases of a narrow gap between the Ombudsman's normative conceptions and those of agencies facilitated compliance with his demands, but normative congruence does not explain away the Ombudsman's impact.

[15] Milton J. Esman, "The Elements of Institution Building," in Joseph W. Eaton, ed., *Institution Building and Development: From Concepts to Application* (Beverly Hills: Sage Publications, 1972), p. 36.

[16] Ralph Braibanti, "External Inducement of Political-Administrative Development: An Institutional Strategy," in Ralph Braibanti, ed., *Political and Administrative Development* (Durham, N.C.: Duke University Press, 1969), p. 55.

Part 3

THE OMBUDSMAN AND HIS PUBLICS

CHAPTER NINE

The Ombudsman's "Victims": The Bureaucrats

THE preceding Part's treatment of the Ombudsman's relationships with the two sets of environmental actors with whom he has the most contact—clients and bureaucrats—approached the institution's study from an exchange perspective. As valuable as this perspective is, however, it alone provides an insufficient base for assessing the Ombudsman's institutionalization. This Part supplements the sociometric data with reports of interviews that were designed to probe into the bureaucrats' and the parliamentarians' opinions of and attitudes toward the Ombudsman.

One of the institution's characteristics that commands the attention of students of political power and bureaucracy is the Ombudsman's effectiveness despite minimal coercive capabilities. The Swedish and Finnish Ombudsmen have the primarily vestigial authority to prosecute administrators, but the essence of the modern institution—which was transferred to New Zealand—is the Ombudsman's ability to investigate citizens' complaints and recommend that bureaucratic decisions be altered. Making such a recommendation is ordinarily the most "negative situational sanction," the most "severe deprivation," with which the Ombudsman can threaten a government agency. Many theorists would consider this to be his strongest and perhaps only source of "power."[1] Thus, the Ombudsman must establish a positive affective relationship with the bureaucrats whom he superintends.

[1] Talcott Parsons, "Rejoinder to Bauer and Coleman," *Public Opinion Quarterly* 27 (Spring 1963), 90; and Harold D. Lasswell and Abraham Kaplan, *Power and Society* (New Haven: Yale University Press, 1950), p. 76.

In this chapter we attempt to measure that relationship through interviews with those bureaucrats. The substantive aspects of the relationship treated here include the perceptual context of the Ombudsman-departmental nexus, a measurement of the bureaucrats' psychosocial distance from the Ombudsman, perceptions of the Ombudsman's impact upon the public service, evaluation of the Ombudsman's jurisdiction, and general affect for the Ombudsman.

I interviewed the permanent or department heads (permanent secretaries in British parlance) of the following nineteen government departments: Social Welfare, Inland Revenue, Education, Customs, State Services Commission, Health, Housing Corporation, Labor, Works and Development, Justice, Police, Post Office, Railways, Superannuation, Agriculture and Fisheries, Transport, Treasury, External Affairs, Government Printer. The first thirteen were chosen because their departments were those against which there had been the most complaints. The six additions were selected either because their departments also had substantial experience with the Ombudsman, because their departments were for other reasons intrinsically important, or because the incumbents were particularly well regarded as experienced and knowledgeable public servants. Usually more than one reason was operable.

A subsidiary purpose of the investigation was to determine if the department's extent of interaction with the Ombudsman affected the respondent's perceptions of him. It was decided arbitrarily that respondents whose departments had more than one hundred complaints against them at the time of interviewing would be dubbed "high interactors" while those having fewer would be "low interactors." (In the previous paragraph's list of departments, Justice was the final high interactor and Police was the first low one.) Approximately equal subgroups of ten and nine, respectively, were created.

Because of the small cells that often resulted, the subsequent analysis usually reports differences only when they are clearly delineated.

The interviews were normally at least an hour in length and ranged from about forty-five minutes to two and one-half hours. The strategy used was to attempt to postpone the scheduled interview with the permanent head until other junior officers—usually those who actually handled the flow of work with the Ombudsman and other appeals agents—had been interviewed, relevant files had been examined, and reports and the like had been collected. (Sometimes, however, this was not possible when a Minister's secretary or another permanent head scheduled the next appointment so close that there was little time for preliminaries.) The dual reasoning behind the strategy was that this procedure would make it easier to interpret, and sometimes even to check the truth of, replies to questions; therefore, it was an attempt to increase the interviewer's credibility. It was hypothesized that an administrator might respond differently to an interviewer who he knew had already done considerable research in his department than to one whom he might regard as an ignorant American with a long list of tiresome and possibly irrelevant questions.

The Perceptual Context

Before exploring the parameters of the permanent heads' orientations toward the Ombudsman, it is necessary to set the scene. Specifically, the relationship between the bureaucracy's administrative values and those of the Ombudsman must be probed. Furthermore, structural and attitudinal aspects of the Ombudsman's rank require investigation.

Talcott Parsons has proclaimed: "The most important *single* condition of the integration of an interaction system is a *shared* basis of *normative* order."[2] Prior to the appointment of the Ombudsman, New Zealand's civil service was conceded to be efficient, and such values as honesty, fairness, equality, justice, and the like were distributed widely. As mentioned above, nothing even approaching the celebrity of Britain's (mild by American standards) Crichel Down scandal of 1954 had been suggested in New Zealand. The Ombudsman was established not to alter the value system but to supplement the already existing value-maintaining agents. One indication of the extent to which these values are shared can be found in the department heads' responses to the following attitude statement: "As one of the effects of modern government, we have to expect that not every grievance can be remedied." Sixteen (84 percent) *disagreed,* and none strongly agreed with it.

Another question's results provide further insights: "How would you evaluate the possible agencies open to the citizen with a complaint against the government? First, what do you think is the most effective action the citizen can take?" This was not a difficult question for them to answer. Fifteen (79 percent) volunteered that appealing to the department itself was the citizen's most effective recourse. The following quotations are representative:

—We rectify genuine grievances that come to us. There is no profit in doing something stupid or wrong.
—You must expect errors in a department such as ours when we have thousands of daily contacts with the public. We make them right.
—What the citizen should always do is to go to the local office where the decision was made and ask for a hearing; it will be disposed of there.

[2] Talcott Parsons, "Interaction: Social Interaction," *International Encyclopedia of the Social Sciences,* Vol. 7 (New York: Macmillan and Free Press, 1968), p. 437.

—If we have done a man an injustice in one of our offices—this is almost always at the lowest level—why, we ought to be given the first chance to correct it.

Conflicts between departments and the Ombudsman do not arise over competing values, but rather over competing interpretations of how to implement the shared values. Although such competition may sometimes become fairly intense, the "subjective psychological costs of compliance"[3] with the Ombudsman are low; this basic congruence of values is an important and perhaps vital[4] component of the Ombudsman's authority.

The Ombudsman stands outside the traditional flow of authority which stems downward from the Minister, through the permanent head, into the department at large. Although he interposes himself into that traditional relationship, his power does not extend to the nullification of administrative decisions. He may only recommend changes; this puny power, which is not at all congruent with his sweeping warrant for investigations, may be appealed by the department to their Minister, the Prime Minister, and ultimately to Parliament.

It would be surprising if the Ombudsman's structurally ambiguous position were not reflected in the department heads' perceptions. Perceived rank, which correlates highly with willingness to respect an authority figure,[5] was probed by the following open-ended question: "What are your ideas on the Ombudsman's true position in the political system? How important is he as compared

---

[3] Robert A. Dahl, *Modern Political Analysis* (Englewood Cliffs, N.J.: Prentice-Hall, 1963), p. 43.

[4] The ombudsman has been widely proposed in developing countries as an anticorruption device. While this will be an interesting experiment, grounds exist for questioning whether an ombudsman could by *himself* alter a system's established value pattern.

[5] Terence K. Hopkins, *The Exercise of Influence in Small Groups* (Totowa, N.J.: Bedminster Press, 1964), pp. 157–82.

with some other officials, such as a Supreme Court Justice, the Solicitor-General, an M.P., a Minister, or a department head?"

It is clear from the replies that the Ombudsman is highly respected, and he was compared to a Supreme Court Judge—an eminently respected official in New Zealand—more often than to any other. Although many respondents were fascinated by the question and several mulled it over at length, most were unable to formulate an answer! These replies are characteristic: "It's difficult to define; he's a very different type." "He's unique; I don't know who to compare him to," or "Well, he must fit in somewhere, but it's hard to say just where." Thus, the fact that the Ombudsman and New Zealand bureaucrats share basic norms would seem to predispose them toward perceptions and actions favorable to him. Nonetheless, the structural and attitudinal ambiguities of his authority cloud those expectations.

Psychosocial Distance from the Ombudsman

The concept of social distance attempts to measure "grades and degrees of understanding and intimacy."[6] The usual measurement technique is a scale that defines an affective continuum. The existing scales were inappropriate, however, and it did not prove feasible to develop a scale that could measure the bureaucrats' social distance from the Ombudsman. Instead, three individual questions investigated this dimension. The first inquired:

"In your day-to-day work how often would you say you have occasion to think of the Ombudsman?"

Very Seldom	Sometimes on Cases	When He Writes	Often	Total
57% (11)	16% (3)	16% (3)	11% (2)	100% (19)

[6] William J. Goode and Paul K. Hatt, *Methods in Social Research* (New York: McGraw-Hill, 1952), Chapter 16.

One of the eleven who replied that they very seldom thought of him said, "Never! Except in 196– when I took over, I rang him up and assured him of my cooperation." Another assured the interviewer, "He's no concern to us at all." A senior head said, "To be perfectly frank, I don't think of him. I'm a lawyer, and in our training we get a lot of ethics." It is interesting that 70 percent of the high interactors contended that they seldom or never thought of the Ombudsman as compared with only 40 percent of the low interactors. This appears to be a classic instance of the defense mechanism of displacement.

Three respondents said they sometimes thought of him in dealing with specific cases, as the following quotations indicate:

—Only a month ago a case came up, a staff matter; I said, if we decide it this way and he takes it to the Ombudsman, we won't have a leg to stand on.

—About six times a year. I usually think of him when I explain to a junior member of the staff why something isn't on.

Three others said they thought of him only in connection with the work they had to do to answer his letters; one of them said that he only thought of the Ombudsman at the moment he signed his officers' replies. Only two claimed to think of him often.

The next question was

"What do you do about the Ombudsman's annual *Reports*?"

Nothing in Particular	Check for Reported Performance	Object to Scorekeeping	Total
36% (7)	32% (6)	32% (6)	100% (19)

Subsequent probes made it clear that the objective was to gather a variety of reactions to the *Reports*. Seven of the respondents had no apparent interest in them; as would be expected, six of them were low interactors. One said, "They're water under the bridge, why should I be interested?" Another replied that he had not seen the most recent *Report* (then six months old) and said, "You've got it there in your bag, let's see how we did." The remaining 64 percent, however, did look at the *Reports*. Six of them said they checked their rating with him; one specifically mentioned that while he read them, he did not send them out to his officers: "They are not waiting with bated breath for the result." Another took just the opposite view and circulated them in all the district offices: "It's good to familiarize them with situations of complaint. He has wasted a lot of our time, but that's all part of the caper." Six others (five were high interactors) regularly scrutinized the *Reports* and also objected to the Ombudsman's scorekeeping of "justified" cases. For example, one fumed, "This score is inflated, because most of these people hadn't complained to us first. I am sensitive to this because I want it to be known that we do what is right."[7]

Twelve of the department heads were asked the final social distance question, "Do you know Sir Guy Powles personally?" Of those, seven said they did; and three of them said they knew him prior to his appointment. One had worked in the same law firm with him at the beginning of their careers. Only two flatly said that they did not know him. Three others who did not feel that the knew Sir Guy personally said they had met him. One of them commented that he occasionally met Sir Guy at cocktail parties, and they made small talk without really talking about their jobs. Thus, the majority of those asked felt that they had at least some personal linkage with the Ombudsman.

[7] A subsequent question asking whether they recalled as particularly significant any of the Ombudsman's cases with other departments was met with blank stares. Not one of them was sufficiently interested to read about or to comment upon other departments' cases.

The Ombudsman's Impact upon the Civil Service

According to the Ombudsman's most recent *Report* (for 1967) at the time interviewing began, his impact upon the government departments would appear to be quantitatively minor. An analysis of the *Report* reveals that, even for the high interactors, a mean of only 17.5 cases per department had been classified as "justified" from the Ombudsman's inception in 1962; the mean was only 5 cases per department for the low interactors. Of course, these few cases may have been considered quite important by the departments, or they may have been sorely irritated by his other investigations that were classified as "not justified," "declined," "discontinued," or "withdrawn." The analysis turns to the Ombudsman's perceived impact upon the civil service.

A matter considered crucial by many is the Ombudsman's impact upon the traditionally sacrosanct institution of ministerial responsibility. Permanent heads were asked:

"What effect has the Ombudsman had on your relationship with your Minister?"

None	Slight Effect	Total
79% (15)	21% (4)	100% (19)

Several replies were quite interesting, and it was often apparent that the subject had never been thought of. Supplementary questions probed into various aspects of the relationship, especially whether they might have become more careful in their advice to their Ministers. One carefully thought-out negative reply was:

—No, I don't worry about the Ombudsman. I give the Minister the various options, but still make a firm recommendation. Of course, I take *his* preferences into account, but the Ombudsman doesn't figure in.

We have mentioned the Ombudsman probably two or three times since 1962, but we have never discussed any specific case.

Another commented that there had been no effect, but that just yesterday in discussing a difficult case his Minister had said, "I wish he'd take this to the Ombudsman and get it off our plates." Some of the respondents were defensive, as if the question suggested that they might let illegitimate factors influence their advice.

In a different vein, a head of an important but not very "political" department said, "My time with my Minister is extremely limited. We wouldn't spend it talking about the Ombudsman." A very "political" colleague agreed that the Ombudsman had had no effect on his relationship with the Minister, but added,

—I can get very annoyed with the Ombudsman, of course. I worry about to what extent he can go into a case and my advice and the Minister's decision. I don't know how far he can go and don't think he does either; he has such wide powers. Even so, I would never think of getting a direction from my Minister; that would be wrong in principle.

Although four of the group felt the Ombudsman had had some effect on their relation with their Minister, only two gave any indication that the effect might be in the direction of weakening the aura of trust and responsibility that is supposed to be the key to that relationship. One of them said, "Once or twice we have been quite annoyed. He evades his jurisdiction and examines the Minister's decision by looking at our advice.[8] We think he has made some mistakes and that it is our duty to fight back."

[8] The Ombudsman does not have jurisdiction over the Ministers' independent decisions. He may, however, examine departments' recommendations to their Ministers.

A radically different effect was mentioned by a colleague who at first denied any impact: "I *have* asked the Minister to put something in writing to put it out of the Ombudsman's reach so he couldn't investigate it. Right now I can't think of an example, but it has happened once or twice."

Only one mentioned using this as a ploy to gain immunity from the Ombudsman. More of them specifically said that no such effect·had resulted. Finally, a highly respected officer mentioned an interesting possibility that was not expressed by any of the others:

> —What worries me is the right of the Ombudsman to examine the department's advice to a Minister. This doesn't worry me because of the possibility of exposing departmental machinations, but because sometimes Ministers' decisions are made *against* departmental advice. I think it would be damaging to democracy if the public were to know (say, in the case of a tragedy) that in order to cut costs the Minister made a technical decision against the advice of his experts in the field.

The following item requested:

"What effect has the Ombudsman had on your department's policies?"

Some	None	Total
32% (6)	68% (13)	100% (19)

Although almost one-third agreed that the Ombudsman had had an effect upon their department's policies, in almost every case that agreement was halting. For example, one replied:

> —None; the cases he has taken up have been predominantly sort of personal cases. No. . . . There *was* one thing that could be called policy that we changed as a result of his investigation. Another one

may have seemed to have changed. On another we made sure that the ruddy politicians understood the reasons for our policy.

Another permanent head admitted that the Ombudsman had had an effect on "some details, some inconsistencies in minor regulations." He added, "The Ombudsman's inquiries have sharpened us up on a few things; these things he forces us to rethink are minor, but still those small matters are important." From the other point of view, a new permanent head retorted, "No. None whatever. Very definitely not!" A more experienced colleague replied, "No, we have varied our decisions and made exceptions for him, but I don't think he has clean-bowled us yet (but you aren't a cricketer)." Most simply contended that there had been no effect on policy matters.

Another item designed to measure a specific impact was:

"Have any special directives on the Ombudsman gone out in this department?"

No	Yes	Don't Know	Not Asked	Total
36% (7)	32% (6)	16% (3)	16% (3)	100% (19)

Seven replied no, and some of these were defensive about the suggestion that it was possible that something should be so seriously wrong in their department that internal comment should be necessary. One replied tersely, "Quite clearly, no!" A colleague agreed, "No! I deliberately do not use him as a bogyman. I have good people in my department and don't need to scare them." Six respondents (as would be expected, four were high interactors) reported, however, that they had sent memoranda to their staff as a result of the Ombudsman's investigations—memoranda on such matters as recording telephone conversations and speeding the flow of correspondence. One confided, "I did use the Ombudsman to get my people to answer their mail quickly. I told them you must have at least an interim reply to citizens within two weeks because if you don't they may complain to the Ombudsman or the Minister and that will give you *more* work." Three respondents professed not to know and said to ask their staff.

Further attempting to measure the Ombudsman's departmental impact, I asked:

"What effect has the Ombudsman had on your staff?"

None	None, But Aware of Him	Somewhat More Careful	Total
47% (9)	21% (4)	32% (6)	100% (19)

About half maintained that the Ombudsman's existence had made no difference to their staff. Several were quite defensive, as the following examples suggest. "We only work on the merits of the case. We don't work in terms of the Ombudsman." Another agreed and added that "It's only the chap who wants to get the last drop who complains to him." Four permanent heads felt that the Ombudsman made no real difference to their staff but that there was a general awareness of him. They talked of a general consciousness of him and of a psychological awareness.

Six of the officials thought the Ombudsman *had* had an effect such as the following:

> —It would be hard to prove, but the fact that your treatment of a specific case may now be scrutinized by an outsider is bound to have an effect. I'm not talking about a big effect—just being more careful to record other files and telephone calls and generally being more precise and meticulous. Our people don't lose any sleep over him.

One replied that he thought the Ombudsman had been useful in "keeping my bureaucrats in line," but the following balanced view is more representative: "He has probably had the effect of making some of the staff more careful about making decisions, especially people with technical training who were promoted to administrative positions. But on the rest of the staff he has made little difference."

It is important to note that none answered this question in terms of the Ombudsman having the stifling effect of making the staff cling more cautiously to established rules and procedures. Nor were increased paperwork and delay mentioned, although the administrative burden of replying to the Ombudsman was commented upon a few times in answering other questions.

The final departmental impact question was, "What effect has the Ombudsman had on your relationships with the public?" Seventy-five percent (14) did not perceive any effect from the Ombudsman. The following statement would probably be subscribed to by the majority: "We figure that we have at least four million face-to-face contacts with the public each year. The Ombudsman would be brought into an infinitesimally small number of them." The five who perceived that the Ombudsman had an effect upon their relationships with the public were all high interactors, and all saw the Ombudsman as *helpful* to public relations. One dissenter exalted, "He puts us in clear so often and tells our toughest customers to stop grizzling that I wouldn't stop people from complaining if I could." Echoing a similar sentiment, a colleague speculated, "This is pure guesswork, but the Ombudsman has good press coverage and, since most of our complaints are not upheld, this probably helps our image." It seems highly significant that none of the respondents expressed the view that the existence of the Ombudsman had acted as a magnet to draw out potential complainants and increase bothersome work.

In addition to measuring the Ombudsman's impact upon their own department, the following question was posed: "Aside from your own department, what do you feel has been the overall impact of the Ombudsman on the public service?" Five of the respondents claimed to have no knowledge about what went on in other departments—particularly with regard to something as esoteric as the Ombudsman. A representative comment from those is, "I don't know that I've heard anyone else mention him; he just causes letter-work." Only one asserted that he had no effect, and it is significant to observe that only one indicated that he felt that the Ombudsman had made some civil servants overly cautious. The remainder thought they perceived—albeit dimly—some positive consequences. Four thought, in the words of one, that his effect has been "to show that he was not needed. He does cause us a lost of work; but I suppose he may be useful for some other departments." The largest single number, eight, suggested some effect on decision making. One commented, "It's a good experiment; he keeps the departments on their toes and counters the tendency toward arbitrary decisions which may adversely affect citizens. The public servant always has the notion that he is there."

Evaluation of the Ombudsman's Jurisdiction

The data in Table 9-1 record the responses of the permanent heads to four attitude statements on the Ombudsman's jurisdiction.[9] The first was stated rather boldly, and it appeared that most of them felt that the Ombudsman's truncated jurisdiction did not prevent him

[9] The respondents were asked to rank each statement on a continuous scale from 1 (indicating strongly agree) to 6 (indicating strongly disagree). There was no middle or neutral category on the scale in order to allow the answers to be dichotomized, but in computing *mean* scores 3.5 would be the theoretical midpoint. Means above that point indicate disagreement, and those below indicate agreement of some extent or other.

from doing "a lot more good." It might be hypothesized that civil servants would resent the apparent discrimination the Ombudsman's Act prescribed in which their advice to the Minister but not his decisions could be investigated. There was little agreement, however, that the Ombudsman should be given the additional jurisdiction. It seems that their perception of the proper constitutional roles outweighed thoughts of personal advantage. Not a single respondent agreed that it would be desirable to filter complaints through Members of Parliament, and the rate of disagreement was the strongest of the four questions. Finally, there was disagreement that, like the British Ombudsman, theirs should be stripped of a large part of his powers by removing discretionary decisions from his jurisdiction. This seems to be an important indicator of his acceptance in the system.

Thus, the permanent heads were unwilling to accede to any of the proposed alterations of the Ombudsman's jurisdiction. What is most apparent from the table is that in each case the high interactors disagreed more strongly than the low group. Their consistency in opposing not only expansions but also contractions—in spite of their greater experience—is striking and indicative of positive affect for the Ombudsman.

These statements were interspersed among several others on different subjects. They were printed on small cards and were handed to the respondents with the following introduction: "Now here are some statements that various people have made about government and politics in general. Would you please read each statement and place it on this agree-disagree scale where it belongs according to how much you agree or disagree with it." When he finished, the interviewer placed them in the properly marked pocket of an envelope for later recording and reshuffling. The procedure followed was similar to that described in Franklin B. Kilpatrick, Milton C. Cummings, Jr., and M. Kent Jennings, *Source Book of a Study of Occupational Values and the Image of the Federal Service* (Washington, D.C.: Brookings Institution, 1964). See Chapter 2.

THE BUREAUCRATS

TABLE 9-1
Department Heads' Attitudes on Ombudsman's Jurisdiction (N = 19)

Statement	Mean for Interactors High	Mean for Interactors Low
1. "Many complaints to the Ombudsman are rejected on technical grounds; he could do a lot more good if he had wider powers."	5.1	4.1
2. "The Ombudsman should be able to investigate the actions of Ministers as well as civil servants' recommendations to them."	5.7	4.3
3. "It would be better if the British system of filtering complaints to the Ombudsman through Members of Parliament were adopted in New Zealand."[a]	5.7	5.1
4. "The Ombudsman's powers should be reduced as in Britain where he only has jurisdiction over maladministration, not discretionary decisions."	4.3	4.1

Key:
  Agree strongly = 1
  Midpoint = 3.5
  Disagree strongly = 6

[a] Two "Don't know" responses to this statement are excluded from the analysis.

General Affect for the Ombudsman

Table 9-2 contains the responses to seven statements designed to probe the parameters of department heads' attitudes toward the Ombudsman. Disagreement with the first, which advocated Parliament's keeping a closer watch on the Ombudsman, was quite strong for the entire group. That high rate of disagreement as well as the one for the next item, which accused the Ombudsman of empire building, at least indicated that the department

TABLE 9-2
Department Heads' Mean Responses to Ombudsman
Attitude Statements (N = 19)

	Mean for Interactors	
Statement	High	Low
1. "Parliament should supervise more closely the work of its Parliamentary Commissioner."[a]	5.0	4.9
2. "The Ombudsman himself is an empire builder who is trying to improve his position by getting his name before the people in press releases and speeches."[a]	5.0	5.0
3. "A high percent of those who go to the Ombudsman are quarrelsome people with no real complaint."	4.0	4.1
4. "The Ombudsman is basically a foreign institution that does not fit into New Zealand's traditions."	5.3	5.1
5. "Though the name was borrowed from Scandinavia, New Zealand's Ombudsman is basically a native product."	4.8	2.9
6. "Though the parties differ somewhat on the ideal limits of the Ombudsman's jurisdiction, the institution is not a party matter."	2.2	1.7
7. "Knowledge of the presence of the Ombudsman acts as a sort of 'conscience' over the actions of the civil service."	3.2	2.8

Key:
Agree strongly = 1
Midpoint = 3.5
Disagree strongly = 6

[a] One "Don't know" response to these statements is excluded from the analysis.

heads did not perceive the Ombudsman to be a dangerous intruder in their midst. In spite of occasional thrusts from civil servants about repetitious work caused by the Ombudsman, there was disagreement with the description of the Ombudsman's complainants as "quarrelsome people with no real complaint."

The strongest rate of disagreement came in response to the fourth item, that the Ombudsman was too foreign for New Zealand. Nevertheless, it is clear from the mean for item five that department heads believed the Ombudsman was transferred from Scandinavia and was not "basically a native product." The means for this statement reflect by far the greatest split between high and low interactors. Probably viewing the Ombudsman as a "foreigner" was a way of displacing frustrations created by their frequent interaction. It also seems surprising that the permanent heads would so strongly refuse to identify the Ombudsman as a partisan matter. The fact that they do not may mean that they act as if it is a permanent institution that must be reckoned with rather than an ephemeral one. (The National Party, which instituted the Ombudsman, had at the time of interviewing held power continually since then.) Nonetheless, they only slightly agreed that the Ombudsman acted as their conscience. Taking into account the defensiveness reported in responses to earlier questions, an even stronger response had been expected. Considering item five as somewhat of an exception, the table offers striking evidence of the attitudinal agreement between the high and low interactors. The mean deviation between the two groups on all seven statements is only .4 of a scale point.

The department heads' ordering of the Ombudsman attitude statements listed in Tables 9-1 and 9-2 also can be usefully examined in another fashion. It is possible to analyze all eleven statements in the two tables on an internal basis, using measures of dispersion. The eleven statements were designed to reveal a coherent set of attitudes about the Ombudsman, and they are here interpreted as a pro-Ombudsman index.[10] Each department head's answers on the eleven items were simply totaled without weighting; the mean was found,[11] and that number became his index score.

Thus, in order to score most favorably on the index (1 would be the most pro-Ombudsman score possible and 6 the most anti-Ombudsman), the respondent would have to consistently and strongly favor the extension of the Ombudsman's jurisdiction, oppose its limitation, oppose Parliament's closer supervision, defend the Ombudsman's attraction of publicity, underscore his domesticity, defend the genuineness of the complainants' grievances, emphasize the Ombudsman's independence of party politics, view him as a conscience over the bureaucracy, and endorse his success in becoming integrated into New Zealand politics.

The requirements of the above list are so demanding that we would not expect even extreme advocates of the Ombudsman to place each statement in the most pro-Ombudsman position; but, in the result, there was one perfect score. Likewise, it would be surprising if even the Ombudsman's most adamant opponent were strongly opposed to him on every statement; hence, at the other end of the range, the most anti-Ombudsman score was only 4—two full scale points below the maximum. The mean pro-Ombudsman index score for the permanent heads was 2.9. This relatively favorable score confirms the earlier pattern of responses on individual questions. Only three permanent heads—all of whom were high interactors—had scores over 3.5, so that they would be counted as anti-Ombudsman.

[10] The statements were arbitrarily determined to elicit basic orientations about the Ombudsman, and it is contended that they have considerable "face" validity. They were not scaled in the sense of a technique such as Guttman scaling.

[11] The scores of the negatively stated items three and four of Table 9-1 and one through four in Table 9-2 simply were inverted.

There are differences between the index scores (3.1 and 2.6, respectively) of the high and low interactors; the difference seems to be a real one, although it is not possible to denote statistical significance to it. This finding is supported by the following correlation: First, the nineteen departments were ranked from highest to lowest in terms of actual interaction with the Ombudsman. Then this rank was compared with the permanent head's score on the pro-Ombudsman index. For comparison purposes, rankings on the index scores were from most anti-Ombudsman to most pro-Ombudsman. Using Spearman's rho, the coefficient of rank correlation was .4.[12] Thus, there is a positive relationship that appears to be moderately strong between interaction and decreased affect for the Ombudsman. Of course, these data do not prove causation, but they—along with the other results and impressions—lead in that direction. Certainly we have a stronger justification for this assumption than that usually assumed in the popular view, "Propinquity breeds contempt."

Conclusions

This investigation of the qualitative relationship between New Zealand's bureaucrats and the Ombudsman has revealed that department heads generally share positively affective orientations toward the Ombudsman. The investigation has been a particularly interesting one, because its context includes shared norms but ambiguous authority. To the extent that we have measured the department heads' social distance from the Ombudsman, it is at least clear that he is not considered a pariah. Few felt that the Ombudsman had had any appreciable—much less a deleterious—effect upon the public service. While it is

[12] The range for this statistic is from -1 to $+1$ (perfect negative correlation to perfect positive correlation). Zero indicates no association. The data do not satisfy the assumptions for tests of statistical significance.

evident that there was no belief that the transfer of the Ombudsman had been a particular boon to the departments, it is highly significant that not one believed that it had been a great mistake.[13] Clearly, the permanent heads were not preoccupied by the Ombudsman. There was, for example, no enthusiasm for either extending or curtailing his jurisdiction. Nonetheless, it developed that many of them were "Ombudsman-conscious" when the need arose: the results of the pro-Ombudsman index showed that they harbored generally favorable attitudes toward the institution.

Affect for the Ombudsman tended to *decrease* as interaction with him *increased*. The decrease was, however, only relative; it must be recalled that only three of the nineteen scores extended into the anti-Ombudsman range. Considering the total characteristics of the permanent heads' perceptual relationships with the Ombudsman, they would be best described as respectful and responsive, if not enthusiastic and extensive. Thus, the Ombudsman may use his political skills to build upon this authority base.*

[13] The findings reported here appear not to be incongruent in significant respects to those reported in Kent M. Weeks, "Public Servants in the New Zealand Ombudsman System," *Public Administration Review* 29 (November/December 1969), 633–38. This article primarily was based upon mailed questionnaires sent out while the present research was under way.

* This chapter is revised from "Affect and Interaction in an Ambiguous Authority Relationship: New Zealand's Bureaucrats and the Ombudsman," *The Journal of Comparative Administration* 4 (May 1972), pp. 35–58, by permission of the publisher, Sage Publications, Inc.

CHAPTER TEN

Honorable Members and the Ombudsman

SWEDEN'S *Justitieombudsman* was created as Parliament's rival to the King's Ombudsman, and the importance of the institution's legislative linkages often has been emphasized. For example, the *Encyclopaedia Britannica* defines an ombudsman as "a legislative commissioner for investigating citizens' complaints of bureaucratic abuse."[1] Similarly, Donald C. Rowat has asserted that "the Ombudsman is an independent and nonpartisan officer of the legislature, provided for in the constitution or by law, who supervises the administration."[2] During New Zealand's debate on whether or not to adopt an ombudsman, the office's potential to restore to Parliament more effective control over Ministers' actions was extolled.[3] But it was decided not to make this new ombudsman responsible to a particular parliamentary committee; he would file his reports with Parliament as a whole. This was a departure from tradition, for all of the Scandinavian officials were linked to the legislature through a specific committee of Parliament. Nevertheless, this first Anglo-Saxon ombudsman definitely was conceived of as a Parliamentary official. This status was confirmed by his legal title; he was dubbed the Parliamentary Commissioner (Ombudsman).

[1] Stanley V. Anderson, "Ombudsman," *Encyclopaedia Britannica, Micropaedia*, 1974, Vol. 7, 530.
[2] Preface to Second Edition, in Rowat, ed., *The Ombudsman: Citizen's Defender*, rev. ed. (Toronto: University of Toronto Press, 1968), p. xxiv.
[3] See, for instance, *New Zealand Parliament, Parliamentary Debates*, CCCXXX (26 July 1962), 1071–75.

An investigation of Parliament's attitude toward this new institution was important for several reasons. Not the least of them was the possibility that the Members of Parliament might come to perceive the Ombudsman as a threat to the traditionally close relations with their constituents. This possibility did not become an important issue during the New Zealand Ombudsman's adoption, but it has elsewhere. About five years after the New Zealand appointment, Britain created a truncated version of the institution in which complaints to their Parliamentary Commissioner for Administration were required to be filtered through Members of Parliament. Furthermore, the most often cited objection of American legislators to an ombudsman was the fear that this new grievance handler would replace them in the affections of their voters.

Thus, the possibility existed that M.P.s could view the Ombudsman as a rival. Whether or not they did was crucial to his institutionalization, for the Ombudsman was entirely Parliament's creature. He was dependent upon it for operating funds, for projected extensions of jurisdiction, for referrals of complaints, and for prestige. This chapter measures parliamentary-Ombudsman relations through personal interviews with each of the Members. The interviews were usually fifty to sixty minutes long, but they often included lunch or tea and lasted two hours or more. Below are reported the responses of the twenty-six National Party ordinary Members and those of the thirty-six Labor Party Members.[4] Separate interviews

[4] In order to make comparisons by party, the interview with the single Social Credit Party Member has been excluded from this analysis.

The major work on the New Zealand Parliament is Robert N. Kelson, *The Private Member of Parliament and the Formation of Public Policy: A New Zealand Case Study* (Toronto: University of Toronto Press, 1964); see also K. J. Scott, *The New Zealand Constitution* (Oxford: Clarendon Press, 1962); Austin Mitchell, *Government by Party* (Wellington: Whitcombe and Tombs, 1966); and Alan Robinson, *Notes on New Zealand Politics* (Wellington: School of Political Science and Public Administration, Victoria University, 1970).

with the Ministers of the Crown are reported in the following chapter.

Putting the Ombudsman in Context

In an attempt to determine to what extent the Ombudsman had come to be perceived by the ordinary Member of Parliament as an important part of the grievance machinery, the first substantive question inquired:

> I would first like to explore the New Zealander's relationship to the government by discussing grievance procedures. Of course, a lot depends on the individual case, but all things being equal, generally how would you evaluate the possible agencies open to the citizen with a complaint against the government? First, what do you think is the most effective action the citizen can take?

As a deliberate strategic maneuver, no clue had been given that the interviewer was interested in the Ombudsman. Four-fifths of the respondents viewed themselves as the preeminent appeals agent (recall that a similar proportion of the permanent heads regarded *themselves* as the best appeals agent). Eleven percent of both parties thought of the government departments as occupying this position, and this choice exhausted the range of candidates offered by Labor. *Not one Labor Member nominated the Ombudsman, whereas four National ones did.* Quite surprisingly, no one mentioned Ministers or the courts as possibilities.

Less than two-fifths mentioned a second-best appeals action; and of those just over half, who had not previously done so, nominated Members of Parliament. Another 30 percent mentioned the departments, and three respondents now mentioned Ministers. The Ombudsman was not volunteered by anyone as a second-choice appeals agent, nor was he proposed by any of the approximately

10 percent of the entire group who offered a third choice. On the basis of these results it should be clear that the Ombudsman had not yet assumed such a status as an appeals agent that he was automatically thought of when the subject of citizens' grievances came to parliamentarians' minds.

These findings are not surprising, for New Zealand Members of Parliament long have been noted as highly oriented toward constituency services. Lord Bryce even described the Member as the "slave of his constituents."[5] The responses to the question "Do you have a set time in your electorate to interview constituents?" confirmed these general impressions. About half of each party reported that they made a special effort to meet with citizens on a regular, weekly basis—usually on Monday, a day when Parliament does not sit—in what are called surgeries in Britain. There is no such term in general use in New Zealand, but "surgery" is sometimes used. An additional one-sixth reported that they held surgeries irregularly but they regularly traveled in their district and solicited complaints. Somewhat more National than Labor Members reported such trips; this is due to the fact that National has more Members in territorially large rural constituencies. The pattern is that they advertise in a local newspaper that they will receive people in one or two towns on a Saturday or Monday and then cover other towns on following weeks.

A further one-seventh of the respondents, primarily older Members, said they were so well known in their district that constituents always came directly to them, so it was unnecessary to search for complaints. Eight percent, principally those from small, urban Labor constituencies, said they preferred to collect letters and telephone messages during the week and then visit the

[5] James Bryce, *Modern Democracies* (New York: Macmillan, 1924), Vol. 2, p. 319. See also Kelson, *The Private Member*, Chapter 2.

complainants on the week-end. This, they claimed, gave them the opportunity to make direct observations about such matters as living conditions, saved them from possible difficulties in getting rid of the complainant, and was a political plus because complainants and their neighbors were impressed to see their M.P. on the job helping people. Only one-tenth of the Members reported they had abandoned the practice of surgeries, either because they were unworkable or because too many people came with unimportant problems. These were, again, mainly older M.P.s; and even they were not necessarily unconcerned with citizens' grievances. Only two M.P.s, both elderly ones, seemed really disinterested in the problems of constituents.

The responses to the question "About how many constituents bring grievances to you each week?" indicate how busy M.P.s are kept with such matters. A total of one-fifth of the Members reported receiving "only a few" or 0–5 grievances per week, but the two political parties are not equally involved. National's Members were more than four times more likely than Labor's to report such a small number of citizen approaches. Somewhat over half of the parliamentarians estimated that they processed 6–20 grievances each week, and about one-fifth reported receiving more than that or an imprecise "many."

Having established that Members are deeply involved in grievance handling, let us turn to the next matter inquired about: the most usual kinds of citizen grievances they received. An analysis of the matters that they volunteered as "grievances" indicates that Members do not sharply differentiate them from other types of citizen approaches. Included as grievances was a broad gamut of types of representations including requests for information and referral, for preferment, for small favors, and for policy advice. When those citizen approaches that did appear to be complaints against government actions were

TABLE 10-1
Subjects of the Three Most Usual Grievances Brought to M.P.s (percents)[a]

Ranking	Housing: Housing Corporation Loans & Capitalization of Family Benefits	Housing: State House Allocation & Maintenance	Social Welfare: Pensions & Superannuation	Social Welfare: Emergency Benefits, Widows, Deserted Wife, etc.	Import Licensing and Other Commercial Matters	Education Problems	Immigration Problems	Land Problems	Other	Total
Most Usual	18	34	10	13	10	3	—	11	12	100
Second Most Usual	16	16	26	26	7	2	2	—	7	100
Third Most Usual	3	18	11	15	11	4	8	—	31	100

[a] N = 62.

separated from the others, their subject-matter formed the pattern revealed in Table 10-1.

For the entire group, social welfare complaints clearly predominate. Adding together the table's first four columns, three-quarters of the Members report that such welfare matters as housing and social welfare are their most usual types of grievances. In keeping with the types of constituencies of the two political parties, Labor's Members were more likely to mention these problems than were National's. To learn that one-third of their representatives list the rather pedestrian matters of State House allocation and maintenance as the problems most often brought to them may come as a surprise to many New Zealanders. These data should establish that Members handle a great many complaints that are similar in character to those routed to the Ombudsman, but it is not possible to come to precise conclusions about the extent to which the two institutions duplicate each others' functions. An essential barrier to such a comparison is that in reporting citizen approaches to the interviewer there was no consensus among Members as to when a particular matter was a genuine grievance that would be similar to a typical complaint received by the Ombudsman or when it was only a misunderstanding or other problem with a government agency.

Thus far, we have seen that much of the day-to-day work of New Zealand Members revolves around helping constituents; we shall continue that line of investigation and also inquire into the extent of personal commitment to such work. Some indications can be gleaned from the response to the following statement: "As one of the effects of modern government we have to expect that not every grievance can be remedied." Two-thirds of the Members, very evenly divided between the parties, overcame the response-set bias toward agreement and disagreed. Furthermore, 94 percent (excluding "Don't know" responses) agreed with the following statement:

"New Zealand Members of Parliament function as 'grievance men' to a greater extent than do British M.P.s" A clear majority *strongly* concurred with that statement.

The following question probed Members' prescriptive attitudes on grievances: "All in all, do you think the New Zealand citizen is well protected by the existing procedures or do you think some new ones are needed?" Since it was felt that the four alterations that had been mooted in the 1960 election campaign often would be suggested, the possibilities of a written constitution, a bill of rights, a second chamber of Parliament, and an administrative court were written into the questionnaire for convenience in coding. Not one of the M.P.s, however, suggested any of those improvements! Most surprisingly, over one-quarter of the entire sample and nearly four-fifths of the National Members felt that the citizen was already *overly* protected, at least in some respects, or that caution was needed to avoid placing him in a further quantity of "cotton wool," as was often said. About half simply indicated that citizens were well enough catered to and that no new measures were desired; only 15 percent suggested a specific improvement. Of those who did, local government, bureaucracy and legislation, and administrative tribunals were criticized—but usually only mildly.

Nevertheless, most respondents to the question "Did you (or would you have) vote(d) for or against the Ombudsman in 1962? Why?" had a favorable recollection of the Ombudsman proposal. But party differences were important: only Labor Members admitted to having been opposed to the Ombudsman (over one-third recalled that they were); and only they claimed to have forgotten their opinion on the matter. Not surprisingly, National Members found it impossible to recall any opposition they may have felt at the time. The most usual reasons given for favoring the Ombudsman were that he was needed to deal with the problem of "bureaucracy" and that he could be an aid for M.P.s. This general satisfaction with

New Zealand's grievance procedures and reported favorable image of the Ombudsman—except among a segment of the Labor Party—at the time he was being proposed helps to put in perspective the data presented in the following sections.

Psychosocial Distance from the Ombudsman

The same questions or ones very similar to those that probed into the bureaucrats' emotional involvement with the Ombudsman were used to measure this aspect of the M.P.'s relationship with the institution. The first inquired, "In your day-to-day work how often would you say you have occasion to think of the Ombudsman?" Over two-fifths of the Members maintained that they *never* thought of him. A representative reply was that of the following National Member: "I don't think of him at all; he's the servant of the citizen, not the M.P." Another laughed at the question and said, "Why, no more than the average citizen. When I'm interviewing a constituent with a problem, the thought doesn't flash through my mind, 'Is this one for the Ombudsman?'" Additionally, nearly half reported that their thoughts of him were so fleeting that they could best be described as coming either only very seldom or not often. One experienced Labor M.P. replied, "The only time I'd ever think of the Ombudsman would be if a citizen persisted and persisted; then I might consider sending him to the Ombudsman to pacify him." Seven percent mentioned that they thought of him only when his annual *Report* was presented to Parliament. The same proportion claimed to think of the Ombudsman quite often. The political parties' responses to this question were very close together, although Labor's answers were clustered closer to the "never" end of the scale than were those of National.

The next question asked of the parliamentarians: "How many of the Ombudsman's annual *Reports* have you read?" Supplementary questions probed their general familiarity with the *Reports*. Forty-six percent—rather evenly distributed between the parties—freely admitted that they did not usually look at or generally paid little attention to the *Reports*. Several pointed to a tall and ever-growing stack of reports of government departments on the floor or on a table and commented that it was comforting to get one that didn't *have* to be read as a part of the never-ending search for political ammunition. About one-third of the Members reported that they usually browsed through, skimmed, or glanced at the Ombudsman's account of his activities. And about one-tenth of the Labor Members and nearly a quarter of the National Members claimed to be avid fans of the reports. It is my opinion that these M.P.s tended to be among the most dynamic of both parties. One National respondent said: "I read them all carefully. It's interesting to see if you have similar complaints, and he gives you a pattern to go by." A colleague reported that he put it in his stack of bed reading: "That is, it's interesting; I read it for pleasure, not as part of my work." Nevertheless, based upon Members' familiarity with the Ombudsman's major means of publicity, his annual *Report*, it cannot be said that most are deeply involved in his fortunes.

Continuing with the subject of the Ombudsman's *Report*, the question was asked, "Do any of the cases he has handled stand out as particularly significant?" Only two Labor and three National Members had sufficient interest in any particular case to mention one specifically, and these were ones that had arisen in their electorates.

In an attempt to determine the degree of perceived intimacy between the Member and the Ombudsman, the following question inquired: "Do you know Sir Guy Powles personally? If yes, did you know him prior to 1962?" Only eight Members from each party reported any degree of personal relationship with the Ombudsman. A total of eight said they knew Sir Guy before he became Ombudsman, and three claimed to have come to know him since that time. Five others mentioned that they had met him either socially or professionally, but the other 70 percent who responded did not report feeling any degree of personal relationship with him.

In the context of attempting to determine Members' psychical involvement with the Ombudsman it is interesting to note how familiarly they were able to pronounce this foreign term. Eighty percent could get it out in a reasonably intelligible fashion and without strain. Eight Labor M.P.s and four of National's could not, however; they either quite innocently mistook the word's structure—producing variants such as "Omsman" or "Omnibusman"—or were unable, no matter how much they tried, to approximate an intelligible rendition of the term. Since none of them had noticeable speech impediments, this would seem to indicate either a general difficulty with foreign terms or, more probably, a lack of familiarity with the Ombudsman.

Interaction with the Ombudsman

When the M.P.s were describing their role as grievance agents, they were asked the following open-ended question: "Again it depends upon the case, but when you get a complaint from a citizen, which of your possible actions do you consider to be most effective?" Supplementaries probed for a second and a third choice. Members reported that they most often took problems brought to them to the local office of the government department involved (47 percent), or to the main office in Wellington (19 percent), or to the Minister of that department (32 percent). Not surprisingly, National Members were more likely (42 percent) than Labor's (25 percent) to see the Minister as their best alternative.[6] Only one M.P., from

[6] Nevertheless, Labor Members do not necessarily feel alientated from Ministers, as the fact that 50 percent of them disagreed with the following statement indicates: "Regardless of which party is in power,

the National Party, mentioned the Ombudsman as his first choice.

The Minister (58 percent) and then the department's head office (27 percent) were overwhelmingly perceived as the Member's second most effective avenues. While the asking of a parliamentary question and encouraging a parliamentary petition were mentioned as a second choice by about one-tenth of the group, the Ombudsman was not listed as a second choice by anyone. The Minister and parliamentary questions accounted for 75 percent of the specifications for third most effective action, and at this point two Labor and one National Member mentioned the Ombudsman. The fact that the Ombudsman does not ordinarily come to the minds of M.P.s when they are devising strategy for dealing with a particular complaint is a preliminary indication of their perception of him as an interaction partner.

The replies to the following question furnish some clues as to why the Ombudsman might not be used more often. M.P.s were asked, "What can [the Ombudsman] do that you can't do?" Further probes attempted to determine the full extent of their knowledge of his powers. One-fifth of the total respondents and about one-third of the Labor Members professed to think that the Ombudsman could do nothing that the Member of Parliament could not do. One of the latter concluded: "If I can't get something for a constituent, I'm damn sure the Ombudsman can't." Another 15 percent suggested that the Ombudsman's high status gave him an important degree of influence, but they did not know of anything he could do that they could not. Almost half of the Labor respondents fell in the two above categories. An additional 15

Opposition Members have a more difficult time in remedying a grievance than Government Members." All of the ordinary Members, party notwithstanding, were closely split on this question, and 52 percent of the entire group disagreed with it.

percent of the M.P.s professed not to know the answer to the question.

Only 44 percent of the total mentioned the salient power differential: the Ombudsman's right of access to departmental files.[7] Some M.P.s saw this as crucial. For example, one Labor respondent said, "I probably couldn't get a file; no Minister has ever given me a departmental file to study, but once the staff let me look at one in his presence." Again Labor Members were less likely to mention this distinction than National's. Two National Members erroneously felt that he had the power to adjudicate and make binding decisions. The extent of this lack of knowledge of the Ombudsman's powers helps to explain why M.P.s seldom think of him as someone with whom they might interact.

The first test of actual interaction with the Ombudsman came when the M.P.s were discussing the effectiveness of the various grievance channels open to them. With regard to the option of recommending that the citizen take the matter to the Ombudsman, they were asked, "Have you ever advised anyone to see the Ombudsman?" And then, "How many times have you given this advice and with what results?" The preponderance of the Members claimed to have given such advice at least once. Over one-third of the entire group (relatively evenly distributed between the parties) said, however, they never had advised a citizen to see the Ombudsman. One new M.P. replied, "I've never mentioned his name or heard anyone else mention it to me." A more experienced colleague said, "I never do, but if they want to try the Ombudsman, I leave it to them. By then I have investigated their case and have seen that it is impossible. Why bother him?" About one-third of the Labor respondents who said they

---

[7] It is not necessarily true that all of the others were unaware of this aspect of the Ombudsman's powers, for a few openly denigrated this distinction. It appears that some knew that he could see the files, but felt that this made no substantive difference and answered "nothing."

never had advised anyone to see the Ombudsman also took the opportunity to criticize some aspect of the Ombudsman as an institution.

But a total of 44 percent of the M.P.s, a number very nearly equally divided between the parties, reported having advised from one to five constituents to contact the Ombudsman. Just less than one-fifth, again almost equally divided on party lines, said they had suggested him to six or more troubled complainants. Almost a quarter recalled that at least one constituent had reported his interaction with the Ombudsman, and of those about half said they had been helped while the others had not. The remainder of those who had encouraged someone to try the Ombudsman said that their constituents had not reported back to them.

As a further and, of course, much more intimate measure of interaction with the Ombudsman, all of the parliamentarians were asked: "Have you ever directly referred a case to him?" Only eight recalled having done so. One claimed "It's not that kind of an office." Another felt that this was a personal decision for the citizen and concluded obscurely, "I don't get any questions like that; mine is a working-class district." Five of Labor's and only one of National's Members had referred one case, and two Labor M.P.s recalled directly referring two cases to him; perhaps this disparity is due to Labor Members feeling less confidence in the actions of Ministers. One M.P. was offended by what he saw as the question's implication: "No! I have never supported a citizen's claim. You should not put political pressure on the Ombudsman."

In an attempt to measure another aspect of the Members' interactions in the Ombudsman's system, they were asked, "Have any constituents come to you after failing to get help from the Ombudsman?" Only 36 percent indicated that this had happened to them, and none could recall more than three such occurrences. The feelings of many were summed up by one who said, "People realize that the Ombudsman is the end of the road." Of those who had experienced such contacts, 70 percent—about equally divided between the parties—said they had been unable to help these constituents, who often were called "no hopers." Thirty-eight percent of the Labor respondents who reported this type of citizen appeal, however, claimed to have been able to help at least one constituent who had failed with the Ombudsman; a note of superiority often could be detected in their replies. Only one National M.P. reportedly was able to help someone who had been unsuccessful with the Ombudsman. The replies indicate that the M.P.s have not been often reminded of the existence of the Ombudsman through having to reexamine the problems of people who previously have complained to him.

The Ombudsman's Impact upon Political Life

In beginning an attempt to measure the Members' assessments of the Ombudsman's effect upon New Zealand political life, they were asked two questions about his impact upon their own jobs. The first inquired, "Do you think that he has had an effect on the role of the M.P.?" Nearly three-quarters felt that he had *no* effect on their role. The following reply of one National Member is representative of a large body of opinion in both parties: "Not in my electorate, because the pattern there is to go to the M.P. first. Some might have then gone over my head. But if this has happened it might be one case over the years." National's M.P.s were considerably more sanguine about his effects than were Labor's. Three times as many National (35 percent) as Labor (11 percent) respondents volunteered their perception that the Ombudsman had improved the position of the M.P. either through acting as a "backstop" for him, through slightly relieving his workload of citizen's grievances, or through reducing the volume of petitions to Parliament. One Labor M.P.

motioned to a letter in his hand and said that the creation of the Ombudsman took some of the strain of dealing with cranks off him: "I've got this one already labeled 'Nut File' and I may fob her off on the Ombudsman; she has a long history of writing to M.P.s and now she is picking on me because of a 'wonderful' speech I made."[8] It is apparent that Members did not think that the adoption of the Ombudsman had ushered in a new millennium for them. But what is most significant about these responses is that no Member answered that the Ombudsman had *adversely* affected him—an option deliberately left open by the question.

As a supplement to the previous question, the parliamentarians were asked, "Have M.P.s' complaints gone up or down?" Four-fifths felt that the Ombudsman had had *no effect* upon the volume of complaints they received. Labor's Members were 20 percent more of this opinion than were National's, and several of them were quite emphatic about it. Only one Labor Member opined that the workload might have slightly *decreased* with the advent of the Ombudsman, but about one-sixth of National's felt this to be the case. Three even suggested that the creation of the Ombudsman might have slightly *increased* their volume of complaints, since the publicity surrounding his operations had tended to focus popular attention upon the possibility of complaining about government decisions. Answers to both the general question about the Ombudsman's impact upon their role and to

[8] It is noteworthy that the Ombudsman seldom has been a subject of Members' speeches. When asked, "Have you ever mentioned [the Ombudsman] in a campaign speech," 81 percent of the Labor M.P.s replied "not ever," as did 62 percent of National's. One National M.P. commented, "He is accepted for what he is, a person divorced from politics." Another flatly said, "No! There's not a vote in him." In total, only about one-fifth replied that they themselves had either mentioned the Ombudsman in a speech or that a constituent had raised a question about him from the floor. One National M.P. reported, however, that he always cited the Ombudsman in listing the party's accomplishments.

the more specific one about his effect on their workload indicate that from their own perspective, M.P.s do not see the Ombudsman as having occasioned great changes.

Members next were asked for their opinions about the Ombudsman's impact upon the bureaucracy: "Do you think that the Ombudsman has had much effect on the civil service and the departments? What?" Almost half were confident that he had had the effect of making civil servants more careful in considering decisions involving citizens.[9] Nearly three-quarters of the National group felt this was so, but less than one-third of Labor concurred. The analogy of the Ombudsman as a traffic cop often was mentioned. Diverse opinions were expressed: although he conceded that "the Ombudsman might have had some effect on top leaders," one respondent contended "but it probably hasn't filtered down to the bottom." Conversely, another stated, "I have a feeling that he may have affected the lower strata; some of them really throw their weight around, and his existence and their knowledge of it acts as a deterrent."

An additional one-sixth of the respondents, evenly split between the parties, thought the Ombudsman *probably* had made administrators more careful, but they were not sure. It should be noted, however, that over a quarter of the Labor respondents felt—some of them adamantly— that the Ombudsman had had *no effect* on civil servants or departments, while only one Government Member expressed this opinion. The high rate of no opinion answers, 18 percent, is indicative of the fact that most Members had not thought deeply about this subject. One National

[9] It should be stressed that this evaluation took place in a context in which civil servants were highly respected. In responding to the following statement, 82 percent disagreed: "Public servants have got too much power and are exploiting the situation in their own interests." One Labor Member commented: "Our civil service has one serious fault; it's too often right. They were already so careful in their decisions that it's hard to say that he makes them more careful; he has certainly reversed few decisions."

M.P. volunteered that he thought the administrators were pleased that the Ombudsman had vindicated them.

A further question, asked of 44 percent of the parliamentarians, was directed at their understanding of the Ombudsman's impact upon the traditional workings of ministerial responsibility: "What about the constitutional situation? Has the Ombudsman had much effect on such conventions as ministerial responsibility?" All but eight Members felt that he had no effect upon this hallowed institution. Most would have agreed with the Labor M.P. who claimed, "No Minister of the Crown gives a damn for the Ombudsman in terms of his own portfolio." Four felt that he had had some effect in making departments more carefully consider their advice to Ministers, and the other four admitted that they knew nothing about the details of the subject. It is of special interest that *no one believed that the Ombudsman had contravened the doctrine of ministerial responsibility by interposing himself between Minister and permanent head,* a fear that was often expressed by Ombudsman opponents—especially in Britain.

The following question probed for opinion about another dimension of the Ombudsman's relationships—those with the public at large. Members were asked: "What kind of relationship would you say exists between the general public and the Ombudsman?" Many felt, often regretfully, that the Ombudsman was not really very well known; only two-fifths believed that the institution was well accepted. In toto, over half of the respondents estimated that either the public was only vaguely aware of his existence (36 percent) or there was little or no relationship between the public and the Ombudsman (17 percent). One Labor respondent suggested, "People without grievances would think he was a sprinter in the sixth race at Trentham." A colleague said in support, "You could go down on Lambton Quay and ask the first ten people who came along about him and they wouldn't have a clue." Quite clearly, Labor thought of him as less well known than did National; over half of the Government Members described him as well accepted with the man-on-the-street. Even so, 40 percent of their colleagues were willing to express the opinion that the average Kiwi's perception of him was vague at best.

The Ombudsman's Effectiveness, Status, and Jurisdiction

The Members' perceptions of the Ombudsman's performance were probed by the following question: "Strictly from the citizen's point of view of effectiveness in remedying grievances, how does the Ombudsman rate?" The general evaluation of more than three-quarters of the M.P.s was favorable, although just over two-fifths of the Labor respondents either expressed reservations about his effectiveness or felt that he was ineffective. None of the National camp expressed any opinion disloyal to this creature spawned by their party. About one-third of those who evaluated the Ombudsman positively spoke of his effectiveness in superlative terms. For example, an experienced National M.P. said: "I feel perhaps that the citizen doesn't value the worth of the Ombudsman. But we know as Members that we have only to say to a department head, 'I'll have to advise this constituent to spend a quid with the Ombudsman,' and this has a marked effect. He has made a difference in changing the tone of the administration." Another one-sixth of this group volunteered the opinion that the Ombudsman had had the effect of making government departments more careful in decision making. One said, "Yes, I'm sure that he is making them more cautious. That bureaucrat thinks twice, by hell, with the Ombudsman in the background." Others rated the institution as adequate or submitted that the existence of the Ombudsman gave the citizen an extra psychological assurance that someone was watching the bureaucracy.

In an attempt to measure the Ombudsman's perceived

status, Members were asked the following question: "Some people think that all these questions about the Ombudsman are a tempest in a teacup. What are your ideas on his true position or status in the political system? How important is he as compared with some other officials, such as a Supreme Court Justice, the Solicitor-General, an M.P., a Minister, or a department head?" The question was stated in a somewhat peculiar way because in the preliminary interviews it was apparent that some M.P.s quickly tired of talking about the Ombudsman or had no more ideas about him. Several suggested that the interviewer answer all the questions on the Ombudsman for them, since it was clear from the detailed nature of the questions that he knew more about the office than they did. The question's wording was designed to help convince those respondents that the interviewer was aware that the Ombudsman was not New Zealand's most important official. However they finally answered the question, very few Members had a ready answer. Ranking the Ombudsman was a question neither his supporters nor his detractors had previously concerned themselves with. Many thought long and hard before giving a reply that often began and sometimes ended with statements such as "He's in a class by himself"; "He is sort of in a space apart"; "I can't say; that is a difficult one"; "He is unique"; "I haven't thought about that one before; let's see, is he as important as a Minister?" The Ombudsman generally was thought of as a high status office, but Labor's opinion was considerably lower than National's. One-quarter of the respondents ranked him below the M.P. or low in status, and three times more Labor than National Members did so.[10] As was true of the above-reported re-

[10] One National Member answered this question by referring to a subject mentioned by several others, the matter of the Ombudsman's salary (there was some unhappiness over his attempt to have his salary placed at the level of a Supreme Court Judge), and by inserting a partisan thrust: "Parliament in its wisdom has approved a salary equal to

plies of the bureaucrats, the largest single category of respondents (29 percent) could not rank the Ombudsman in order of importance with any other official; they gave him a high but indeterminate ranking.

The largest category of definite opinion expressed (23 percent) was that the Ombudsman was about equal in status to a Supreme Court Judge. The granting of this status was not, however, distributed evenly between the political parties. The National M.P.s were over 40 percent more likely to make this comparison than were their Labor colleagues, but one Labor respondent—who was no friend of the Ombudsman—did accord him this status. He commented: "The Ombudsman is placed on a pedestal and decisions by him are much more respected than say those of a Minister; he is considered as a judicial officer, and the judiciary in New Zealand is very highly regarded." A further 7 percent located the Ombudsman between a magistrate and a Supreme Court Justice. An additional body of opinion (about one-seventh of the respondents) placed him intermediately between the M.P. and either a judge or a Minister of the Crown. Surprisingly, only two individuals regarded him as being closest in status to the Controller and Auditor-General, the office with which he is most often officially compared.

An indirect method of discerning the Members' opinions of the Ombudsman's effectiveness is to ask about the possibility of altering his jurisdiction, and six questions were directed toward this end. The first inquired generally, "Do you think that any changes ought to be made in the jurisdiction and operation of the Ombudsman?" A majority (53 percent) of those asked this question thought

---

that of the Controller and Auditor-General, but frankly he doesn't rank anywhere near him. Potentially he could, but there is not the same need for him because of the high standards of our civil service. It's a good thing their standards are so high, because if Labor gets in power some civil servants will practically run the country. Labor has some very weak front-benchers."

that the jurisdiction should be extended to include local bodies. The remaining Members were roughly divided between those who thought no change was needed and those who had no opinion. Responses to earlier questions have depicted Labor Members as notably less enthusiastic about the Ombudsman than National. Thus, the fact that Labor Members were more strongly in favor of extending the jurisdiction to local bodies than National's (57 percent as compared with 47 percent) may seem surprising. This finding is a consequence of the often expressed Labor view: "If we are going to have an Ombudsman, let's give him something to do."

A further question, "Do you think that if the Labor Party becomes the Government, they would make any changes in the Ombudsman?" was asked of nearly half of the parliamentarians; it later was dropped because Labor's policy to extend the Ombudsman's jurisdiction to include local bodies was formulated during the interviewing. Of those who were asked, only two Labor Members suggested that their party should reevaluate the question of whether or not an Ombudsman was worthwhile. All others opted either to maintain the present jurisdiction or to extend it; none of the National respondents speculated that Labor would eliminate the Ombudsman.

Table 10-2 contains the M.P.s' responses to the four questions on the Ombudsman's jurisdiction, which also were asked of the bureaucrats. First: party differences in the Members' perceptions of the adequacy of the Ombudsman's powers were pronounced. National respondents apparently believed the question implied that "their" Ombudsman was unnecessarily restricted, while Labor's slightly agreed that a wider scope—probably including local bodies—was desirable. Second: the disagreement with a proposed major revision—giving the Ombudsman jurisdiction over Ministers' decisions—was rather strong. As an out-group, Labor's disagreement was

TABLE 10-2
Members' Attitudes on the Ombudsman's Jurisdiction (N = 62)[a]

Statement	Mean for Members Labor	National
1. "Many complaints to the Ombudsman are rejected on technical grounds; he could do a lot more if he had wider powers."	3.3	4.3
2. "The Ombudsman should be able to investigate the actions of Ministers as well as civil servants' recommendations to them."	4.6	5.3
3. "It would be better if the British system of filtering complaints to the Ombudsman through Members of Parliament were adopted in New Zealand."	3.7	5.2
4. "The Ombudsman's powers should be reduced as in Britain where he only has jurisdiction over maladministration, not discretionary decisions."	4.2	4.5

Key:
Agree strongly = 1
Midpoint = 3.5
Disagree strongly = 6

[a] "Don't know" responses are excluded from the analysis.

substantially less strong than National's. Third: if M.P.s had felt threatened by the Ombudsman, they probably would have agreed that complaints should be filtered through them as is done in the United Kingdom. Many Labor Members were not so sure that this was a bad idea, but such a revision was never seriously proposed in New Zealand by Labor or any other group. Fourth: there was little sentiment for removing discretionary decisions from the Ombudsman's purview, and it was not apparent to the interviewer that any of the few who endorsed the proposal had thought about it before seeing the statement.[11]

Affection for the Ombudsman

Table 10-3 contains the M.P.s' responses to the seven Ombudsman attitude statements that also were asked of the bureaucrats, the results of which are reported in the previous chapter. Since it could be hypothesized that Members elected before the Ombudsman took office might be hostile to someone they could regard as a usurper of their functions and that those elected later might tend more to accept him as a "given" part of the job, this factor is tested as the independent variable.

General disagreement with the first item, that Parliament should supervise the Ombudsman more closely, was evident for all of the groups; mean differences between the total pre- and the total post-Ombudsman groups were, however, relatively slight. Party differences were interesting, though; Labor's post-Ombudsman Members were more in favor of leaving the Ombudsman unfettered than were their elders, yet National's pattern was exactly the opposite! Those National Members who were in Parliament at the time of the Ombudsman's creation were very strongly opposed to restricting him, but their newer colleagues were far more inclined to endorse closer control. The explanation for this is not clear, but it may reflect an alteration in recruitment into the National Parliamentary Party after the Ombudsman's appointment. Impressionistic evidence suggests that an increasing number of those recruited were more concerned than

[11] It was often obvious that the respondent had no clear idea about the distinction that administrative lawyers sometimes make between maladministration and discretionary decisions. In those cases the respondent probably interpreted the question as asking whether in some technical sense he wanted the Ombudsman to have less power like the English Ombudsman.

TABLE 10-3
M.P.s' Mean Responses to Ombudsman Attitude Statements

	Elected Pre-Ombudsman			Elected Post-Ombudsman		
Statements	Labor	National	Total	Labor	National	Total
1. "Parliament should supervise more closely the work of its Parliamentary Commissioner."	4.1	5.3	4.5	4.4	4.3	4.4
2. "The Ombudsman himself is an empire builder who is trying to improve his position by getting his name before the people in press releases and speeches."	4.0	5.3	4.5	3.3	5.4	4.5
3. "The Ombudsman is basically a foreign institution that does not fit into New Zealand's traditions."	4.6	5.6	4.9	4.3	5.1	4.7
4. "A high percent of those who go to the Ombudsman are quarrelsome people with no real complaint."	3.2	4.3	3.6	4.3	4.5	4.4
5. "Though the parties differ somewhat on the ideal limits of the Ombudsman's jurisdiction, the institution is not a party matter."	1.9	2.1	2.0	2.6	1.6	2.1
6. "Knowledge of the presence of the Ombudsman acts as a sort of 'conscience' over the actions of the civil service."	3.3	1.7	2.7	2.3	2.7	2.5
7. "Though the name was borrowed from Scandinavia, New Zealand's Ombudsman is basically a native product."	4.5	3.6	4.2	3.4	2.6	3.0
(Mean number responding)	(24)	(14)	(38)	(10)	(12)	(22)

Key: Agree strongly = 1; Midpoint = 3.5; Disagree strongly = 6.

some previous Members had been with restoring the importance of Parliament's role in the political system, and this question may have seemed to express that concern.

Both the M.P.s elected before the Ombudsman was appointed and those elected afterward were generally unwilling to agree with item two's characterization of the Ombudsman as an empire builder. New National Members defended him most staunchly. The mean response of their Labor counterparts, however, was over the line into the agreement category. It may be that Labor's lack of experience with the institution and their lesser degree of understanding about how it operates may have made them less tolerant of what seemed to them to be the techniques of a publicity hound. One of them said, for example, "He seems to spend all of his time making speeches, and he's been out of the country twice that I know of; I wonder when he does any work."

The total mean rates of disagreement for item three, which identified the Ombudsman as foreign and unsuitable for New Zealand, were the highest among the table's items; and the means for both generations of M.P.s were relatively close together. Again, National's defense of the Ombudsman was considerably stronger than Labor's. The final negatively stated item identified the Ombudsman's complainants as cranks rather than as people with legitimate grievances and by implication deprecated the institution. Both parties' Members elected since the Ombudsman's appointment disagreed more intensely than their more experienced colleagues about the seriousness of the Ombudsman's complainants. The older Labor Members agreed somewhat that the Ombudsman got a large share of cranks, but their junior colleagues definitely disagreed.

Of the table's positively stated items, the first (item five), which claimed party agreement on the Ombudsman, gained the greatest degree of assent; the total means for the older and the newer M.P.s were quite close. On an intraparty basis the newer Labor Members were less sure of the Ombudsman's nonpartisan nature than their elders. But the extent of this difference is exaggerated by the very strong intensity of agreement of the latter group. That intensity may reflect the recollection of the older Labor Members that the passage of the Ombudsman Bill occasioned little partisanship, whereas Labor's newer Members probably perceived the question in terms of their willingness to go further than National in extending the Ombudsman's jurisdiction. National's new Members were more sure of the degree of the Ombudsman's nonpartisanness than were their elders. Perhaps older National M.P.s liked to stress their party's identification with this seemingly popular institution and wanted to retain it as "a party matter."

The sixth item, which described the Ombudsman as a "conscience" for the civil service, won agreement from all groups. Those whose agreement was weakest, however, were the pre-Ombudsman Labor Members. Many of them probably felt that agreement would carry with it the implication that the civil service, of which they were the consistent political defender, was in need of a "conscience": this they were unwilling to admit. The pre-Ombudsman National Members, who had used the item's argument for proposing the Ombudsman, were most strongly in agreement that the awareness of the Ombudsman acted as a restraining device on the bureaucrats. Their junior colleagues agreed, but less strongly. Labor's new Members more strongly endorsed the Ombudsman as a restraining influence on the bureaucracy than did the equivalent National group. It is understandable that they should be in closer agreement than the pre-Ombudsman Labor Members, since they had never served under a Labor Government and thus had less reason to defend the civil service, but why they should agree more strongly than post-Ombudsman *National* Members is not apparent.

THE OMBUDSMAN AND HIS PUBLICS

In spite of the general disagreement with item three and the narrow degree of difference between veteran and new legislators as to its branding of the Ombudsman as foreign and unsuitable for New Zealand, many veteran M.P.s of both parties disagreed with statement seven, which identified the Ombudsman as "basically a native product." Probably the willingness of veteran legislators to admit the Ombudsman's "foreignness" was a consequence of their greater familiarity with the actual process by which the institution, and not just the name, was borrowed from Scandinavia. Those elected later were probably reacting to their interpretation of how the institution had evolved in New Zealand. Thus, each party's new Members were at least an entire scale point more strongly convinced of the Ombudsman's indigenous nature than were their respective elders. Consistent and radical party differences also can be seen; Labor clearly perceives of the Ombudsman as more foreign than National.

When the Members' responses to the items in Tables 10-2 and 10-3 were combined to form the pro-Ombudsman index as was done above for the permanent heads, the tabulations revealed that *the mean scale scores of all of the principal subgroups under study were well under the scale's theoretical midpoint of 3.5.* Thus, all of them can be described as pro-Ombudsman. The scores of the four subgroups were narrowly clustered: the pre-Ombudsman National M.P.s were most pro-Ombudsman (2.4), followed by their junior colleagues (2.6), who were followed by Labor's post-Ombudsman M.P.s (2.7), who preceeded their more experienced colleagues (3.2). As an indication of the uniform character of the distribution, the median (2.7) and the mean (2.8) scores for the entire group were almost identical.

On an individual basis, only nine of Parliament's sixty-two ordinary Members had anti-Ombudsman index scores. Only one of that group was a member of the National Party. Seven were Labor Members who were already in Parliament at the time the Ombudsman was adopted; since most of the latter group was near retirement age, one would expect Labor opinions of the Ombudsman to become more favorable over time.

Finally, it should be noted that whether the opinions articulated on the Ombudsman were favorable or not, they seldom were expressed intensely. Qualitative analysis of the interviews reveals that only twelve M.P.s expressed really intense opinions about the Ombudsman. Members making intense statements usually were pro-Ombudsman. *Eight of the twelve were extremely enthusiastic about the institution, and six of the eight were Labor Members.* The two National singers of praise for the Ombudsman were the only ones of their party to display any real emotion on the subject, and Labor monopolized the four intensely unfavorable Ombudsman statements such as, "If we retain this high level of expenditure, I'm damn sure that he has to be made a lot more effective."

Conclusions

Important aspects of Members of Parliament's orientations toward the Ombudsman can be recapitulated briefly. First: Despite the Ombudsman's arrival on the scene, M.P.s thought of themselves and the internal processes of the government agencies as New Zealand's principal mechanisms for processing citizens' administrative complaints, and they continued their involvement—which often was so deep as to be labeled a preoccupation—with grievance handling. Second: Few Members could be accurately described as feeling very concerned in a personal sense with the Ombudsman's fortunes. Third: The rate of interaction—especially when measured in terms of case referrals—between M.P.s and the Ombudsman is low. Fourth: In evaluating the impact of the Ombudsman upon their own roles, the public service, ministerial responsibility, and the general public, Members were generally favorable but most believed the impact to be minimal. Fifth: The Ombudsman's performance as a citizens' grievance agent was rated as effective by most Members. Sixth: As was true of the permanent heads, M.P.s' scores on the pro-Ombudsman index indicated a high level of support for the institution; if few were greatly enamored of the Ombudsman, it is also true that few intensely disliked him.

Because Members of Parliament are potentially, at least, such important actors in the Ombudsman's authority system, one aspect of M.P.s' pro-Ombudsman attitudes merits emphasis: their view of the institution's impact upon the parliamentary role. A principal reason for individual citizens being denied access to Britain's Parliamentary Commissioner for Administration[12] and for the inclusion of a similar provision in Congressman Henry Reuss's proposed administrative Counsel for the American Congress[13] was the fears of both countries' legislators that a true ombudsman might adversely affect their constituency caseload. Such citizen contacts traditionally are viewed by legislators as unparalleled opportunities to build up obligations that can be cashed in at the next election, and it is well known among students of the subject that the above-mentioned fears are the covert (and sometimes overt) factor that has inhibited legislative bodies during the consideration of ombudsman legislation.

The possibility of the Ombudsman usurping the jobs of New Zealand Members was not raised to any significant

[12] A thorough exposition of this theme can be found in Frank Stacey, *The British Ombudsman* (Oxford: Clarendon Press, 1971); see for example p. 45.

[13] For an analysis of the Reuss scheme see Walter Gellhorn, *When Americans Complain: Governmental Grievance Procedures* (Cambridge, Mass.: Harvard University Press, 1966), pp. 87–94.

extent at the time of the institution's creation, and the crucial finding from the interviews is that Members do not perceive of the Ombudsman as a rival. Nearly three-quarters felt he had no effect upon the parliamentary role, and all of those who believed he had some effect mentioned a favorable one. How can the New Zealand M.P.s' lack of antipathy toward what would appear to be a natural rival for their constituents' affections be explained? The simplest interpretation is that they are secure in the performance of their own roles as citizens' grievance men. The small size of the electorates, about 16,000 voters, makes attentive constituency-nursing feasible, and it appears, impressionistically, that New Zealand Members pay more attention to this role than do their counterparts in many other countries. They know that during the Ombudsman's tenure their caseload has not been affected; citizens have continued to bring them so many problems that most M.P.s routinely work at nearly full capacity. In such a situation, the Ombudsman does not prey upon latent insecurities and appear as a threatening specter.

CHAPTER ELEVEN

The Queen's Ministers and the Ombudsman

BECAUSE Ministers of the Crown hold strategic power positions, their opinions of the Ombudsman are of obvious importance. Ministers' acquiescence was required for his continued existence, but their active support was necessary for the institution to take root and grow. Would they regard the Ombudsman as a rival in the performance of their own "grievance man" role? Did they feel that he had interfered with the revered convention of ministerial responsibility? And how did they evaluate his performance as a complaints mechanism? Since the Ombudsman was a National Party creation one would expect the National Ministers' public remarks about the institution to be complimentary, but their private views might differ. To probe those private opinions, interviews similar in nature to those with the M.P.s were conducted with each of the sixteen Ministers of the Crown.[1]

MINISTERS AS GRIEVANCE MEN

The job of Minister in New Zealand is a many-faceted executive role in which time must be divided among various sectors, including Cabinet and its committees, the government departments (the usual load is two or more departments per Minister), Parliament and its debates and committees, the party and its caucus and caucus

[1] Because of his unique position, the Prime Minister was asked a separate list of questions. To present some of his views while preserving his anonymity, a few of his opinions about the Ombudsman are interspersed below among those of other Ministers.

committees, and the electorate and constituents. The triennial election of Parliament requires Ministers to pay almost continual attention to the cultivation of their own constituents. And to them the Minister remains their individual grievance man. The Ministers vary considerably on such matters as the nature of their portfolios and the distance of their districts from Wellington, but they all reported that they allocated a significant amount of time to their local constituents.

One senior Minister, a farmer, said he held office hours in his electorate from 10:00 to 11:00 A.M. each Saturday morning: "My people don't understand that my time is more limited now that I'm a Minister and that they should make fewer demands." Another regretted that he was unable to service his constituents as he would have liked, but he was normally at home from Friday night until Sunday night and received people then. An urban colleague said he received all comers the first Saturday of each month—"a rule I have not broken in seven years." His constituency service had slipped, and his constituents resented it, admitted a Minister from a large electorate. Whereas he used to appear once a month in the main towns of his district, he now managed to get around to each of them only about once every three months.

Not only are Ministers grievance men for their own constituents, but as the previous chapter noted they also were highly ranked by M.P.s as grievance agents for citizens at large and as referral agents for Members. In order to place such matters in the context of their total role, Ministers were asked:

"Would it be possible to say what proportion of your job concerns citizens' grievances?"

Very Little	Moderate Amount	Large Segment	Total
44% (7)	25% (4)	31% (5)	100% (16)

Of those in the most numerous category, one said that he had to deal with only "a few crackpots." Another replied, "Not much; I send them straight to the department. Very rarely do I take one up myself, but I do deal with every firing by the department." (The department was one of New Zealand's largest employers.) Another reported he did very little, but he focused upon the usefulness of complaints: "If I get too many complaints on one particular matter, I jump on my officers; we must at all costs give John Q. Citizen his just due." Of those who felt that such matters occupied a moderate amount of their time, one reported, "There is a continual flow from individual citizens; the department drafts replies for my signature, but I frequently amend them—not for political ammunition, but to answer more sympathetically or to suggest a possible other solution." Another replied, "A fair amount; I don't refuse to see anyone who insists on talking to me."

None of the Ministers felt besieged, but about one-third perceived this function as demanding. One responded, "I have a fairly heavy correspondence on these matters; I try to get the department to intervene and lighten my load." A colleague replied, "A fair percentage. About half of my paper work—not of my time, which is at least seventy hours per week—would be spent on these kinds of matters." Another said that a large part of his time, especially with regard to one portfolio, was devoted to complaints. Several commented that they were too accessible to the people, and that they should have larger staffs. There was no apparent relationship between Ministers' answers and the types of departments they presided over. That the proportion of their job that Ministers felt they devoted to citizens' grievances varied considerably could be expected from the varying natures of the portfolios. Some have little to do with the public, but others have hundreds of thousands of citizen contacts every year. Despite the varying proportions, it was apparent that Ministers were oriented toward serving citizens and were generally concerned to consider carefully any complaints within the time available. They did not seem to be apologists for their departments.

The Ombudsman and Ministerial Responsibility

Like most other constitutional conventions, New Zealand imported ministerial responsibility from Britain without making many structural adaptations. Perhaps the most significant adaptation is that Ministers have their offices in Parliament Building but do not have offices in the departmental quarters. This physical distance promotes psychological distance as well between Ministers and agencies. Also Ministers do not have political staffs, although they can call upon speech writers, publicists, and researchers who are employed by the party. Only one, the Minister of Agriculture, enjoyed a Parliamentary Undersecretary at the time these interviews were conducted. The remainder did not have even a single *political* assistant. Their staff work was accomplished by two or three civil servants who were on loan from the respective departments. Because of the physical separation of Ministers from departments, these assistants play key roles in the communications process between politicians and administrators.

When asked "What is the essential meaning of ministerial responsibility in New Zealand?" followed by the supplementary "How does it differ from the British doctrine?" the Ministers referred to collective and individual responsibility in terms that would be familiar to British students of constitutional processes. With regard to their individual obligations, one senior respondent commented: "A Minister is responsible for everything that happens in his department whether he knows about it or not; he is responsible for any mistake, even for those of a junior administrative officer. This is not tough; it's good. Someone must take responsibility—fair enough?

So you keep tabs on what goes on in your departments and rectify mistakes so they won't happen again." Another mentioned that one of his departments was then involved in two large construction projects. Because of ministerial responsibility, he complained, "I must accept complete accountability; it does seem hard that I can't blame engineers or accountants for their mistakes; I can't duck it."

Despite these claims, however, New Zealand Ministers are not likely to be held as tightly accountable for their subordinates' actions as the British tradition recommends. If a situation similar to Britain's Crichel Down case were to arise in New Zealand, it is probable that the relevant Minister would not resign.[2] One Minister, who was particularly well informed in the area of constitutional practices, commented: "For matters of policy there is a binding personal responsibility, and we are answerable in Parliament on such matters. I don't think it extends to minor administrative acts. If the occasion arises to reprimand some officer in public, I do. But if it's a major matter, I accept responsibility."[3] Although the shape of the convention is somewhat modified in New Zealand, it is nevertheless true that the doctrine of individual accountability is very much alive.

[2] One of the respondents mentioned with approval, however, Sir Thomas Dugdale's resignation over the "Christian Daws" (sic) case as an illustration of the proper functioning of ministerial responsibility. Some Ministers were well informed about British practices; others obviously were not. One frankly admitted that he knew nothing about them. For a sketch of Crichel Down see Herbert Morrison, *Government and Parliament: A Survey From the Inside* (London: Oxford University Press, 1964), pp. 333–34. It should be mentioned that British constitutional scholars are divided on the questions of whether Dugdale should necessarily have resigned and of whether the responsible Minister would be likely to resign if a similar case were to recur.

[3] The mention of public reprimands for civil servants is not heretical. K. J. Scott's discussion of ministerial responsibility contains the subheading, "Blaming Public Servants." See *The New Zealand Constitution* (Oxford: Clarendon Press, 1962) pp. 131–32.

THE QUEEN'S MINISTERS

As was observed in Chapter 3, during New Zealand's Ombudsman debate the institution never was publicly depicted as a threat to the status of Ministers of the Crown. This specter was, however, raised in the privacy of the Cabinet Committee on Legislation and in the National Party Caucus, and the nascent Ombudsman's powers were restrained in ways designed to insure that he would not be a threat to Ministers' constitutional positions. Particularly, he was denied jurisdiction over the personal decisions of Ministers. But considerable potential for mischief remained in the provision that allowed him to investigate the recommendations of civil servants to their Ministers. The intent of this measure was to prevent administrators from hiding behind their Ministers' authority, but the practical result was to lay bare the components of ministerial decision making to the Ombudsman's—and eventually to the public's—scrutiny.

The following three questions were designed to probe the Ministers' opinions of the Ombudsman's impact upon the traditional concept of ministerial responsibility. The first inquired generally:

"How would you describe your relations with the Ombudsman?"

Superlative	Good	Adequate but Nonexistent	Total
31% (5)	38% (6)	31% (5)	100% (16)

Ministers divided almost equally into thirds and claimed to have either superlative, or good, or adequate but really nonexistent relationships with the Ombudsman. What is most significant about the answers is that no one described their relations in predominantly negative terms. One of those who reported most enthusiastically upon their relationship commented, "I'm keen to see him succeed." Another related gratification over two instances in which the Ombudsman had supported the Minister's decision which overruled departmental recommendations. A third claimed that "he frequently comes up to discuss a case or talk about general matters." Yet another reported, "I deal with him on quite a few cases and our relations are first-class."

One of the Ministers who described their relations as basically good stated, "I used the Ombudsman to twit Ministers four times myself when I was a back-bencher; in two cases I even paid the fee myself." He was also happy to report that he had not yet run afoul of him as a Minister. A senior colleague also said, "I've never been in any trouble with the Ombudsman; he pays me a social visit each year and I hope to keep it at that." One Minister reminisced, "I called him in once on a case I inherited from my predecessor. This was an impossible one and the file was a foot high; I asked him to take it away and said, 'Here's the pound' [the Ombudsman's fee]. But he decided it was out of his jursidiction." In a more negative vein, another said he believed that the Ombudsman was at present "after" one of his departments, but that he thought the Ombudsman had chosen a bad case to use as a vehicle for the attack. Nevertheless, he seemed to regard this as the only blemish on their relationship.

Almost a third of the Ministers claimed to have no relationship with the Ombudsman; they used language such as "None; I haven't had any problems," or "I don't know where he lives." In spite of the lack of perceptual and, apparently, physical interaction, they were not anti-Ombudsman. One even claimed that although they were personal friends, they really had no professional relationship. A junior colleague, who also reported no significant interaction, nevertheless commented favorably, "We are fortunate in having Guy Powles' wisdom; I think he performs a useful function." It was often apparent that even those who reported excellent relationships had relatively little real interest in the institution. One respondent accused the interviewer of being "obsessed" with the subject. Another asked, "Why are you so interested in the damn Ombudsman?"

The matter of the Ombudsman's impact upon the convention of ministerial responsibility was directly raised in the next question: "Has he affected your relationship with your department head?" *Not one Minister thought that the Ombudsman had had any long-term effect upon the traditionally close relationship between him and his permanent head.* This opinion was usually expressed quite briefly, sometimes with a sense of amusement that such a question should even be asked. Often Ministers were emphatic in their responses, such as: "No, not the slightest—we welcome him"; "No, and I don't think my [permanent] heads really resent the fact that he can investigate their recommendations to me"; "I'm quite sure this has not occurred, but perhaps it has with others"; and "We have discussed some of the Ombudsman's cases; we have always been in agreement about whether or not to accept his recommendations."

Four Ministers who concurred with their fellows that the Ombudsman had not really affected their general relationship with a department head did cite at least one instance in which there was some disagreement over the Ombudsman. The extent of the conflict ranged from the report of one Minister who said, "I had one permanent head who couldn't bear the Ombudsman," to that of the colleague who reported, "He has on occasion caused me to change an administrative decision; then I have managed to persuade my head to agree." In all four cases the conflict centered around the Ombudsman's recommendation to the Minister to overrule a departmental decision. All of them also reported that they supported the Ombudsman's recommendation over the department's. One mentioned that he "mostly" accepted the Ombudsman's suggestions as a matter of course. It is interesting that such actions by the Ombudsman were not regarded as intrusive by Ministers, and it is also significant that few of them thought their simple negative replies needed any elaboration.

The final test of the Ministers' opinions about the Ombudsman's relationship to their own role occurred when they were asked to respond to the statement, "The Ombudsman should be able to investigate the actions of Ministers as well as civil servants' recommendations to them." Only 25 percent (4) of them agreed, and many of the remainder intensely disagreed with what seemed to be a preposterous proposal. One extravagantly exclaimed, "Why, if the Ombudsman could investigate Ministers' decisions, we would have a dictatorship!" To buttress his disagreement, another somewhat more realistically pointed to the superfluity of such a change: "In point of fact, he can now get to us through seeing whether we accepted or rejected the department's recommendation; also, his Act entitles him to confer with me." However clearly the answers to the two preceding questions might indicate the Ministers' belief that the Ombudsman had not interfered with the traditions of ministerial responsibility, the reaction to the proposed inclusion of their decisions in his jurisdiction shows that there are apparent limits to their tolerance of the Ombudsman.

Assessing the Ombudsman

In addition to exploring with the Ministers their own activities as complaints men and their perceptions of the Ombudsman's impact upon their jobs, they also were asked to evaluate the institution from several perspectives.

The first such question inquired in general terms, "How effective would you say the Ombudsman is in settling grievances?" (Five Ministers gave multiple responses.) None of the Ministers depicted the Ombudsman as ineffective; and only one, who commented that "he may not be as important as he thinks he is," was even reserved in his reaction. Six testified to the Ombudsman's effectiveness in quite general terms, such as "Outstandingly successful! No genuine and sincere civil servant need fear an Ombudsman"; and "I think quite effective. Yes, I think it's a good institution; everybody is agreed on this, aren't they?"

Five of their colleagues chose to describe his effectiveness in terms of his vindication of civil servants, even though the question was phrased in terms of the aggrieved citizen. One said, "He has been of great value for the public service because he explains the validity of decisions." Another replied, "I think the end product is that he has had the effect of giving prestige to the public service; to me it's interesting to note the number of times the Ombudsman finds there is no case. When the idea was brought up, there was some opposition from the public service to the idea of him crawling around; he has actually strengthened the responsibility of the public service." When one recalls that Ministers bear individual responsibility for administrators' decisions, their satisfaction with such a vindication is not unexpected.

Five Ministers felt that the Ombudsman's effectiveness lay in the psychological reassurance his presence gave to citizens. One commented, "His investigations are very thorough; but in terms of righting wrongs, no mistake is usually revealed. However, he does a good job for the citizen in relieving frustration." Others also described his impact on the public service as minimal but contended that the sense of security his existence gave to many citizens fully justified his expense.

Five other Ministers discussed his effectiveness in terms of the prevention of possible abuses by civil servants. He was often called a "watchdog" and a "deterrent," and the following response was representative: "He has had a good psychological effect on departments in that they now have one more think before they decide something that could go to the Ombudsman." A subtle use of him from the Minister's point of view was mentioned: "You can get a Minister who will give a department head too great a sway, but we have worked hard to develop a team and eliminate problems. I'm glad he's there because I can say, "Let's get this cleaned up in case the Ombudsman investigates." Thus, Ministers' reactions to the Ombudsman's effectiveness were favorable, even if they were usually not couched in terms of the settlement of grievances.

The Ministers' responses to the four attitude statements on the Ombudsman's jurisdiction, which also were presented to the permanent heads and to the back-bench Members of Parliament, are arrayed in Table 11-1. Perhaps because of their experientially based understanding of how the Ombudsman operates, the Ministers did not feel that the institution's powers were insufficient; they were, however, not strongly committed to this view, and several spontaneously endorsed the inclusion of local government in the Ombudsman's jurisdiction. Self-interest surely is a principal explanation for Minister's disagreement with item two, but their general disagreement with the expansion of the Ombudsman's jurisdiction as suggested by statements one and two did not indicate that they were amenable to the clipping of his wings, after the fashion of the British counterpart, which was envisioned by items three and four.

Also arrayed in Table 11-1 are the ministerial responses to the seven Ombudsman attitude statements; the responses of the bureaucrats and the ordinary Members of Parliament were reported in the two previous chapters. The pattern of the Ministers' replies was similar to that of the National Party back-benchers. That is, they disagreed that the Ombudsman needed closer supervision, disagreed more strongly that he was a self-aggrandizing empire builder, and disagreed more strongly still that he was so foreign that he did not fit into New Zealand. Ministers were not far from agreement, however, with item four, which labeled many of the Ombudsman's complainants

TABLE 11-1
Ministers' Mean Responses to Ombudsman Attitude Statements (N = 16)

Jurisdiction Statements	Mean	Affect Statements	Mean
1. "Many complaints to the Ombudsman are rejected on technical grounds; he could do a lot more good if he had wider powers."[a]	3.6	1. "Parliament should supervise more closely the work of its Parliamentary Commissioner."	4.9
2. "The Ombudsman should be able to investigate the actions of Ministers as well as civil servants' recommendations to them."	5.5	2. "The Ombudsman himself is an empire builder who is trying to improve his position by getting his name before the people in press releases and speeches."	5.3
3. "It would be better if the British system of filtering complaints to the Ombudsman through Members of Parliament were adopted in New Zealand."	5.6	3. "The Ombudsman is basically a foreign institution that does not fit into New Zealand's traditions."	5.5
4. "The Ombudsman's powers should be reduced as in Britain where he only has jurisdiction over maladministration, not discretionary decisions."	4.8	4. "A high percent of those who go to the Ombudsman are quarrelsome people with no real complaint."	3.6
		5. "Though the parties differ somewhat on the ideal limits of the Ombudsman's jurisdiction, the institution is not a party matter."	2.1
		6. "Knowledge of the presence of the Ombudsman acts as a sort of 'conscience' over the actions of the civil service."	1.8
		7. "Though the name was borrowed from Scandinavia, New Zealand's Ombudsman is basically a native product."	3.5

Key:
Agree strongly = 1
Midpoint = 3.5
Disagree strongly = 6

[a] One "Don't know" response to this question is excluded from the analysis.

as "quarrelsome people with no real complaint." They also agreed rather strongly, as did the other populations, that the Ombudsman was primarily nonpartisan, although one insisted that it was a National Party gimmick. Furthermore, they strongly agreed that the Ombudsman acted as a "conscience" for the civil service; from their perspective this was seen as a valuable attribute. Finally, Ministers' mean scores were exactly at the midpoint, 3.5, on the question of whether or not the Ombudsman was "basically a native product." Probably this is a reflection of the fact that many of them were well aware of how directly the institution was transferred from Denmark, and therefore they had difficulty deciding.

In terms of the overall eleven-item pro-Ombudsman scale composed of all statements in Table 11-1, the mean for Ministers was 2.5. Of the populations surveyed, only the National Party M.P.s elected before the Ombudsman's appointment had a more favorable score, 2.4. Only one Minister had an index score that was anti-Ombudsman; and even it was 3.9, not far over the midpoint.

Conclusions

It is clear from the interviews with National's Ministers that these central political actors, whose attitudes and behaviors were crucial to the Ombudsman's success, were supportive of the institution. They believed that the Ombudsman had adversely affected neither their own roles as citizens' grievance men nor the traditionally close nexus between Minister and permanent head. Furthermore, they had experienced little interaction with the Ombudsman, but they had formed positive evaluations of the institution's effectiveness as well as positive emotional attachments to it.[4]

[4] The Ombudsman's principal claim to the status of parliamentary official arises from Ministers' and M.P.s' psychological identification of

For the first decade of the Ombudsman's existence, the office enjoyed the protective umbrella of its creator—the National Party. But at the end of 1972, National lost an election to Labor, which governed for the next three years until National regained the Treasury benches at the conclusion of our study. During its years as the Loyal Opposition Labor had decided to promote the extension of the Ombudsman's jurisdiction to include complaints against all local authorities, and once in office the new Government did amend the legislation so as to include them. Although the Labor Government was supportive and took no actions that threatened the Ombudsman, this first major change in the office's political environment was a significant test for the institution. Recall that on many questions about emotional involvement with the Ombudsman, about interaction with him, about the evaluation of his impact, his status, and his jurisdiction, and about affection for him, the responses of the Labor Members were considerably less favorable than those of National's parliamentarians.[5]

---

him as Parliament's man. He has seldom been the subject of parliamentary debate (although most of that body's formal discussion of the Ombudsman has been a consideration of just how far and how fast his jurisdiction should be extended), and thus far he had has little impact upon the parliamentary petitions process. For extended discussions see Larry B. Hill, *Parliament and the Ombudsman in New Zealand*, Legislative Research Series Monograph Number 8 (Norman: University of Oklahoma Bureau of Government Research, 1974), pp. 52–90; and Larry B. Hill, "Parliamentary Petitions, the Ombudsman, and Political Change in New Zealand," *Political Studies* 22 (September 1974), 337–46.

[5] One other assessment of the New Zealand parliamentary-Ombudsman relationship has been undertaken: Kent M. Weeks, "Members of Parliament and the New Zealand Ombudsman System," *Midwest Journal of Political Science*, 14 (November 1970), 673–87. This article, which was based upon mailed questionnaires distributed while the interviews reported here were under way, is generally corroborative of the findings presented. An important difference should be mentioned, however. Labor's reported attitudes toward the Om-

Apparently the Ombudsman passed the test; all indications are that during its governmental tenure Labor was quite satisfied with the institution's performance. This is indicated, for example, by the following comment by the then Prime Minister, the Rt. Hon. W. E. Rowling, during his opening address to the Conference of Australasian and Pacific Ombudsmen in Wellington in 1974:

> It is because my Government recognises the tremendous work, on the basis of experience, of the Ombudsman in this field and also that they [sic] act, I believe, as a valuable safety valve in the community, that legislation has now been introduced into Parliament to extend the office into the field of local authorities and to provide for an additional appointment. We believe it will make the system even more effective than that which is functioning at the present time.[6]

It seems likely that some Labor Members' doubts—many of which were based upon misinformation or lack of information—about the institution were mollified by positive experience with it while their party was in power.

One should remember, however, that Labor's conversion to the Ombudsman principle was on pragmatic rather than ideological grounds; it simply appeared to the party's leaders that there was more political mileage in endorsing than in deploring the Ombudsman. The original decision to advocate the extension of his jurisdiction

---

budsman are more favorable than the pattern presented here. This could be attributed to the circumstance that not all of the universe of Labor opinion was represented: whereas 84 percent of the National Members returned their questionnaires, only 50 percent of the Labor Members did so (p. 674).

[6] *Official Record of Proceedings of the Conference of Australasian and Pacific Ombudsmen,* Wellington, New Zealand, 19–22 November 1974 (Wellington: Office of Ombudsman, 1975), p. 3.

was taken despite the personal reservations of several top party leaders. One can speculate that if an Ombudsman were to pursue difficult cases—cases that would ultimately impinge upon areas of party policy—during a Labor Government's tenure, the Ministers might feel fewer compunctions than their National counterparts in scotching one of his investigations. Nonetheless, it appears that Labor has become so committed to the Ombudsman that his existence would be preserved in any foreseeable circumstances; but the institution's authority is founded upon so slender a power base that a future Government could easily vitiate the Ombudsman's effectiveness through such devices as subtly communicating to administrative agencies that it did not demand their enthusiastic cooperation with his investigations.

The Ombudsman is, however, a peculiarly nonpartisan mechanism—perhaps a better word would be "ambipartisan." Despite Labor's lack of proprietary interest in it, the office is compatible with party ideology. It was proposed in Britain by the Labor Party as a gesture to indicate that the Left was sensitive to the problems that the huge governmental bureaucracies, created or fostered by them, posed for individuals (the further assumption that those on society's lower social and economic rungs were likely to be most in need of an ombudsman's assistance was congruent with party policy). This also is the interpretation of the Ombudsman's uses toward which the New Zealand Labor Party has evolved, as the following statement by Mr. Rowling illustrates:

"If, as will be the case under an activist Government, the State services are galvanised into action, the impact upon the general public will be very considerable indeed. That is the task of Government. In the process, however, when this happens there are certain to be individuals who feel that they have been badly treated by the State. It is the right of such individuals to have their complaints impartially investigated. Thus it becomes [the Ombudsman's] task to help us to ensure that the Government is human and personal as well as vigorous and enlightened."[7]

[7] Ibid., p. 5.

Part 4
EPILOGUE

CHAPTER TWELVE

Evaluations: Program, Institutionalization, and Transfer

It is therefore the chronicler's task to finish his account by a comprehensive, synthetic coup d'oeil upon the institution described.
—BRONISLAW MALINOWSKI, *Argonauts of the Western Pacific*

THIS book is a modern saga—a story of the originally Scandinavian ombudsman's introduction to New Zealand and of the first twelve and one-half years of his life there. Romantic though they may be, the historicity of the ancient sagas recounting the adventures of Scandinavia's legendary champions often is questionable. This ombudsman saga contains few truly heroic exploits, but the narrative is solidly based upon materials gathered at firsthand whose authenticity is verifiable. Rather than the chronological storytelling method favored by the traditional sagaman, I have organized my story of the ombudsman around the sorts of analytical categories that modern social scientists find congenial. But this method was not devised to escape the rigorous demands of creating biography. It was, instead, intended to be a more powerful—if less lyrical—means of conveying institutional biography.

The genuine sagas were not morality plays, and I too have shunned didacticism. At the end of each chapter I have pointed to some possible implications of that part of our story, but in the main, like the sagaman, I have been content to be a dispassionate narrator allowing readers to form their own moral judgments about the ombudsman. Having told my story, I now depart from the conventional format of the saga and draw some general conclusions from my tale. In doing so, I am somewhat less ambitious

EPILOGUE

than Raymond Firth's anthropologist who uses his small sample of human behavior to "reach out with hypotheses—about family, marriage, magic, or morals—to put a question mark against the whole of human culture." Nevertheless, I employ my "microcosm to illuminate the macrocosm, the particular to illustrate the general."[1]

Program Evaluation

Even if it is only implicit, some sort of evaluation (the process of assessing, judging, or weighing) is an inherent aspect of any worthwhile investigation of human society. But it is only recently that scholars have begun to undertake research specifically designed to evaluate social policies. Interest in such research has been stimulated by the immense growth of government agencies that are intended to have an impact upon society. Policy makers and administrators have an understandable desire to assess the effectiveness of their ambitious and costly social schemes, and the field of *program evaluation*—part academic subdiscipline, part administrative specialty—has grown up to accommodate the desire. Although program evaluation, or evaluation research, is a new field whose techniques are developing rapidly, there is general agreement among practitioners about its scope. Few would quarrel with Carol Weiss's statement of objectives: "the purpose of evaluation research is to measure the effects of a program against the goals it set out to accomplish as a means of contributing to subsequent decision making about the program and improving future programming."[2]

In large measure, this book constitutes a program evaluation of an ombudsman. In the opening chapter the

[1] Raymond Firth, *Elements of Social Organization* (New York: Philosophical Library, 1951), p. 18.
[2] *Evaluation Research: Methods for Assessing Program Effectiveness* (Englewood Cliffs, N.J.: Prentice-Hall, 1972), p. 4.

office was introduced as a goal-oriented mechanism for ameliorating citizen-bureaucratic relations, and several alleged virtues were listed: righting specific administrative wrongs, bringing humanity into bureaucracy, lessening popular alienation from government, reforming administration, acting as a bureaucratic watchdog, and vindicating civil servants when they were unjustly accused of maladministration—all were mentioned as goals for an ombudsman. The subsequent chapters investigated—albeit not always systematically—how well the New Zealand official performed in attempting to fulfill these objectives. Furthermore, our research design for monitoring the ombudsman's effectiveness was of a type that is endemic among professional evaluators: system analysis. We examined the office's inputs and the identities of those who complained; we examined the investigative methods used in processing the complaints; and we examined that central feature of evaluation research—the outcomes of the ombudsman's investigations. In keeping with the conventional assumption that people's attitudes are related to their behavior, we also asked bureaucrats and politicians for their interpretations of the ombudsman's effectiveness.

This program evaluation has demonstrated that an ombudsman can have an impact upon the character of the relationships that develop between citizens and government bureaucracies. In short: *the New Zealand Ombudsman has been a success.* Social scientists often are leery of committing themselves to such unambiguous generalizations, but an examination of the evidence presented in the preceding chapters supports the conclusion.

Judged in terms of what an ombudsman reasonably might be expected to accomplish, the New Zealand official's performance seems impressive. His achievements in two crucial arenas—relationships with citizens and with the administrative system—can be stated succinctly. First: the office has become identified as a national symbol to whom numbers of citizens, possessing a wide range of sociological characteristics, have complained; and the Ombudsman has dealt with these clients in a humane and sympathetic fashion and has managed to help materially about one-sixth of those who complained against agencies within his jurisdiction. Second: the Ombudsman has enlisted the cooperation and gained the respect of bureaucrats and politicians, and he has succeeded in reforming some administrative policies that he believed were unjust or inconsistent. It would be an exaggeration to claim that the Ombudsman has fundamentally restructured the relationships between the governors and the governed in New Zealand, and the above generalizations are appropriately qualified in the text. Nevertheless, the accomplishments cited are real and socially significant.[3]

In measuring the effects of a program, evaluators not only consider beneficial impacts; they also count the costs. Our evaluation has indicated that the Ombudsman's benefits do not appear to be accompanied by any important undesirable administrative or political consequences, as some have feared. Particularly, no evidence was uncovered indicating that the Ombudsman has seriously disrupted the administrative process or that fear of him has made civil servants timid or inclined them toward ensnarling citizens in more "red tape." When costs are mentioned, monetary costs come quickly to mind. Although some predicted that the office would be-

[3] This evaluation has focused upon the Ombudsman's consequences, which were linked only loosely with the office's intended effects. Any attempt to operationalize those statements of organizational intent which were described above as the Ombudsman's goals would indicate that they are vague at best, and some are mutually incompatible—as is often true of the "goals" of social programs. Many evaluators would deplore but tolerate this laxity; others would insist upon making a rigorous attempt to specify the Ombudsman's goals, so that the extent of their attainment could be measured systematically. See Harley E. Hinricks and Graeme H. Taylor, *A Primer on Benefit-Cost Analysis and Program Evaluation* (Pacific Palisades, Calif.: Goodyear, 1972), p. 150.

come in itself a large, expensive bureaucracy, the Ombudsman has been a cheap program. The maximum size of the staff has been eleven—including clerical personnel—and the office's operating budget has remained under 100,000 dollars (N.Z.) per year—including the Ombudsman's salary and an estimate for the office rent. (Of course, the new functions, discussed below, that the revised Ombudsmen Act assigned to the office in 1975 will cause the size of the staff and budget to increase.) According to this summarized accounting, the benefits that have accrued to New Zealand from having an Ombudsman appear to have greatly outweighed the social and financial costs.

Among program evaluations our study is exceptional, because it indicates that the Ombudsman has been a success. "An evaluation study does not generally come up with final and unequivocal findings about the worth of a program," Carol Weiss concludes; "its results often show small, ambiguous changes, minor effects, outcomes influenced by the specific events of the place and moment."[4] That the Ombudsman could be demonstrated to be successful is all the more remarkable when one considers the original state of the New Zealand administrative environment: before an Ombudsman was created, public agencies already performed at a high level. Because they were generally competent, uncorrupted, and concerned for citizens' welfare, the Ombudsman scored few easy and dramatic victories. In such a situation, Peter Rossi has noted that social innovations usually "can be expected to yield only disproportionately small improvements over existing programs. Hence cost-to-benefit ratios can be expected to be relatively high and also to

[4] *Evaluation Research*, p. 3. The commonplace finding of negative results dismays many evaluators, who often have a personal stake in the "progressive" social programs which they study. Weiss acknowledges (pp. 127–28), "the emotional effect of much evaluation is to give aid and comfort to the barbarians. . . ."

EPILOGUE

rise as target problems represent increasingly hard core' phenomena."[5]

The users of evaluation research often are critical of some of the genre's shortcomings, including the above-mentioned inconclusiveness and the high cost of many reports. A further common point of dissatisfaction is the evaluations' methodological base. Studies performed by "outsiders" are sometimes criticized as superficial; perhaps brief observation occurred and a "scorecard" was filled in, or perhaps high-powered analytical techniques were simply applied to a set of aggregate data. On the other hand, "insiders"—employees of the agency being evaluated—are likely to be knowledgeable and to do a thorough analysis, but their objectivity always is suspect. Self-evaluations usually are self-justifications.[6] Whatever its shortcomings may be, this study's utilization of the viewpoint that was labeled in Chapter 2 the political-anthropological approach has made it possible to maximize the advantages while avoiding the main pitfalls of both the outsider and the insider perspectives.

If some potential users of this research are convinced of its epistemological soundness, they may feel, nonetheless, that it is insufficiently programmatic. Unlike conventional program evaluations, little direct guidance is given above for improving the operations of the New Zealand Ombudsman or for devising a more effective version of the ombudsman model. Several hints for those who wish to undertake such tasks can be gleaned from the foregoing chapters, but my purposes have not been those of the institutional engineer. Having laid the normative groundwork for assuming that the ombudsman is a

[5] "Testing for Success and Failure in Social Action," in Peter H. Rossi and Walter Williams, eds., *Evaluating Social Programs: Theory, Practice, and Politics* (New York: Seminar Press, 1972), pp. 21–22.

[6] For a discussion of the "outsider-insider" controversy see Francis G. Caro, Introduction to Caro, ed., *Readings in Evaluation Research* (New York: Russell Sage Foundation, 1971), p. 19.

worthwhile subject for study, I devoted much attention to the public policy question of what the consequences of one ombudsman have been for individuals, bureaucrats, politicians, and the total political system.[7] But the office's policy implications were pursued not just as ends in themselves, but also as manifestations of more generalized political phenomena. I have viewed the ombudsman as an interesting means of exploring a fascinating aspect of social change, political institutional transfer—most especially institutionalization.

Alternative Measures of Institutionalization

If, as our data indicate, the New Zealand Ombudsman has worked, has performed its intended mission, does

[7] Of course, my findings about the New Zealand Ombudsman cannot necessarily be extended to ombudsmen around the world—especially to those which are structurally dissimilar to the classical office or which have been introduced to inhospitable administrative-political environments. Readers will have to draw their own conclusions about the possible applicability of the New Zealand experience to the situation in other jurisdictions. Nevertheless, based upon relatively short periods of time and incomplete study, it appears that the new ombudsmen in the American and Australian states and the Canadian provinces, at least, have performed much like the New Zealand model. For personal testimonies, see the statements by the ombudsmen of Hawaii, Victoria, South Australia, Western Australia, and Saskatchewan in the *Official Record of Proceedings of the Conference of Australasian and Pacific Ombudsmen*, Wellington, New Zealand, 19–22 November 1974 (Wellington: Office of Ombudsman, 1975). See also Alan J. Wyner, *The Nebraska Ombudsman: Innovation in State Government* (Berkeley: University of California, Institute of Governmental Studies, 1974); Alan J. Wyner, "American Ombudsmen and Their Political Environment" (Paper delivered at the 70th Annual Meeting of the American Political Science Association, Chicago, 29 August to 2 September 1974); John E. Moore, "The Ombudsman Activities Project's Internal Evaluation of the New Ombudsmen" (Paper delivered at the 70th Annual Meeting of the American Political Science Association, Chicago, 29 August to 2 September 1974); and Karl A. Friedmann's forthcoming study of the Alberta Ombudsman.

EPILOGUE

this in itself mean that the office has become institutionalized? No: mission effectiveness is a positive omen, but it is neither a necessary nor a sufficient condition of institutionalization. In Chapter 2, institutionalization was defined as a "process that occurs over time in which the organization creates authority relationships vis-à-vis the environmental actors." On the one hand, Organization X might utterly fail at performing its intended functions but, nonetheless, become institutionalized—succeed at making a place for itself in the environment—perhaps by delivering other services. On the other hand, even though Organization Y effectively fulfilled its assigned tasks, it might fail to become institutionalized and have to rely upon coercion rather than authority to ensure compliance.

Neither fate befell the New Zealand Ombudsman. The preceding chapters record the office's development of bonds of authority with clients, with bureaucrats, and with politicians. The strength of the Ombudsman's authority relationships with each set of environmental actors has been adequately traced, and it is unnecessary to recapitulate. Instead, let us briefly look at our data through a new set of lenses. Let us look at the Ombudsman's institutionalization from some theoretical perspectives other than those that were adopted as principal focal points for this study.

Because Samuel P. Huntington's conception of institutionalization has strongly affected the way social scientists perceive of the phenomenon, it is worthwhile to place the Ombudsman in context within his categories. According to Huntington, an organization's level of institutionalization can be measured by two internal, structural criteria—complexity and coherence—and by two environmental criteria which are defensive in nature—autonomy and adaptability. His criteria were designed to enable scholars to "make meaningful comparisons of the levels of political institutionalization of different countries or of the same country at different times."[8] To be sure, the examples used in elaborating the four criteria indicate that they were intended to be applied to large organizations, but the following analysis will reveal that they also are useful in gauging the level of institutionalization of such a small organization as the Ombudsman.

Complexity, as Huntington uses the term, includes not only such structural matters as the numbers and types of subunits, but also the concept of organizational multifunctionality. He contends: "The more complicated an organization is, the more highly institutionalized it is." Complexity is said to allow an organization "to secure and maintain the loyalties of its members."[9] Huntington never explains this phrase; perhaps he means that complexity enables members to aspire to promotions within and among the subunits of large organizations. Furthermore, having diversified purposes supposedly makes an organization less vulnerable to the loss of any particular purpose. Although complexity is an internal, structural concept, Huntington is principally concerned with it as an indicator of an organization's ability to adjust to changing environmental demands (adaptability is, however, a separate criterion of institutionalization).

For at least the first decade of its existence, the Ombudsman receives a low score on the complexity criterion. The office has been a minimal organization; until 1972, it did not possess even a single administrative subunit. There has been some functional specialization on types of cases (e.g., social welfare, taxation, land matters), and staff members were given formal job classifications (e.g., Legal Officer, First Assistant, Investigating Officer). But everyone, including the Ombudsman, has taken a leading role in investigating some complaints. Although the organization's basic function of processing citizens'

[8] Samuel P. Huntington, "Political Development and Political Decay," *World Politics* 17 (April 1965), 404.
[9] Ibid., p. 399.

complaints against maladministration has not changed in significant respects, the office has proved capable of taking on additional functions.

Government has asked the Ombudsman to undertake a few special investigations of an *ad hoc* character. As examples: Sir Guy was requested in 1968 to act as Chairman of the Commission of Inquiry into some aspects of Scientology, set up following the report of a parliamentary committee upon a petition; and the office's 1970 investigation into allegations of "police brutality" in handling the demonstrations against United States Vice President Spiro Agnew resulted in a special report which was the only official inquiry into the allegations (it was, however, initiated by normal citizen complaints rather than by government). Furthermore, during 1971 and early 1972—while a National Government remained in power—Sir Guy was asked to collaborate with a senior magistrate in conducting a thorough investigation into the treatment of prisoners at the Paremoremo maximum security prison; their report, which was widely publicized, has served as a blueprint for prison reform. Finally, Sir Guy conducted a lengthy investigation of the Security Intelligence Service for Labor's Prime Minister during 1975. Thus, the Ombudsman has come to be viewed as a prestigious, multipurpose investigative tool—something like a readily available "mini" Royal Commission.

A more regularized additional function taken on by the Ombudsman was the role of Race Relations Conciliator. Following the passage of a 1970 Act of Parliament, the Ombudsman was appointed to the position as a temporary, additional assignment. A branch office, staffed by an Executive Officer–Race Relations and a secretary on a full-time basis and by a magistrate appointed as a part-time Deputy Conciliator, was opened during 1972 in Auckland—where most Polynesians live. After less than one and one-half years, the Ombudsman concluded that he did not have the time or energy to wear both hats; also he had not succeeded in convincing the government to appoint a full-time deputy for each position; and he resigned the post of Conciliator.

Apart from the short-lived increase in structural complexity just mentioned, the Ombudsman's internal growth during twelve and one-half years was slight. At the end of 1968, the office's jurisdiction was expanded to include the actions of local education and hospital boards, but this long-awaited development immediately caused only one additional staff member to be added, and at the conclusion of our period of study the size of the office staff was only eleven. But Parliament's passage of the Ombudsmen Act 1975 has already had considerable effect upon the office's structure; the future impact will be even greater.

On 10 October 1975, Sir Guy Powles was designated Chief Ombudsman, and the appointment of two additional Ombudsmen (one was a temporary appointment) also was announced. These appointments were designed to cope with the increase in workload that was expected when the office's jurisdiction over all local government complaints came into effect on 1 April 1976. The plan was to triple the size of the staff and open regional offices in Auckland and Christchurch.[10] Sir Guy has detailed the proposed structure of the office as follows:

[10] This planning was based upon the assumption, which is supported by overseas experience, that about as many complaints will be lodged against local government as have been against central government. Furthermore, it is expected, again on the basis of overseas experience, that the average local government case will require about twice as many man-hours of investigation as central government complaints; this expectation is attributed to a combination of the following factors: "(a) In most cases the complaint will have to be investigated on the spot, whereas in most cases Central Government complaints can be dealt with in Wellington; (b) The hierarchical structure of Central Government permits ease of investigation, whereas in the case of a number of local authorities various different officers and persons, committee mem-

EPILOGUE

The statutory duties of the Chief Ombudsman include the coordination of the work of the Ombudsmen and the allocation of work between them. In addition, the Chief Ombudsman functions as an Ombudsman, and all Ombudsmen have equal and co-extensive powers and jurisdiction. As a matter of administrative arrangement I propose that the Ombudsman stationed in Auckland will, in the main, deal with local authority complaints for the northern half of New Zealand, whereas the Ombudsman stationed in Wellington will do the same for the southern half. The office in Christchurch will not at the moment be headed by an Ombudsman but by a senior officer. The Chief Ombudsman will be stationed in Wellington and, with the Wellington Ombudsman, will manage the work of dealing with complaints against the central government organisations and departments. It is hoped that the arrangements between the three Ombudsmen and the three offices will be sufficiently flexible to enable them to assist one another. It is also hoped that there will be substantial contact between local authority complaint handling and central government complaint handling, resulting in a transfer of administrative practices from central government to local government, to the benefit of the latter.[11]

Although the organizational structure of the amended office remains somewhat amorphous—much may depend upon the attitude of the new National Government that

---

bers, etc., may have to be approached; (c) Replies and decisions on complaints against local bodies may well take longer to come forward than would a decision from a Central Government department—a one-man decision as against a committee or council decision." *Report of the Ombudsman* (Wellington: Government Printer, 1975), p. 12.

[11] Office memorandum from Sir Guy Powles to fellow ombudsmen around the world and to other interested parties, 15 October 1975.

EVALUATIONS

was elected at the end of 1975[12]—it is certain that the developments discussed above augur well for the Ombudsman's transformation into a much more complex (hence more highly institutionalized in Huntington's terms) organization. Its increases in complexity can be interpreted as rewards for superior performance.

Coherence is Huntington's second internal criterion of institutionalization; he offers disunity as the appropriate antonym.[13] Consensus, morale, unity, and discipline are said to be necessary attributes of successful organizations. It seems apparent that small organizations, which have few worries about superintending subunits, attain coherence—unlike complexity—easier than large ones.

The Ombudsman office has been operated on hierarchical principles; thus far, it has been small enough that the Ombudsman could scrutinize most actions of the entire staff and screen most communications with environmental actors. Nearly all letters to bureaucrats and complainants have gone out over his signature after receiving his approval. Employees have been carefully selected

[12] At the Conference of Australasian and Pacific Ombudsmen in 1974, the Hon. R. D. Muldoon—then Leader of the Opposition and a man not noted for engaging in idle speculation—emphasized his party's origination of the Ombudsman and reaffirmed National's commitment to the concept but, at the same time, suggested the possibility of incorporating the office of Ombudsman within the larger structure of a Human Rights Commission: "This would have some such functions as: (1) The exploratory investigation of public, private, and Government administration at executive level; (2) An educational role to advise the individual of his rights, how to implement them, and to whom to complain; (3) The Ombudsman's role and in addition the administration of racial, industrial, local government, and victimisation complaints. . . . I believe that serious consideration should be given in this country to the establishment of a Human Rights Commission with functions somewhat as I have set down, but decided in detail following a closer study of the concept." *Official Record of Proceedings of the Conference of Australasian and Pacific Ombudsmen,* p. 8.

[13] Huntington, "Political Development and Political Decay," p. 403.

329

from the ranks of those who have substantial experience in government and share the office's ideological orientations. Because they have tended to serve in the small office for lengthy periods, members have had time to become thoroughly socialized into the organization's *esprit*. The underlying value consensus has contributed to discipline and efficiency, and the generally acknowledged success of the office has had a reciprocal impact upon morale and unity. In short: the Ombudsman has been highly coherent.

The extent to which the office's coherence will fall victim to its decentralization and increase in scope remains to be seen, but maintaining coherence in the face of increases in complexity has been recognized as a problem. Sir Guy addressed himself to the issue in his 1975 *Report* (p. 15; see Appendix A) as follows:

> The deliberate choice for the extended jurisdiction of a collegiate system of Ombudsmen—each one exercising full jurisdiction, and being equal, and having the division of their functions settled almost wholly by agreement—is a better solution than attempting to build a hierarchical structure with authority stemming from the Chief Ombudsman down through successive layers. The collegiate system has worked well in Sweden, and there is no reason why it should not work well here. There will be ample scope for the Ombudsmen to develop their individual approaches while keeping within a co-ordinated and co-operative framework.

Thus, it has been decided that losing a limited degree of coherence is more acceptable than limiting flexibility by creating a rigid, hierarchical structure. Despite the allusion to the Swedish precedent, in choosing this organizational solution to the problem the New Zealand institution is embarking upon a structural innovation. Because the Swedish *Justitieombudsmen* are all housed in the same building in Stockholm and served by a common staff, rather than working independently in different cities as the New Zealanders will be, the Swedish experience is not a reliable guide.

No organization can exist in a vacuum; always some accommodations must be reached with the environment. Obviously, not even the organization's internal structure can be built if it is not let alone. Organizations must develop defensive capabilities.

Autonomy is one defensive measure of institutionalization suggested by Huntington.[14] Autonomous organizations are independent of and can be clearly differentiated from other organizations and social groupings. An organization that is highly vulnerable to influences from various political forces cannot be thought of as institutionalized. If representatives of class interests, politicians, or bureaucrats penetrate an organization and dictate its actions, then the organization will reflect the interests and values of the groups that have the closest access. Such a structure would be a subordinate organization rather than an autonomous institution.

Functional autonomy is a structural characteristic of the Ombudsman—a characteristic that can be used to differentiate the office from other similar organizations, such as inspectors general. That is, the Ombudsman is not the direct subordinate of any elected or appointed official. Although he is in technical terms a legislative creature, in fact he is expected to be an independent investigator beholden to no person or political persuasion. Our findings indicate that the Ombudsman has, indeed, been autonomous. Neither the National Party, which established the innovation, nor the Labor Party, which came to power after the office had been operating for ten years, has at-

[14] Ibid., pp. 401–03.

EPILOGUE

tempted to use the Ombudsman for partisan purposes.[15] A consensus has developed between the two main political parties—the principal potential threats to the office's autonomy—that they will not try to influence the consideration of complaints. As we have seen, Parliament has left the institution almost entirely alone. Bureaucrats, judges, and powerful social forces such as labor unions also could try to interfere with the Ombudsman's autonomy; but we have found that the office is the servant of none of these groups. Universalistic criteria—including abstract principles of justice—are utilized in investigating complaints, so no one point of view is favored over others. Furthermore, the clients' sociological origins cut across society's various strata; therefore the Ombudsman

[15] Nevertheless, a provision (Section 13[5]; see Appendix B) in the Ombudsmen Act 1975, which was not in the original statute, should be mentioned: "The Prime Minister may, with the consent of the Chief Ombudsman, refer to an Ombudsman for investigation and report any matter, other than a matter concerning a judicial proceeding, which the Prime Minister considers should be investigated by an Ombudsman. Where a matter is referred to an Ombudsman pursuant to this subsection, he shall, notwithstanding anything to the contrary in this Act, forthwith investigate that matter and report thereon to the Prime Minister, and may thereafter make such report to Parliament on the matter as he thinks fit. Nothing in section 22 of this Act shall apply in respect of any investigation or report made under this subsection."

This provision obviously could compromise the Ombudsman's autonomy—at least slightly—through permitting a Prime Minister to affect the Ombudsman's investigative agenda. The reference to Section 22 is obscure, but it appears to allow secret reports to the Prime Minister by eliminating the requirement that the accused agency or individual be notified of the Ombudsman's criticisms and permitted to reply. It should be noted, however, that Section 13 (4), which permits a parliamentary committee to require the Ombudsman to investigate a petition, also suspends the protections of Section 22 for those under investigation. The latter provision was a part of the original statute, and it appears that when the Prime Minister was authorized to ask the Ombudsman to undertake special investigations he was simply given the same powers as could be exercised by a parliamentary committee. As far as I am aware, no case has yet arisen in which a report was presented to a House committee without allowing those affected to respond.

is autonomous in that he is not a particularistic spokesman for a limited group.

Adaptability is a second defensive criterion of institutionalization developed by Huntington, who considers that adaptability equals environmental challenges plus age. Age can be measured in three ways: by the passage of time, by generational changes, and by functional changes.

Time is mentioned in virtually all definitions of institutionalization, and Huntington lists chronological age as an index of the phenomenon: "The older an organization is, the more likely it is to continue to exist through any specified future time period."[16] The fact that the New Zealand Ombudsman has survived, while building up its authority, for twelve and one-half years is prima facie evidence of its institutionalization. The Ombudsman's life span has constituted a significant portion of the careers of civil servants and politicians, and enough time has passed so that many who may not have accommodated themselves to the new organization's norms have retired from the scene. New recruits have been socialized into a milieu in which they perceive the Ombudsman as a part of the status quo, and even those at mid-career who may be less than enthusiastic appear to have accepted the office as a permanent part of the environment. Some of the environmental challenges to which the Ombudsman has successfully adapted during the period include the following: serving under two National and two Labor Prime Ministers; the change from a National to a Labor Government in 1972; and survival during a period of budget tightening occasioned by the worldwide drop of commodity prices, which particularly affected New Zealand's exports of wool, meat, and dairy products, in the late 1960s and again in the early 1970s. While none of these were fundamental challenges to the

[16] Huntington, "Political Development and Political Decay," p. 395.

EPILOGUE

office's existence, they allowed the Ombudsman to demonstrate that it did possess an adaptive capacity.

The Ombudsman remains young, however, when age is measured in generational terms. The first incumbent, Sir Guy Powles, remained at the helm from the office's embarkation through the course of this study, and it is likely that he will continue as Chief Ombudsman for the first year or two of the new jurisdictional-structural arrangements. Huntington maintains that mere replacement of leaders is not a very stringent measure of adaptability and that the real test occurs when a younger generation of leaders replaces the original ones. The appointment of Mr. George R. Laking to the additional permanent position of Ombudsman represented in generational terms an evolutionary rather than a radical change, as he was 63 years of age—seven years younger than Sir Guy.[17] Considerable turnover has already occurred among the office staff; only two remain from the original staff, and most of the newer members are of a younger generation than those whom they replaced. As the staff expands to meet the workload generated by

[17] Moreover, Laking's appointment represented in another sense—probably a more important one—continuity with Sir Guy's tenure as Ombudsman: the appointment was a distinguished one and can be taken as a signal of the high regard in which the Labor Government had come to hold the office. A résumé of the public service positions Laking has held will be indicative of his administrative experience and of the trust that has been placed in his competence: member of the Secretariat of the War Cabinet (during World War II), N.Z. delegate to the League of Nations and to the General Assembly of the United Nations, N.Z. member of the United Nations mission in East Africa, Counselor and Minister at the N.Z. Embassy in Washington, Deputy Secretary of Foreign Affairs, Ambassador to the European Economic Community, Acting N.Z. High Commissioner at London, Ambassador to the United States, and Secretary of Foreign Affairs and Permanent Head of the Prime Minister's Department.

The temporary Ombudsman position is to be filled by Mr. A. E. Hurley, a respected Wellington lawyer who has many years of experience serving as counsel to various local authorities.

EVALUATIONS

the new jurisdiction, the opportunity to hire a number of younger employees will be presented.

Precisely how the Ombudsman will adapt to its increased responsibilities and its larger and more complex structure cannot now be predicted with any degree of confidence. That these developments are perceived of as problems for the office's continuing institutionalization is indicated by the following cautious commentary by the Chief Ombudsman upon an earlier draft of this chapter:

> The passage and implementation of the Ombudsmen Act 1975 makes a profound change in the whole institution. It will never be the same again. I think the great test of whether the Ombudsman has become institutionalized is yet to come, and it may be that we do indeed have to wait for the succession to office of a completely new generation of Ombudsmen working under new structural and collegiate arrangements before any sound judgment can be formed as to the status of the institution. All that I can do is to attempt to construct some blueprints and as it were to put appropriate front runners at the starting barrier and to start them off pointed in the right direction, but whether they will go in that direction or in some totally different one is a matter over which I shall have no control whatever—which is probably just as well.[18]

Finally, Huntington contends that functional changes are a measure of an organization's adaptability. In discussing the Ombudsman's complexity above, we noted that the office has taken on some additional duties: it has acquired capabilities as a general-purpose investigative tool that is readily available to government; it also became—for a time—a body for the investigation of complaints of racial discrimination; and it has had many organs of local government added to the jurisdiction. To be

[18] Personal communication from Sir Guy Powles to the author, 22 October 1975.

sure, these are functional adaptations, but they are, in the main, extensions of existing functions. None are radical departures, and none were occasioned by environmental changes—which are the stimuli for the kinds of adaptations Huntington has in mind. After observing that organizations usually are created to perform a specific function, Huntington says: "When that function is no longer needed, the organization faces a major crisis. It either finds a new function or reconciles itself to a lingering death. An organization which has adapted itself to changes in its environment and has survived one or more changes in its principal functions is more highly institutionalized than one that has not."[19]

Sociologists have studied a number of organizations that have replaced their goals because the original ones were achieved or obviated by changing circumstances, and political scientists are aware of the difficulties involved in transforming a "subversive" party of national independence into an effective governing body. Huntington seems to believe that such crucial functional crises will beset all organizations. Perhaps given enough time all will be affected, but it seems unlikely in the foreseeable future that the Ombudsman will solve all of the problems that arise between citizens and the bureaucracy or that such problems will go out of fashion to the extent that no one complains. Hence, the remoteness of the possibility that the Ombudsman's functions will become obsolete should be taken into account before downgrading the organization's adaptability on the grounds that it has faced no major functional crises.

Taken as a whole, the preceding application of Huntington's four criteria to the New Zealand Ombudsman has corroborated our earlier conclusions, which were based upon a longitudinal analysis of the office's development of offensive, authoritative capabilities: institutionalization appears to have occurred, despite the

[19] Huntington, "Political Development and Political Decay," p. 396.

EVALUATIONS

Ombudsman's small size thus far (which makes complexity difficult to achieve) and despite its definite mission and relative youth (which inhibit the scores on functional and generational adaptability). Furthermore, if we were systematically to apply to the Ombudsman the categories developed by Milton Esman or by Ralph Braibanti, those exercises, too, would indicate that institutionalization has occurred. (Many of their categories have been subsumed in others utilized above.)[20]

Finally, if we were to base a judgment of the Ombudsman upon Philip Selznick's definition, which underlies so much of the writing about institutionalization, we would again conclude that the office has become institutionalized. Our data indicate that the Ombudsman

[20] Milton J. Esman ("The Elements of Institution Building," in Joseph W. Eaton, ed., *Institution Building and Development: From Concepts to Application* [Beverly Hills: Sage Publications, 1972], p. 36) suggests four criteria. An organization moving toward institutionality will be characterized by increases in 1) technical capacity, the organization's competence to deliver services; 2) normative commitments, the staff's internalization of the organization's mission; 3) innovative thrust, the ability to learn and adapt to changing political circumstances; and 4) environmental image, the valuing of the organization by the larger society.

Ralph Braibanti ("External Inducement of Political-Administrative Development: An Institutional Strategy," in Braibanti, ed., *Political and Administrative Development* [Durham, N.C.: Duke University Press, 1969], pp. 59–62) proposes seven indices. The adequacy of an institution's performance can be measured by its 1) autonomy, the capacity to function independently while retaining compatibility with the architectonics of the whole political system and coordination with its parts; 2) reception, the ability to accept new norms from other institutions; 3) reformulation, the ability to integrate the new norms with the old ones; 4) internal viability, the mechanical aspects of job performance; 5) balance, maintaining a harmony between the institution's interest and the public interest; 6) congruence, a measure of the relationship between the institution's stated goals and its actual behavior; and 7) roles, the congruence among the role perceptions of the institution's members, those ascribed by the structure, and members' actual role behavior.

EPILOGUE

has developed with environmental actors authority relationships that are based not just upon respect and deference but also upon "prizing" and "value-infusion." According to Selznick's summary statement of the differences between organizations and institutions, the New Zealand Ombudsman has developed sufficiently that it falls into the latter category: "Organizations are technical instruments, designed as means to definite goals. They are judged on engineering premises; they are expendable. Institutions, whether conceived as groups or practices, may be partly engineered, but they have also a 'natural' dimension. They are products of interaction and adaptation; they become the receptacles of group idealism; they are less readily expendable."[21]

Of Time and the Threshold of Institutionalization

Institutionalization is generally conceded to be time-based, but time itself has not in actuality played a key role in analysis of the phenomenon.[22] Some, such as Uphoff and Ilchman, have simply viewed time as a strategic resource to be manipulated by the institution builder.[23] More common is Huntington's straightforward usage: "the longer an organization or procedure has been in existence, the higher the level of institutionalization."[24] As-

[21] Philip Selznick, *Leadership in Administration: A Sociological Interpretation* (New York: Harper and Row, 1957), pp. 21–22.

[22] Milton J. Esman has acknowledged that his original institution-building model "has little to say on the duration of the process, the synchronization and sequences of activities, or the stages of development, except to recognize time in its many dimensions as a problem." "Some Issues in Institution Building Theory," in D. Woods Thomas, Harry R. Potter, William L. Miller, and Adrian F. Aveni, eds., *Institution Building: A Model for Applied Social Change* (Cambridge, Mass.: Schenkman, 1972), p. 72.

[23] Norman T. Uphoff and Warren F. Ilchman, "The Time Dimension in Institution Building," in Eaton, ed., *Institution Building and Development*, pp. 111–35.

[24] Huntington, "Political Development and Political Decay," p. 395.

suredly, if we are comparing organizations' degrees of institutionalization, it seems reasonable (other factors being equal) to rank new ones below those that have been in existence for some years. But in measuring the extent to which any particular organization fulfills whatever definitional criteria are being employed, how does one determine if *enough* time has elapsed so that institutionalization has occurred? Over just how long a period must an organization maintain a stable pattern of authority relations, be prized or considered to be value-infused and nonexpendable by other environmental actors, adapt to important environmental challenges, etc., in order to qualify as "institutionalized"? Because such questions raise important conceptual problems, they usually are not directly confronted by writers on institutionalization.

It certainly would simplify matters if we could conclude that the process of institutionalization requires five, ten, fifteen, or some other definite number of years to reach fruition. Unfortunately, though, the mention of any specific period immediately makes one wonder if the time suggested is not arbitrary. For instance, Duncan and Pooler's estimate that the institution-building process requires at least eight years seems suspect: why eight, rather than seven or nine?[25] Not only may the choice of any absolute length of time seem arbitrary, but also it appears that the time required for institutionalization would vary among organizations—e.g., technically based organizations probably achieve institutionalization more quickly than those that require high degrees of political input and support. Furthermore, it seems obvious that during any given period, organizations might face environmental challenges of quite different orders of mag-

---

[25] Richard Duncan and William Pooler, "Technical Assistance and Institution Building," mimeographed (Pittsburgh: University of Pittsburgh, Institution Building Headquarters, 1967); cited in Esman, "Some Issues in Institution Building Theory," p. 72.

nitude; surely this factor would have a profound impact upon the temporal requirements for institutionalization.

Another conceptual barrier that has tended to inhibit researchers from attempting to make definitive judgments at Time X about whether or not an organization really has become institutionalized is the assumption, which may seem implicit in the question, that institutionalization is a rigid, terminal state. As we have seen, such an assumption would be rejected by many authors who prefer to depict institutionalization as a dynamic, continuous, even a reversible process. Although I have stipulated in Chapter 2 and elsewhere my general agreement with this interpretation, it seems to me that a middle ground can be found between those who perceive of institutionalization as a never-ending process of "becoming" and those who see it as a static end point.

Institutionalization embraces certain aspects of an organization's behavior, the perception of the behavior by other actors in the environment, and their reactions to the behavior. Any of these activities may change over time. A methodological difficulty of analyzing such a phenomenon is that there are no activities that relate uniquely to it: one establishes criteria of relevance, observes behavior patterns, and draws inferences about the apparent extent of institutionalization at that time. Thus, institutionalization is not an either/or process. *I suggest that it is best thought of as a threshold phenomenon.*

To be sure, the institutional analyst is in a far less enviable position than the physiologist who has merely to measure the intensity of pain that can be inflicted upon a subject so that he barely perceives it as pain—the subject's pain threshold. But the analyst of institutions has a similar mission. Does observation of an organization reveal the existence of a relatively stable pattern of activity that has been defined as pertaining to institutionalization? When the relevant activity pattern (the creation of authority relationships, according to the definition preferred here) can be identified as a pattern at its lowest level, then it can be said that the organization has reached the threshold of institutionalization.[26]

Reaching the threshold, the lowest measurable level, of institutionalization is fraught with significance for the organization. Nevertheless there is, of course, no guarantee that the process will continue—e.g., authority relations may be weakened by changes in personnel, by errors in strategies of leadership, or by the disaffection of powerful constituents. Such occurrences could halt institutionalization and even bring about the organization's death. Excepting such dramatic eventualities, however, it is likely that once the minimal conditions for institutionalization have been established the process will continue toward institutional maturity. It is commonly noted that organizations are extremely resilient; even when they serve no apparent purpose and perform badly, they tend to survive and sometimes even to prosper.[27] I hypothesize that those organizations that are so successful that they reach the threshold of institutionalization will have accumulated a quantity of "reserve support," which will tend to insulate them from day-to-day environmental challenges.[28] Furthermore, once the institutionalization threshold has been crossed, challenges of crisis proportions are seldom likely to occur, because the organization will have become established as a authority figure; and other actors will perceive it as an institution—presuming that its demands are legitimate.

Having said that institutionalization is a continual pro-

[26] I have in mind something quite different from what Anthony Downs refers to as a bureau's "initial survival threshold," *Inside Bureaucracy* (Boston: Little, Brown, 1966), p. 9.

[27] William H. Starbuck even contends, "nearly all organizations, nearly all of the time, find survival easy." "Organizational Growth and Development," in James G. March, ed., *Handbook of Organizations* (Chicago: Rand McNally, 1965), p. 464.

[28] See David Easton, "An Approach to the Analysis of Political Systems," *World Politics* 9 (April 1957), 396–97.

cess does not necessarily imply that it is unilinear. Even a developed institution will experience secular changes in the strengths of the authority bonds it has forged with other actors, or—to use Huntington's criteria—its degrees of complexity, coherence, autonomy, and adaptability will fluctuate considerably over time. In fact, an extended longitudinal study of several institutions might even reveal that the process is typically dialectical rather than unilinear.

The general assessment that—according to alternative definitions of the phenomenon—the New Zealand Ombudsman has become institutionalized was made in the previous section. Can we determine the precise point during the office's twelve and one-half year history at which it crossed over the threshold of institutionalization? Of course, the most imposing barrier to making such determinations is that standardized tests of the strength of organizations' authority relationships, etc., are not administered on a regular schedule. Instead, organizations face highly varied environmental challenges or other milestones, whose import may be obscure, at irregular intervals. In the case of the New Zealand Ombudsman, the substantial rise in complaint levels, which occurred after 1971, and the successful accommodation to the demands of a Labor Government, beginning at the end of 1972, were both important developments. Using these indicators, we would conclude that the Ombudsman had crossed the threshold of institutionalization after about a decade of existence.

While I do not believe that judgments about institutionalization that are based upon much less than a decade of experience are very firmly grounded, it may be that the Ombudsman reached the threshold somewhat earlier. Recall from Chapter 8 that for the first four and one-half years, formal recommendations had to be issued to government departments in about one-third of the total of the "rectified" and "recommendation made" cases;

EVALUATIONS

since then the proportion of recommendations has dipped to one-tenth. Although they were not tested by crisis, it appears that the Ombudsman began to forge authority bonds with environmental actors at a relatively early stage of his existence, and during additional years of regularized interaction these authority relationships have been reinforced.

TRANSFER, TRANSFORMATION, AND THE FUTURE

Following New Zealand's decision in 1962 to create a grievance man to be modeled after the Scandinavian ombudsmen, an organization that was initially, at least, structurally very similar to that of those officials was legally founded and put into operation. Furthermore, as established in the preceding chapters, the new organization so thrived in the antipodal environment that after twelve and one-half years we can conclude it has become an institution. In terms of the communications model proposed in Chapter 2, a message about an exogenous institution was received by the host political system, which decoded the signal and encoded a response. Not only did the response become a viable institution, but also it was an *Ombudsman* institution. That is, it closely resembled the original Scandinavian source in both structure and function.[29] Although some minor modulations occurred, a genuine institutional transfer was the result.[30]

---

[29] Compare Walter Gellhorn's chapter on New Zealand with those concerning Sweden, Finland, Denmark, and Norway. *Ombudsmen and Others: Citizens' Protectors in Nine Countries* (Cambridge, Mass.: Harvard University Press, 1966). Also see Larry B. Hill, "The International Transfer of the Ombudsman," in Richard L. Merritt, ed., *Communication in International Politics* (Urbana: University of Illinois Press, 1972), pp. 295–317.

[30] Transfer necessarily entails some adaptations, such as those experienced by the New Zealand Ombudsman and detailed above. Cf. Homer G. Barnett, *Innovation: The Basis of Culture Change* (New York: McGraw-Hill, 1953), p. 331: "The bodily transfer of a thing, even if it

EPILOGUE

Thus far, the New Zealand Ombudsman has existed for only a few years beyond the point at which it has become possible to assert with some confidence that the office was institutionalized. What, then, can we predict about the institution's future? Taking a long-term view, it is always possible that extra- or intraorganizational changes that cannot now be anticipated will cause the Ombudsman's demise or his transformation into some quite different institution.[31] But when one considers the resilience of institutions in general and the protective capabilities of this particular one, such fates seem unlikely. Goal displacement is, however, another possible future that organization theorists might forecast for the Ombudsman. Sociologists long have observed that new organizations tend to be dominated by zealots, committed champions of the goals the organization was created to espouse; yet with the passage of time these external purposes tend to

---

remains intact, does not mean that acceptance has been passive and noncreative; for the integration of a thing demands that it be imbedded in a new context which has varying degrees of resemblance to, but never complete identity with, the one out of which it was taken." In several obvious respects, the New Zealand socio-political environment is similar to that in Scandinavia; this surely was an asset during institutionalization.

[31] Transformation is acknowledged to be a common consequence of attempts at transfer. See Walton H. Hamilton, "Institution," *Encyclopaedia of the Social Sciences*, Vol. 8 (New York: Macmillan, 1932), p. 86: "The act of borrowing merely gives the opportunity for [the institution's] transformation. The nucleus is liberated from its cultural matrix and takes on the character of the usages among which it is set down." Transfers from relatively developed to undeveloped societies are especially likely to result in transformation. See Daniel Lerner, "The Transformation of Political Institutions," in William B. Hamilton, ed., *The Transfer of Institutions* (Durham, N.C.: Duke University Press, 1964), p. 8. Institutional transformation is very nearly the same phenomenon that organization theorists refer to as goal succession. For a theoretically rich case study see Mayer N. Zald, *Organizational Change: The Political Economy of the YMCA* (Chicago: University of Chicago Press, 1970).

be deflected, or displaced, as members receive gratification from following the organization's procedures, from social relations within the organization, from striving for promotions, etc.[32]

Even though the Ombudsman was created as a reform mechanism precisely because administrative agencies were said to be afflicted by this organizational pathology—means came to be regarded as ends in themselves—there is, of course, no guarantee that an Ombudsman will not succumb to the malady and become as rigid, formalistic, and insensitive to the needs of citizens as the remainder of the "bureaucracy" was alleged to be. The Ombudsman's small size, which makes the proliferation of complex procedures ridiculous beyond a certain point and which limits opportunities for status enhancement, seems to mitigate against the likelihood of goal displacement becoming a serious problem. Furthermore, the high probability that unusual care will continue to be taken to recruit as Ombudsmen and staff members those persons who are thoroughly committed to the institution's program would appear to promote goal continuity.

But the structure of the institution itself is the strongest insurance against goal displacement: a constant flow of complaints keeps the Ombudsman oriented toward the demands of citizens. Because clients virtually never lodge multiple complaints, the office has only one opportunity to satisfy each client. Before a particular complaint is disposed of, others arrive; so the organization is not allowed to stagnate or to concentrate its energies upon internal concerns. Furthermore, the Ombudsman's principal contacts, under ordinary circumstances his only type of contacts, with bureaucrats and their superintend-

---

[32] A succinct review of much of the literature on goal displacement is David L. Sills, "Voluntary Associations: Sociological Aspects," *International Encyclopedia of the Social Sciences*, Vol. 16 (New York: Macmillan and Free Press, 1968), pp. 369–72.

ing politicians are adversarial in nature. Agencies respond to his inquiries, which are really challenges, and he makes a determination about the complaint. Relations are then severed until the next complaint arises against that agency. Unlike the American regulatory commissions, to cite a notorious example, the Ombudsman does not share with other powerful actors the responsibility for developing and administering a sector of policy. Because nonadversarial contacts hardly exist, few opportunities occur for agencies to coopt the Ombudsman. In combination, these various factors have thus far preserved the New Zealand Ombudsman's institutional integrity.

Barring cataclysmic events, it is likely that the office will follow the example set by the Swedish Ombudsman during more than a century and a half in reaching succeedingly higher levels of institutionalization. Under auspicious circumstances, it is possible that an Ombudsman that has the structural and functional characteristics attributed in Chapter 1 to the classical model of the office and that reaches the threshold of institutionalization could operate into the indefinite future.

The long-term fates of the many new ombudsmen in North America and elsewhere, most of which were copied—directly or indirectly—from the New Zealand model, will test such speculations. If in these new environments the office proves to be a perpetual reform institution that delivers significant individual and social benefits, then the world will owe yet another debt of gratitude to New Zealand—the "laboratory of democracy."

APPENDIX A*

In Retrospect
A Commentary by Sir Guy Powles

With the new Ombudsmen Bill proceeding through the House, but not passed when this report is being written, it is clear that a fundamental change will come over the functions and methods of operation of the office. It is useful, therefore, to recall some of the important features of the last 12½ years' work.

The legislation setting up the office, which came into force on 1 October 1962, was the product of a very careful and considered process. The original Parliamentary Commissioner Bill was introduced into the House in 1961, but was subjected to a good deal of adverse public criticism. It was withdrawn, completely redrafted and revised, and then reintroduced in 1962 in a considerably improved form. It is now an open secret that it was personally redrafted at a weekend meeting of a high-level group consisting of those gentlemen then holding, respectively, the posts of Minister of Justice, Secretary for Justice, Solicitor-General, and Law Draftsman. It has stood the test of time and its wisdom and clarity have been copied in a number of jurisdictions overseas. It was obviously a seminal piece of legislation which in its own field has made its mark upon the English-speaking world. It has never yet been before the courts for interpretation, partly because of its own clarity, and partly because no one has seen fit to challenge the office's official interpretation of its own statute. This, of course, is not to say that there have not been difficulties, but over the years the

* Reprinted from *Report of the Ombudsman* (Wellington: Government Printer, 1975), pp. 13–15.

APPENDIX

office seems to have worked out to general satisfaction interpretations of its minor obscurities. The principal problem has been how to define "relating to a matter of administration" as the keynote of the jurisdiction, but careful pragmatism does seem to have produced acceptable answers.

The co-operation of the departments in the work of the office has been another outstanding feature, and has indeed meant that, compared with many Ombudsmen offices overseas, the New Zealand office has been able to operate with a comparatively small staff and yet deal with a comparatively large case load. The general principle of inviting departments to co-operate in the investigation of complaints against themselves has proved itself time and time again—it has lightened the load of the Ombudsman's office and it has served to build a firm structure of confidence between the office and the departments which has undoubtedly been in the national interest. It has exemplified the high standard of probity which exists in our Government departments—indeed it has been said by its modern commentators that the Ombudsman system will not work well unless it is applied to a public service which shares the ideals of the office. It should, however, be noted in passing, that recent United Kingdom experience with local authorities is that these bodies are not able to provide this investigatory assistance to the same degree as are departments or agencies of the Central Government. This is not due to any lack of willingness on the part of these bodies, but merely to the physical dispersion of the various administrative structures and the comparatively non-hierarchical nature of many of them. This comment will need to be borne in mind in New Zealand in the future.

As I remarked in one of my earlier annual reports,[1] the Ombudsman system is a complaint-based system—that is

[1] *Report of the Ombudsman*, 31 March 1973, page 14.

A COMMENTARY BY SIR GUY POWLES

to say it requires an active complaint from some individual to set the machinery in motion. There is provision in the legislation for the Ombudsman to take up matters of his own motion, but in New Zealand this has been used very sparingly because so much of the time and energy of the Ombudsman and his officers has been taken up in investigating the actual complaints which are continually being lodged with the office. Operating a complaint-based system, the office needs to be sufficiently well known for people to be moved to complain to it and to utilise its services. This question of publicity is one which has been a source of concern over the years, and there has been an endeavour to strike some form of balance between oblivion and overexposure. It has been found that the intake of complaints usually increases after any important public reference to the Ombudsman or his work. This leads one to suspect that the system does not, in fact, yet touch as many of the potential complaint sufferers as it ought to. Ombudsmen in other parts of the world are increasingly finding it necessary to adopt deliberate publicity measures, such as the issue of pamphlets and the making of appropriate press releases and public statements. The recently established United Kingdom local authority Ombudsman system has launched itself by this means. It will therefore be necessary for the office in future to make sure that it really does reach those people who are most in need of its services.

The office's method of operation, which is wholly investigatory and not adversarial, has lent itself to an objective pursuit of the truth in each case, and in so doing has generated confidence in those persons, be they complainants or departmental officers, whose actions may ultimately be found to be open to criticism. The suggestion that there should be hearings or confrontations between the parties has been resisted, although it is known that some Ombudsmen have used this method occasionally. In cases where obdurate disputes of facts have emerged

APPENDIX

they have been solved by an intensification of the investigatory process, or the investigation has been discontinued upon the ground that a resort to the courts and the well known principles of cross-examination would provide the best solution. The investigatory procedure can take time, and in some cases that the office has handled over the years the time taken has really been very long—much longer than one would initially have hoped. On the other hand, the adversarial procedure, once the court is reached, produces a quick and definite decision. The investigatory method, in addition to taking time, does not produce a decision, only a recommendation. Nevertheless, it has distinct advantages, and in the experience of this office it is the only method which can enable the Ombudsman adequately to fulfil his functions.

This investigatory method has been adopted for use in certain major and special inquiries which were undertaken by the office during the past years. For instance, there were the two special investigations into prison complaints and general conditions at Paremoremo Prison. In these two cases collaboration with an experienced ex-magistrate did not in any way compromise the integrity of the office, or hinder its proper functions—indeed the reverse was the case. There was also the special investigation into complaints against Police conduct during the demonstrations in Auckland in January 1970, and the major inquiry into a "battered baby" case, to mention just two. The procedures followed in these cases were wholly investigatory, as were those in the special inquiry undertaken at the request of the Prime Minister into a difficult issue concerning an aspect of allowances in the Foreign Service. On the other hand I took part in an adversarial inquiry when I sat as one member of a two-man Commission of Inquiry into allegations against the Hubbard Scientology Organisation in New Zealand. The investigatory method, plus the recommendation as its end product, leads to, and can become, a process of conciliation. It is not surprising that this method was chosen for the Race Relations Act, that important procedural sections from the Ombudsman Act were transferred into the Race Relations Act, and that the Ombudsman was chosen as the first Race Relations Conciliator (regretfully having to relinquish it later).

Over the years the relationship which complaints found to be justified bear to the number of complaints investigated has proved strikingly steady—between 20 and 30 percent. Even more striking still is the fact that this seems to be approximately the relationship which exists in all other Ombudsmen jurisdictions for which comparable figures are available. This relationship does not seem to vary according to the total number of complaints received, or the relationship that this number bears to, for example, the total population.

Finally there is the personal factor which, of course, is mentioned with diffidence. The office began with one Ombudsman. The essentials of secretary and administrative assistant were soon added, followed by legal officer, investigating officer, etc., until after 12½ years, and with a massive extension of jurisdiction in contemplation, and already requiring planning arrangements, the office comprises one Ombudsman, one first assistant, one legal counsel, one senior investigating officer, three investigating officers, one administrative assistant, one secretary, and three shorthand typists. This steady period of growth has meant the development of new practices, and the construction of a whole new ethos of administrative procedures. When the office was established there were only three others in the world and not one of them was in an English-speaking community. There are now more than 40 others in the English-speaking world alone. There has therefore been a sense of isolation and solitude about the office—lack of being able to confer with colleagues. This is now largely a thing of the past, and the holding of the regional Ombudsmen Conference in Wellington in

APPENDIX

November of last year ended the era of isolation. However, it is clear that, with able advice and assistance from his staff, the Ombudsman has, in fact, built his own office. With the increasing case load, however, this personal influence will be diminished. The deliberate choice for the extended jurisdiction of a collegiate system of Ombudsmen—each one exercising full jurisdiction, and being equal, and having the division of their functions settled almost wholly by agreement—is a better solution than attempting to build a hierarchical structure with authority stemming from the Chief Ombudsman down through successive layers. The collegiate system has worked well in Sweden, and there is no reason why it should not work well here. There will be ample scope for the Ombudsmen to develop their individual approaches while keeping within a co-ordinated and co-operative framework.

Thus the future will indeed be interesting, and it will be carefully watched by administrators throughout the English-speaking world, just as was the initial New Zealand experiment of establishing the office of Ombudsman in an English-speaking country.

APPENDIX B

The Ombudsmen Act 1975

ANALYSIS

Title
1. Short Title and commencement
2. Interpretation

Ombudsmen

3. Ombudsmen
4. Ombudsmen to hold no other office
5. Term of office of Ombudsmen
6. Removal or suspension from office
7. Filling of vacancy
8. Temporary appointments of Ombudsmen
9. Salaries and allowances of Ombudsmen
10. Oath to be taken by Ombudsmen
11. Staff
12. Superannuation or retiring allowances of Ombudsmen and staff

Functions of Ombudsmen

13. Functions of Ombudsmen
14. Limitation of time for certain complaints in respect of local organisations
15. House of Representatives may make rules for guidance of Ombudsmen
16. Mode of complaint
17. Ombudsman may refuse to investigate complaint
18. Proceedings of Ombudsmen
19. Evidence
20. Disclosure of certain matters not to be required
21. Ombudsmen and staff to maintain secrecy
22. Procedure after investigation
23. Ombudsmen may require publication of summary of report
24. Complainant to be informed of result of investigation
25. Proceedings not to be questioned or to be subject to review
26. Proceedings privileged

Miscellaneous Provisions

27. Power of entry on premises
28. Delegation of powers by Ombudsman
29. Annual report
30. Offences
31. Money to be appropriated by Parliament for purposes of this Act
32. Power to amend First Schedule by Order in Council
33. Repeals, amendment, and savings
Schedules

1975, No. 9

An Act to consolidate and amend the Parliamentary Commissioner (Ombudsman) Act 1962 [*26 June 1975*]

BE IT ENACTED by the General Assembly of New Zealand in Parliament assembled, and by the authority of the same, as follows:

1. Short Title and commencement—(1) This Act may be cited as the Ombudsmen Act 1975.

(2) Part III of the First Schedule to this Act, and sections 13, 18, and 22 of this Act so far as they relate to that

APPENDIX

Part, shall come into force on a date to be appointed by the Governor-General by Order in Council.

(3) Except as provided in subsection (2) of this section, this Act shall come into force upon its passing.

2. Interpretation—In this Act, unless the context otherwise requires,—

> "Ombudsman," in relation to any function, power, or duty under this Act, means the Ombudsman for the time being investigating the complaint in respect of which the function, power, or duty is being exercised.

Ombudsmen

3. Ombudsmen—(1) There shall be appointed, as officers of Parliament and Commissioners for Investigations, one or more Ombudsmen.

(2) Subject to the provisions of section 7 of this Act, each Ombudsman shall be appointed by the Governor-General on the recommendation of the House of Representatives.

(3) No person shall be deemed to be employed in the service of Her Majesty for the purposes of the State Services Act 1962 or the Superannuation Act 1956 by reason of his appointment as an Ombudsman.

(4) One of the Ombudsmen shall be so appointed as Chief Ombudsman, and shall be responsible for the administration of the office, and the co-ordination and allocation of the work between the Ombudsmen.

(5) In any case where the Governor-General is satisfied that the Chief Ombudsman is incapacitated by illness, absence, or other sufficient cause from performing the duties of his office, the Governor-General may appoint one of the other Ombudsmen to act for the Chief Ombudsman during his incapacity.

(6) No appointment of an acting Chief Ombudsman

and no acts done by him as such, shall in any proceedings be questioned on the ground that the occasion for his appointment had not arisen or had ceased.

Cf. 1962, No. 10, s. 2

4. Ombudsmen to hold no other office—An Ombudsman shall not be capable of being a member of Parliament or of a local authority, and shall not, without the approval of the Prime Minister in each particular case, hold any office of trust or profit, other than his office as an Ombudsman, or engage in any occupation for reward outside the duties of his office.

Cf. 1962, No. 10, s. 3

5. Term of office of Ombudsmen—(1) Except as otherwise provided in this Act, every Ombudsman shall hold office for a term of 5 years.

(2) Unless his office sooner becomes vacant, every person appointed as an Ombudsman shall hold office until his successor is appointed. Every such person may from time to time be reappointed.

(3) Any Ombudsman may at any time resign his office by writing addressed to the Speaker of the House of Representatives, or to the Prime Minister if there is no Speaker or the Speaker is absent from New Zealand, and (except in the case of an Ombudsman appointed under section 8 of this Act) shall so resign his office on attaining the age of 72 years.

Cf. 1962, No. 10, s. 4

6. Removal or suspension from office—(1) Any Ombudsman may at any time be removed or suspended from his office by the Governor-General, upon an address from the House of Representatives, for disability, bankruptcy, neglect of duty, or misconduct.

(2) At any time when Parliament is not in session, any Ombudsman may be suspended from his office by the

APPENDIX

Governor-General in Council for disability, bankruptcy, neglect of duty, or misconduct proved to the satisfaction of the Governor-General; but any such suspension shall not continue in force beyond 2 months after the beginning of the next ensuing session of Parliament.

Cf. 1962, No. 10, s. 5

7. Filling of vacancy—(1) If any Ombudsman dies, or resigns his office, or is removed from office, the vacancy thereby created shall be filled in accordance with this section.

(2) If any vacancy in the office of an Ombudsman occurs at any time while Parliament is in session, it shall be filled by the appointment of an Ombudsman by the Governor-General on the recommendation of the House of Representatives:

Provided that if the vacancy occurs less than 2 months before the close of that session and no such recommendation is made in that session, the provisions of subsection (3) of this section shall apply as if the vacancy had occurred while Parliament was not in session.

(3) If any such vacancy occurs at any time while Parliament is not in session, the following provisions shall apply:

(a) The Governor-General in Council may appoint an Ombudsman to fill the vacancy, and the person so appointed shall, unless his office sooner becomes vacant, hold office until his appointment becomes vacant, hold office until his appointment is confirmed by the House of Representatives:

(b) If the appointment is not so confirmed within 2 months after the commencement of the next ensuing session, the appointment shall lapse and there shall be deemed to be a further vacancy in the office of an Ombudsman.

Cf. 1962, No. 10, s. 6

8. Temporary appointments of Ombudsmen—(1) The Governor-General may, at any time during the illness or absence of any Ombudsman, or for any other temporary purpose whatsoever, appoint an Ombudsman to hold office in accordance with this section, and every such Ombudsman shall be paid such salary, not exceeding the amount payable in accordance with section 9 of this Act to an Ombudsman other than the Chief Ombudsman, as the Governor-General thinks fit.

(2) The power conferred by this section shall be exercised only on a certificate signed by the Chief Ombudsman to the effect that, in his opinion, it is necessary for the due conduct of the business of the Ombudsmen under this Act that an additional Ombudsman should be temporarily appointed.

(3) Subject to sections 5 to 7 of this Act, every Ombudsman appointed under this section on account of the illness or absence of an Ombudsman shall hold office during the pleasure of the Governor-General, and every other Ombudsman appointed for a temporary purpose shall hold office for such period, not exceeding 2 years, as may be specified in his warrant of appointment.

(4) An Ombudsman appointed under this section may from time to time be reappointed, but no Ombudsman shall hold office under this section for more than 5 years in the aggregate.

(5) The provisions of section 7 of this Act shall apply, with any necessary modifications, to the temporary appointment of an Ombudsman under this section as if the Ombudsman were being appointed under that section to fill a vacancy.

9. Salaries and allowances of Ombudsmen—(1) There shall be paid to each Ombudsman out of the Consolidated Revenue Account, without further appropriation than this section, a salary at such rate as the Governor-

APPENDIX

General, by Order in Council, from time to time determines, and the rate so determined for the Chief Ombudsman may be higher than that for the other Ombudsmen.

(2) The salary of an Ombudsman is not to be diminished by an Order in Council under this section during the continuance of his appointment.

(3) Any Order in Council under this section, and any provision of any such order, may be made so as to come into force on a date to be specified in that behalf in the order, being the date of the making of the order or any other date, whether before or after the date of the making of the order or the date of the commencement of this Act.

(4) Every Order in Council under this section, and every provision of any such order, in respect of which no date is specified as aforesaid shall come into force on the date of the making of the order.

(5) The provisions of section 8 of the Regulations Act 1936 (which relates to the laying of regulations before Parliament) shall extend and apply to every Order in Council made under this section.

(6) There shall be paid to each Ombudsman, in respect of time spent in travelling in the exercise of his functions, travelling allowances and expenses in accordance with the Fees and Travelling Allowances Act 1951, and the provisions of that Act shall apply accordingly as if the Ombudsman were a member of a statutory Board and the travelling were in the service of a statutory Board.

Cf. 1962, No. 10, s. 7; 1970, No. 96, s. 2

10. Oath to be taken by Ombudsmen—(1) Before entering upon the exercise of the duties of his office an Ombudsman shall take an oath that he will faithfully and impartially perform the duties of his office, and that he will not, except in accordance with section 21 of this Act, divulge any information received by him under this Act.

(2) The oath shall be administered by the Speaker or the Clerk of the House of Representatives.
Cf. 1962, No. 10, s. 8

11. Staff—(1) Subject to the provisions of this section, the Chief Ombudsman may appoint such officers and employees as may be necessary for the efficient carrying out of the functions, powers, and duties of the Ombudsmen under this Act.

(2) The number of persons that may be appointed under this section, whether generally or in respect of any specified duties or class of duties, shall from time to time be determined by the Prime Minister.

(3) The salaries of persons appointed under this section, and the terms and conditions of their appointments, shall be such as are approved by the Minister of Finance.

(4) No person shall be deemed to be employed in the service of Her Majesty for the purposes of the State Services Act 1962 or the Superannuation Act 1956 by reason of his appointment under this section.
Cf. 1962, No. 10, s. 9

12. Superannuation or retiring allowances of Ombudsmen and staff—There may from time to time be paid sums by way of contributions or subsidies to the National Provident Fund or any Fund or scheme approved by the Governor-General in Council for the purpose of providing superannuation or retiring allowances for any Ombudsman and any officer or employee appointed under this Act.
Cf. 1962, No. 10, s. 10

Functions of Ombudsmen

13. Functions of Ombudsmen—(1) Subject to section 14 of this Act, it shall be a function of the Ombudsmen to

APPENDIX

investigate any decision or recommendation made, or any act done or omitted, whether before or after the passing of this Act, relating to a matter of administration and affecting any person or body of persons in his or its personal capacity, in or by any of the Departments or organisations named or specified in Parts I and II of the First Schedule to this Act, or by any committee (other than a committee of the whole) or subcommittee of any organisation named or specified in Part III of the First Schedule to this Act, or by any officer, employee, or member of any such Department or organisation in his capacity as such officer, employee, or member.

(2) Subject to section 14 of this Act, and without limiting the generality of subsection (1) of this section, it is hereby declared that the power conferred by that subsection includes the power to investigate a recommendation made, whether before or after the passing of this Act, by any such Department, organisation, committee, subcommittee, officer, employee, or member to a Minister of the Crown or to any organisation named or specified in Part III of the First Schedule to this Act, as the case may be.

(3) Each Ombudsman may make any such investigation either on a complaint made to an Ombudsman by any person or of his own motion; and where a complaint is made he may investigate any decision, recommendation, act, or omission to which the foregoing provisions of this section relate, notwithstanding that the complaint may not appear to relate to that decision, recommendation, act, or omission.

(4) Without limiting the foregoing provisions of this section, it is hereby declared that any Committee of the House of Representatives may at any time refer to an Ombudsman, for investigation and report by an Ombudsman, any petition that is before that Committee for consideration, or any matter to which the petition relates. In any such case, an Ombudsman shall, subject to any

special directions of the Committee, investigate the matters so referred, so far as they are within his jurisdiction, and make such report to the Committee as he thinks fit. Nothing in section 17 or section 22 or section 24 of this Act shall apply in respect of any investigation or report made under this subsection.

(5) Without limiting the foregoing provisions of this section, it is hereby declared that at any time the Prime Minister may, with the consent of the Chief Ombudsman, refer to an Ombudsman for investigation and report any matter, other than a matter concerning a judicial proceeding, which the Prime Minister considers should be investigated by an Ombudsman. Where a matter is referred to an Ombudsman pursuant to this subsection, he shall, notwithstanding anything to the contrary in this Act, forthwith investigate that matter and report thereon to the Prime Minister, and may thereafter make such report to Parliament on the matter as he thinks fit. Nothing in section 22 of this Act shall apply in respect of any investigation or report made under this subsection.

(6) The powers conferred on Ombudsmen by this Act may be exercised notwithstanding any provision in any enactment to the effect that any such decision, recommendation, act, or omission shall be final, or that no appeal shall lie in respect thereof, or that no proceeding or decision of the person or organisation whose decision, recommendation, act, or omission it is shall be challenged, reviewed, quashed, or called in question.

(7) Nothing in this Act shall authorise an Ombudsman to investigate—

    (a) Any decision, recommendation, act, or omission in respect of which there is, under the provisions of any Act or regulation, a right of appeal or objection, or a right to apply for a review, available to the complainant, on the merits of the case, to any Court, or to any tribunal constituted by or under any enactment, whether or not that right of ap-

APPENDIX

peal or objection or application has been exercised in the particular case, and whether or not any time prescribed for the exercise of that right has expired:

Provided that the Ombudsman may conduct an investigation (not being an investigation relating to any decision, recommendation, act, or omission to which any other paragraph of this subsection applies) notwithstanding that the complainant has or had such right if by reason of special circumstances it would be unreasonable to expect him to resort or have resorted to it:

(b) Any decision, recommendation, act, or omission of any person in his capacity as a trustee within the meaning of the Trustee Act 1956:

(c) Any decision, recommendation, act, or omission of any person acting as legal adviser to the Crown pursuant to the rules for the time being approved by the Government for the conduct of Crown legal business, or acting as counsel for the Crown in relation to any proceedings:

(d) Any decision, recommendation, act, or omission of any member of the Police that may be the subject of an inquiry under section 33 of the Police Act 1958, unless a complaint in relation thereto has been made or conveyed to a member of the Police superior in rank to the member to whom the complaint relates; and

    (i) The complaint has not been investigated; or

    (ii) The complaint has been investigated and the complainant is dissatisfied with the final result.

(8) Nothing in this Act shall authorise an Ombudsman to investigate any matter relating to any person who is or was a member of or provisional entrant to the New Zea-

land Naval Forces, the New Zealand Army, or the Royal New Zealand Air Force, so far as the matter relates to—
   (a) The terms and conditions of his service as such member or entrant; or
   (b) Any order, command, decision, penalty, or punishment given to or affecting him in his capacity as such member or entrant.

(9) If any question arises whether an Ombudsman has jurisdiction to investigate any case or class of cases under this Act, he may, if he thinks fit, apply to the Supreme Court for a declaratory order determining the question in accordance with the Declaratory Judgments Act 1908, and the provisions of that Act shall extend and apply accordingly.

Cf. 1962, No. 10, s. 11; 1968, No. 138, s. 2

14. Limitation of time for certain complaints in respect of local organisations—Nothing in section 13 of this Act shall permit an Ombudsman to investigate any decision or recommendation made, or any act done or omitted, in or by any committee or subcommittee of any organisation named or specified in Part III of the First Schedule to this Act (other than an Education Board or a Hospital Board), or by any officer, employee, or member of any such organisation to which this subsection applies in his capacity as such officer, employee, or member, unless the decision or recommendation was made, or the act or omission occurred or continued within 6 months before Part III of the First Schedule to this Act came into force.

15. House of Representatives may make rules for guidance of Ombudsmen—(1) The House of Representatives may from time to time, if it thinks fit, make general rules for the guidance of the Ombudsmen in the exercise of their functions, and may at any time in like manner revoke or vary any such rules.

APPENDIX

(2) Any such rules may authorise an Ombudsman from time to time, in the public interest or in the interests of any person or Department or organisation, to publish reports relating generally to the exercise of his functions under this Act or to any particular case or cases investigated by him, whether or not the matters to be dealt with in any such report have been the subject of a report to Parliament under this Act.

(3) All rules made under this section shall be printed and published in accordance with the Regulations Act 1936.

Cf. 1962, No. 10, s. 12

16. Mode of complaint—(1) Every complaint to an Ombudsman shall be made in writing.

(2) Notwithstanding any provision in any enactment, where any letter appearing to be written by any person in custody on a charge or after conviction of any offence, or by any patient of any hospital within the meaning of the Mental Health Act 1969, is addressed to an Ombudsman it shall be immediately forwarded, unopened, to the Ombudsman by the person for the time being in charge of the place or institution where the writer of the letter is detained or of which he is a patient.

Cf. 1962, No. 10, s. 13

17. Ombudsman may refuse to investigate complaint—(1) An Ombudsman may—
- (a) Refuse to investigate a complaint that is within his jurisdiction or to investigate any such complaint further if it appears to him that under the law or existing administrative practice there is an adequate remedy or right of appeal, other than the right to petition Parliament, to which it would have been reasonable for the complainant to resort; or

(b) Refuse to investigate any such complaint further if in the course of the investigation of the complaint it appears to him that, having regard to all the circumstances of the case, any further investigation is unnecessary.

(2) Without limiting the generality of the powers conferred on Ombudsmen by this Act, it is hereby declared that an Ombudsman may in his discretion decide not to investigate, or, as the case may require, not to investigate further, any complaint if it relates to any decision, recommendation, act, or omission of which the complainant has had knowledge for more than 12 months before the complaint is received by the Ombudsman, or if in his opinion—
  (a) The subject-matter of the complaint is trivial; or
  (b) The complaint is frivolous or vexatious or is not made in good faith; or
  (c) The complainant has not a sufficient personal interest in the subject-matter of the complaint.

(3) In any case where an Ombudsman decides not to investigate or make further investigation of a complaint he shall inform the complainant of that decision, and shall state his reasons therefor.

Cf. 1962, No. 10, s. 14

18. Proceedings of Ombudsmen—(1) Before investigating any matter under this Act, an Ombudsman shall inform the Permanent Head of the Department affected, or, as the case may require, the principal administrative officer of the organisation affected, of his intention to make the investigation.

(2) Every investigation by an Ombudsman under this Act shall be conducted in private.

(3) An Ombudsman may hear or obtain information from such persons as he thinks fit, and may make such inquiries as he thinks fit. It shall not be necessary for an

APPENDIX

Ombudsman to hold any hearing, and no person shall be entitled as of right to be heard by an Ombudsman:

Provided that if at any time during the course of an investigation it appears to an Ombudsman that there may be sufficient grounds for his making any report or recommendation that may adversely affect any Department or organisation or person, he shall give to that Department or organisation or person an opportunity to be heard.

(4) In the case of an investigation relating to a Department or organisation named or specified in Parts I and II of the First Schedule to this Act, an Ombudsman may in his discretion at any time during or after the investigation consult a Minister who is concerned in the matter of the investigation, and an Ombudsman shall consult any Minister who so requests or to whom a recommendation which is the subject of the investigation has been made, after the Ombudsman has made the investigation and before he has formed a final opinion on any of the matters referred to in subsection (1) or subsection (2) of section 22 of this Act.

(5) In the case of an investigation relating to an organisation named or specified in Part III of the First Schedule to this Act, an Ombudsman may in his discretion at any time during or after the investigation consult the Mayor or Chairman of the organisation concerned, and an Ombudsman shall consult the Mayor or Chairman of the organisation who so requests or to whom a recommendation which is the subject of the investigation has been made, after the Ombudsman has made the investigation and before he has formed a final opinion on any of the matters referred to in subsection (1) or subsection (2) of section 22 of this Act.

(6) If, during or after any investigation, a Commissioner is of opinion that there is substantial evidence of any significant breach of duty or misconduct on the part of any officer or employee of any Department or organisa-

tion, he shall refer the matter to the appropriate authority.

(7) Subject to the provisions of this Act and of any rules made for the guidance of Ombudsmen by the House of Representatives and for the time being in force, an Ombudsman may regulate his procedure in such manner as he thinks fit.

Cf. 1962, No. 10, s. 15

19. Evidence—(1) Subject to the provisions of this section and of section 20 of this Act, an Ombudsman may from time to time require any person who in his opinion is able to give any information relating to any matter that is being investigated by the Ombudsman to furnish to him any such information, and to produce any documents or papers or things which in the Ombudsman's opinion relate to any such matter as aforesaid and which may be in the possession or under the control of that person. This subsection shall apply whether or not the person is an officer, employee, or member of any Department or organisation, and whether or not such documents, papers, or things are in the custody or under the control of any Department or organisation.

(2) An Ombudsman may summon before him and examine on oath—
   (a) Any person who is an officer or employee or member of any Department or organisation named or specified in the First Schedule to this Act and who in the Ombudsman's opinion is able to give any such information as aforesaid; or
   (b) Any complainant; or
   (c) With the prior approval of the Attorney-General in each case, any other person who in the Ombudsman's opinion is able to give any such information—

and for that purpose may administer an oath. Every such examination by the Ombudsman shall be deemed to be a

APPENDIX

judicial proceeding within the meaning of section 108 of the Crimes Act 1961 (which relates to perjury).

(3) Subject to the provisions of subsection (4) of this section, no person who is bound by the provisions of any enactment, other than the State Services Act 1962 and the Official Secrets Act 1951, to maintain secrecy in relation to, or not to disclose, any matter shall be required to supply any information to or answer any question put by an Ombudsman in relation to that matter, or to produce to an Ombudsman any document or paper or thing relating to it, if compliance with that requirement would be in breach of the obligation of secrecy or non-disclosure.

(4) With the previous consent in writing of any complainant, any person to whom subsection (3) of this section applies may be required by an Ombudsman to supply information or answer any question or produce any document or paper or thing relating only to the complainant, and it shall be the duty of the person to comply with that requirement.

(5) Every person shall have the same privileges in relation to the giving of information, the answering of questions, and the production of documents and papers and things as witnesses have in any Court.

(6) Except on the trial of any person for perjury within the meaning of the Crimes Act 1961 in respect of his sworn testimony, no statement made or answer given by that or any other person in the course of any inquiry by or any proceedings before an Ombudsman shall be admissible in evidence against any person in any Court or at any inquiry or in any other proceedings, and no evidence in respect of proceedings before an Ombudsman shall be given against any person.

(7) No person shall be liable to prosecution for an offence against the Official Secrets Act 1951 or any enactment, other than this Act, by reason of his compliance with any requirement of an Ombudsman under this section.

(8) Where any person is required by an Ombudsman to attend before him for the purposes of this section, the person shall be entitled to the same fees, allowances, and expenses as if he were a witness in a Court, and the provisions of any regulations in that behalf made under the Summary Proceedings Act 1957 and for the time being in force shall apply accordingly. For the purposes of this subsection an Ombudsman shall have the powers of a Court under any such regulations to fix or disallow, in whole or in part, or increase the amounts payable thereunder.

Cf. 1962, No. 10, s. 16

20. Disclosure of certain matters not to be required—(1) Where the Attorney-General certifies that the giving of any information or the answering of any question or the production of any document or paper or thing—
- (a) Might prejudice the security, defence, or international relations of New Zealand (including New Zealand's relations with the Government of any other country or with any international organisation), or the investigation or detection of offences; or
- (b) Might involve the disclosure of the deliberations of Cabinet; or
- (c) Might involve the disclosure of proceedings of Cabinet, or of any committee of Cabinet, relating to matters of a secret or confidential nature, and would be injurious to the public interest—

an Ombudsman shall not require the information or answer to be given or, as the case may be, the document or paper or thing to be produced.

(2) Subject to the provisions of subsection (1) of this section, the rule of law which authorises or requires the withholding of any document or paper, or the refusal to answer any question, on the ground that the disclosure of the document or paper or the answering of the question

APPENDIX

would be injurious to the public interest shall not apply in respect of any investigation by or proceedings before an Ombudsman.

Cf. 1962, No. 10, s. 17

21. Ombudsmen and staff to maintain secrecy— (1) Every Ombudsman and every person holding any office or appointment under the Chief Ombudsman shall be deemed for the purposes of the Official Secrets Act 1951 to be persons holding office under Her Majesty.

(2) Every Ombudsman and every such person as aforesaid shall maintain secrecy in respect of all matters that come to their knowledge in the exercise of their functions.

(3) Every person holding any office or appointment under the Chief Ombudsman shall, before he begins to perform any official duty under this Act, take an oath, to be administered by an Ombudsman, that he will not divulge any information received by him under this Act except for the purpose of giving effect to this Act.

(4) Notwithstanding anything in the foregoing provisions of this section, an Ombudsman may disclose such matters as in his opinion ought to be disclosed for the purposes of an investigation or in order to establish grounds for his conclusions and recommendations. The power conferred by this subsection shall not extend to any matter that might prejudice the security, defence, or international relations of New Zealand (including New Zealand's relations with the Government of any other country or with any international organisation) or the investigation or detection of offences, or that might involve the disclosure of the deliberations of Cabinet.

Cf. 1962, No. 10, s. 18

22. Procedure after investigation—(1) The provisions of this section shall apply in every case where, after making any investigation under this Act, an Ombudsman is of

THE OMBUDSMEN ACT 1975

opinion that the decision, recommendation, act, or omission which was the subject-matter of the investigation—
- (a) Appears to have been contrary to law; or
- (b) Was unreasonable, unjust, oppressive, or improperly discriminatory, or was in accordance with a rule of law or a provision of any Act, regulation, or bylaw or a practice that is or may be unreasonable, unjust, oppressive, or improperly discriminatory; or
- (c) Was based wholly or partly on a mistake of law or fact; or
- (d) Was wrong.

(2) The provisions of this section shall also apply in any case where an Ombudsman is of opinion that in the making of the decision or recommendation, or in the doing or omission of the act, a discretionary power has been exercised for an improper purpose or on irrelevant grounds or on the taking into account of irrelevant considerations, or that, in the case of a decision made in the exercise of any discretionary power, reasons should have been given for the decision.

(3) If in any case to which this section applies an Ombudsman is of opinion—
- (a) That the matter should be referred to the appropriate authority for further consideration; or
- (b) That the omission should be rectified; or
- (c) That the decision should be cancelled or varied; or
- (d) That any practice on which the decision, recommendation, act, or omission was based should be altered; or
- (e) That any law on which the decision, recommendation, act, or omission was based should be reconsidered; or
- (f) That reasons should have been given for the decision; or
- (g) That any other steps should be taken—

the Ombudsman shall report his opinion, and his reasons

therefor, to the appropriate Department or organisation, and may make such recommendations as he thinks fit. In any such case he may request the Department or organisation to notify him, within a specified time, of the steps (if any) that it proposes to take to give effect to his recommendations. The Ombudsman shall also, in the case of an investigation relating to a Department or organisation named or specified in Parts I and II of the First Schedule to this Act, send a copy of his report or recommendations to the Minister concerned, and, in the case of an investigation relating to an organisation named or specified in Part III of the First Schedule to this Act, send a copy of his report or recommendations to the Mayor or Chairman of the organisation concerned.

(4) If within a reasonable time after the report is made no action is taken which seems to an Ombudsman to be adequate and appropriate, the Ombudsman, in his discretion, after considering the comments (if any) made by or on behalf of any Department or organisation affected, may send a copy of the report and recommendations to the Prime Minister, and may thereafter make such report to Parliament on the matter as he thinks fit.

(5) The Ombudsman shall attach to every report sent or made under subsection (4) of this section a copy of any comments made by or on behalf of the Department or organisation affected.

(6) Subsections (4) and (5) of this section shall not apply in the case of an investigation relating to an organisation named or specified in Part III of the First Schedule to this Act.

(7) Notwithstanding anything in this section, an Ombudsman shall not, in any report made under this Act, make any comment that is adverse to any person unless the person has been given an opportunity to be heard.

Cf. 1962, No. 10, s. 19

23. Ombudsman may require publication of summary of report—(1) Where an Ombudsman has prepared a report under subsection (3) of section 22 of this Act relating to any organisation named or specified in Part III of the First Schedule to this Act, he may prepare and send to the principal administrative officer of that organisation a written summary of the contents of his report and require that officer to make copies of that summary available during ordinary business hours for inspection by members of the public without charge. Any member of the public may make a copy of the whole or any part of the summary.

(2) Before forwarding any such written summary to the appropriate principal administrative officer under subsection (1) of this section, the Ombudsman shall send a copy of it in draft form to the organisation to which it relates for perusal, and shall, as far as practicable, incorporate in the summary any comments made to him by the organization.

(3) Within one week after the report is received by the organisation, the principal administrative officer of that organisation shall, at the expense of the organisation, give public notice in such form and in such newspapers as the Ombudsman shall require of the availability of the report for inspection and of the places where it may be inspected.

(4) Every such report shall be made available for a period of 4 weeks from the date of the first publication of the public notice.

24. Complainant to be informed of result of investigation—(1) Where, on any investigation following a complaint, an Ombudsman makes a recommendation under subsection (3) of section 22 of this Act, and no action which seems to the Ombudsman to be adequate and appropriate is taken thereon within a reasonable time, the Ombudsman shall inform the complainant of his recommendation, and may make such comments on the matter as he thinks fit.

(2) The Ombudsman shall in any case inform the com-

plainant, in such manner and at such time as he thinks proper, of the result of the investigation.
Cf. 1962, No. 10, s. 20.

25. Proceedings not to be questioned or to be subject to review—No proceeding of an Ombudsman shall be held bad for want of form, and, except on the ground of lack of jurisdiction, no proceeding or decision of an Ombudsman shall be liable to be challanged, reviewed, quashed, or called in question in any Court.
Cf. 1962, No. 10, s. 21

26. Proceedings privileged—(1) Except in the case of proceedings for an offence against the Official Secrets Act 1951,—
- (a) No proceedings, civil or criminal, shall lie against any Ombudsman, or against any person holding any office or appointment under the Chief Ombudsman, for anything he may do or report or say in the course of the exercise or intended exercise of his functions under this Act, unless it is shown that he acted in bad faith:
- (b) No Ombudsman, and no such person as aforesaid, shall be called to give evidence in any Court, or in any proceedings of a judicial nature, in respect of anything coming to his knowledge in the exercise of his functions.

(2) Anything said or any information supplied or any document, paper, or thing produced by any person in the course of any inquiry by or proceedings before an Ombudsman under this Act shall be privileged in the same manner as if the inquiry or proceedings were proceedings in a Court.

(3) For the purposes of clause 5 of the First Schedule to the Defamation Act 1954, any report made by an Ombudsman under this Act shall be deemed to be an official report made by a person holding an inquiry under the authority of the legislature of New Zealand.
Cf. 1962, No. 10, s. 22

THE OMBUDSMEN ACT 1975

Miscellaneous Provisions

27. Power of entry on premises—(1) For the purposes of this Act, but subject to the provisions of this section, an Ombudsman may at any time enter upon any premises occupied by any of the Departments or organisations named or specified in the First Schedule to this Act and inspect the premises and, subject to the provisions of sections 19 and 20 of this Act, carry out therein any investigation that is within his jurisdiction.

(2) Before entering upon any such premises an Ombudsman shall notify the Permanent Head of the Department or, as the case may require, the principal administrative officer of the organisation by which the premises are occupied.

(3) The Attorney-General may from time to time by notice to the Chief Ombudsman exclude the application of subsection (1) of this section to any specified premises or class of premises, if he is satisfied that the exercise of the power conferred by this section might prejudice the security, defence, or international relations of New Zealand, including New Zealand's relations with the Government of any other country or with any international organisation.

Cf. 1962, No. 10, s. 23

28. Delegation of powers by Ombudsman—(1) With the prior approval of the Prime Minister, any Ombudsman may from time to time, by writing under his hand, delegate to any person holding any office under him any of his powers under this Act, except this power of delegation and the power to make any report under this Act.

(2) Any delegation under this section may be made to a specified person or to the holder for the time being of a specified office or to the holders of offices of a specified class.

(3) Every delegation under this section shall be revo-

APPENDIX

cable at will, and no such delegation shall prevent the exercise of any power by an Ombudsman.

(4) Any such delegation may be made subject to such restrictions and conditions as the Ombudsman thinks fit, and may be made either generally or in relation to any particular case or class of cases.

(5) Until any such delegation is revoked, it shall continue in force according to its tenor. In the event of the Ombudsman by whom it was made ceasing to hold office, it shall continue to have effect as if made by his successor.

(6) Any person purporting to exercise any power of an Ombudsman by virtue of a delegation under this section shall, when required to do so, produce evidence of his authority to exercise the power.

Cf. 1962, No. 10, s. 24

29. Annual report—Without limiting the right of an Ombudsman to report at any other time, but subject to the provisions of subsection (7) of section 22 of this Act and to any rules for the guidance of the Ombudsmen made by the House of Representatives and for the time being in force, the Ombudsmen shall in each year make a report to Parliament on the exercise of their functions under this Act.

Cf. 1962, No. 10, s. 25

30. Offences—Every person commits an offence against this Act and is liable on summary conviction to a fine not exceeding $200 who—
- (a) Without lawful justification or excuse, wilfully obstructs, hinders, or resists an Ombudsman or any other person in the exercise of his powers under this Act:
- (b) Without lawful justification or excuse, refuses or wilfully fails to comply with any lawful require-

ment of an Ombudsman or any other person under this Act:
(c) Wilfully makes any false statement to or misleads or attempts to mislead an Ombudsman or any other person in the exercise of his powers under this Act:
(d) Represents directly or indirectly that he holds any authority under this Act when he does not hold that authority.
Cf. 1962, No. 10, s. 26

31. Money to be appropriated by Parliament for purposes of this Act—Except as otherwise provided in this Act, all salaries and allowances and other expenditure payable or incurred under or in the administration of this Act shall be payable out of money to be appropriated by Parliament for the purpose.
Cf. 1962, No. 10, s. 27

32. Power to amend First Schedule by Order in Council—(1) Where any Department or organisation named or specified in the First Schedule to this Act is abolished, or its name is altered, or where any new Department of State is created, the Governor-General may, by Order in Council, make such amendments to the said Schedule as may be necessary to give effect to the abolition or alteration, or to include the name of the new Department therein.

(2) The Governor-General may from time to time, by Order in Council, amend Part II or Part III of the First Schedule to this Act by—
(a) Including therein the name of any local organisation or other organisation or the description of any class of local organisations or other organisations:

APPENDIX

(b) Omitting from the said Part II or Part III the name of any local organisation or other organisation or the description of any class of local organisations or other organisations, whether that name or description appeared in that Part as initially enacted or was included therein by any other Act or any Order of Council.

Cf. 1962, No. 10, s. 28

33. Repeals, amendment, and savings—(1) Subject to subsection (5) of this section, the enactments specified in the Second Schedule to this Act are hereby repealed.

(2) Section 63 of the Mental Health Act 1969 is hereby amended by omitting from subsection (1) the words "the Ombudsman," and substituting the words "an Ombudsman."

(3) The provisions of this Act are in addition to the provisions of any other enactment or any rule of law under which any remedy or right of appeal or objection is provided for any person or any procedure is provided for the inquiry into or investigation of any matter, and nothing in this Act shall limit or affect any such remedy or right of appeal or objection or procedure as aforesaid.

(4) Notwithstanding the repeal of subsection (1) of section 4 of the Parliamentary Commissioner (Ombudsman) Act 1962, any appointment made pursuant to a recommendation under that subsection shall continue in full force and effect until the dissolution or expiration of the Parliament that is in existence at the commencement of this Act.

(5) The enactments specified in the Second Schedule to this Act shall continue in force in relation to the organisations specified in Part III of the Schedule to the Parliamentary Commissioner (Ombudsman) Act 1962, as added by section 2 (6) of the Parliamentary Commissioner (Ombudsman) Amendment Act 1968, until Part III of the First Schedule to this Act comes into force.

THE OMBUDSMEN ACT 1975

SCHEDULES

Section 13   FIRST SCHEDULE

DEPARTMENTS AND ORGANISATIONS TO WHICH THIS ACT APPLIES

Part I—Government Departments

The Audit Department.
The Crown Law Office.
The Customs Department.
The Department of Education.
The Department of Health.
The Department of Internal Affairs.
The Department of Justice.
The Department of Labour.
The Department of Lands and Survey.
The Department of Scientific and Industrial Research.
The Department of Social Welfare.
The Department of Statistics.
The Department of Trade and Industry.
The Export Guarantee Office.
The Government Life Insurance Office.
The Government Printing Office.
The Housing Corporation of New Zealand.
The Inland Revenue Department.
The Legislative Department.
The Maori and Island Affairs Department.
The Maori Trust Office.
The Mines Department.
The Ministry of Agriculture and Fishers.
The Ministry of Civil Defence.
The Ministry of Defence.
The Ministry of Energy Resources.
The Ministry of Foreign Affairs.
The Ministry of Recreation and Sport.
The Ministry of Transport.

APPENDIX

FIRST SCHEDULE—*continued*

The Ministry of Works and Development.
The New Zealand Electricity Department.
The New Zealand Forest Service.
The New Zealand Government Railways Department.
The Office of the State Services Commission.
The Parliamentary Counsel Office.
The Police Department.
The Post Office.
The Prime Minister's Department.
The Public Trust Office.
The Rural Banking and Finance Corporation of New Zealand.
The State Insurance Office.
The Tourist and Publicity Department.
The Treasury.
The Valuation Department.

Part II—Organisations Other than Local Organisations

The Accident Compensation Commission.
The Agricultural Chemicals Board.
The Animal Remedies Board.
The Board of Maori Affairs.
The Board of Trustees of the National Art Gallery, the National Museum, and the National War Memorial.
The Canteen Fund Board.
The Children's Health Camps Board.
The Decimal Currency Board.
The Earthquake and War Damage Commission.
The Fire Service Commission.
The Government Stores Board.
The Government Superannuation Board.
The Land Settlement Board.
Management Council and Special Councils under the National Art Gallery, Museum, and War Memorial Act 1972.

THE OMBUDSMEN ACT 1975
FIRST SCHEDULE—continued

The Maori Education Foundation.
The Maori Purposes Fund Board.
The Maori Trustee.
The Marginal Lands Board.
The National Civil Defence Committee.
The National Hydatids Council.
The National Parks Authority.
The National Provident Fund Board.
The National Roads Board.
The National Water and Soil Conservation Authority.
The New Zealand Army.
The New Zealand Council for Recreation and Sport.
The New Zealand Defence Council.
The New Zealand Historic Places Trust.
The New Zealand Maori Arts and Crafts Institute.
The New Zealand Naval Board.
The New Zealand Naval Forces.
The New Zealand Patriotic Fund Board.
The New Zealand Trades Certification Board.
The Pacific Islands Polynesian Education Foundation Board.
The Pest Destruction Council.
The Poisons Committee.
The Police.
The Queen Elizabeth the Second Arts Council of New Zealand.
The Rehabilitation Board.
The Royal New Zealand Air Force.
The Social Security Commission.
The Soil Conservation and Rivers Control Council.
The Standards Council.
The State Insurance Investment Board.
The State Services Commission.
The Technicians Certification Authority of New Zealand.
The Urban Public Passenger Transport Council.

APPENDIX

FIRST SCHEDULE—*continued*

The Vocational Training Council.
The Water Resources Council.

Part III—*Local Organisations*

Airport Authorities.
Approved organisations under the Hydatids Act 1968.
Borough Councils.
Camp Committees under the Children's Health Camps Act 1972.
Catchment Boards.
Catchment Commissions.
City Councils.
Committees of Management of Secondary Schools.
County Councils.
District Councils.
District Roads Councils.
Domain Boards.
Drainage Boards.
Education Boards.
Electric Power Boards.
Fire Boards.
Governing bodies of Community Colleges.
Governing bodies of Secondary Schools.
Governing bodies of Teachers' Colleges.
Governing bodies of Technical Institutes.
Harbour Boards.
Hospital Boards.
Irrigation Boards.
Licensing Trusts.
Nassella Tussock Boards.
National Park Board Committees.
National Park Boards.
Pest Destruction Boards.
Provincial Patriotic Councils.
Public reserves special Boards, Trusts, or Trust Boards.

THE OMBUDSMEN ACT 1975

FIRST SCHEDULE—continued

Regional Civil Defence Committees.
Regional Councils.
Regional Planning Authorities.
Regional Water Boards.
River Boards.
Scenic Boards.
Secondary Schools Councils.
Town Councils.
United Councils.
The Auckland Harbour Bridge Authority.
The Auckland Institute and Museum Trust Board.
The Auckland Regional Authority.
The Canterbury Museum Trust Board.
The Christchurch Drainage Board.
The Christchurch-Lyttelton Road Tunnel Authority.
The Christchurch Transport Board.
The Dunedin Drainage and Sewerage Board.
The Hauraki Gulf Maritime Park Board.
The Hawke's Bay Crematorium Board.
The Hutt Valley Drainage Board.
The Marlborough Forestry Corporation.
The Masterton Trust Lands Trust.
The North Shore Drainage Board.
The Ohai Railway Board.
The Otago Museum Trust Board.
The Rangitaiki Drainage Board.
The Riccarton Bush Trustees.
The Rotorua Area Electricity Supply Authority.
The Selwyn Plantation Board.
The South Canterbury Wallaby Board.
The Waikato Valley Authority.
The Waimakariri-Ashley Water Supply Board.
The Wairarapa Cadet Training Farm Trust Board.
The Wellington Regional Water Board.

APPENDIX

SECOND SCHEDULE   Section 33 (1)

Enactments Repealed

1962, No. 10—The Parliamentary Commissioner (Ombudsman) Act 1962.
1964, No. 50—The Export Guarantee Act 1964: Section 24.
1965, No. 47—The State Advances Corporation Act 1965: So much of the Second Schedule as relates to the Parliamentary Commissioner (Ombudsman) Act 1962.
1965, No. 124—The Decimal Currency Amendment Act 1965: Section 10.
1967, No. 135—The Water and Soil Conservation Act 1967: Section 39.
1967, No. 159—The Finance Act (No. 2) 1967: Section 3.
1968, No. 14—The Maori and Island Affairs Department Act 1968: So much of the Schedule as relates to the Parliamentary Commissioner (Ombudsman) Act 1962.
1968, No. 39—The Ministry of Transport Act 1968: So much of the Second Schedule as relates to the Parliamentary Commissioner (Ombudsman) Act 1962.
1968, No. 138—The Parliamentary Commissioner (Ombudsman) Amendment Act 1968.
1969, No. 121—The Parliamentary Commissioner (Ombudsman) Amendment Act 1969.
1970, No. 96—The Parliamentary Commissioner (Ombudsman) Amendment Act 1970.
1971, No. 52—The Defence Act 1971: So much of the Second Schedule as relates to the Parliamentary Commissioner (Ombudsman) Act 1962.

THE OMBUDSMEN ACT 1975

SECOND SCHEDULE—*continued*

1971, No. 60—The Department of Social Welfare Act 1971: Section 28.

1971, No. 154—The Water and Soil Conservation Amendment Act (No. 2) 1971: Section 23 (1).

1972, No. 3—The Ministry of Agriculture and Fisheries Amendment Act 1972: Section 3 (5).

1972, No. 4—The Ministry of Transport Amendment Act 1972: So much of the First Schedule as relates to the Parliamentary Commissioner (Ombudsman) Act 1962.

1972, No. 12—The Ministry of Energy Resources Act 1972: So much of the Second Schedule as relates to the Parliamentary Commissioner (Ombudsman) Act 1962.

1972, No. 43—The Accident Compensation Act 1972: So much of the Third Schedule as relates to the Parliamentary Commissioner (Ombudsman) Act 1962.

1974, No. 3—The Rural Banking and Finance Corporation Act 1974: So much of the Schedule as relates to the Parliamentary Commissioner (Ombudsman) Act 1962.

1974, No. 19—The Housing Corporation Act 1974: So much of the First Schedule as relates to the Parliamentary Commissioner (Ombudsman) Act 1962.

This Act is administered in the Department of Justice.

Select Bibliography

Ombudsman Works

Abraham, Henry J. "The Danish Ombudsman." *Annals of the American Academy of Political and Social Sciences* 377 (May 1968): 55–61.

———. "A Peoples' Watchdog Against Abuse of Power." *Public Administration Review* 20 (Summer 1960): 152–57.

Aikman, Colin C. "The New Zealand Ombudsman." *Canadian Bar Review* 42 (September 1964): 399–432.

Aikman, Colin C., and Clark, Roger S. "Some Developments in Administrative Law." *New Zealand Journal of Public Administration* 27 (1965): 45–55.

Anderson, Stanley V. "Ombudsman." *Encyclopaedia Britannica, Micropaedia*, 1974, Vol. 7, p. 530.

———. *Ombudsman Papers: American Experience and Proposals.* Berkeley: University of California, Institute of Governmental Studies, 1969.

———. "The Scandinavian Ombudsman." *The American-Scandinavian Review* 52 (December 1964): 403–09.

———, ed. *Ombudsmen for American Government?* Englewood Cliffs, N.J.: Prentice-Hall, 1968.

Bexelius, Alfred. "The Swedish Institution of the Justitieombudsman." *International Review of the Administrative Sciences* 27 (1961): 243–56.

Christensen, Bent. "The Danish Ombudsman." *University of Pennsylvania Law Review* 109 (June 1961): 1100–26.

Clark, Roger Stenson. *A United Nations High Commissioner for Human Rights.* The Hague: Martinus Nijhoff, 1972.

BIBLIOGRAPHY

Combe, Gordon D. "Characteristics of Complaint Investigation Against Government Departments, Statutory Authorities and Local Authorities." In *Official Record of Proceedings of the Conference of Australasian and Pacific Ombudsmen*, Wellington, New Zealand, 19–22 November 1974. Wellington: Office of Ombudsman, 1975.

Davis, A. G. "The Ombudsman in New Zealand." *Journal of the International Commission of Jurists* 4 (Summer 1962): 51–62.

———. "The Ombudsman in New Zealand (Part II)." *Journal of the International Commission of Jurists* 4 (Summer 1963): 316–22.

Dillon, John V. "Publicity and the Ombudsman." In *Official Record of Proceedings of the Conference of Australasian and Pacific Ombudsmen*, Wellington, New Zealand, 19–22 November 1974. Wellington: Office of Ombudsman, 1975.

Doi, Herman S. "Work, Staffing and Administration of an Ombudsman's Office." In *Official Record of Proceedings of the Conference of Australasian and Pacific Ombudsmen*, Wellington, New Zealand, 19–22 November 1974. Wellington: Office of Ombudsman.

Frank, Bernard. "The British Parliamentary Commissioner for Administration—The Ombudsman." *Federal Bar Journal* 28 (Winter 1968): 1–24.

———. "The Ombudsman and Human Rights." *Administrative Law Review* 22 (April 1970): 467–92.

Friedmann, Karl A. "Commons, Complaints, and the Ombudsman." *Parliamentary Affairs* 21 (Winter 1967): 38–47.

Gellhorn, Walter. "The Ombudsman in New Zealand." *California Law Review* 53 (December 1965): 1155–1211.

———. *Ombudsmen and Others: Citizens' Protectors in Nine Countries*. Cambridge, Mass.: Harvard University Press, 1966.

BIBLIOGRAPHY

———. *When Americans Complain: Governmental Grievance Procedures*. Cambridge, Mass.: Harvard University Press, 1966.

Gregory, Roy, and Hutchesson, Peter. *The Parliamentary Ombudsman: A Study in the Control of Administrative Action*. London: Allen and Unwin, 1975.

Gwyn, William B. "The British PCA: 'Ombudsman or Ombudsmouse?'." *Journal of Politics* 35 (February 1973): 45–69.

———. "Transferring the Ombudsman." In *Ombudsmen for American Government?*, edited by Stanley V. Anderson. Englewood Cliffs, N.J.: Prentice-Hall, 1968.

Hanan, Ralph J. "How To Be an Ombudsman," *Manchester Guardian Weekly*, 7 January 1965, p. 15.

Hidén, Mikael J. V. *The Ombudsman in Finland: The First Fifty Years*. Translated by Aaron Bell. Edited and with a Foreword by Donald C. Rowat. Berkeley: University of California, Institute of Governmental Studies, 1973.

Hill, Larry B. "Affect and Interaction in an Ambiguous Authority Relationship: New Zealand's Bureaucrats and the Ombudsman." *Journal of Comparative Administration* 4 (May 1972): 35–58.

———. "Complaining to the Ombudsman as an Urban Phenomenon: An Analysis of the New Zealand Ombudsman's Clients." *Urban Affairs Quarterly* 8 (September 1972): 123–27.

———. "Institutionalization, the Ombudsman, and Bureaucracy." *American Political Science Review* 68 (September 1974): 1075–85.

———. "The International Transfer of the Ombudsman." In *Communication in International Politics*, edited by Richard L. Merritt. Urbana: University of Illinois Press, 1972.

———. "The New Zealand Ombudsman's Authority System." *Political Science* 20 (September 1963): 40–51. Revised and reprinted in *Readings in New Zealand*

BIBLIOGRAPHY

Government, edited by Alan D. Robinson and Les Cleveland. Wellington: Reed, 1971.

———. *Parliament and the Ombudsman in New Zealand*. Legislative Research Series Monograph Number 8. Norman: University of Oklahoma Bureau of Government Research, 1974.

———. "Parliamentary Petitions, the Ombudsman, and Political Change in New Zealand." *Political Studies* 22 (September 1974): 337–46.

———. "The Role of Pressure Groups in the Policy Process: The New Zealand Public Service Association and the Adoption of the Ombudsman." *New Zealand Journal of Public Administration* 34 (March 1972): 46–58.

———. "The Transference of the Institution of Ombudsman, with Special Reference to Britain." Master's thesis, Tulane University, 1966.

Hurwitz, Stephan. "Control of the Administration in Denmark." *Journal of the International Commission of Jurists* 1 (Spring-Summer 1958): 224–43.

———. "Control of the Administration in Denmark: The Danish Parliamentary Commissioner for Civil and Military Government Administration." *Public Law* 3 (Autumn 1958): 236–53.

———. "The Danish Ombudsman and His Office." *The Listener* 63 (1960): 835–38.

———. "Denmark's Ombudsmand: The Parliamentary Commissioner for Civil and Military Government Administration." *Wisconsin Law Review* (March 1961): 169–99.

———. "The Folketingets Ombudsmand." *Parliamentary Affairs* 12 (Winter 1959): 199–208.

———. *The Ombudsman*. Copenhagen: Det Danske Selskab, 1961.

———. "The Scandinavian Ombudsman." *Political Science* 12 (September 1960): 121–42.

Jägerskiöld, Stig. "The Swedish Ombudsman." *Univer-*

sity of Pennsylvania Law Review 109 (June 1961): 1077–99.

Keith, K. J. "A Matter of Administration." In *Official Record of Proceedings of the Conference of Australasian and Pacific Ombudsmen*, Wellington, New Zealand, 19–22 November 1974. Wellington: Office of Ombudsman, 1975.

———. "The Ombudsman and 'Wrong' Decisions." *New Zealand Universities Law Review* 4 (October 1971): 361–93.

Marsh, Norman S. "The Ombudsman in New Zealand and in the United Kingdom." *New Zealand Universities Law Review* 1 (September 1963): 71–76.

Marshall, Geoffrey. "The British Parliamentary Commission for Administration." *Annals of the American Academy of Political and Social Sciences* 377 (May 1968): 87–96.

———. "The New Zealand Parliamentary Commissioner (Ombudsman) Act, 1962." *Public Law* (Spring 1963): 20–22.

Moore, John E. "Ombudsman and the Ghetto." *Connecticut Law Review* 1 (December 1968): 244–48.

Northey, J. F. "A New Zealand Ombudsman?" *Public Law* (Spring 1962): 43–51.

———. "New Zealand's Parliamentary Commissioner." In *The Ombudsman: Citizen's Defender*, 2d ed., edited by Donald C. Rowat. Toronto: University of Toronto Press, 1968.

Official Record of Proceedings of the Conference of Australasian and Pacific Ombudsmen, Wellington, New Zealand, 19–22 November 1974. Wellington: Office of Ombudsman, 1975.

Official Record of Proceedings of the Conference of Australasian and Pacific Ombudsmen, Wellington, New Zealand, 19–22 November 1974. *Supplement*. Wellington: Office of Ombudsman, 1975.

O'Neill, David P. "New Zealand Ombudsman." *America*, 30 January 1965, pp. 166–68.

"The Parliamentary Commissioner for Investigations." *New Zealand Law Journal* 37 (3 October 1961): 273–74.

Paterson, D. E. "The New Zealand Ombudsman as a Protector of Citizen's Rights." *Revue des Droits de l'Homme* 2 (1969): 395–451.

Payne, James E. "Ombudsman Roles for Social Workers." *Social Work* 17 (January 1972): 94–100.

Powles, Sir Guy. "Aspects of the Search for Administrative Justice with Particular Reference to the New Zealand Ombudsman." *Canadian Journal of Public Administration* 9 (June 1966): 133–57.

———. "The Citizen's Rights Against the Modern State and Its Responsibilities to Him." *International and Comparative Law Quarterly* 13 (July 1964): 761–97; *Public Administration* 23 (1964): 42–68.

———. "Common Justice." *The Guardian*, 14 May 1964, p. 10.

———. "The Office of Ombudsman in New Zealand." *Journal of Administration Overseas* 7 (January 1968): 287–92.

———. "The Office of Ombudsman in New Zealand: Its Origin and Operation." Address to Canadian Bar Association, 1 September 1964, Montreal.

———. "The Role of the New Zealand Ombudsman in Penal Complaints: An Individual Approach." In *Official Record of Proceedings of the Conference of Australasian and Pacific Ombudsmen*, Wellington, New Zealand, 19–22 November 1974. Wellington: Office of Ombudsman, 1975.

Purchase, C. E. "The Parliamentary Commissioner for Investigations." *New Zealand Law Journal* (7 August 1962): 321–24.

Roberts, John. "The Ombudsman and Local Government." In *Official Record of Proceedings of the Conference of Australasian and Pacific Ombudsmen*, Wellington, New Zealand, 19–22 November 1974. Wellington: Office of Ombudsman, 1975.

Rowat, Donald C. "Ombudsman for North America." *Public Administration Review* 24 (December 1964): 230–33.

―――. *The Ombudsman Plan: Essays on the Worldwide Spread of an Idea*. Toronto: Carleton Library No. 67, McClelland and Stewart, 1973.

―――. "Recent Developments in Ombudsmanship." *Canadian Journal of Public Administration* 10 (1967): 35–46.

―――, ed. *The Ombudsman: Citizen's Defender*. 2d ed. Toronto: University of Toronto Press, 1968.

Salier, W. A. "The New Zealand Ombudsman." *Sydney Law Review* 4 (August 1964): 416–22.

Sawer, Geoffrey. "The Ombudsman and Related Institutions in Australia and New Zealand." *Annals of the American Academy of Political and Social Sciences* 377 (May 1968): 62–72.

―――. *Ombudsmen*. Rev. ed. Victoria: Melbourne University Press, 1964.

Stacey, Frank A. *The British Ombudsman*. Oxford: Clarendon Press, 1971.

Tikaram, Moti. "The Ombudsman and the Exercise of Discretionary Powers." In *Official Record of Proceedings of the Conference of Australasian and Pacific Ombudsmen*, Wellington, New Zealand, 19–22 November 1974. Wellington: Office of Ombudsman, 1975.

"Value of Ombudsman Proved in New Zealand." *The Times* (London), 15 May 1964, p. 12.

Weeks, Kent M. "Members of Parliament and the New Zealand Ombudsman System." *Midwest Journal of Political Science* 14 (November 1970): 673–87.

BIBLIOGRAPHY

———. "Public Servants in the New Zealand Ombudsman System." *Public Administration Review* 29 (November/December 1969): 633–38.

Whyatt, Sir John. *The Citizen and the Administration: The Redress of Grievances—A Report by Justice.* London: Stevens, 1961.

Wolkon, George H., and Moriwaki, Sharon. "The Ombudsman Programme: Primary Prevention of Psychological Disorders." *International Journal of Social Psychiatry* 19 (Autumn/Winter 1973): 220–25.

Wyner, Alan J. *The Nebraska Ombudsman: Innovation in State Government.* Berkeley: University of California, Institute of Governmental Studies, 1974.

———, ed. *Executive Ombudsmen in the United States.* Berkeley: University of California, Institute of Governmental Studies, 1973.

Zweig, Franklin M. "The Social Worker as Legislative Ombudsman." *Social Work* 14 (January 1969): 25–33.

New Zealand Works

Aikman, Colin C. "Administrative Law—I." In *New Zealand: The Development of Its Laws and Constitution*, edited by J. L. Robson. 2d ed. London: Stevens, 1967.

Ausubel, David P. *The Fern and the Tiki: An American View of New Zealand National Character, Social Attitudes and Race Relations.* New York: Holt, Rinehart and Winston, 1960.

Brown, Bruce. *The Rise of New Zealand Labour: A History of the New Zealand Labour Party from 1916 to 1940.* Wellington: Price Milburn, 1962.

Bryce, James. *Modern Democracies.* Vol. 2. New York: Macmillan, 1924.

Campbell, Peter. "The New Zealand Public Service Commission." *Public Administration* 34 (Summer 1956): 157–68.

BIBLIOGRAPHY

———. "Politicians, Public Servants, and the People in New Zealand, II." *Political Studies* 4 (1956): 18–29.

Chapman, R. M.; Jackson, W. K.; and Mitchell, A. V. *New Zealand Politics in Action: The 1960 General Election.* London: Oxford University Press, 1962.

Condliffe, J. B. *New Zealand in the Making.* 2d ed. London: Allen and Unwin, 1959.

Frontin-Rollet, Robin. "Questions in the House of Representatives." Honors research paper, Victoria University of Wellington, 1967.

Hill, Larry B. "Political Culture-and-Personality: Theoretical Perspectives on Democratic Stability from the New Zealand Pattern." In *The Social Psychology of Political Life,* edited by Samuel A. Kirkpatrick and Lawrence K. Petitt. Belmont, Calif.: Duxbury Press, 1972.

Jackson, Keith. *New Zealand: Politics of Change.* Wellington: Reed, 1973.

Jones, P. E. R. "A Sociological Note on the Role of the Ombudsman." In *New Zealand Society: Contemporary Perspectives,* edited by Stephen D. Webb and John Collette. Sydney: John Wiley Australasia Pty., 1973.

Kelson, Robert N. *The Private Member of Parliament and the Formation of Public Policy: A New Zealand Case Study.* Toronto: University of Toronto Press, 1964.

Levine, Stephen, ed. *New Zealand Politics: A Reader.* Melbourne: Cheshire, 1975.

Lipson, Leslie. *The Politics of Equality.* Chicago: University of Chicago Press, 1948.

Milne, R. S. *Political Parties in New Zealand.* Oxford: Clarendon Press, 1966.

———, ed. *Bureaucracy in New Zealand.* Wellington: New Zealand Institute of Public Administration, 1957.

Mitchell, Austin. *Government by Party.* Wellington: Whitcombe and Tombs, 1966.

———. "Politics." In *The Pattern of New Zealand Cul-*

ture, edited by A. L. McLeod. Ithaca, N.Y.: Cornell University Press, 1968.

———. *Politics and People in New Zealand*. Christchurch: Whitcombe and Tombs, 1969.

New Zealand. Department of Statistics. *New Zealand Statistics of Justice—1965*. Wellington: Government Printer, 1967.

New Zealand Census of Population and Dwellings, 1966—Increase and Location of Population. Wellington: Department of Statistics, 1967.

New Zealand Census of Population and Dwellings— 1966: Summary Results. Wellington: Department of Statistics, 1968.

O'Brien, Peter V. "Parliamentary Control of Administrative Action in New Zealand: Questions to Ministers 1946–67." LL.B thesis, Victoria University School of Law, in preparation 1968.

Orr, Gordon. *Report on Administrative Justice in New Zealand*. Wellington: Government Printer, 1964.

Polaschek, R. J. *Government Administration in New Zealand*. Wellington: New Zealand Institute of Public Administration, 1958; London: Oxford University Press, 1958.

Riddiford, D. J. "A Citizen's Point of View." In *Bureaucracy in New Zealand*, edited by R. S. Milne. Wellington: New Zealand Institute of Public Administration, 1957.

Robinson, Alan D. "Class Voting in New Zealand: A Comment on Alford's Comparison of Class Voting in the Anglo-American Political Systems." In *Party Systems and Voter Alignments*, edited by Seymour M. Lipset and Stein Rokkan. New York: Free Press, 1967.

———. *Notes on New Zealand Politics*. Wellington: School of Political Science and Public Administration, Victoria University, 1970.

Robinson, Alan D., and Ashenden, A. H. "Mass Communications and the 1963 Election: A Preliminary Report." *Political Science* 16 (September 1964): 7–22.

Robson, J. L., ed. *New Zealand: The Development of Its Laws and Constitution*. London: Stevens, 1954.

———, ed. *New Zealand: The Development of Its Laws and Constitution*. 2d ed. London: Stevens, 1967.

Robson, J. L., and Scott, K. J. "Public Administration and Administrative Law." In *New Zealand: The Development of Its Laws and Constitution*, edited by J. L. Robson. London: Stevens, 1954.

Scott, K. J. *The New Zealand Constitution*. Oxford: Clarendon Press, 1962.

Siegfried, André. *Democracy in New Zealand*. London: G. Bell, 1913.

Smith, Thomas B. *The New Zealand Bureaucrat*. Wellington: Cheshire, 1974.

Westrate, C. *Portrait of a Modern Mixed Economy: New Zealand*. Wellington: Sweet and Maxwell, 1959.

Theoretical Works

Barnett, Homer G. *Innovation: The Basis of Culture Change*. New York: McGraw-Hill, 1953.

Bendix, Reinhard. "Bureaucracy." In *International Encyclopedia of the Social Sciences*, Vol. 2. New York: Macmillan and Free Press, 1968.

Berelson, Bernard R.; Lazarsfeld, Paul F.; and McPhee, William N. *Voting: A Study of Opinion Formation in a Presidential Campaign*. Chicago: University of Chicago Press, 1954.

Blau, Peter M., and Scott, W. Richard. *Formal Organizations: A Comparative Approach*. San Francisco: Chandler, 1962.

Braibanti, Ralph. "External Inducement of Political-Administrative Development: An Institutional Strategy." In *Political and Administrative Develop-*

BIBLIOGRAPHY

ment, edited by Ralph Braibanti. Durham, N.C.: Duke University Press, 1969.

Buck, Gary L., and Jacobson, Alvin L. "Social Evolution and Structural-Functional Analysis: An Emprical Test." *American Sociological Review* 33 (June 1968): 343–55.

Caiden, Gerald E. *Administrative Reform*. Chicago: Aldine, 1969.

Caro, Francis G. *Readings in Evaluation Research*. New York: Russell Sage Foundation, 1971.

Dahl, Robert A. *Modern Political Analysis*. Englewood Cliffs, N.J.: Prentice-Hall, 1963.

Danet, Brenda. "The Language of Persuasion in Bureaucracy: 'Modern' and 'Traditional' Appeals to the Israel Customs Authorities." *American Sociological Review* 36 (October 1971): 847–59.

Danet, Brenda, and Hartman, Harriet. "Coping with Bureaucracy: The Israeli Case." *Social Forces* 51 (September 1972): 7–22.

Dolbeare, Kenneth. *Trial Courts in Urban Politics: State Court Policy Impact and Functions in a Local Political System*. New York: John Wiley, 1967.

Downs, Anthony. *Inside Bureaucracy*. Boston: Little, Brown, 1966.

Easton, David. "An Approach to the Analysis of Political Systems." *World Politics* 9 (April 1957): 381–400.

Eaton, Joseph W., ed. *Institution Building and Development: From Concepts to Application*. Beverly Hills: Sage Publications, 1972.

Epstein, A. L., ed. *The Craft of Social Anthropology*. London: Tavistock Publications, 1967.

Esman, Milton J. "The Elements of Institution Building." In *Institution Building and Development: From Concepts to Application*, edited by Joseph W. Eaton. Beverly Hills: Sage Publications, 1972.

———. "Some Issues in Institution Building Theory." In *Institution Building: A Model for Applied Social*

BIBLIOGRAPHY

Change, edited by D. Woods Thomas, Harry R. Potter, William L. Miller, and Adrian F. Aveni. Cambridge, Mass.: Schenkman, 1972.

Esman, Milton J., and Blaise, Hans C. "Institution Building Research: The Guiding Concepts." Mimeographed. Pittsburgh: University of Pittsburgh, Graduate School of Public and International Affairs, 1966.

Evans-Pritchard, E. E. *Social Anthropology and Other Essays.* New York: Free Press, 1962.

Firth, Raymond. *Elements of Social Organization.* New York: Philosophical Library, 1951.

Fortes, Meyer. *The Dynamics of Clanship Among the Tallensi.* London: Oxford University Press, 1945.

Freilich, Morris, ed. *Marginal Natives: Anthropologists at Work.* New York: Harper and Row, 1970.

Gerth, Hans H., and Mills, C. Wright. *From Max Weber: Essays in Sociology.* New York: Oxford University Press, 1946.

Gluckman, Max. "Ethnographic Data in British Social Anthropology." *Sociological Review* 9 (March 1961): 5–17.

Hamilton, Walton H. "Institution." In *Encyclopaedia of the Social Sciences,* Vol. 8. New York: Macmillan, 1932.

Hill, Larry B. "The Inter-Systematic Transfer of Political Institutions: A Communications Strategy for the Analysis of Political Change." Paper delivered at the 66th Annual Meeting of the American Political Science Association, Los Angeles, 8–12 September 1970.

Hinricks, Harley E., and Taylor, Graeme H. *A Primer on Benefit-Cost Analysis and Program Evaluation.* Pacific Palisades, Calif.: Goodyear, 1972.

Hopkins, Terence K. *The Exercise of Influence in Small Groups.* Totowa, N.J.: Bedminster Press, 1964.

Huntington, Samuel P. "Political Development and Political Decay." *World Politics* 17 (April 1965): 386–430.

———. *Political Order in Changing Societies*. New Haven: Yale University Press, 1969.
Jacob, Herbert. *Debtors in Court: The Consumption of Government Services*. Chicago: Rand McNally, 1969.
Katz, Daniel, and Kahn, Robert L. *The Social Psychology of Organizations*. New York: John Wiley, 1966.
Katz, Elihu, and Danet, Brenda. "Petitions and Persuasive Appeals: A Study of Official-Client Relations." *American Sociological Review* 31 (December 1966): 811–22.
Kornhauser, William. "The Politics of Mass Society." In *Comparative Politics–A Reader*, edited by Harry Eckstein and David E. Apter. New York: Free Press, 1965.
Kushner, Gilbert. "The Anthropology of Complex Societies." In *Biennial Review of Anthropology, 1969*, edited by Bernard J. Siegel. Stanford, Calif.: Stanford University Press, 1970.
Laski, Harold. "Bureaucracy." In *Encyclopaedia of the Social Sciences*, Vol. 3. New York: Macmillan, 1930.
Lasswell, Harold D. "The Structure and Function of Communication in Society." In *The Communication of Ideas*, edited by Lyman Bryson. New York: Harper, 1948.
Lasswell, Harold D., and Kaplan, Abraham. *Power and Society*. New Haven: Yale University Press, 1950.
Lerner, Daniel. "The Tranformation of Political Institutions." In *The Transfer of Institutions*, edited by William P. Hamilton. Durham, N.C.: Duke University Press, 1964.
Leys, Colin. "Petitioning in the Nineteenth and Twentieth Centuries." *Political Studies* 3 (1955): 45–64.
Lorch, Robert S. *Democratic Process and Administrative Law*. Detroit: Wayne State University Press, 1969.
Mair, Lucy. *An Introduction to Social Anthropology*. 2d ed. Oxford: Clarendon Press, 1972.
Malinowski, Bronislaw. *Argonauts of the Western Pacific: An Account of Native Enterprise and Adventure in the*

Archipelagoes of Melanesian New Guinea. New York: E. P. Dutton, 1922; New York: E. P. Dutton, Everyman Paperback, 1961.

———. *The Dynamics of Culture Change: An Inquiry Into Race Relations in Africa.* Edited by Phyllis M. Kaberry. New Haven: Yale University Press, 1945.

Mayhew, Leon H. *Law and Equal Opportunity: A Study of the Massachusetts Commission Against Discrimination.* Cambridge, Mass.: Harvard University Press, 1968.

Paige, Glenn D. "The Rediscovery of Politics." In *Approaches to Development: Politics, Administration, and Change,* edited by John D. Montgomery and William J. Siffin. New York: McGraw-Hill, 1966.

Parsons, Talcott. "How Are Clients Integrated into Service Organizations?" In *Organizations and Clients: Essays in the Sociology of Service,* edited by William R. Rosengren and Mark Lefton. Columbus: Charles E. Merrill, 1970.

———. "Interaction: Social Interaction." In *International Encyclopedia of the Social Sciences,* Vol. 7. New York: Macmillan and Free Press, 1968.

———. "Rejoinder to Bauer and Coleman." *Public Opinion Quarterly* 27 (Spring 1963): 87–92.

———. *The Social System.* Glencoe, Ill.: Free Press, 1951.

———. *Structure and Process in Modern Societies.* New York: Free Press, 1960.

Polsby, Nelson W. "The Institutionalization of the U.S. House of Representatives." *American Political Science Review* 62 (March 1968): 144–68.

Powdermaker, Hortense. "Field Work." In *International Encyclopedia of the Social Sciences,* Vol. 5. New York: Macmillan and Free Press, 1968.

Robson, William A. *The Governors and the Governed.* Baton Rouge: Louisiana State University Press, 1964.

Rogers, Everett M. *Modernization Among Peasants: The*

Impact of Communication. New York: Holt, Rinehart and Winston, 1969.

Rossi, Peter H. "Testing for Success and Failure in Social Action." In *Evaluating Social Programs: Theory, Practice and Politics*, edited by Peter H. Rossi and Walter Williams. New York: Seminar Press, 1972.

Scott, W. Richard. "Field Methods in the Study of Organizations." In *Handbook of Organizations*, edited by James G. March. Chicago: Rand McNally, 1965.

Selznick, Philip. *Leadership in Administration: A Sociological Interpretation*. New York: Harper and Row, 1957.

Shannon, Claude E., and Weaver, Warren. *The Mathematical Theory of Communication*. Urbana: University of Illinois Press, 1939.

Sills, David L. "Voluntary Associations: Sociological Aspects." In *International Encyclopedia of the Social Sciences*, Vol. 16. New York: Macmillan and Free Press, 1968.

Skinner, B. F. *Beyond Freedom and Dignity*. New York: Alfred A. Knopf, 1971.

Sjoberg, Gideon; Brymer, Richard A.; and Farris, Buford. "Bureaucracy and the Lower Class." *Sociology and Social Research* 50 (April 1966): 325–37.

Starbuck, William H. "Organizational Growth and Development." In *Handbook of Organizations*, edited by James G. March. Chicago: Rand McNally, 1965.

Swartz, Marc J.; Turner, Victor W.; and Tuden, Arthur, eds. *Political Anthropology*. Chicago: Aldine, 1966.

Thomas, D. Woods; Potter, Harry R.; Miller, William L.; and Aveni, Adrian F., eds., *Institution Building: A Model for Applied Social Change*. Cambridge, Mass.: Schenkman, 1972.

Thompson, James D. *Organizations in Action*. New York: McGraw-Hill, 1967.

Thompson, Victor A. *Modern Organization*. New York: Alfred A. Knopf, 1961.

Uphoff, Norman T., and Ilchman, Warren F. "The Time Dimension in Institution Building." In *Institution Building and Development: From Concepts to Application,* edited by Joseph W. Eaton. Bevery Hills: Sage Publications, 1972.

Van Velsen, J. *The Politics of Kinship: A Study in Social Manipulation Among the Lakeside Tonga of Nyasaland.* Manchester: Manchester University Press for the Rhodes-Livingston Institute, 1964.

Wax, Rosalie H. *Doing Fieldwork: Warnings and Advice.* Chicago: University of Chicago Press, 1971.

———. "Reciprocity as a Field Technique." *Human Organization* 11 (Fall 1952): 34–37.

Weber, Max. *The Theory of Social and Economic Organization.* Translated by A. M. Henderson and Talcott Parsons. Edited by Talcott Parsons. New York: Oxford University Press, 1947.

Weiss, Carol. *Evaluation Research: Methods for Assessing Program Effectiveness.* Englewood Cliffs, N.J.: Prentice-Hall, 1972.

Zald, Mayer N. *Organizational Change: The Political Economy of the YMCA.* Chicago: University of Chicago Press, 1970.

Index

Abraham, Henry J., 14n
administrative tribunals, 64–67
Agriculture and Fisheries, 156, 246
Aikman, C. C., 62n
Alberta Ombudsman, 9, 323n
American Bar Association, 9, 11
Anderson, Stanley V., 9n, 12n, 15n, 154n, 267n
anthropology and ombudsman study, 16–26, 318, 322; and fieldwork, 16–17, 26–34, 42; and research design, 35–46; theoretical perspectives, 18–26. *See also* Bronislaw Malinowski
appeals agencies, administrative tribunals, 64–66; courts, 61–64; departments, 57–58; Members of Parliament, 52–55, 140; Ministers, 55–57; other channels, 66; parliamentary petitions, 58–61
Argonauts of the Western Pacific, 16–17, 317
Ashenden, A. H., 110n
Auckland, 107, 326–27
Auckland Star, 71
Audit Department, 215
Australian ballot, 19–20
Ausubel, David P., 49n, 50
Aveni, Adrian F., 338n

Bendix, Reinhard, 8
Berkley, George E., 7n
Blaise, Hans C., 37n
Blau, Peter M., 87–89
Braibanti, Ralph, 19n, 24n, 241n, 337n

British Broadcasting Corporation, 69
British Ombudsman, The, 9n
Brown, Laurie, 141
Bryce, James, 270
Brymer, R. A., 128n
Bryson, Lyman, 21n
Buck, Gary L., 47n
bureaucracy, 3, 50–52, 73–74, 79–80, 99, 101, 128, 134, 149, 153–55, 290; images of, 4–8, 136; and ombudsman impact, 185–86, 188–204, 212–37, 283–85; and ombudsman relationship, 153–55, 182–84, 245; and views of ombudsman, 245–52
bureaucracy-ombudsman relationship, 153–55, 182–84, 245; and client-attending departments, 89–93, 123, 164–70; and client-serving departments, 89–93, 158–64; correspondence, 103, 130–33, 138–39, 146–47, 151, 172–73; and departmental reaction, 179–82; and discretion, 174–75; incidence of investigations, 155–56; and locus of decisions, 176–77; and non-client-oriented departments, 89–93, 158, 170–72; and ombudsman's demands, 177–79; and other interaction, 173–74; responsibility focus, 177; targets of complaints, 81–86, 156–72; and threats, 174–76, 183
bureaucrats' views of ombudsman, 245–47, 266, 320;

405

INDEX

bureaucrats' views (*cont.*) disagreement, 261–65; favorable, 261–65; and jurisdiction evaluation, 259–61; in perceptual context, 247–50; and public service impact, 252–59; and social distance, 250–52

Cabinet Committee on Legislation, 303
Caiden, Gerald E., 205n
Campbell, Peter, 50n, 58n
Caro, Francis G., 322n
Chapman, R. M., 70n
Christchurch, 107, 327
Christchurch *Press*, 71
clients' identities, 125–26; businesses, 105–106; organizations, 105; political groups, 106; pressure groups, 106
clients of ombudsman, 43, 101–104, 125–29, 245; ages, 110–12, 197; civil service personnel, 124–25, 199, 201; class-occupation, 119–24, 139, 142, 199–200; demographic origins, 106–109, 197; education, 112–14, 198; identities, 105–106, 125–26; marital status, 114–16, 143, 198; racial-ethnic origins, 116–19, 144, 198; sexual composition, 109–110, 197. *See also* complaints
common law, 61–62
complaints, 79, 99–100; departmental classification of, 87–93; and documentary evidence, 139; fee for, 146–49; and financial appeals, 141–43; levels of, 80–81; subjects of, 93–99; targets, 81–86, 156–71. *See also* clients of ombudsman *and* ombudsman-client relationship

Conference of Australasian and Pacific Ombudsmen, 312, 329n
Constitutional Society, 70
Court of Arbitration, 48
courts, 61–64
Crichel Down scandal, 248, 302
Crown Law Office, 209, 215
Cummings, Milton C., Jr., 260n
customs duties, 106
Customs office, 158, 246

Dahl, Robert A., 249n
Danet, Brenda, 102, 104n
Debtors in Court: The Consumption of Government Services, 3n, 101n
decentralization, 330
Decimal Currency Board, 215
dehumanization, 6–7
deinstitutionalization, 26
democracy, 3
demonstrations, 81, 326
Denmark Ombudsman, 8, 67–69, 71–73
Department of Defense, 156
departments, 57–58; client-attending, 89–93, 123, 164–70, 214–15; client-serving, 89–93, 158–64, 214; non-client-oriented, 89–93, 158, 170–72, 215. *See also under department names*
diffusionists, 20n
Doi, Herman S., 10
Dolbeare, Kenneth, 103n
Downs, Anthony, 341n
Dugdale, Sir Thomas, 302n
Duncan, Richard, 339n
Dunedin, 107

Easton, David, 341
Eaton, Joseph W., 25n
Education Department, 84, 98, 109, 158, 161–62, 202n, 218–23;

INDEX

Child Welfare Division of, 161–63, 163n; interview, 246
Eisenstadt, S. N., 26, 38n
Esman, Milton J., 25n, 37n, 240–41, 337, 338n
evaluation of ombudsman, costs, 320–22; and future, 343–46; and institutionalization, 323–43; program, 318–23; and social change, 323; success, 319–21. *See also* institutionalization of ombudsman
External Affairs Department, 156, 246

Family Allowance Act, 48
Farris, B., 128n
Fiji, 11
Finland Ombudsman, 8–9, 69, 245
Firth, Raymond, 29n, 318
Forest Service, 109
Fortes, Meyer, 36n
France, 11
Frank, Bernard, 11n
Freilich, Morris, 31
Friedmann, Karl A., 323n

Gellhorn, Walter, 9, 14n, 15n, 102n, 133n, 193n, 296n, 343n
Gerth, H. H., 5n
Gluckman, Max, 40–42n
Goode, William J., 250n
government health care, 48
Government Life Insurance Department, 48, 84, 214–15
Government and Parliament: A Survey From the Inside, 302n
Government Printing Office, 215, 246
Great Britain Ombudsman, 9, 11
Gregory, Roy, 15n
grievance agents, 75, 343
Guyana, 11
Gwyn, William B., 13n, 15n, 154n

Hallett, G., 59n
Hamilton, 233
Hamilton, Walton H., 344n
Hanan, J. R., 71–72
Hartman, Harriet, 102, 144n
Harvard Student Legislative Research Bureau, 9
Hatt, Paul K., 250n
Hawaii Ombudsman, 9–10, 323n
Health Department, 109, 158, 163–64, 202n, 217, 226–28, 231, 235; interview, 246
Henderson, A. M., 7, 24n
Hill, Larry B., 21n, 37n, 47n, 59n, 68n, 71n, 107n, 124n, 311n, 343n
Hinricks, Harley E., 320n
Hopkins, Terence K., 249n
Housing Corporation, 158, 215, 246
Human Rights Commission, 329n
Huntington, Samuel P., 22n, 23, 26, 74n, 324, 325n, 329, 331–36
Hurwitz, Stephan, 68–69
Hutchesson, Peter, 15n
Hutt, 108

Ilchman, Warren F., 338n
impact of ombudsman, 185–86, 235, 239–41
  on administrative reform, 204–206; and annual report, 206–209; and case disposition, 236–37; and clients, 237–39; content of, 217–18, 231–35; costs of compliance, 235–36; dimensions of, 209–13; and selected major targets (chart), 218–31; targets of, 213–17
  helping and correlates, 194–96; and case classification, 196–97; and client iden-

407

INDEX

impact of ombudsman (*cont.*) tities, 197–200; and complaint characteristics, 200–202; and complaint targets, 202–203; on selected targets (chart), 218–31
meaning of decisions: "declined," 188–91, 253; "discontinued," 191, 253; "justified," 192–93, 204, 212, 237; "not justified," 187–88, 237, 239, 253; time and case classifications, 193–94; "withdrawn," 191–92, 239, 253
import restrictions, 106
Inland Revenue, 83–87, 158, 202n, 233, 246
inputs, *see* complaints
institutionalization, 8, 18–26, 39, 44, 48, 74–75, 126n, 183, 193, 240–41, 245, 268
alternative measures of: 323–24; adaptability, 333–38; autonomy, 331–33; coherence, 329–31; complexity, 325–29
time and threshold of, 338–43. *See also* evaluation of ombudsman
institution building, 18n, 37n
Internal Affairs Department, 156, 216
International Bar Association, 11
Israel, 11

Jackson, W. K., 70n
Jacob, Herbert, 3n, 101n
Jennings, M. Kent, 260n
Justice Department, 83–85, 164–66, 223–25, 246; commercial affairs division, 164–65; courts division, 164–65; land and deeds division, 164, 166; patents division, 164, 166; penal division, 164; registrar-general division, 164–65

Katz, Elihu, 144n
Kelson, Robert N., 53n, 60n, 61n, 268n
Kilpatrick, Franklin B., 260n
Kirkpatrick, Samuel A., 47n
Kornhauser, William, 108n
Kushner, Gilbert, 38n

Labor Department, 109, 158, 166–68, 230–31, 233, 246
Labor Party, 68, 70, 268–71, 286–87n; and ombudsman, 273–95, 311–13, 342
Laking, George R., 334
Lands and Survey Department, 156
Laski, Harold, 6
Lasswell, Harold D., 21n, 245n
lawyers, 64, 67, 105, 140, 290n
Legislative Department, 215
letters of complaint, 130–33, 138–39, 146–47, 151, 172–73
Leys, Colin, 59n
Lipson, Leslie, 50n
Listener, 69
Lorch, Robert S., 8

maladministration, 96
Malinowski, Bronislaw, 39, 41–42n; and anthropology, 16, 17n, 39n. *See also* anthropology and ombudsman study
Manapuri power station, 171
Maori Affairs Board, 215
Maori Affairs Committee, 117
Maori and Island Affairs, 214
Maori Land Courts, 117
Maoris, 28, 116–17, 126, 129, 198, 285
Maori Trust Office, 215

408

INDEX

March, James G., 28n, 341n
Marine Department, 215
Marshall, J. R., 70
Mason, H. G. R., 68
Masterton, 108
Mauritius, 11
Mayhew, Leon H., 103n
Merritt, Richard L., 343n
Miller, William L., 338n
Mills, C. Wright, 5n
Milne, R. S., 52n
Mines Department, 215
Minister of Agriculture, 301
Ministers of the Crown, 55–57, 298, 310–13; and assessment of ombudsman, 306–10; as grievance men, 298–301 (for constituents, 299; for other citizens, 299–301); and ministerial responsibility, 301–306; and relations with ombudsman, 303–306
Ministry of Works and Development, *see* Works and Development
Mitchell, Austin, 70n, 268n
Moore, John E., 15n, 323n
Moriwaki, Sharon, 152
Morrison, Herbert, 302n
Muldoon, R. D., 329n

Nader, Ralph, 9
National Party, 70, 263, 268–71, 286–87n, 308–13; and ombudsman, 273–95, 298
National Party Caucus, 303
National Roads Board, 234
Nelson, 108
New Zealand, 27–29, 47–48, 83, 113–15, 129, 136, 167–68, 184, 212, 233, 250, 264–65; appeals agencies, 52–67; biracial society, 116–19; and citizen grievances, 81, 269–71; and civil service, 248; and innovativeness, 48–50, 74; judiciary, 287; mail, 147; occupational classes, 119–25; and ombudsman, 8, 16, 19, 29, 48–76, 99–103, 128, 154, 245; population, 109–10; prime minister, 56–57, 249; rural, 108; schools, 161–62; urban, 107; women, 109, 126. *See also* New Zealand Ombudsman
New Zealand Constitution, The, 268n, 302n
New Zealand Ombudsman, 8–16, 19, 29, 73–76, 99–100, 128, 154, 245, 267–68, 317, 330, 343–46; and appeals agencies, 53–67; clients, 43, 101–29; compared to Supreme Court judge, 250, 287; impact on political system, 186; and Ministers of the Crown, 55–57, 298–313; and politics of transfer, 67–73; receptivity, 48–53; success, 319–21; viewed as foreign, 263, 292–94. *See also* New Zealand
New Zealand Parliament, Parliamentary Debates, 267n
New Zealand Politics in Action: The 1960 General Election, 70n
Northern Ireland, 11
Norway Ombudsman, 9
nuclear power stations, 171

O'Brien, Peter V., 55n
Official Secrets Act, 104
Old Age Pensions Act, 48
ombudsman, 3–4; as client-serving institution, 149, 152; concept of, 10–15; as empire builder, 292; future, 343–46; as governmental institution, 153–85; and institutionalization, 323–43; origin of, 8–10; as parliamentary official, 310–11n;

409

INDEX

ombudsman (*cont.*)
 political-anthropological approach to, 16–46; success, 319–21; widespread use of, 10–11. *See also* New Zealand Ombudsman
Ombudsman Act of 1962, 43, 209
ombudsman-client relationship: client attitudes, 135–38; and client perceptions of, 132–35; and client strategies, 138–44, 151; complaint timing, 137–38; nature of, 145–49; and quantity of interactions, 130–31
Ombudsmen Act of 1975, 332n, 335, 353–85
Ombudsmen for American Government?, 9n, 13n

Paige, Glenn D., 75n
Paremoremo prison probe, 81, 326
Parliament and ombudsman, 52–55, 260–61, 267–69, 295–97, 308; and affection, 290–94; interaction, 277–81; and Labor Party, 268–71, 286–87n, 273–95; and National Party, 268–71, 273–95, 286–87n; and ombudsman effectiveness, jurisdiction, 285–90; and ombudsman status, 269–75; and political life impact, 281–85; and psychosocial distance, 275–77; and ruling appeals, 249
Parsons, Talcott, 7, 24n, 75n, 150n, 245n, 247–48n
Peel, Roy V., 12n
Petitt, Lawrence K., 47n
Polaschek, R. J., 50n, 62n, 63n
Police Department, 109, 158, 164, 168–70, 231, 246
political-anthropological approach, *see* anthropology and ombudsman study

political institutions, 21n, 48
Polsby, Nelson W., 22n
Polynesian Islanders, 118, 326
Pooler, William, 339n
Post Office, 158, 235, 246; and Social Welfare case, 207–209, 211, 213
Potter, Harry R., 338n
Powdermaker, Hortense, 16, 17n
Powles, Sir Guy, 10, 29–30, 60, 64, 75, 131, 134–35, 182n, 193n, 212n, 326–27, 330, 335n; age, 334; and bureaucrats, 252–53; commentary by, 347–52
Prime Minister, 249, 298n
Prime Minister's Department, 215
Public Law (journal), 68
Public Service Association, 71
Public Trust Office, 48, 84

race relations, 81, 326
railways, 158, 246
Rehabilitation Board, 214
Report of the Committee on Administrative Tribunals and Enquiries in the United Kingdom, 65n
Reports, ombudsman's, 98n, 157n, 166, 195, 206–209, 212, 330; bureaucracy's views of, 251–53, 275–76
Reuss, Henry, 296
Riddiford, D. J., 53n, 73
Robinson, Alan D., 110n, 268n
Robson, J. L., 48n, 64n, 68–71
Robson, William A., 6n
Rossi, Peter, 321, 322n
Rotorura, 233
Rowat, Donald C., 11n, 12n, 81n, 267
Rowling, the Rt. Hon. W. E., 312–13
Russett, Bruce M., 47n, 107n

410

INDEX

Scandinavian ombudsmen, 3, 8, 10, 19, 72, 81, 129, 263, 294, 317, 343
Scientific and Industrial Research, 215
Scientology, 326
Scott, K. J., 61n, 64n, 268n, 302n
Scott, W. Richard, 27–28n, 87–89
Selznick, Philip, 25n, 337, 338n
Seminar on Judicial and Other Remedies Against the Illegal Exercise or Abuse of Administrative Authority, 68, 69n
Shannon, Claude E., 21n
Siegel, Gilbert, 38n
Siegfried, André, 49
Sills, David L., 345n
Sjoberg, G., 128n
Skinner, B. F., 79n
Social Anthropology, 28n
Social Credit Party member, 268n
Social Security, 63, 161
Social Welfare Department, 83, 87–88, 109, 158–61, 167, 171, 204, 207–209, 217, 225–26, 231; benefits, 159; interview, 246
Soil Conservation and Rivers Control Council, 109, 215
Stacy, Frank A., 9n, 15n, 296n
Starbuck, William H., 341n
State Insurance Office, 156
State Services Commission, 125, 158, 246
Statistics Department, 215
Superannuation Fund Board, 125, 158, 216, 246
Swartz, Marc J., 36n
Sweden Ombudsman, 8–9, 69, 73, 245, 267, 330–31; clients, 102

Tanzania, 11
Tauranga, 233
taxation, taxes, 5, 79, 106, 197, 325
Tax Court, 83–84, 158

Taylor, Graeme H., 320
Thomas, D. Woods, 338n
Thompson, James D., 37n
Thompson, Victor A., 5n
time and threshold of institutionalization, 338–43
Tongariro power station, 171
Tourist and Publicity Department, 84, 215
Trade and Industry, 215
transfer of institutions, 18–26, 343–46
Transport Department, 156, 216, 246
Treasury and Statistics, 89, 158, 246
Trobriand Islanders, 16
Tuden, Arthur, 36n
Turner, Victor W., 36n

Uphoff, Norman T., 338n
unicameral legislature, New Zealand's, 48
urbanism, 5, 197

Valuation Department, 211n, 215
Wax, Rosalie H., 33n, 45n
Weaver, Warren, 21n
Weber, Max, 4–7, 22n
Weeks, Kent M., 266n, 311–12n
Weiss, Carol, 318, 321
Wellington, 107–108, 136, 299, 312
Wellington *Evening Post*, 71
Westrate, C., 47n
Whyatt Report, 72
Williams, Walter, 322
Wolkon, George H., 152
women's suffrage, 48
Works and Development, 109, 158, 170–72, 228–31, 246
writs, 63, 66
Wyner, Alan J., 15n, 323n

Zweig, F. M., 129n

411

Library of Congress Cataloging in Publication Data

Hill, Larry B
   The model ombudsman.

   Based on the author's thesis, Tulane University, 1970.
   Bibliography: p.
   Includes index.
   1. Ombudsman—New Zealand.   I. Title.
JQ5829.04H53   354'.931'091   76-3258
ISBN 0-691-07579-4